DATE DUE

JAN 0 2 2002			

THE MACMILLAN COMPANY
NEW YORK · BOSTON · CHICAGO · DALLAS
ATLANTA · SAN FRANCISCO

MACMILLAN & CO., LIMITED
LONDON · BOMBAY · CALCUTTA
MELBOURNE

THE MACMILLAN CO. OF CANADA, LTD.
TORONTO

MODERN ESSAYS

SELECTED AND EDITED

BY

JOHN MILTON BERDAN, Ph.D.

ASSISTANT PROFESSOR OF ENGLISH IN YALE UNIVERSITY

JOHN RICHIE SCHULTZ, Ph.D.

PROFESSOR OF ENGLISH AT ALLEGHENY COLLEGE

AND

HEWETTE ELWELL JOYCE, M.A.

ASSISTANT PROFESSOR OF ENGLISH AT DARTMOUTH COLLEGE

New York

THE MACMILLAN COMPANY

1922

PREFACE

In the difficult problem of teaching the principles of exposition, the need of a volume of illustrations to accompany the rhetoric has been increasingly felt. These illustrations, moreover, if the student is to write an essay, rather than a bundle of paragraphs, should themselves be complete essays. And if the student is to learn to write naturally, it seems logical that the essays should be chosen from the writers of his own time. For, no matter how perfect theoretically may be the "style" of the *Spectator*, the fact remains that, as Addison lived in the early eighteenth century, such a paper to-day would be an anachronism. This is not a statement of preference; it is a statement of fact. In the following pages, therefore, the essays selected are taken from contemporary authors, the great majority of whom are still alive. Still more, they are among the most able writers of the age. To enable both teacher and pupil to estimate the relative reputation of each, short biographical accounts are appended in the index. Each author here, then, has something worth while to tell his age. The question is not of the truth or the validity of his statements. The compilers of this volume assume no responsibility for the opinions expressed. The essays were chosen because in their opinion the author succeeded in saying forcibly what he wished to say; the emphasis is on the form, not on

v

the facts ; on the method, not the content. The student, by analyzing these methods, will be enabled to express his own ideas.

In the following pages, also, will be found a wide range both in treatment and in subject matter. None of these essays is recommended as a perfect model, nor have the editors the hallucination that they have selected the " best " essays in the English language. Each has been selected, however, because in their opinion it offered a suggestive treatment for its particular subject and its particular audience. And each, of course, has the defects of its qualities. Although the epigrammatic brilliance of Whistler is as far removed as the poles from the closely coördinated reasoning of Professor Sumner, yet each succeeded in the particular object for which it was designed. The value, therefore, of a sympathetic study of such a collection is for the student to perceive clearly exactly what in each case is gained and what is lost, in order that he may profit in his own work. In the hope that he may be aided to this end, brief notes are prefixed to each essay, suggesting the scope and limitations of the type. And to the whole a general theoretical introduction has been prefixed, to explain the point of view.

The editors take pleasure in acknowledging their indebtedness to the various authors who have so generously given permission for the use of their essays and who, by many helpful suggestions, have aided greatly in making the selection. Their thanks are due also to the following publishers, who have very kindly permitted the use of valuable copyrighted material : D. Appleton and Company, The Century Company, Dodd, Mead and Company, George H. Doran Company, Harper and Brothers, John Lane Company, Longmans, Green, and Company,

The Macmillan Company, G. P. Putnam's Sons, Charles Scribner's Sons, Frederick A. Stokes Company, *The New York Sun*, The Yale University Press; to the editors of *The Yale Review* and of *The Yale Alumni Weekly*, for permission to reprint; and to Miss Clara B. Underwood and Mr. Hamilton J. Smith, for assistance in reading proof.

TABLE OF CONTENTS

TABLE OF CONTENTS

INTRODUCTION

To a teacher of rhetoric, or written composition, there are two factors in relation to the subject that seem of paramount interest. The first is the great popularity that it at present enjoys in educational institutions. Books dealing with it in whole or part — rhetorics, manuals, guides — pour daily from the press. No publisher seems really respectable without at least one upon his list, and large firms carry several. The demand for this sort of book seems inexhaustible. But just here comes the second factor, that among trained writers there exists a definite hostility toward the subject. Nor is this hostility merely negative. It is quite conceivable that to the advanced writer, who has forgotten his own youth, the elementary stages might seem a waste of time. But this is not the attitude. In an editorial in a great modern periodical, the impression was conveyed that certain work had "a deftness and power such as college instruction can never give." A subsequent editorial, in which this statement was emphasized, adds the limitation that "there are some men strong enough to survive even the 'composition course' of our modern colleges." This is not merely negative, this is positive. In the opinion of the editors of that periodical the composition course in a modern college is not only a waste of time, it is actually hurtful. Nor is that particular editor alone in his belief. And to a teacher of the subject it is scarcely a bracing thought that those that feel thus about his work are apt to be themselves very able writers !

What is the explanation of this apparent paradox? It seems to me that the reason lies in the type of teaching done in the name of rhetoric. An author, or a teacher, devises certain rules that he gives to the students both as guides to composition and as criteria for judgment. One may feel that the "split infinitive" is the mark of a lost soul; another may see all salvation in the placing of commas; the third may feel that the proper use of "only" differentiates the sheep from the goats. The value of such tests is that they are easy of application. This explains the irritation of the professional writer when dealing with a cub fresh from the class room. He finds his brilliant work condemned because of imaginary improprieties, and he feels that the college has debauched the lad by teaching him to lay major stress upon minor detail. The story is told of Leonardo, that when his pupils were called in to see the completed picture of the Last Supper, they fell in ecstasies over the tracery on the border of the tablecloth. Whereat the angry artist, with a sweep of his brush, annihilated the beautiful tracery, exclaiming, "Fools! look at the Master's face!" Is it not possible that our pupils also have been trained to see only the tracery? Has not much of our criticism been destructive, rather than constructive, our teaching what to avoid, rather than how to do?

In the country at large, however, there seem to be rather hazy notions concerning even the aim of such a course. When the pupil is asked why he has elected this subject, the almost invariable reply is that he wishes to learn how to express himself. But this is scarcely accurate. Mere self-expression is vocal. When one unexpectedly hits his thumb with a hammer, the first impluse is not to seize pen and paper, — it is to say something! The act of writing, then, presupposes more than the simple desire for self-expression; it assumes a desire to transmit the writer's thoughts and emotions to another. The sentence is a medium of communication between two individuals as surely as is a telephone wire. And the self-expression theory fails to account for the person at the other end. Thus the fact that a given piece is written posits for that piece two parties, the author and the reader. Even the most private diary is composed to be read, although by the writer, yet by the writer changed by a lapse of time. If this be true in so purely personal a matter, much more so is it true in any writing intended to be published. Obviously there the reader must be considered.

But with the introduction of the reader-element into the theory, a number of new deductions must be made. And the first of these is that in judging any work it is the opinion of the reader, not that of the author, that counts. In fact, the author is apt to be the worst judge of his own work. He knows what he has wished to say, and in the thrill of creation feels that he has said it. He is necessarily partial. But the measure of his success or failure is seen only in its effect upon the reader. In spite of the numerous canons of criticism, devised to enable an author to write perfectly, the reader remains the master of the situation, and works written by rule are deemed splendidly null and thrown on the scrap heap. Here, then, is an axiom in the teaching of composition. Stress positives rather than negatives. One *do* is worth ten *don'ts*. Explain to the pupil how to get his effect; avoid making him memorize faults. And, if possible, enable him to see the effect of his work upon a class of his own contemporaries. Composition so taught ceases to be an abstract terror, and becomes both vital and practical.

But if the study of composition is to be vital, each particular theme must be alive, that is, it must be interesting. The unpardonable sin in writing is dullness. But since, to make a subject interesting to others, you must first be interested in it yourself, it is better to allow pupils to choose the subjects for their own themes. Each pupil is then confronted with a definite problem. And the teacher has a real basis for criticism, because of the very fact that supposedly the writer was himself interested. By this means, also, the pupil learns to discriminate between the encyclopedic collection of unrelated facts and an article where all material is subordinated to a predetermined end, by watching the effect of both on the members of the class. He realizes that an "easy" subject is not the one on which he can pour forth an undigested mass of irrelevant material, but rather the one with which he can make a definite appeal. He learns practically the truth of the proverb that easy writing makes hard reading. And he begins his long apprenticeship in the art of composition.

Thus not the least for the pupil to learn is that interest is more apt to lie in the treatment than in the choice of the subject. Although certainly some topics are inherently more interesting than are others, there are very few that cannot be ruined by clumsy handling. And of those few rarely are any in the possession of the college undergraduate! If he is to hold the attention of the class, he will realize that he must do that not by what he writes, but by the manner in which he writes. Thus there is no *one* way to write. Every piece of written work represents an equation with three unknown quantities, the personality of the author, the peculiarity of the subject, and the presumed point of view of the imagined reader. The first is only the old philosophical maxim, Know thyself. He must learn the excellences and the limitations of his own mind, what he can do and what he had better let alone. And this can be learned only through long and painful practice. The second and the third are obviously more variable. The interest in a subject like "The Making of Bricks," for example, is narrowly circumscribed, and appeals only to a limited public. Theoretically such a subject can be best treated with perfect clarity. Yet here the question of the public must be considered. It is quite comprehensible that to an association of brick makers, the subject might be one of intense interest. But equally for such an association the treatment should be technical. This same reason applies equally to every possible composition. An editorial, if it be a successful editorial, should differ radically in tone from that of an essay on the same subject in a magazine, because the attention of the readers of the newspaper is distracted and fragmentary, whereas the magazine can assume comparative leisure and quiet. An academic address is rightfully different in the nature of its appeal from a popular essay. What is right for the one would be wrong for the other.

In general, the prime object of all expository writing may be said to be clarity, that the reader after he has finished may know exactly what the author intended. The simplest form, therefore, resembles a catalogue, wherein the author says I think so-and-so because of (a), (b), (c), etc. It is definite and clear, but it also lacks interest. That must be sought by the individual treatment of each factor, and the value of the whole depends upon the comprehensiveness of the list. Emphasis may to a measure be attained by a careful gradation of the various factors, the most important reserved to the last. At the worst, this type of essay separates into a number of disjointed paragraphs, or even sentences, bound together merely by the fact that they all treat of a common subject. Thus the reason why much of Emerson is such hard reading is not that his thought is so profound, but that the sequence of his thought is not expressed, and sometimes is non-existent. Consequently, the effect of the essay as a whole is lost. On the other hand, the value of this method of composition lies in the suggestiveness of the individual sentence, or the individual paragraph. And as the student presumably has neither the brilliance of Whistler, the profundity of Emerson, or the analytic power of Bryce, therein lies the danger. Yet it is the normal form.

Surer of its effect than the catalogue form, and yet more difficult to write, is that type of essay wherein the thought either starts with a generalization in the first paragraph and narrows to a particular in the last, or, on the contrary, starts with a particular in the first paragraph and expands in the last to a generalization. Either of these forms assumes that the whole essay has been conceived as a unit, that before the first word is written the last is clearly in mind, — in short, in Walter Pater's words, "that architectural conception of work, which foresees the end in the beginning and never loses sight of it, and in every part is conscious of all the rest, till the last sentence does but, with undiminished vigour, unfold and justify the first." This quality of "mind in style" is obviously powerful, as Mr. Pater himself has shown. It is an ideal to be held before the young writer. The difficulty here is, however, that it presupposes not only a trained mind in the writer, but also a trained mind in the reader. Both, to appreciate the bearing of the last sentence, must be conscious of all preceding sentences back to the first. There must be no trifling by the way. And unless the reader is willing to surrender himself completely, there is the unhappy possibility that he will never arrive at the last unfolding sentence! Yet for the chosen reader, compared to this all other forms seem futile.

But not only is the question of the form in which the thought is to be cast to be considered, there is also the problem of the development of the thought within the form. Here the student must watch the value of the concrete versus the abstract, the utility of the illustration, and the necessity for its restraint. And as these principles hold equally whether the composition be written or merely verbal, this is particularly valuable for those considering the profession of teaching. Thus as the concrete is interesting and may always be safely relied on to attract the attention of the class, to what extent may it be used without destroying the emphasis of the whole? In a lecture on the catholicity of Lamb's friendships, for example, how much space may be given to his acquaintance with Wainwright who combined the professions of author and poisoner? There is no doubt that with but little skill the class or the reader will be interested in Wainwright's performances, — only the nominal subject, Lamb, tends to be obscured in the process. Yet surely within limits such an appeal is justifiable. What are the limits?

A somewhat analogous problem is the use of the first person. There is a freshness and a vitality in the treatment of a subject where the first person appears. As I write this, I am aware of a sympathetic connection with you that read it. Not to make use of this obvious advantage seems absurd, and yet it was with pride that a friend of mine, on giving me his book, assured me that the pronoun "I" did not appear once. As the thought in the book was his thought, there was no reason why he should not have said so. The danger, however, of the wearisome repetition of that objectionable pronoun is that the effect will be one of disgusting egotism. The student that continually writes in the first person often trips on his own shadow. In the same way, the narrative of course may be used for expository content, but the writer must beware lest the result be a hybrid, neither a story nor an essay, but an amorphous creation possessing the disadvantages of both and the advantages of neither. And the only way he can learn to handle it is by study and practice.

It was with the aim of furnishing examples to illustrate such problems as these that the present book was compiled. There is no desire here to supersede the study of formal rhetoric, rather to supplement it. Within the last few years the revival of an interest in essays has carried the practice far beyond the bounds of the old regulation type of exposition, represented by "How to make a boat." In life, and it should be in college, there is little demand for the biographical essay where the industry of the author is in inverse proportion to the quantity of his facts. And when payment for an article is based upon the number of words, omission becomes elevated to a high art. Too long has our college teaching debauched our students into believing that a mere flux of words is in itself meritorious. The question that the students should ask is, not how long *must* it be, but how long *may* it be, and, provided always that the desired aim is accomplished, brevity should be considered a cardinal virtue. This means that the student should take the shortest route to his desired end, — namely, to transmit his thought and his emotions to his reader. And since in a free country there is no method of compelling the reader, the question of interest becomes paramount.

MODERN ESSAYS

"TEN O'CLOCK" [1]

BY

James McNeill Whistler

James McNeill Whistler, an American, one of the most eminent and most original of contemporary artists, was asked by the University of Oxford to deliver the following address explaining his theory of art. Here the sentence is the unit of structure. As such, it is rightfully paragraphed by itself. But in so doing, the author, by making a series of aphorisms upon art, has lost any collective effect. Thus the reader puts it down with a confused impression of a number of brilliant statements, but with no one definite single impression. Like a diamond emitting light from each of its facets, each sentence in turn holds the attention, not only in itself, but also regardless of what either precedes or follows. And the sequence of the sentences is largely a matter of indifference. The inference to be drawn from such a form is that it is at all cost to be avoided, since notwithstanding, or really because of, the brilliance of the sentence, the total effect is lost.

LADIES AND GENTLEMEN:

It is with great hesitation and much misgiving that I appear before you, in the character of The Preacher.

If timidity be at all allied to the virtue modesty, and can find favour in your eyes, I pray you, for the sake of that virtue, accord me your utmost indulgence.

I would plead for my want of habit, did it not seem preposterous, judging from precedent, that aught save the most efficient effrontery could be ever expected in connection with my subject — for I will not conceal from

[1] From "The Gentle Art for Making Enemies," by permission of the publishers, G. P. Putnam's Sons, New York and London.

11

you that I mean to talk about Art.   Yes, Art — that has
of late become, as far as much discussion and writing can
make it, a sort of common topic for the tea-table.

Art is upon the Town! — to be chucked under the chin
by the passing gallant — to be enticed within the gates
of the householder — to be coaxed into company, as a
proof of culture and refinement.

If familiarity can breed contempt, certainly Art — or
what is currently taken for it — has been brought to its
lowest stage of intimacy.

The people have been harassed with Art in every guise,
and vexed with many methods as to its endurance.   They
have been told how they shall love Art, and live with it.
Their homes have been invaded, their walls covered with
paper, their very dress taken to task — until, roused at
last, bewildered and filled with the doubts and discomforts
of senseless suggestion, they resent such intrusion, and cast
forth the false prophets, who have brought the very name
of the beautiful into disrepute, and derision upon themselves.

Alas! ladies and gentlemen, Art has been maligned.
She has naught in common with such practices.   She is
a goddess of dainty thought — reticent of habit, abjuring
all obtrusiveness, purposing in no way to better others.

She is, withal, selfishly occupied with her own perfection
only — having no desire to teach — seeking and finding the
beautiful in all conditions and in all times, as did her high
priest Rembrandt, when he saw picturesque grandeur
and noble dignity in the Jews' quarter of Amsterdam, and
lamented not that its inhabitants were not Greeks.

As did Tintoret and Paul Veronese, among the Vene-
tians, while not halting to change the brocaded silks for
the classic draperies of Athens.

As did, at the Court of Philip, Velasquez, whose Infantas, clad in inæsthetic hoops, are, as works of Art, of the same quality as the Elgin marbles.

No reformers were these great men — no improvers of the way of others! Their productions alone were their occupation, and, filled with the poetry of their science, they required not to alter their surroundings — for, as the laws of their Art were revealed to them they saw, in the development of their work, that real beauty which, to them, was as much a matter of certainty and triumph as is to the astronomer the verification of the result, foreseen with the light given to him alone. In all this, their world was completely severed from that of their fellow-creatures with whom sentiment is mistaken for poetry; and for whom there is no perfect work that shall not be explained by the benefit conferred upon themselves.

Humanity takes the place of Art, and God's creations are excused by their usefulness. Beauty is confounded with virtue, and, before a work of Art, it is asked: "What good shall it do?"

Hence it is that nobility of action, in this life, is hopelessly linked with the merit of the work that portrays it; and thus the people have acquired the habit of looking, as who should say, not *at* a picture, but *through* it, at some human fact, that shall, or shall not, from a social point of view, better their mental or moral state. So we have come to hear of the painting that elevates, and of the duty of the painter — of the picture that is full of thought, and of the panel that merely decorates.

A favourite faith, dear to those who teach, is that certain periods were especially artistic, and that nations, readily named, were notably lovers of Art.

So we are told that the Greeks were, as a people, wor-shippers of the beautiful, and that in the fifteenth century Art was engrained in the multitude.

That the great masters lived in common understanding with their patrons — that the early Italians were artists — all — and that the demand for the lovely thing produced it.

That we, of to-day, in gross contrast to this Arcadian purity, call for the ungainly, and obtain the ugly.

That, could we but change our habits and climate — were we willing to wander in groves — could we be roasted out of broadcloth — were we to do without haste, and journey without speed, we should again *require* the spoon of Queen Anne, and pick at our peas with the fork of two prongs. And so, for the flock, little hamlets grow near Hammersmith, and the steam horse is scorned.

Useless! quite hopeless and false is the effort! — built upon fable, and all because "a wise man has uttered a vain thing and filled his belly with the East wind."

Listen! There never was an artistic period.
There never was an Art-loving nation.

In the beginning, man went forth each day — some to do battle, some to the chase; others, again, to dig and to delve in the field — all that they might gain and live, or lose and die. Until there was found among them one, differing from the rest, whose pursuits attracted him not, and so he stayed by the tents with the women, and traced strange devices with a burnt stick upon a gourd.

This man, who took no joy in the ways of his brethren — who cared not for conquest, and fretted in the field — this designer of quaint patterns — this deviser of the beauti-ful — who perceived in Nature about him curious curv-ings, as faces are seen in the fire — this dreamer apart, was the first artist.

And when, from the field and from afar, there came back the people, they took the gourd — and drank from out of it.

And presently there came to this man another — and, in time, others — of like nature, chosen by the Gods — and so they worked together; and soon they fashioned, from the moistened earth, forms resembling the gourd. And with the power of creation, the heirloom of the artist, presently they went beyond the slovenly suggestion of Nature, and the first vase was born, in beautiful proportion.

And the toilers tilled, and were athirst; and the heroes returned from fresh victories, to rejoice and to feast; and all drank alike from the artists' goblets, fashioned cunningly, taking no note the while of the craftsman's pride, and understanding not his glory in his work; drinking at the cup, not from choice, not from a consciousness that it was beautiful, but because, forsooth, there was none other!

And time, with more state, brought more capacity for luxury, and it became well that men should dwell in large houses, and rest upon couches, and eat at tables; whereupon the artist, with his artificers, built palaces, and filled them with furniture, beautiful in proportion and lovely to look upon.

And the people lived in marvels of art — and ate and drank out of masterpieces — for there was nothing else to eat and to drink out of, and no bad building to live in; no article of daily life, of luxury, or of necessity, that had not been handed down from the design of the master, and made by his workmen.

And the people questioned not, *and had nothing to say in the matter.*

So Greece was in its splendour, and Art reigned supreme — by force of fact, not by election — and there was no meddling from the outsider. The mighty warrior would no more have ventured to offer a design for the temple of Pallas Athene than would the sacred poet have proffered a plan for constructing the catapult.

And the Amateur was unknown — and the Dilettante undreamed of!

And history wrote on, and conquest accompanied civilisation, and Art spread, or rather its products were carried by the victors among the vanquished from one country to another. And the customs of cultivation covered the face of the earth, so that all peoples continued to use what *the artist alone produced.*

And centuries passed in this using, and the world was flooded with all that was beautiful, until there arose a new class, who discovered the cheap, and foresaw fortune in the facture of the sham.

Then sprang into existence the tawdry, the common, the gewgaw.

The taste of the tradesman supplanted the science of the artist, and what was born of the million went back to them, and charmed them, for it was after their own heart; and the great and the small, the statesman and the slave, took to themselves the abomination that was tendered, and preferred it — and have lived with it ever since!

And the artist's occupation was gone, and the manufacturer and the huckster took his place.

And now the heroes filled from the jugs and drank from the bowls — with understanding — noting the glare of their new bravery, and taking pride in its worth.

And the people — this time — had much to say in the matter — and all were satisfied. And Birmingham and

Manchester arose in their might — and Art was relegated
to the curiosity shop.

Nature contains the elements, in colour and form, of all
pictures, as the keyboard contains the notes of all music.

But the artist is born to pick, and choose, and group
with science, these elements, that the result may be beautiful — as the musician gathers his notes, and forms his
chords, until he bring forth from chaos glorious harmony.

To say to the painter, that Nature is to be taken as she
is, is to say to the player, that he may sit on the piano. *Yes ?*

That Nature is always right, is an assertion, artistically,
as untrue, as it is one whose truth is universally taken for
granted. Nature is very rarely right, to such an extent
even, that it might almost be said that Nature is usually
wrong: that is to say, the condition of things that shall
bring about the perfection of harmony worthy a picture
is rare, and not common at all.

This would seem, to even the most intelligent, a doctrine almost blasphemous. So incorporated with our
education has the supposed aphorism become, that its
belief is held to be part of our moral being, and the words
themselves have, in our ear, the ring of religion. Still,
seldom does Nature succeed in producing a picture.

The sun blares, the wind blows from the east, the sky is
bereft of cloud, and without, all is of iron. The windows
of the Crystal Palace are seen from all points of London.
The holiday-maker rejoices in the glorious day, and the
painter turns aside to shut his eyes.

How little this is understood, and how dutifully the
casual in Nature is accepted as sublime, may be gathered
from the unlimited admiration daily produced by a very
foolish sunset.

c

The dignity of the snow-capped mountain is lost in distinctness, but the joy of the tourist is to recognise the traveller on the top. The desire to see, for the sake of seeing, is, with the mass, alone the one to be gratified, hence the delight in detail.

And when the evening mist clothes the riverside with poetry, as with a veil, and the poor buildings lose themselves in the dim sky, and the tall chimneys become campanili, and the warehouses are palaces in the night, and the whole city hangs in the heavens, and fairy-land is before us — then the wayfarer hastens home; the working man and the cultured one, the wise man and the one of pleasure, cease to understand, as they have ceased to see, and Nature, who, for once, has sung in tune, sings her exquisite song to the artist alone, her son and her master — her son in that he loves her, her master in that he knows her.

To him her secrets are unfolded, to him her lessons have become gradually clear. He looks at her flower, not with the enlarging lens, that he may gather facts for the botanist, but with the light of the one who sees in her choice selection of brilliant tones and delicate tints, suggestions of future harmonies.

He does not confine himself to purposeless copying, without thought, each blade of grass, as commended by the inconsequent, but, in the long curve of the narrow leaf, corrected by the straight tall stem, he learns how grace is wedded to dignity, how strength enhances sweetness, that elegance shall be the result.

In the citron wing of the pale butterfly, with its dainty spots of orange, he sees before him the stately halls of fair gold, with their slender saffron pillars, and is taught how the delicate drawing high upon the walls shall be traced in tender tones of orpiment, and repeated by the base in notes of graver hue.

In all that is dainty and lovable he finds hints for his own combinations, and *thus* is Nature ever his resource and always at his service, and to him is naught refused.

Through his brain, as through the last alembic, is distilled the refined essence of that thought which began with the Gods, and which they left him to carry out.

Set apart by them to complete their works, he produces that wondrous thing called the masterpiece, which surpasses in perfection all that they have contrived in what is called Nature; and the Gods stand by and marvel, and perceive how far away more beautiful is the Venus of Melos than was their own Eve.

For some time past, the unattached writer has become the middleman in this matter of Art, and his influence, while it has widened the gulf between the people and the painter, has brought about the most complete misunderstanding as to the aim of the picture.

For him a picture is more or less a hieroglyph or symbol of story. Apart from a few technical terms, for the display of which he finds an occasion, the work is considered absolutely from a literary point of view; indeed, from what other can he consider it? And in his essays he deals with it as with a novel — a history — or an anecdote. He fails entirely and most naturally to see its excellences, or demerits — artistic — and so degrades Art, by supposing it a method of bringing about a literary climax.

It thus, in his hands, becomes merely a means of perpetrating something further, and its mission is made a secondary one, even as a means is second to an end.

The thoughts emphasised, noble or other, are inevitably attached to the incident, and become more or less noble, according to the eloquence or mental quality of the writer, who looks the while, with disdain, upon what he holds as "mere execution" — a matter belonging, he believes, to the training of the schools, and the reward of assiduity. So that, as he goes on with his translation from canvas to paper, the work becomes his own. He finds poetry where he would feel it were he himself transcribing the event, invention in the intricacy of the *mise en scène*, and noble philosophy in some detail of philanthropy, courage, modesty, or virtue, suggested to him by the occurrence.

All this might be brought before him, and his imagination be appealed to, by a very poor picture — indeed, I might safely say that it generally is.

Meanwhile, the *painter's* poetry is quite lost to him — the amazing invention that shall have put form and colour into such perfect harmony, that exquisiteness is the result, he is without understanding — the nobility of thought, that shall have given the artist's dignity to the whole, says to him absolutely nothing.

So that his praises are published, for virtues we would blush to possess — while the great qualities, that distinguish the one work from the thousand, that make of the masterpiece the thing of beauty that it is — have never been seen at all.

That this is so, we can make sure of, by looking back at old reviews upon past exhibitions, and reading the flatteries lavished upon men who have since been forgotten altogether — but, upon whose works, the language has been exhausted, in rhapsodies — that left nothing for the National Gallery.

A curious matter, in its effect upon the judgment of these gentlemen, is the accepted vocabulary of poetic symbolism, that helps them, by habit, in dealing with Nature : a mountain, to them, is synonymous with height — a lake, with depth — the ocean, with vastness — the sun, with glory.

So that a picture with a mountain, a lake, and an ocean — however poor in paint — is inevitably "lofty," "vast," "infinite," and "glorious" — on paper.

There are those also, sombre of mien, and wise with the wisdom of books, who frequent museums and burrow in crypts ;   collecting — comparing — compiling — classifying — contradicting.

Experts these — for whom a date is an accomplishment — a hall-mark, success !

Careful in scrutiny are they, and conscientious of judgment — establishing, with due weight, unimportant reputations — discovering the picture, by the stain on the back — testing the torso, by the leg that is missing — filling folios with doubts on the way of that limb — disputatious and dictatorial, concerning the birthplace of inferior persons — speculating, in much writing, upon the great worth of bad work.

True clerks of the collection, they mix memoranda with ambition, and, reducing Art to statistics, they "file" the fifteenth century, and "pigeon-hole" the antique !

Then the Preacher "appointed" !

He stands in high places — harangues and holds forth.

Sage of the Universities — learned in many matters, and of much experience in all, save his subject.

Exhorting — denouncing — directing.

Filled with wrath and earnestness.

Bringing powers of persuasion, and polish of language, to prove — nothing.

Torn with much teaching — having naught to impart.

Impressive — important — shallow.

Defiant — distressed — desperate.

Crying out, and cutting himself — while the gods hear not.

Gentle priest of the Philistine withal, again he ambles pleasantly from all point, and through many volumes, escaping scientific assertion — "babbles of green fields."

So Art has become foolishly confounded with education — that all should be equally qualified.

Whereas, while polish, refinement, culture, and breeding, are in no way arguments for artistic result, it is also no reproach to the most finished scholar or greatest gentleman in the land that he be absolutely without eye for painting or ear for music — that in his heart he prefers the popular print to the scratch of Rembrandt's needle, or the songs of the hall to Beethoven's "C minor Symphony."

Let him have but the wit to say so, and not feel the admission a proof of inferiority.

Art happens — no hovel is safe from it, no Prince may depend upon it, the vastest intelligence cannot bring it about, and puny efforts to make it universal end in quaint comedy, and coarse farce.

This is as it should be — and all attempts to make it otherwise are due to the eloquence of the ignorant, the zeal of the conceited.

The boundary-line is clear. Far from me to propose to bridge it over — that the pestered people be pushed across.

No! I would save them from further fatigue. I would come to their relief, and would lift from their shoulders this incubus of Art.

Why, after centuries of freedom from it, and indifference to it, should it now be thrust upon them by the blind — until wearied and puzzled, they know no longer how they shall eat or drink — how they shall sit or stand — or wherewithal they shall clothe themselves — without afflicting Art.

But, lo! there is much talk without!

Triumphantly they cry, "Beware! This matter does indeed concern us. We also have our part in all true Art! — for, remember the 'one touch of Nature' that 'makes the whole world kin.'"

True, indeed. But let not the unwary jauntily suppose that Shakespeare herewith hands him his passport to Paradise, and thus permits him speech among the chosen. Rather, learn that, in this very sentence, he is condemned to remain without — to continue with the common.

This one chord that vibrates with all — this "one touch of Nature" that calls aloud to the response of each — that explains the popularity of the "Bull" of Paul Potter — that excuses the price of Murillo's "Conception" — this one unspoken sympathy that pervades humanity, is — Vulgarity!

Vulgarity — under whose fascinating influence "the many" have elbowed "the few," and the gentle circle of Art swarms with the intoxicated mob of mediocrity, whose leaders prate and counsel, and call aloud, where the Gods once spoke in whisper!

And now from their midst the Dilettante stalks abroad.

The amateur is loosed. The voice of the æsthete is heard in the land, and catastrophe is upon us.

The meddler beckons the vengeance of the Gods, and ridicule threatens the fair daughters of the land.

And there are curious converts to a weird *culte*, in which all instinct for attractiveness — all freshness and sparkle — all woman's winsomeness — is to give way to a strange vocation for the unlovely — and this desecration in the name of the Graces!

Shall this gaunt, ill-at-ease, distressed, abashed mixture of *mauvaise honte* and desperate assertion call itself artistic, and claim cousinship with the artist — who delights in the dainty, the sharp, bright gaiety of beauty?

No! — a thousand times no! Here are no connections of ours.

We will have nothing to do with them.

Forced to seriousness, that emptiness may be hidden, they dare not smile —

While the artist, in fulness of heart and head, is glad, and laughs aloud, and is happy in his strength, and is merry at the pompous pretension — the solemn silliness that surrounds him.

For Art and Joy go together, with bold openness, and high head, and ready hand — fearing naught, and dreading no exposure.

Know, then, all beautiful women, that we are with you. Pay no heed, we pray you, to this outcry of the unbecoming — this last plea for the plain.

It concerns you not.

Your own instinct is near the truth — your own wit far surer guide than the untaught ventures of thick-heeled Apollos.

What! will you up and follow the first piper that leads

you down Petticoat Lane, there, on a Sabbath, to gather, for the week, from the dull rags of ages wherewith to bedeck yourselves? that, beneath your travestied awkwardness, we have trouble to find your own dainty selves? Oh, fie! Is the world, then, exhausted? and must we go back because the thumb of the mountebank jerks the other way?

Costume is not dress.

And the wearers of wardrobes may not be doctors of taste!

For by what authority shall these be pretty masters? Look well, and nothing have they invented — nothing put together for comeliness' sake.

Haphazard from their shoulders hang the garments of the hawker — combining in their person the motley of many manners with the medley of the mummers' closet.

Set up as a warning, and a finger-post of danger, they point to the disastrous effect of Art upon the middle classes.

Why this lifting of the brow in deprecation of the present — this pathos in reference to the past?

If Art be rare to-day, it was seldom heretofore.

It is false, this teaching of decay.

The master stands in no relation to the moment at which he occurs — a monument of isolation — hinting at sadness — having no part in the progress of his fellow-men.

He is also no more the product of civilisation than is the scientific truth asserted dependent upon the wisdom of a period. The assertion itself requires the *man* to make it. The truth was from the beginning.

So Art is limited to the infinite, and beginning there cannot progress.

A silent indication of its wayward independence from

all extraneous advance, is in the absolutely unchanged condition and form of implement since the beginning of things.

The painter has but the same pencil — the sculptor the chisel of centuries.

Colours are not more since the heavy hangings of night were first drawn aside, and the loveliness of light revealed.

Neither chemist or engineer can offer new elements of the masterpiece.

False again, the fabled link between the grandeur of Art and the glories and virtues of the State, for Art feeds not upon nations, and peoples may be wiped from the face of the earth, but Art *is*.

It is indeed high time that we cast aside the weary weight of responsibility and co-partnership, and know that, in no way, do our virtues minister to its worth, in no way do our vices impede its triumph!

How irksome! how hopeless! how superhuman the self-imposed task of the nation! How sublimely vain the belief that it shall live nobly or art perish.

Let us reassure ourselves, at our own option is our virtue. Art we in no way affect.

A whimsical goddess, and a capricious, her strong sense of joy tolerates no dulness, and, live we never so spotlessly, still may she turn her back upon us.

As, from time immemorial, she has done upon the Swiss in their mountains.

What more worthy people! Whose every Alpine gap yawns with tradition, and is stocked with noble story; yet, the perverse and scornful one will none of it, and the sons of patriots are left with the clock that turns the mill, and the sudden cuckoo, with difficulty restrained in its box!

For this was Tell a hero! For this did Gessler die!

Art, the cruel jade, cares not, and hardens her heart, and hies her off to the East, to find, among the opium-eaters of Nankin, a favourite with whom she lingers fondly — caressing his blue porcelain, and painting his coy maidens, and marking his plates with her six marks of choice — indifferent in her companionship with him, to all save the virtue of his refinement!

He it is who calls her — he who holds her!

And again to the West, that her next lover may bring together the Gallery at Madrid, and show to the world how the Master towers above all; and in their intimacy they revel, he and she, in this knowledge; and he knows the happiness untasted by other mortal.

She is proud of her comrade, and promises that in after-years, others shall pass that way, and understand.

So in all time does this superb one cast about for the man worthy her love — and Art seeks the Artist alone.

Where he is, there she appears, and remains with him — loving and fruitful — turning never aside in moments of hope deferred — of insult — and of ribald misunderstanding; and when he dies she sadly takes her flight, though loitering yet in the land, from fond association, but refusing to be consoled.[1]

With the man, then, and not with the multitude, are her intimacies; and in the book of her life the names inscribed are few — scant, indeed, the list of those who have helped to write her story of love and beauty.

From the sunny morning, when, with her glorious Greek relenting, she yielded up the secret of repeated line, as,

---

[1] And so have we the ephemeral influence of the Master's memory — the afterglow, in which are warmed, for a while, the worker and disciple.

with his hand in hers, together they marked in marble,
the measured rhyme of lovely limb and draperies flowing
in unison, to the day when she dipped the Spaniard's
brush in light and air, and made his people live within
their frames, and *stand upon their legs*, that all nobility
and sweetness, and tenderness, and magnificence should be
theirs by right, ages had gone by, and few had been her
choice.

Countless, indeed, the horde of pretenders! But she
knew them not.

A teeming, seething, busy mass, whose virtue was industry, and whose industry was vice!

Their names go to fill the catalogue of the collection at
home, of the gallery abroad, for the delectation of the
bagman and the critic.

Therefore have we cause to be merry! — and to cast
away all care — resolved that all is well — as it ever
was — and that it is not meet that we should be cried at,
and urged to take measures!

Enough have we endured of dulness! Surely are we
weary of weeping, and our tears have been cozened from
us falsely, for they have called out woe! when there was
no grief — and, alas! where all is fair!

We have then but to wait — until, with the mark of
the Gods upon him — there come among us again the
chosen — who shall continue what has gone before. Satisfied that, even were he never to appear, the story of the
beautiful is already complete — hewn in the marbles of
the Parthenon — and broidered, with the birds, upon the
fan of Hokusai — at the foot of Fusiyama.

TACT [1]

BY

SIR JOHN LUBBOCK

In Lord Avebury's essay, as in the Whistler, there is no one dominating thought. It consists of a series of paragraphs united only by the fact that they deal with a common subject. But whereas in Whistler it was the sentence that was the unit, here it is the paragraph. The order of the paragraphs, however, is of no apparent importance. Thus there is no obvious reason why the paragraph "Have the courage of your opinions" should precede rather than follow that beginning "Be frank, and yet be reserved." Consequently this is not really one essay, but a series of little essays, and the value of the whole is the sum of the values of the component parts. But as no paragraph receives any support from its fellows, one must be very sure of the value of the separate thoughts before he dare risk so loose a structure. On the other hand, it has this advantage that each thought can be considered without relation to the rest. Consequently, while in the hands of a suggestive thinker, it is a perfectly possible form, for the beginner it is very difficult. And yet it is precisely this form that the beginner is moved to attempt!

FOR success in life tact is more important than talent, but it is not easily acquired by those to whom it does not come naturally. Still something can be done by considering what others would probably wish.

Never lose a chance of giving pleasure. Be courteous to all. "Civility," said Lady Montague, "costs nothing and buys everything." It buys much, indeed, which no money will purchase. Try then to win every one you

[1] From "The Use of Life," by permission of The Macmillan Co.

meet. "Win their hearts," said Burleigh to Queen Elizabeth, "and you have all men's hearts and purses."

Tact often succeeds where force fails. Lilly quotes the
old fable of the Sun and the Wind: "It is pretily noted
of a contention betweene the Winde and the Sunne, who
should have the victorye. A Gentleman walking abroad,
the Winde thought to blowe off his cloake, which with
great blastes and blusterings striuing to vnloose it, made
it to stick faster to his backe, for the more the Winde
encreased the closer his cloake clapt to his body: then
the Sunne, shining with his hot beams, began to warm
this gentleman, who waxing somewhat faint in this faire
weather, did not only put off his cloake but his coate, which
the Wynde perceiuing, yeelded the conquest to the Sunne."

Always remember that men are more easily led than
driven, and that in any case it is better to guide than to
coerce.

> "What thou wilt
> Thou rather shalt enforce it with thy smile,
> Than hew to't with thy sword." [1]

It is a good rule in politics, "pas trop gouverner."

Try to win, and still more to deserve, the confidence of
those with whom you are brought in contact. Many a
man has owed his influence far more to character than to
ability. Sydney Smith used to say of Francis Horner,
who, without holding any high office, exercised a remarkable personal influence in the Councils of the Nation,
that he had the Ten Commandments stamped upon his
countenance.

Try to meet the wishes of others as far as you rightly
and wisely can; but do not be afraid to say "No."

[1] Shakespeare.

Anybody can say "Yes," though it is not every one
who can say "Yes" pleasantly; but it is far more difficult
to say "No." Many a man has been ruined because he
could not do so. Plutarch tells us that the inhabitants of
Asia Minor came to be vassals only for not having been
able to pronounce one syllable, which is "No." And if
in the Conduct of Life it is essential to say "No," it is
scarcely less necessary to be able to say it pleasantly. We
ought always to endeavour that everybody with whom we
have any transactions should feel that it is a pleasure to do
business with us and should wish to come again. Business
is a matter of sentiment and feeling far more than many
suppose; every one likes being treated with kindness and
courtesy, and a frank pleasant manner will often clench
a bargain more effectually than a half per cent.

Almost any one may make himself pleasant if he wishes.
"The desire of pleasing is at least half the art of doing
it:"[1] and, on the other hand, no one will please others who
does not desire to do so. If you do not acquire this great
gift while you are young, you will find it much more difficult afterwards. Many a man has owed his outward success in life far more to good manners than to any solid merit;
while, on the other hand, many a worthy man, with a good
heart and kind intentions, makes enemies merely by the
roughness of his manner. To be able to please is, moreover, itself a great pleasure. Try it, and you will not be
disappointed.

Be wary and keep cool. A cool head is as necessary as
a warm heart. In any negotiations, steadiness and coolness are invaluable; while they will often carry you in
safety through times of danger and difficulty.

If you come across others less clever than you are, you

[1] Chesterfield's "Letters."

have no right to look down on them. There is nothing more to be proud of in inheriting great ability, than a great estate. The only credit in either case is if they are used well. Moreover, many a man is much cleverer than he seems. It is far more easy to read books than men. In this the eyes are a great guide. "When the eyes say one thing and the tongue another, a practised man relies on the language of the first." [1]

Do not trust too much to professions of extreme goodwill. Men do not fall in love with men, nor women with women, at first sight. If a comparative stranger protests and promises too much, do not place implicit confidence in what he says. If not insincere, he probably says more than he means, and perhaps wants something himself from you. Do not therefore believe that every one is a friend, merely because he professes to be so; nor assume too lightly that any one is an enemy.

We flatter ourselves by claiming to be rational and intellectual beings, but it would be a great mistake to suppose that men are always guided by reason. We are strange inconsistent creatures, and we act quite as often, perhaps oftener, from prejudice or passion. The result is that you are more likely to carry men with you by enlisting their feelings, than by convincing their reason. This applies, moreover, to companies of men even more than to individuals.

Argument is always a little dangerous. It often leads to coolness and misunderstandings. You may gain your argument and lose your friend, which is probably a bad bargain. If you must argue, admit all you can, but try and show that some point has been overlooked. Very few people know when they have had the worst of an

[1] Emerson.

argument, and if they do, they do not like it. Moreover, if they know they are beaten, it does not follow that they are convinced. Indeed it is perhaps hardly going too far to say that it is very little use trying to convince any one by argument. State your case as clearly and concisely as possible, and if you shake his confidence in his own opinion it is as much as you can expect. It is the first step gained.

Conversation is an art in itself, and it is by no means those who have most to tell who are the best talkers; though it is certainly going too far to say with Lord Chesterfield that "there are very few Captains of Foot who are not much better company than ever were Descartes or Sir Isaac Newton."

I will not say that it is as difficult to be a good listener as a good talker, but it is certainly by no means easy, and very nearly as important. You must not receive everything that is said as a critic or a judge, but suspend your judgment, and try to enter into the feelings of the speaker. If you are kind and sympathetic your advice will be often sought, and you will have the satisfaction of feeling that you have been a help and comfort to many in distress and trouble.

Do not expect too much attention when you are young. Sit, listen, and look on. Bystanders proverbially see most of the game; and you can notice what is going on just as well, if not better, when you are not noticed yourself. It is almost as if you possessed a cap of invisibility.

To save themselves the trouble of thinking, which is to most people very irksome, men will often take you at your own valuation. "On ne vaut dans ce monde," says La Bruyère, "que ce que l'on veut valoir."

Do not make enemies for yourself; you can make nothing worse.

D

"Answer not a fool according to his folly,
Lest thou also be like unto him." [1]

Remember that "a soft answer turneth away wrath;" but even an angry answer is less foolish than a sneer: nine men out of ten would rather be abused, or even injured, than laughed at. They will forget almost anything sooner than being made ridiculous.

"It is pleasanter to be deceived than to be undeceived." Trasilaus, an Athenian, went mad, and thought that all the ships in the Piræus belonged to him, but having been cured by Crito, he complained bitterly that he had been robbed. It is folly, says Lord Chesterfield, "to lose a friend for a jest: but, in my mind, it is not a much less degree of folly, to make an enemy of an indifferent and neutral person for the sake of a bon-mot."

Do not be too ready to suspect a slight, or think you are being laughed at — to say with Scrub in the Stratagem, "I am sure they talked of me, for they laughed consumedly." On the other hand, if you *are* laughed at, try to rise above it. If you can join in heartily, you will turn the tables and gain rather than lose. Every one likes a man who can enjoy a laugh at his own expense — and justly so, for it shows good-humour and good-sense. If you laugh at yourself, other people will not laugh at you.

Have the courage of your opinions. You must expect to be laughed at sometimes, and it will do you no harm. There is nothing ridiculous in seeming to be what you really are, but a good deal in affecting to be what you are not. People often distress themselves, get angry, and drift into a coolness with others, for some quite imaginary grievance.

[1] Proverbs.

Be frank, and yet reserved. Do not talk much about yourself; neither of yourself, for yourself, nor against yourself: but let other people talk about themselves, as much as they will. If they do so it is because they like it, and they will think all the better of you for listening to them. At any rate do not show a man, unless it is your duty, that you think he is a fool or a blockhead. If you do, he has good reason to complain. You may be wrong in your judgment; he will, and with some justice, form the same opinion of you.

Burke once said that he could not draw an indictment against a nation, and it is very unwise as well as unjust to attack any class or profession. Individuals often forget and forgive, but Societies never do. Moreover, even individuals will forgive an injury much more readily than an insult. Nothing rankles so much as being made ridiculous. You will never gain your object by putting people out of humour, or making them look ridiculous.

Goethe in his "Conversations with Eckermann" commended our countrymen. Their entrance and bearing in Society, he said, were so confident and quiet that one would think they were everywhere the masters, and the whole world belonged to them. Eckermann replied that surely young Englishmen were no cleverer, better educated, or better hearted than young Germans. "That is not the point," said Goethe; "their superiority does not lie in such things, neither does it lie in their birth and fortune: it lies precisely in their having the courage to *be* what nature made them. There is no *halfness* about them. They are *complete* men. Sometimes complete fools also, that I heartily admit; but even that is something, and has its weight."

In any business or negotiations, be patient. Many a

man would rather you heard his story than granted his request : many an opponent has been tired out.

Above all, never lose your temper, and if you do, at any rate hold your tongue, and try not to show it.

> "Cease from anger, and forsake wrath :
> Fret not thyself in any wise to do evil." [1]

For

> "A soft answer turneth away wrath :
> But grievous words stir up anger." [2]

Never intrude where you are not wanted. There is plenty of room elsewhere. "Have I not three kingdoms?" said King James to the Fly, "and yet thou must needs fly in my eye." [3]

Some people seem to have a knack of saying the wrong thing, of alluding to any subject which revives sad memories, or rouses differences of opinion.

No branch of Science is more useful than the knowledge of Men. It is of the utmost importance to be able to decide wisely, not only to know whom you can trust, and whom you cannot, but how far, and in what, you can trust them. This is by no means easy. It is most important to choose well those who are to work with you, and under you ; to put the square man in the square hole, and the round man in the round hole.

"If you suspect a man, do not employ him : if you employ him, do not suspect him." [4]

Those who trust are oftener right than those who mistrust.

Confidence should be complete, but not blind. Merlin lost his life, wise as he was, for imprudently yielding to Vivien's appeal to trust her "all in all or not at all."

[1] Psalms.
[2] Proverbs.
[3] Selden's "Table Talk."
[4] Confucius.

Be always discreet. Keep your own counsel. If you do not keep it for yourself, you cannot expect others to keep it for you. "The mouth of a wise man is in his heart; the heart of a fool is in his mouth, for what he knoweth or thinketh he uttereth."

Use your head. Consult your reason. It is not infallible, but you will be less likely to err if you do so.

Speech is, or ought to be silvern, but silence is golden.

Many people talk, not because they have anything to say, but for the mere love of talking. Talking should be an exercise of the brain, rather than of the tongue. Talkativeness, the love of talking for talking's sake, is almost fatal to success. Men are "plainly hurried on, in the heat of their talk, to say quite different things from what they first intended, and which they afterwards wish unsaid: or improper things, which they had no other end in saying, but only to find employment to their tongue.

* * * * * * *

And this unrestrained volubility and wantonness in speech is the occasion of numberless evils and vexations in life. It begets resentment in him who is the subject of it; sows the seed of strife and dissension amongst others; and inflames little disgusts and offences, which, if let alone, would wear away of themselves." [1]

"C'est une grande misère," says La Bruyère, "que de n'avoir pas assez d'esprit pour bien parler, ni assez de jugement pour se taire." Plutarch tells a story of Demaratus, that being asked in a certain assembly whether he held his tongue because he was a fool, or for want of

[1] Dr. Butler's "Sermons."

words, he replied, "A fool cannot hold his tongue."
"Seest thou," said Solomon,

> "Seest thou a man that is hasty in his words?
> There is more hope of a fool than of him." [1]

Never try to show your own superiority: few things
annoy people more than being made to feel small.

Do not be too positive in your statements. You may
be wrong, however sure you feel. Memory plays us
curious tricks, and both ears and eyes are sometimes
deceived. Our prejudices, even the most cherished, may
have no secure foundation. Moreover, even if you are
right, you will lose nothing by disclaiming too great
certainty.

In action, again, never make too sure, and never throw
away a chance. "There's many a slip 'twixt the cup and
the lip."

It has been said that everything comes to those who
know how to wait; and when the opportunity does come,
seize it.

> "He that wills not, when he may;
> When he will, he shall have nay."

If you once let your opportunity go, you may never
have another.

> "There is a tide in the affairs of men,
>   Which taken at the flood, leads on to fortune:
>   Omitted, all the voyage of their life
>   Is bound in shallows and in miseries.
>   On such a full sea are we now afloat:
>   And we must take the current when it serves,
>   Or lose our venture." [2]

[1] Proverbs xxix. 20.   [2] Shakespeare.

Be cautious, but not over-cautious; do not be too much afraid of making a mistake; "a man who never makes a mistake, will make nothing."

Always dress neatly: we must dress, therefore we should do it well, though not too well; not extravagantly, either in time or money, but taking care to have good materials. It is astonishing how much people judge by dress. Of those you come across, many go mainly by appearances in any case, and many more have in your case nothing but appearances to go by. The eyes and ears open the heart, and a hundred people will see, for one who will know you. Moreover, if you are careless and untidy about yourself, it is a fair, though not absolute, conclusion that you will be careless about other things also.

When you are in Society study those who have the best and pleasantest manners. "Manner," says the old proverb with much truth, if with some exaggeration, "maketh Man," and "a pleasing figure is a perpetual letter of recommendation." [1] "Merit and knowledge will not gain hearts, though they will secure them when gained. Engage the eyes by your address, air, and motions; soothe the ears by the elegance and harmony of your diction; and the heart will certainly (I should rather say probably) follow." [2] Every one has eyes and ears, but few have a sound judgment. The world is a stage. We are all players, and every one knows how much the success of a piece depends upon the way it is acted.

Lord Chesterfield, speaking of his son, says, "They tell me he is loved wherever he is known, and I am very glad of it; but I would have him be liked before he is known, and loved afterwards. . . . You know very little of the nature of mankind, if you take those things to be of little

[1] Bacon. [2] Lord Chesterfield.

consequence; one cannot be too attentive to them; it is they that always engage the heart, of which the understanding is commonly the bubble."

The Graces help a man in life almost as much as the Muses. We all know that "one man may steal a horse, while another may not look over a hedge;" and why? because the one will do it pleasantly, the other disagreeably. Horace tells us that even Youth and Mercury, the God of Eloquence and of the Arts, were powerless without the Graces.

BOOK–BUYING [1]

Augustine Birrell

As the student is taught in any rhetoric, an essay to have *unity* must
have one dominating idea, in order that, when the reader finishes, he
may summarize the thought in a single sentence. Theoretically each
paragraph has a definite bearing on that one sentence. Yet in such
an essay as this of Mr. Birrell such a summary is impossible. The
paragraphs are associational, rather than logical. The thought may be
roughly expressed in the following sequence : although the older generation feel that book-buying has gone out of fashion, actually, as is proved
by the prices in the catalogues, it is still done ; private libraries are growing up on all sides ; provided that they are not inherited, each library
expresses the owner ; and yet the owner's possession is merely temporal. Between these thoughts there is no logical sequence. The
author is trying to give the effect of fireside conversation where the
second idea arises from the first but is not caused by it. Consequently
there is no one dominating thought, and equally the relation of the
paragraphs is merely chronological. It is not a series of sentences, like
the Whistler, nor a series of paragraphs like Lord Avebury's " Tact " ; it
has a unity, but that unity is one of emotion, rather than one of thought.
Consequently, however charming may be this particular essay, it is a
dangerous model.

THE most distinguished of living Englishmen, who,
great as he is in many directions, is perhaps inherently
more a man of letters than anything else, has been over-
heard mournfully to declare that there were more book-

---

[1] From "Obiter Dicta," Second Series, by permission of the publishers,
Charles Scribner's Sons.

sellers' shops in his native town sixty years ago, when he
was a boy in it, than are to-day to be found within its
boundaries. And yet the place 'all unabashed' now
boasts its bookless self a city!

Mr. Gladstone was, of course, referring to second-hand
bookshops. Neither he nor any other sensible man puts
himself out about new books. When a new book is
published, read an old one, was the advice of a sound
though surly critic. It is one of the boasts of letters to
have glorified the term 'second-hand,' which other crafts
have "soiled to all ignoble use." But why it has been
able to do this is obvious. All the best books are necessarily second-hand. The writers of to-day need not grumble. Let them 'bide a wee.' If their books are worth
anything, they, too, one day will be second-hand. If
their books are not worth anything there are ancient trades
still in full operation amongst us — the pastrycooks and
the trunkmakers — who must have paper.

But is there any substance in the plaint that nobody
now buys books, meaning thereby second-hand books?
The late Mark Pattison, who had 16,000 volumes, and
whose lightest word has therefore weight, once stated that
he had been informed, and verily believed, that there were
men of his own University of Oxford who, being in uncon-
trolled possession of annual incomes of not less than £500,
thought they were doing the thing handsomely if they expended £50 a year upon their libraries. But we are not
bound to believe this unless we like. There was a touch
of morosity about the late Rector of Lincoln which led him
to take gloomy views of men, particularly Oxford men.

No doubt arguments *a priori* may readily be found to
support the contention that the habit of book-buying is
on the decline. I confess to knowing one or two men,

not Oxford men either, but Cambridge men (and the passion of Cambridge for literature is a by-word), who, on the plea of being pressed with business, or because they were going to a funeral, have passed a bookshop in a strange town without so much as stepping inside "just to see whether the fellow had anything." But painful as facts of this sort necessarily are, any damaging inference we might feel disposed to draw from them is dispelled by a comparison of price-lists. Compare a bookseller's catalogue of 1862 with one of the present year, and your pessimism is washed away by the tears which unrestrainedly flow as you see what *bonnes fortunes* you have lost. A young book-buyer might well turn out upon Primrose Hill and bemoan his youth, after comparing old catalogues with new.

Nothing but American competition, grumble some old stagers.

Well! why not? This new battle for the books is a free fight, not a private one, and Columbia has 'joined in.' Lower prices are not to be looked for. The book-buyer of 1900 will be glad to buy at to-day's prices. I take pleasure in thinking he will not be able to do so. Good finds grow scarcer and scarcer. True it is that but a few short weeks ago I picked up (such is the happy phrase, most apt to describe what was indeed a 'street casualty') a copy of the orginial edition of *Endymion* (Keats's poem — O subscriber to Mudie's! — not Lord Beaconsfield's novel) for the easy equivalent of half-a-crown — but then that was one of my lucky days. The enormous increase of booksellers' catalogues and their wide circulation amongst the trade has already produced a hateful uniformity of prices. Go where you will it is all the same to the odd sixpence. Time was when you could

map out the country for yourself with some hopefulness
of plunder. There were districts where the Elizabethan
dramatists were but slenderly protected. A raid into the
'bonnie North Countrie' sent you home again cheered
with chap-books and weighted with old pamphlets of curious interests; whilst the West of England seldom failed
to yield a crop of novels. I remember getting a complete
set of the Brontë books in the original issues at Torquay,
I may say, for nothing. Those days are over. Your
country bookseller is, in fact, more likely, such tales does
he hear of London auctions, and such catalogues does he
receive by every post, to exaggerate the value of his wares
than to part with them pleasantly, and as a country
bookseller should, "just to clear my shelves, you know,
and give me a bit of room." The only compensation for
this is the catalogues themselves. You get *them*, at least,
for nothing, and it cannot be denied that they make
mighty pretty reading.

These high prices tell their own tale, and force upon us
the conviction that there never were so many private
libraries in course of growth as there are to-day.

Libraries are not made; they grow. Your first two thousand volumes present no difficulty, and cost astonishingly
little money. Given £400 and five years, and an ordinary
man can in the ordinary course, without undue haste or
putting any pressure upon his taste, surround himself with
this number of books, all in his own language, and thence-
forward have at least one place in the world in which it
is possible to be happy. But pride is still out of the
question. To be proud of having two thousand books
would be absurd. You might as well be proud of having
two top-coats. After your first two thousand difficulty
begins, but until you have ten thousand volumes the less

you say about your library the better. *Then* you may begin to speak.

It is no doubt a pleasant thing to have a library left you. The present writer will disclaim no such legacy, but hereby undertakes to accept it, however dusty. But good as it is to inherit a library, it is better to collect one. Each volume then, however lightly a stranger's eye may roam from shelf to shelf, has its own individuality, a history of its own. You remember where you got it, and how much you gave for it; and your word may safely be taken for the first of these facts, but not for the second.

The man who has a library of his own collection is able to contemplate himself objectively, and is justified in believing in his own existence. No other man but he would have made precisely such a combination as his. Had he been in any single respect different from what he is, his library, as it exists, never would have existed. Therefore, surely he may exclaim, as in the gloaming he contemplates the backs of his loved ones, "They are mine, and I am theirs."

But the eternal note of sadness will find its way even through the keyhole of a library. You turn some familiar page, of Shakespeare it may be, and his 'infinite variety,' his 'multitudinous mind,' suggests some new thought, and as you are wondering over it you think of Lycidas, your friend, and promise yourself the pleasure of having his opinion of your discovery the very next time when by the fire you two "help waste a sullen day." Or it is, perhaps, some quainter, tenderer fancy that engages your solitary attention, something in Sir Philip Sydney or Henry Vaughan, and then you turn to look for Phyllis, ever the best interpreter of love, human or divine. Alas! the printed page grows hazy beneath a filmy eye as you suddenly remember that Lycidas is dead — " dead ere his prime " — and that the pale cheek of Phyllis will never again be re-lumined by the white light of her pure enthusiasm. And then you fall to thinking of the inevitable, and perhaps, in your present mood, not unwelcome hour, when the 'ancient peace' of your old friends will be disturbed, when rude hands will dislodge them from their accustomed nooks and break up their goodly company.

> "Death bursts amongst them like a shell,
> And strews them over half the town."

They will form new combinations, lighten other men's toil, and soothe another's sorrow. Fool that I was to call anything *mine!*

ALEXANDER HAMILTON [1]

BY

FREDERIC HARRISON

In the problem presented in reviewing a book, likewise, it is unity of impression that is sought, rather than a definite logical unity of the thought. The reviewer aims rather to record his impression than to prove a case. To us Americans, Mr. Harrison's review of Mr. Oliver's study of Hamilton is interesting as enabling us to see a national figure through foreign eyes. For his English readers, Mr. Harrison starts with discussion of the need for such a work. Then a paragraph dealing with previous writers on Hamilton. Two paragraphs follow criticizing the method of presentation chosen by Mr. Oliver. One paragraph summarizes Hamilton's renown. And the final paragraph denies the application of one of his principles to the British Empire. The English reader must have finished the review with the impression that Mr. Oliver's book was an adequate and suggestive treatment of a character well worth the knowing. And that is the impression that Mr. Harrison wished to convey.

An English study of Alexander Hamilton, in the domain of thought the main Founder of the United States as a cohesive Commonwealth, was urgently needed. His was one of the finest minds of the eighteenth century. For more than a century the great State he did so much to create has been broadening in the lines which he traced for it, and to the ends which his genius foresaw more truly than all his colleagues. His hurried political pamphlets, which brought order out of chaos at the close of

[1] From "Memories and Thoughts," by permission of The Macmillan Co.

the War of Independence, have taken their place amongst
the permanent classics of political science. And yet few
Englishmen have ever opened the *Federalist;* and many
well-read students of history, who know all about his
personal scandals and his tragic end, have no very definite
convictions as to the share in forming the United States,
due to Washington, to Jefferson, Madison, Adams, and
to Hamilton. As philosopher, as publicist, as creative
genius, Hamilton was far the most important. And it
was indeed time that English readers should have the
story told them from the English point of view. His own
son, Senator Cabot Lodge, and other American writers have
amply done him justice. But one fears that standard
American works are not assiduously studied in England.
Mr. Oliver's work, which is not a biography, but "an
essay on American Union," adequately supplies a real
want in political history.

Sir Henry Maine, in his work on *Popular Government,*
1885, devoted the fourth essay to the Constitution of
the United States, which he truly called "much the most
important political instrument of modern times." And
throughout this fourth essay Sir Henry does ample justice
to the sagacity and foresight of Hamilton. He quotes
Chancellor Kent, who compares the *Federalist* (mainly
written by Hamilton) with Aristotle, Cicero, Machiavel,
Montesquieu, Milton, Locke, and Burke; and Maine
declares that such praise is not too high. Talleyrand, a
diplomatist and a cynic, spoke of Hamilton with enthusiasm, and Guizot praised his political writings as of
consummate wisdom and practical sagacity. Mr. Bryce,
in his great work on *The American Commonwealth,* does
full justice to Hamilton. Sir George Trevelyan, in his
American Revolution, calls Hamilton "the most brilliant

and most tragic figure in all the historical gallery of American statesmen." In the new *Cambridge Modern History*, vol. vii., Professor Bigelow truly describes Hamilton as "the master spirit of the Convention which framed the Constitution of the United States." "A nation was to be created and established, created of jarring commonwealths and established on the highest level of right." The accomplishment of this stupendous task by the dominant character of George Washington and the piercing genius of Alexander Hamilton places both amongst the great creative statesmen of the world.

Mr. Oliver's book does not profess to be a history or a biography, but "merely an essay on the character and achievements of a man who was the chief figure in a series of striking events." This is perhaps rather too modest a claim. For the years from 1780 to 1796 — the years when Hamilton first contributed to the task of practical statesmanship down to his drafting Washington's "Farewell Address" — the history of the War and of the Settlement during the two Presidencies of Washington is quite adequately sketched. And as to a biography of Hamilton, a living portrait of the man himself is vigorously drawn in the midst of the historical and political chapters. It is quite true that Hamilton and the circumstances of his career are by no means the exclusive subject. Washington, Jefferson, Madison, Adams, Monroe, Burr, and other prominent politicians have sections of the book to themselves. And the aims and principles of the various parties — Federalists, Democrats, State Rights, Republicans, Patriots, Neutralists — so obscure to us at home, are made clear as the story moves.

This is no doubt the true, perhaps the necessary way of recounting the life-work of Hamilton. He was so closely

E

associated with every phase of the American movement
for the twenty years after the virtual close of the war at
Yorktown, in 1781, that the life of Hamilton is hardly
intelligible unless we read it as part of the history of his
country. And his relations with his colleagues in government, and with his opponents, rivals, and enemies in controversy and intrigue, are so close and so complex that no
true portrait of Hamilton is complete till we have sketches
of his contemporaries. On the whole, Mr. Oliver has set
Alexander Hamilton in his true place, as next to Washington, the leading founder of the United States — the intellectual creator of the great Commonwealth of which
George Washington was the typical father and the moral
hero.

Hamilton is the American Burke in his union of literary
power with political science. If he falls short of Burke
in the majesty of speech and the splendour of many-
sided gifts, he was never hurried into the frantic passions
and fatal blunders which finally ruined Burke's influence
over his age. Hamilton at times exaggerated the dangers
he foresaw, was too pessimist and even unjust to the failings he condemned. But on the whole he made no great
mistake, and all those ideas for which he struggled with
such tenacity and earnestness have in the course of ages
come to a triumphant issue. Hamilton, too, reminds us
of Burke in the sadness of his personal history, in the
poignant disappointments of his career, and in the want
of full recognition of his supreme greatness in his lifetime.
Colleagues whom we now see to have been his inferiors,
both morally and intellectually, men representing lower
ideals, came to the first place in the State he had created,
a seat to which it was quite impossible that he could have
been chosen. Even in America Hamilton has hardly

been judged with full honour. He was too conservative, too anti-democratic, of too philosophic a temperament, too much the idealist, and too little the demagogue ever to attain the popularity which wins the votes of a vast majority.

The book has a moral — somewhat startling, and at the present moment charged with lively interest. The concluding book is occupied with general reflections upon Nationality, Empire, Union, and Sovereignty; and the problem of welding the thirteen American States into a single Commonwealth is applied to the present-day problem of reconciling the British Constitution with our transmarine Empire. Mr. Oliver, if I understand him aright, seems afraid that the British Empire is held together by bonds too loose and undefined, and would urge on it the Hamiltonian doctrine of central Sovereignty and resolute Union. He quotes Washington's maxim: "Influence is not government." He says the tie of affection or kinship is not union. He seems, like Hobbes and Austin, to ask for force as the basis of true union and government. Why, the self-governing Colonies would fly into fifty bits at the mere sound of such a thing. The American Civil War of 1863 would be a flea-bite compared to this. For my part, I quite agree with Washington that "influence is not government," and with Mr. Oliver that sentimental ties are not Union. But the casual conglomeration called the British Empire has nothing else to rest on, and the least attempt to bind it with closer ties would mean immediate and final disruption.

SALAD [1]

BY

CHARLES SEARS BALDWIN

Such an essay as the following by Professor Baldwin differs from the preceding by Mr. Birrell in that, although not overtly expressed, there is one dominating thought implied, namely that salad is excellent. On the face of it, this thought is neither profound, nor capable of elaborate proof. Naturally it is a question of the individual taste. Therefore Professor Baldwin is artistically correct in not stressing any logical connection between his paragraphs. Notice, however, how very careful is the author to preserve the apparent sequence of thought, by closing his paragraphs with his strongest sentence. He then in the first sentence of the succeeding paragraph repeats the final idea of the preceding. By this device — one to be recommended to all young writers — his thought apparently moves to a definite conclusion. And as the essay by its nature is a much-ado-about-nothing, in the very forms of his sentences is an intentionally pedantic cast to give a half humorous effect. The more this essay is studied, the greater will be the appreciation of the author's literary art.

A soup garden is a phrase of the French, too nice for America. Our gardens are indiscriminate; enough distinction merely to have a garden. And indeed, for an American moved to express a further distinction, to assert himself against provincialism, better than a soup garden would be a salad garden. To soup, though it be accepted in too narrow a sense, America is largely converted. Even mountain taverns dispense a diluted tomato sauce that

[1] From "Essays out of Hours," by permission of the publishers, Longmans, Green, & Co.

often has merit of heat. But salad is not even known except to the unrepresentative few.

That salad is gone but a little way, and is still a singularity, appears when American women that read book reviews are found to know it only as involving fowl or lobster, and to buy dressing even for these, as for their boots, by the bottle. She shall not learn the rudiments of this craft who will not forget the grosser mayonnaise. And since, under pressure of convention, as for what is by barbarism called a tea, she will hanker back after the fleshpots, it is oftener he that learns. In matters of food, what moves through man alone stems a tide of distrust slowly.

Nor is this without its worth in supporting the head of the table ; but let the head keep a manly humility. Let that man alone turn to mayonnaise who has labored seven years without mustard, and used eggs as they were golden. It is a woman's dressing, at best offering satiety, like the sugarings of the sex ; at less than best belying the name of salad by making what it touches less savory. The elements of all salads are oil and vinegar, with salt and pepper. Until these are his familiars, let no man try beyond. That the oil be French or Italian marks the fixing of personality. The vinegar may well add tarragon, the pepper be from Nepaul. But none of these is vital ; the proportion of each to the material is all, and the happy hand.

The material is every green herb for the service of man. Fruit salads, though they open many inventions, are but toys to a serious return to nature. First, let him explore all the greens of a large market, and combine boldly among the vegetables carried cold from yesterday's table. Lettuce, though alone among herbs it has vogue, is but ancillary. To use no other is like knowing wine only as champagne. In fact, among herbs lettuce has least character. Therefore, after the delicacy of its first freshness, its use is in conjunction. But water cress and celery should be either very thick in the bowl or very sparse; for they pungently put down other savors. Beyond this frontier is a world without rule, where each man may be a discoverer and a benefactor, if he cast away prejudice. Prejudice cannot consist with salad. They that abjure cabbage are proud stomachs, and they that fear onion have given their souls to their neighbors. Salad without onion is like blank verse; it needs the master hand to prevail without the rhyme. Unprejudiced, he that finds not a salad for every day, or fails of happy solutions, is either improvident or dull.

More practical minds will see thrift as well as variety in the dispossession of flesh meat. Food without fire, pleasant ministry to digestion in despite of the cook, may yet win the mistress. Meantime our hope is for the master. By a knack at the bowl, be it but to use an old savory spoon, or to slice his radishes, or to insinuate garlic or cheese, he keeps his state. His digestion is not arrested by fear; his conversation is secure. Unless he be morose, he may reign at his table.

WORDS THAT LAUGH AND CRY [1]

BY

CHARLES ANDERSON DANA

During the period after the Civil War the New York *Sun* became one of the most influential newspapers of the country and it was certainly one of the best written. This was due largely to the power of its great editor, Charles A. Dana. Although himself a college man, a man of wide cultivation and of much reading, he realized the necessity of precision and conciseness in journalistic editorials. His style is celebrated for its simplicity and for its effect. There is never any doubt as to the meaning. In the following editorial, March 16, 1890, he states vividly the secret of good writing, namely, feel what you write. The first paragraph states concretely the fact that combinations of written words can convey feeling. Two phases of this thought are expanded in two short paragraphs. The fourth, and final, paragraph emphasizes the thought that the feeling must first be in the writer, returning in the last sentence to the thought of the first paragraph. There is no proof, nor any reasoned development of the thought. Nor is any necessary. It is a model for the simplest form of exposition.

DID it ever strike you that there was anything queer about the capacity of written words to absorb and convey feelings ! Taken separately they are mere symbols with no more feeling to them than so many bricks, but string them along in a row under certain mysterious conditions and you find yourself laughing or crying as your eye runs over them. That words should convey mere ideas is not

[1] From "Casual Essays of the *Sun*," by permission of the New York *Sun*.

so remarkable. "The boy is fat," "the cat has nine tails," are statements that seem obviously enough within the power of written language. But it is different with feelings. They are no more visible in the symbols that hold them than electricity is visible on the wire; and yet there they are, always ready to respond when the right test is applied by the right person. That spoken words, charged with human tones and lighted by human eyes, should carry feelings, is not so astonishing. The magnetic sympathy of the orator one understands; he might affect his audience, possibly, if he spoke in a language they did not know. But written words: How can they do it! Suppose, for example, that you possess remarkable facility in grouping language, and that you have strong feelings upon some subject, which finally you determine to commit to paper. Your pen runs along, the words present themselves, or are dragged out, and fall into their places. You are a good deal moved; here you chuckle to yourself, and half a dozen of lines further down a lump comes into your throat, and perhaps you have to wipe your eyes. You finish, and the copy goes to the printer. When it gets into print a reader sees it. His eye runs along the lines and down the page until it comes to the place where you chuckled as you wrote; then he smiles, and six lines below he has to swallow several times and snuffle and wink to restrain an exhibition of weakness. And then some one else comes along who is not so good a word juggler as you are, or who has no feelings, and swaps the words about a little, and twists the sentences; and behold the spell is gone, and you have left a parcel of written language duly charged with facts, but without a single feeling.

No one can juggle with words with any degree of success

without getting a vast respect for their independent ability. They will catch the best idea a man ever had as it flashes through his brain, and hold on to it, to surprise him with it long after, and make him wonder that he was ever man enough to have such an idea. And often they will catch an idea on its way from the brain to the pen point, turn, twist, and improve on it as the eye winks, and in an instant there they are, strung hand in hand across the page and grinning back at the writer: "This is our idea, old man; not yours!"

As for poetry, every word that expects to earn its salt in poetry should have a head and a pair of legs of its own, to go and find its place, carrying another word, if necessary, on its back. The most that should be expected of any competent poet in regular practice is to serve a general summons and notice of action on the language. If the words won't do the rest for him it indicates that he is out of sympathy with his tools.

But you don't find feelings in written words unless there were feelings in the man who used them. With all their apparent independence they seem to be little vessels that hold in some puzzling fashion exactly what is put into them. You can put tears into them, as though they were so many little buckets; and you can hang smiles along them, like Monday's clothes on the line, or you can starch them with facts and stand them up like a picket fence; but you won't get the tears out unless you first put them in. Art won't put them there. It is like the faculty of getting the quality of interest into pictures. If the quality exists in the artist's mind he is likely to find means to get it into his pictures, but if it isn't in the man no technical skill will supply it. So, if the feelings are in the writer and he knows his business, they will get

into the words; but they must be in him first. It isn't
the way the words are strung together that makes Lincoln's Gettysburg speech immortal, but the feelings that
were in the man. But how do such little, plain words
manage to keep their grip on such feelings? That is
the miracle.

NATIONAL CHARACTERISTICS AS MOULDING PUBLIC OPINION [1]

BY

JAMES BRYCE

The noticeable feature in the following essay by Ambassador Bryce is that each paragraph is an independent little essay by itself. The thought of the paragraph normally is expressed in the first sentence; for example, "All the world knows that they are a humorous people." This thought, then, is repeated, expanded, and illustrated in the following sentences. Consequently the total thought of the essay may be gained by summarizing the first sentences of all the paragraphs; the Americans are (a) good-natured, (b) humorous, (c) hopeful, (d) democratic, etc. Obviously, the value of such an extreme form of the catalogue structure depends upon the completeness of the catalogue. The interest consists first in the personal element, what such a man as Ambassador Bryce, one of the most acute thinkers of living Englishmen, predicates of us Americans; secondly, in the interest of the individual paragraphs, in the illustrations, and in the anecdotes. It is, therefore, both an easy and dangerous form for the beginner to attempt. For, although he can without difficulty construct his essay, yet, having neither the analytic power nor the background of Ambassador Bryce, he will fail to interest the reader.

As the public opinion of a people is even more directly than its political institutions the reflection and expression of its character, we may begin the analysis of opinion in America by noting some of those general features of national character which give tone and colour to the

[1] Chapter 80 of "The American Commonwealth," 1911. Reprinted by permission of The Macmillan Co.

people's thoughts and feelings on politics. There are, of course, varieties proper to different classes, and to different parts of the vast territory of the Union; but it is well to consider first such characteristics as belong to the nation as a whole, and afterwards to examine the various classes and districts of the country. And when I speak of the nation, I mean the native Americans. What follows is not applicable to the recent immigrants from Europe, and, of course, even less applicable to the Southern negroes.

definite

The Americans are a good-natured people, kindly, helpful to one another, disposed to take a charitable view even of wrongdoers. Their anger sometimes flames up, but the fire is soon extinct. Nowhere is cruelty more abhorred. Even a mob lynching a horse thief in the West has consideration for the criminal, and will give him a good drink of whisky before he is strung up. Cruelty to slaves was unusual while slavery lasted, the best proof of which is the quietness of the slaves during the war when all the men and many of the boys of the South were serving in the Confederate armies. As everybody knows, juries are more lenient to offences of all kinds but one, offences against women, than they are anywhere in Europe. The Southern "rebels" were soon forgiven; and though civil wars are proverbially bitter, there have been few struggles in which the combatants did so many little friendly acts for one another, few in which even the vanquished have so quickly buried their resentments. It is true that newspapers and public speakers say hard things of their opponents; but this is a part of the game, and is besides a way of relieving their feelings: the bark is sometimes the louder in order that a bite may not follow. Vindictiveness shown by a public man excites general disapproval, and the maxim of letting bygones be bygones is pushed so far that an offender's misdeeds are often forgotten when they ought to be remembered against him.

All the world knows that they are a humorous people. They are as conspicuously the purveyors of humour to the nineteenth century as the French were the purveyors of wit to the eighteenth. Nor is this sense of the ludicrous side of things confined to a few brilliant writers. It is diffused among the whole people; it colours their ordinary life, and gives to their talk that distinctively new flavour which a European palate enjoys. Their capacity for enjoying a joke against themselves was oddly illustrated at the outset of the Civil War, a time of stern excitement, by the merriment which arose over the hasty retreat of the Federal troops at the battle of Bull Run. When William M. Tweed was ruling and robbing New York, and had set on the bench men who were openly prostituting justice, the citizens found the situation so amusing that they almost forgot to be angry. Much of President Lincoln's popularity, and much also of the gift he showed for restoring confidence to the North at the darkest moments of the war, was due to the humorous way he used to turn things, conveying the impression of not being himself uneasy, even when he was most so.

That indulgent view of mankind which I have already mentioned, a view odd in a people whose ancestors were penetrated with the belief in original sin, is strengthened by this wish to get amusement out of everything. The want of seriousness which it produces may be more apparent than real. Yet it has its significance; for people become affected by the language they use, as we see men grow into cynics when they have acquired the habit of talking cynicism for the sake of effect.

They are a hopeful people. Whether or no they are

right in calling themselves a new people, they certainly seem to feel in their veins the bounding pulse of youth. They see a long vista of years stretching out before them, in which they will have time enough to cure all their faults, to overcome all the obstacles that block their path. They look at their enormous territory with its still only half-explored sources of wealth, they reckon up the growth of their population and their products, they contrast the comfort and intelligence of their labouring classes with the condition of the masses in the Old World. They remember the dangers that so long threatened the Union from the slave power, and the rebellion it raised, and see peace and harmony now restored, the South more prosperous and contented than at any previous epoch, perfect good feeling between all sections of the country. It is natural for them to believe in their star. And this sanguine temper makes them tolerant of evils which they regard as transitory, removable as soon as time can be found to root them up.

They have unbounded faith in what they call the People and in a democratic system of government. The great States of the European continent are distracted by the contests of Republicans and Monarchists, and of rich and poor, — contests which go down to the foundations of government, and in France are further embittered by religious passions. Even in England the ancient Constitution is always under repair, and while some think it is being ruined by changes, others hold that further changes are needed to make it tolerable. No such questions trouble native American minds, for nearly everybody believes, and everybody declares, that the frame of government is in its main lines so excellent that such reforms as seem called for need not touch those lines, but are required only to protect the Constitution from being perverted by the parties. Hence a further confidence that the people are sure to decide right in the long run, a confidence inevitable and essential in a government which refers every question to the arbitrament of numbers. There have, of course, been instances where the once insignificant minority proved to have been wiser than the majority of the moment. Such was eminently the case in the great slavery struggle. But here the minority prevailed by growing into a majority as events developed the real issues, so that this also has been deemed a ground for holding that all minorities which have right on their side will bring round their antagonists, and in the long run win by voting power. If you ask an intelligent citizen why he so holds, he will answer that truth and justice are sure to make their way into the minds and consciences of the majority. This is deemed an axiom, and the more readily so deemed because truth is identified with common sense, the quality which the average citizen is most confidently proud of possessing.

This feeling shades off into another, externally like it, but at bottom distinct — the feeling not only that the majority, be it right or wrong, will and must prevail, but that its being the majority proves it to be right. This idea, which appears in the guise sometimes of piety and sometimes of fatalism, seems to be no contemptible factor in the present character of the people. It will be more fully dealt with in a later chapter.

The native Americans are an educated people, compared with the whole mass of the population in any European country except Switzerland, parts of Germany, Norway, Iceland, and Scotland; that is to say, the average of knowledge is higher, the habit of reading and thinking more generally diffused, than in any other country. They know the Constitution of their own country, they follow public affairs, they join in local government and learn from it how government must be carried on, and in particular how discussion must be conducted in meetings, and its results tested at elections. The Town Meeting was for New England the most perfect school of self-government in any modern country. In villages, men used to exercise their minds on theological questions, debating points of Christian doctrine with no small acuteness. Women in particular, pick up at the public schools and from the popular magazines far more miscellaneous information than the women of any European country possess, and this naturally tells on the intelligence of the men. Almost everywhere one finds women's clubs in which literary, artistic, and social questions are discussed, and to which men of mark are brought to deliver lectures.

That the education of the masses is nevertheless a superficial education goes without saying. It is sufficient to enable them to think they know something about the great problems of politics : insufficient to show them how little they know. The public elementary school gives everybody the key to knowledge in making reading and writing familiar, but it has not time to teach him how to use the key, whose use is in fact, by the pressure of daily work, almost confined to the newspaper and the magazine. So we may say that if the political education of the average American voter be compared with that of the average voter in Europe, it stands high ; but if it be compared with the functions which the theory of the American government lays on him, which its spirit implies, which the methods of its party organization assume, its inadequacy is manifest. This observation, however, is not so much a reproach to the schools, which generally do what English schools omit — instruct the child in the principles of the Constitution — as a tribute to the height of the ideal which the American conception of popular rule sets up.

For the functions of the citizen are not, as has hitherto been the case in Europe, confined to the choosing of legislators, who are then left to settle issues of policy and select executive rulers. The American citizen is one of the governors of the Republic. Issues are decided and rulers selected by the direct popular vote. Elections are so frequent that to do his duty at them a citizen ought to be constantly watching public affairs with a full comprehension of the principles involved in them, and a judgment of the candidates derived from a criticism of their arguments as well as a recollection of their past careers. The instruction received in the common schools and from the newspapers, and supposed to be developed by the practice of primaries and conventions, while it makes the voter deem himself capable of governing, does not fit him to weigh the real merits of statesmen, to discern the true grounds on which questions ought to be decided, to note the drift of events and discover the direction in which parties are being carried. He is like a sailor who knows the spars and ropes of the ship and is expert in working her, but is ignorant of geography and navigation; who can perceive that some of the officers are smart and others dull, but cannot judge which of them is qualified to use the sextant or will best keep his head during a hurricane.

They are a moral and well-conducted people. Setting aside the *colluvies gentium* which one finds in Western mining camps, now largely filled by recent immigrants, and which popular literature has presented to Europeans as far larger than it really is, setting aside also the rabble

F

of a few great cities and the negroes of the South, the average of temperance, chastity, truthfulness, and general probity is somewhat higher than in any of the great nations of Europe. The instincts of the native farmer or artisan are almost invariably kindly and charitable. He respects the law; he is deferential to women and indulgent to children; he attaches an almost excessive value to the possession of a genial manner and the observance of domestic duties.

They are also — and here again I mean the people of native American stock, especially in the Eastern and Middle States — on the whole, a religious people. It is not merely that they respect religion and its ministers, for that one might say of Russians or Sicilians, not merely that they are assiduous church-goers and Sunday-school teachers, but that they have an intelligent interest in the form of faith they profess, are pious without superstition, and zealous without bigotry. The importance which some still, though all much less than formerly, attach to dogmatic propositions, does not prevent them from feeling the moral side of their theology. Christianity influences conduct, not indeed half as much as in theory it ought, but probably more than it does in any other modern country, and far more than it did in the so-called ages of faith.

Nor do their moral and religious impulses remain in the soft haze of self-complacent sentiment. The desire to expunge or cure the visible evils of the world is strong. Nowhere are so many philanthropic and reformatory agencies at work. Zeal outruns discretion, outruns the possibilities of the case, in not a few of the efforts made, as well by legislation as by voluntary action, to suppress vice, to prevent intemperance, to purify popular literature.

Religion apart, they are an unreverential people. I do not mean irreverent, — far from it; nor do I mean that they have not a great capacity for hero-worship, as they have many a time shown. I mean that they are little disposed, especially in public questions — political, economical, or social — to defer to the opinions of those who are wiser or better instructed than themselves. Everything tends to make the individual independent and self-reliant. He goes early into the world; he is left to make his way alone; he tries one occupation after another, if the first or second venture does not prosper; he gets to think that each man is his own best helper and adviser. Thus he is led, I will not say to form his own opinions, for few are those who do that, but to fancy that he has formed them, and to feel little need of aid from others towards correcting them. There is, therefore, less disposition than in Europe to expect light and leading on public affairs from speakers or writers. Oratory is not directed towards instruction, but towards stimulation. Special knowledge, which commands deference in applied science or in finance, does not command it in politics, because that is not deemed a special subject, but one within the comprehension of every practical man. Politics is, to be sure, a profession, and so far might seem to need professional aptitudes. But the professional politician is not the man who has studied statesmanship, but the man who has practised the art of running conventions, and winning elections.

Even that strong point of America, the completeness and highly popular character of local government, contributes to lower the standard of attainment expected in a public man, because the citizens judge of all politics by the politics they see first and know best, — those of

their township or city, — and fancy that he who is fit
to be selectman, or county commissioner, or alderman, is
fit to sit in the great council of the nation. Like the
shepherd in Virgil, they think the only difference between
their town and Rome is in its size, and believe that what
does for Lafayetteville will do well enough for Washington. Hence when a man of statesmanlike gifts appears,
he has little encouragement to take a high and statesmanlike tone, for his words do not necessarily receive weight
from his position. He fears to be instructive or hortatory,
lest such an attitude should expose him to ridicule; and
in America ridicule is a terrible power. Nothing escapes
it. Few have the courage to face it. In the indulgence
of it even this humane race can be unfeeling.

They are a busy people. I have already observed that
the leisured class is relatively small, is in fact confined
to a few Eastern cities. The citizen has little time to
think about political problems. Engrossing all the
working hours, his avocation leaves him only stray
moments for this fundamental duty. It is true that he
admits his responsibilities, considers himself a member
of a party, takes some interest in current events. But
although he would reject the idea that his thinking should
be done for him, he has not leisure to do it for himself,
and must practically lean upon and follow his party.
It astonished me in 1870 and 1881 to find how small
a part politics played in conversation among the best
educated classes and generally in the cities. Since 1896
there has been a livelier and more constant interest in
public affairs; yet even now business matters so occupy
the mind of the financial and commercial classes, and
athletic competitions the minds of the uneducated classes
and of the younger sort in all classes, that political ques-

tions are apt, except at critical moments, to fall into the background.[1] In a presidential year, and especially during the months of a presidential campaign, there is, of course, abundance of private talk, as well as of public speaking, but even then the issues raised are largely personal rather than political in the European sense. But at other times the visitor is apt to feel — more, I think, than he feels anywhere in Britain — that his host has been heavily pressed by his own business concerns during the day, and that when the hour of relaxation arrives he gladly turns to lighter and more agreeable topics than the state of the nation. This remark is less applicable to the dwellers in villages. There is plenty of political chat round the store at the cross roads, and though it is rather in the nature of gossip than of debate, it seems, along with the practice of local government, to sustain the interest of ordinary folk in public affairs.[2]

The want of serious and sustained thinking is not confined to politics. One feels it even more as regards economical and social questions. To it must be ascribed the vitality of certain prejudices and fallacies which could scarcely survive the continuous application of such

[1] The increased space given to athletics and games of all sorts in the newspapers marks a change in public taste no less striking here than it is in Britain. As it is equally striking in the British Colonies, one may take it as a feature common to the modern English-speaking world, and to that world only, for it is scarcely discernible in Continental Europe.

[2] The European country where the common people best understand politics is Switzerland. That where they talk most about politics is, I think, Greece. I remember, for instance, in crossing the channel which divides Cephalonia from Ithaca, to have heard the boatmen discuss a recent ministerial crisis at Athens, during the whole voyage, with the liveliest interest and apparently some knowledge.

vigorous minds as one finds among the Americans. Their quick perceptions serve them so well in business and in the ordinary affairs of private life that they do not feel the need for minute investigation and patient reflection on the underlying principles of things. They are apt to ignore difficulties, and when they can no longer ignore them, they will evade them rather than lay siege to them according to the rules of art. The sense that there is no time to spare haunts an American even when he might find the time, and would do best for himself by finding it.

Some one will say that an aversion to steady thinking belongs to the average man everywhere. True. But less is expected from the average man in other countries than from a people who have carried the doctrine of popular sovereignty further than it has ever been carried before. They are tried by the standard which the theory of their government assumes. In other countries statesmen or philosophers do, and are expected to do, the solid thinking for the bulk of the people. Here the people are supposed to do it for themselves. To say that they do it imperfectly is not to deny them the credit of doing it better than a European philosopher might have predicted.

They are a commercial people, whose point of view is primarily that of persons accustomed to reckon profit and loss. Their impulse is to apply a direct practical test to men and measures, to assume that the men who have got on fastest are the smartest men, and that a scheme which seems to pay well deserves to be supported. Abstract reasonings they dislike, subtle reasonings they suspect; they accept nothing as practical which is not plain, downright, apprehensible by an ordinary understanding. Although open-minded, so far as willingness to listen goes, they are hard to convince, because they have really made up their minds on most subjects, having adopted the prevailing notions of their locality or party as truths due to their own reflection.

It may seem a contradiction to remark that with this shrewdness and the sort of hardness it produces, they are nevertheless an impressionable people. Yet this is true. It is not their intellect, however, that is impressionable, but their imagination and emotions, which respond in unexpected ways to appeals made on behalf of a cause which seems to have about it something noble or pathetic. They are capable of an ideality surpassing that of Englishmen or Frenchmen.

They are an unsettled people. In no State of the Union is the bulk of the population so fixed in its residence as everywhere in Europe; in some it is almost nomadic. Except in the more stagnant parts of the South, nobody feels rooted to the soil. Here to-day and gone to-morrow, he cannot readily contract habits of trustful dependence on his neighbours. Community of interest, or of belief in such a cause as temperance, or protection for native industry, unites him for a time with others similarly minded, but congenial spirits seldom live long enough together to form a school or type of local opinion which develops strength and becomes a proselytizing force. Perhaps this tends to prevent the growth of variety in opinion. When a man arises with some power of original thought in politics, he is feeble if isolated, and is depressed by his insignificance, whereas if he grows up in favourable soil with sympathetic minds around him, whom he can in prolonged intercourse permeate with his ideas, he learns to speak with confidence and soars on the wings of his disciples. One who considers the variety of conditions under which men live in America may certainly find ground for surprise that there should be so few independent schools of opinion.

But even while an unsettled, they are nevertheless an associative, because a sympathetic people. Although the atoms are in constant motion, they have a strong attraction for one another. Each man catches his neighbour's sentiment more quickly and easily than happens with the English. That sort of reserve and isolation, that tendency rather to repel than to invite confidence, which foreigners attribute to the Englishman, though it belongs rather to the upper and middle class than to the nation generally, is, though not absent, yet less marked in America.[1] It seems to be one of the notes of difference between the two branches of the race. In the United States, since each man likes to feel that his ideas raise in other minds the same emotions as in his own, a sentiment or impulse is rapidly propagated and quickly conscious of its strength. Add to this the aptitude for organization which their history and institutions have educed, and one sees how the tendency to form and the talent to work combinations for a political or any other object has become one of the great features of the country. Hence, too, the immense strength of party. It rests not only on interest and habit and the sense of its value as a means of working the government, but also on the sympathetic element and instinct of combination ingrained in the national character.

[1] I do not mean that Americans are more apt to unbosom themselves to strangers, but that they have rather more adaptiveness than the English, and are less disposed to stand alone and care nothing for the opinion of others. It is worth noticing that Americans travelling abroad seem to get more easily into touch with the inhabitants of the country than the English do; nor have they the English habit of calling those inhabitants — Frenchmen, for instance, or Germans — "the natives."

They are a changeful people. Not fickle, for they
are if anything too tenacious of ideas once adopted, too
fast bound by party ties, too willing to pardon the errors
of a cherished leader. But they have what chemists call
low specific heat; they grow warm suddenly and cool as
suddenly; they are liable to swift and vehement outbursts
of feeling which rush like wildfire across the country,
gaining glow, like the wheel of a railway car, by the
accelerated motion. The very similarity of ideas and
equality of conditions which makes them hard to convince
at first makes a conviction once implanted run its course
the more triumphantly. They seem all to take flame
at once, because what has told upon one, has told in the
same way upon all the rest, and the obstructing and
separating barriers which exist in Europe scarcely exist
here. Nowhere is the saying so applicable that nothing
succeeds like success. The native American or so-called
Know-nothing party had in two years from its foundation
become a tremendous force, running, and seeming for a
time likely to carry, its own presidential candidate. In
three years more it was dead without hope of revival.
Now and then, as for instance in the elections of 1874–75,
and again in those of 1890, there comes a rush of feeling
so sudden and tremendous, that the name of Tidal Wave
has been invented to describe it.

After this it may seem a paradox to add that the Americans are a conservative people. Yet any one who observes the power of habit among them, the tenacity with
which old institutions and usages, legal and theological
formulas, have been clung to, will admit the fact.
Moreover, prosperity helps to make them conservative.
They are satisfied with the world they live in, for they
have found it a good world, in which they have grown rich

and can sit under their own vine and fig tree, none making them afraid. They are proud of their history and of their Constitution, which has come out of the furnace of civil war with scarcely the smell of fire upon it. It is little to say that they do not seek change for the sake of change, because the nations that do this exist only in the fancy of alarmist philosophers. There are nations, however, whose impatience of existing evils, or whose proneness to be allured by visions of a brighter future, makes them under-estimate the risk of change, nations that will pull up the plant to see whether it has begun to strike root. This is not the way of the Americans. They are no doubt ready to listen to suggestions from any quarter. They do not consider that an institution is justified by its existence, but admit everything to be matter for criticism. Their keenly competitive spirit and pride in their own ingenuity have made them quicker than any other people to adopt and adapt inventions: telephones were in use in every little town over the West, while in the city of London men were just beginning to wonder whether they could be made to pay. The Americans have doubtless of late years become, especially in the West, an experimental people, so far as politics and social legislation are concerned. Yet there is also a sense in which they are at bottom a conservative people, in virtue both of the deep instincts of their race and of that practical shrewdness which recognizes the value of permanence and solidity in institutions. They are conservative in their fundamental beliefs, in the structure of their governments, in their social and domestic usages. They are like a tree whose pendulous shoots quiver and rustle with the lightest breeze, while its roots enfold the rock with a grasp which storms cannot loosen.

a perfect ending

firmness & conservatism

radicalness & change

AMERICAN MANNERS [1]

BY

Wu Tingfang

The following essay should be compared with the preceding one by
Lord Bryce, because of its similar structure, and the fact that the problem
is the same in each case — a sympathetic study of certain American
characteristics by a distinguished foreigner. In the first paragraph the
statement is made that Americans have been accused of bad manners;
in the second, that Chinese manners have also been adversely criticized,
but for directly opposite reasons. This gives the key to the plan of
the whole essay, which in nearly every paragraph brings out some particular characteristic of American manners by contrast with the Chinese.
This contrast is shown by illustration and personal experience. American manners, the author concludes, are the result of two predominant
characteristics, a love of independence and equality, and an abhorrence
of waste of time. This is stated about the middle of the essay, and after
further elaboration, again at the close. Thus the form of the essay is a
catalogue, tied in the middle and at the end with the one unifying thought
which is deduced from the material given.

MUCH has been written and more said about American
manners, or rather the American lack of manners. Americans have frequently been criticized for their bad breeding,
and many sarcastic references to American deportment
have been made in my presence. I have even been told,
I do not know how true it is, that European diplomats

[1] From "America Through the Spectacles of an Oriental Diplomat,"
by permission of the publishers, Frederick A. Stokes Co. and Mr.
William Morrow, literary representative of Dr. Wu Tingfang.

dislike being stationed in America, because of their aversion to the American way of doing things.

Much too has been written and said about Chinese
manners, not only by foreigners but also by Chinese.
One of the classics, which our youth have to know by
heart, is practically devoted entirely to manners. There
has also been much adverse criticism of our manners or
our excess of manners, though I have never heard that
any diplomats have, on this account, objected to being
sent to China. We Chinese are therefore in the same
boat as the Americans. In regard to manners neither of
us find much favor with foreigners, though for diametri-
cally opposite reasons : the Americans are accused of
observing too few formalities, and we of being too formal.

The Americans are direct and straightforward. They
will tell you to your face that they like you, and occasionally they also have very little hesitation in telling you
that they do not like you. They say frankly just what
they think. It is immaterial to them that their remarks
are personal, complimentary or otherwise. I have had
members of my own family complimented on their good
looks as if they were children. In this respect Americans
differ greatly from the English. The English adhere with
meticulous care to the rule of avoiding everything personal.
They are very much afraid of rudeness on the one hand,
and of insincerity or flattery on the other. Even in the
matter of such a harmless affair as a compliment to a
foreigner on his knowledge of English, they will precede
it with a request for pardon and speak in a half-apologetic
manner, as if complimenting were something personal.
The English and the Americans are closely related, they
have much in common, but they also differ widely, and
in nothing is the difference more conspicuous than in

their conduct. I have noticed curiously enough that English Colonials, especially in such particulars as speech and manners, follow their quondam sister colony, rather than the mother country. And this, not only in Canada, where the phenomenon might be explained by climatic, geographic, and historic reasons, but also in such antipodean places as Australia and South Africa, which are so far away as to apparently have very little in common either with America or with each other. Nevertheless, whatever the reason, the transplanted Englishman, whether in the arctics or the tropics, whether the Northern or the Southern Hemisphere, seems to develop a type quite different from the original stock, yet always resembling his fellow emigrants.

The directness of Americans is seen not only in what they say but in the way they say it. They come directly to the point, without much preface or introduction, much less is there any circumlocution or "beating about the bush." When they come to see you they say their say and then take their departure, moreover they say it in the most terse, concise and unambiguous manner. In this respect what a contrast they are to us! We always approach each other with preliminary greetings. Then we talk of the weather, of politics or friends, of anything, in fact, which is as far as possible from the object of the visit. Only after this introduction do we broach the subject uppermost in our minds, and throughout the conversation polite courtesies are exchanged whenever the opportunity arises. These elaborate preludes and interludes, may, to the strenuous ever-in-a-hurry American, seem useless and superfluous, but they serve a good purpose. Like the common courtesies and civilities of life they pave the way for the speakers, especially if they are strangers; they improve their tempers, and place them generally on terms of mutual understanding. It is said that some years ago a Foreign Consul in China, having a serious complaint to make on behalf of his national, called on the Taotai, the highest local authority in the port. He found the Chinese official so genial and polite that after half an hour's conversation, he advised the complainant to settle the matter amicably without troubling the Chinese officials about the matter. A good deal may be said in behalf of both systems. The American practice has at least the merit of saving time, an all important object with the American people. When we recall that this remarkable nation will spend millions of dollars to build a tunnel under a river, or to shorten a curve in a railroad, merely that they may save two or three minutes, we are not surprised at the abruptness of their speech. I, as a matter of fact, when thinking of their time-saving and abrupt manner of address, have been somewhat puzzled to account for that peculiar drawl of theirs. Very slowly and deliberately they enunciate each word and syllable with long-drawn emphasis, punctuating their sentences with pauses, some short and some long. It is almost an effort to follow a story of any length — the beginning often becomes cold before the end is reached. It seems to me that if Americans would speed up their speech after the fashion of their English cousins, who speak two or three times as quickly, they would save many minutes every day, and would find the habit not only more efficacious, but much more economical than many of their time-saving machines and tunnels. I offer this suggestion to the great American nation for what it is worth, and I know they will receive it in the spirit in which it is made, for they have the saving sense of humor.

Some people are ridiculously sensitive. Some years ago, at a certain place, a big dinner was given in honor of a notable who was passing through the district. A Chinese, prominent in local affairs, who had received an invitation, discovered that though he would sit among the honored guests he would be placed below one or two whom he thought he ought to be above, and who, he therefore considered, would be usurping his rightful position. In disgust he refused to attend the dinner, which, excepting for what he imagined was a breach of manners, he would have been very pleased to have attended. Americans are much more sensible. They are not a bit sensitive, especially in small matters. Either they are broad-minded enough to rise above unworthy trifles, or else their good Americanism prevents their squabbling over questions of precedence, at the dinner table or elsewhere.

Americans act up to their Declaration of Independence, especially the principle it enunciates concerning the equality of man. They lay so much importance on this that they do not confine its application to legal rights, but extend it even to social intercourse. In fact, I think this doctrine is the basis of the so-called American manners. All men are deemed socially equal, whether as friend and friend, as President and citizen, as employer and employee, as master and servant, or as parent and child. Their relationship may be such that one is entitled to demand, and the other to render, certain acts of obedience, and a certain amount of respect, but outside that they are on the same level. This is doubtless a rebellion against all the social ideas and prejudices of the old world, but it is perhaps only what might be looked for in a new country, full of robust and ambitious manhood, disdainful of all traditions which in the least savor of monarchy or hier-

archy, and eager to blaze as new a path for itself in the
social as it has succeeded in accomplishing in the political
world.   Combined with this is the American characteristic
of saving time.   Time is precious to all of us, but to
Americans it is particularly so.   We all wish to save time,
but the Americans care much more about it than the rest
of us.   Then there are different notions about this question of saving time, different notions of what wastes
time and what does not, and much which the old world
regards as politeness and good manners Americans consider as sheer waste of time.   Time is, they think, far
too precious to be occupied with ceremonies which appear
empty and meaningless.   It can, they say, be much more
profitably filled with other and more useful occupations.
In any discussion of American manners it would be unfair
to leave out of consideration their indifference to ceremony
and their highly developed sense of the value of time, but
in saying this I do not forget that many Americans are
devout ritualists, and that these find both comfort and
pleasure in ceremony, which suggests that after all there
is something to be said for the Chinese who have raised
correct deportment almost to the rank of a religion.

The youth of America have not unnaturally caught the
spirit of their elders, so that even children consider themselves as almost on a par with their parents, as almost on
the same plane of equality; but the parents, on the other
hand, also treat them as if they were equals, and allow
them the utmost freedom.   While a Chinese child renders
unquestioning obedience to his parents' orders, such
obedience as a soldier yields to his superior officer, the
American child must have the whys and the wherefores
duly explained to him, and the reason for his obedience
made clear.   It is not his parent that he obeys, but

expediency and the dictates of reason. Here we see the clear-headed, sound, common-sense business man in the making. The early training of the boy has laid the foundation for the future man. The child too has no compunction in correcting a parent even before strangers, and what is stranger still the parent accepts the correction in good part, and sometimes even with thanks. A parent is often interrupted in the course of a narrative, or discussion, by a small piping voice, setting right, or what it believes to be right, some date, place, or fact, and the parent, after a word of encouragement or thanks, proceeds. How different is our rule that a child is not to speak until spoken to! In Chinese official life under the old régime it was not etiquette for one official to contradict another, especially when they were unequal in rank. When a high official expressed views which his subordinates did not endorse, they could not candidly give their opinion, but had to remain silent. I remember that some years ago some of my colleagues and I had an audience with a very high official, and when I expressed my dissent from some of the views of that high functionary, he rebuked me severely. Afterward he called me to him privately, and spoke to me somewhat as follows: "What you said just now was quite correct. I was wrong, and I will adopt your views, but you must not contradict me in the presence of other people. Do not do it again." There is of course much to be said for and against each system, and perhaps a blend of the two would give good results. Anyhow, we can trace in American customs that spirit of equality which pervades the whole of American society, and observe the germs of self-reliance and independence so characteristic of Americans, whether men, women, or children.

G

Even the domestic servant does not lose this precious American heritage of equality. I have nothing to say against that worthy individual, the American servant (if one can be found); on the contrary, none is more faithful or more efficient. But in some respects he is unique among the servants of the world. He does not see that there is any inequality between him and his master. His master, or should I say, his employer, pays him certain wages to do certain work, and he does it, but outside the bounds of this contract, they are still man and man, citizen and citizen. It is all beautifully, delightfully, legal. The washerwoman is the "wash-lady," and is just as much a lady as her mistress. The word "servant" is not applied to domestics, "help" is used instead, very much in the same way that Canada and Australia are no longer English "colonies," but "self-governing dominions."

We of the old world are accustomed to regard domestic service as a profession in which the members work for advancement, without much thought of ever changing their position. A few clever persons may ultimately adopt another profession, and, according to our antiquated conservative ways of thinking, rise higher in the social scale, but, for the large majority, the dignity of a butler, or a housekeeper is the height of ambition, the crowning point in their career. Not so the American servant. Strictly speaking there are no servants in America. The man, or the woman as the case may be, who happens for the moment to be your servant, is only servant for the time being. He has no intention of making domestic service his profession, of being a servant for the whole of his life. To have to be subject to the will of others, even to the small extent to which American servants are subordinate, is offensive to an American's pride of citizenship, it is contrary to his conception of American equality. He is a servant only for the time, and until he finds something better to do. He accepts a menial position only as a stepping stone to some more independent employment. Is it to be wondered at that American servants have different manners from their brethren in other countries? When foreigners find that American servants are not like servants in their own country, they should not resent their behavior: it does not denote disrespect, it is only the outcrop of their natural independence and aspirations.

All titles of nobility are by the Constitution expressly forbidden. Even titles of honor or courtesy are but rarely used. "Honorable" is used to designate members of Congress; and for a few Americans, such as the President and the Ambassadors, the title "Excellency" is permitted. Yet, whether it is because the persons entitled to be so addressed do not think that even these mild titles are consistent with American democracy, or because the American public feels awkward in employing such stilted terms of address, they are not often used. I remember that on one occasion a much respected Chief Executive, on my proposing, in accordance with diplomatic usage and precedent, to address him as "Your Excellency," begged me to substitute instead "Mr. President." The plain democratic "Mr." suits the democratic American taste much better than any other title, and is applied equally to the President of the Republic and to his coachman. Indeed, the plain name John Smith, without even "Mr.," not only gives no offense, where some higher title might be employed, but fits just as well, and is in fact often used. Even prominent and distinguished men do not resent nicknames; for example, the celebrated person whose name is so intimately connected with that delight of American children and grown-ups — the "Teddy Bear." This characteristic, like so many other American characteristics, is due not only to the love of equality and independence, but also to the dislike of any waste of time.

In countries where there are elaborate rules of etiquette concerning titles and forms of address, none but a Master of Ceremonies can hope to be thoroughly familiar with them, or to be able to address the distinguished people without withholding from them their due share of high-sounding titles and epithets; and, be it whispered, these same distinguished people, however broad-minded and magnanimous they may be in other respects, are sometimes extremely sensitive in this respect. And even after one has mastered all the rules and forms, and can appreciate and distinguish the various nice shades which exist between "His Serene Highness," "His Highness," "His Royal Highness," and "His Imperial Highness," or between "Rt. Rev." and "Most Rev.," one has yet to learn what titles a particular person has, and with what particular form of address he should be approached, an impossible task even for a Master of Ceremonies, unless he always has in his pocket a Burke's Peerage to tell him who's who. What a waste of time, what an inconvenience, and what an unnecessary amount of irritation and annoyance all this causes. How much better to be able to address any person you meet simply as Mr. So-and-So, without unwittingly treading on somebody's sensitive corns! Americans have shown their common sense in doing away with titles altogether, an example which the sister Republic of China is following. An illustrious name loses nothing for having to stand by itself without prefixes and suffixes, handles and tails. Mr. Gladstone was no less himself for not prefixing his name with Earl, and the other titles to which it would have entitled him, as he could have done had he not declined the so-called honor. Indeed, like the "Great Commoner," he, if that were possible, endeared himself the more to his countrymen because of his refusal. A name, which is great without resorting to the borrowed light of titles and honors, is greater than any possible suffix or affix which could be appended to it.

In conclusion, American manners are but an instance or result of the two predominant American characteristics to which I have already referred, and which reappear in so many other things American. A love of independence and of equality, early inculcated, and a keen abhorrence of waste of time, engendered by the conditions and circumstances of a new country, serve to explain practically all the manners and mannerisms of Americans. Even the familiar spectacle of men walking with their hands deep in their trousers' pockets, or sitting with their legs crossed needs no other explanation, and to suggest that, because Americans have some habits which are peculiarly their own, they are either inferior or unmanly, would be to do them a grave injustice.

Few people are more warm-hearted, genial, and sociable than the Americans. I do not dwell on this, because it is quite unnecessary. The fact is perfectly familiar to all who have the slightest knowledge of them. Their kindness and warmth to strangers are particularly pleasant, and are much appreciated by their visitors. In some other countries, the people, though not unsociable, surround themselves with so much reserve that strangers are at first chilled and repulsed, although there are no pleasanter or more hospitable persons anywhere to be found when once you have broken the ice, and learned to know them; but it is the stranger who must make the first advances, for they themselves will make no effort to become acquainted, and their manner is such as to discourage any efforts on the part of the visitor. You may travel with them for hours in the same car, sit opposite to them, and all the while they will shelter themselves behind a newspaper, the broad sheets of which effectively prohibit any attempts at closer acquaintance. The following instance, culled from a personal experience, is an illustration. I was a law student at Lincoln's Inn, London, where there is a splendid law library for the use of the students and members of the Inn. I used to go there almost every day to pursue my legal studies, and generally sat in the same quiet corner. The seat on the opposite side of the table was usually occupied by another law student. For months we sat opposite each other without exchanging a word. I thought I was too formal and reserved, so I endeavored to improve matters by occasionally looking up at him as if about to address him, but every time I did so he looked down as though he did not wish to see me. Finally I gave up the attempt. This is the general habit with English gentlemen. They will not speak to a stranger without a proper introduction; but in the case I have mentioned surely the rule would have been more honored by a breach than by the observance. Seeing that we were fellow students, it might have been presumed that we were gentlemen and on an equal footing. How different are the manners of the American! You can hardly take a walk, or go for any distance in a train, without being addressed by a stranger, and not infrequently making a friend. In some countries the fact that you are a foreigner only thickens the ice, in America it thaws it. This delightful trait in the American character is also traceable to the same cause as that which has helped us to explain the other peculiarities which have been mentioned. To good Americans, not only are the citizens of America born equal, but the citizens of the world are also born equal.

FRANKLIN [1]

BY

HENRY CABOT LODGE

The catalogue form may be used also as a convenient summary for a man's achievements. On the two hundredth anniversary of Franklin's birth Henry Cabot Lodge, the brilliant Senator from Massachusetts, was asked to contribute an appreciation. Evidently there were eight features in Franklin's life and character that he felt significant: (a) Franklin's temperament, (b) his character, (c) the breadth of his interest, etc. This, the real essay, is introduced by two paragraphs of general appreciation, and three paragraphs in which the background is indicated. The same general scheme is followed also within the paragraph development. The first sentence usually summarizes the preceding thought, and the second introduces the main thought of the paragraph. Then this is expanded and explained.

MANY years ago, when in London for the first time, I remember being filled with the indignant astonishment of which youth alone is capable at seeing upon the pedestal of a statue placed in a public square the single word "Franklin." A Boston boy, born within a stone's throw almost of the birthplace of "Poor Richard," I had never deemed it possible that any Franklin but one could be referred to by that name alone without further definition or qualification. I knew, of course, who the subject of the British statue was, a brave naval officer and bold explorer, who had lost his life in a futile effort to achieve an almost equally futile object. But I had a vague impres-

[1] From "A Frontier Town and Other Essays," by permission of the publishers, Charles Scribner's Sons.

sion that "heroic sailor souls" had very fortunately been
not uncommon among English-speaking people, whereas
I had supposed that men like Benjamin Franklin had
been rather rare among the people of any race. I have
passed the British statue many times since then. My
youthful and indignant astonishment has long since
vanished, and the humor of the inscription has become
very apparent to me. I know now that the inscription
merely represents a solid British habit of claiming everything, ignoring the rest of mankind, and enlarging to the
utmost their own achievements, both great and small,
upon the entirely sound principle that a constant and fearless assertion of one's own virtues will lead a considerable
proportion of a very busy and somewhat indifferent world
to take one at one's own valuation. The highly humorous
side of describing Sir John as the only Franklin, and
relegating to obscurity a man who achieved greatness in
literature, in science, in politics, and in diplomacy, and
who was one of the most brilliant figures in a brilliant
century, has come in the lapse of time to give me no little
real pleasure.

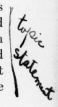

I have also learned that my early estimate of the man
commonly referred to outside of England as "Franklin"
was not only vague, but, although right in direction, was
still far short of the truth, which a better knowledge enables
me to substitute for an ill-defined belief. Two hundred
years have elapsed since his birth in the little house on
Milk Street in Boston, and as the anniversary of that
event is now being celebrated, it is well worth while to
pause for a moment and consider him. Few men, be
it said, better deserve consideration, for he not only
played a great part in shaping events and influencing
human thought, but he represents his time more com-

pletely, perhaps, than any other actor in it, something which is always in and of itself a memorable feat.

Franklin's time was the eighteenth century, which his long life nearly covered. When he was born Anne was Queen, and England, agitated by dynastic struggles, was with difficulty making head against the world-wide power of Louis XIV. When Franklin died France had been driven from North America, the British Empire had been divided, his own being one of the master hands in the division, the United States of America had started on their career as a nation, and the dawning light of the French Revolution was beginning to redden the skies. Marvellous changes these to be enclosed within the span of one brief human life, and yet they were only part of the story. The truth is that the eighteenth century was a very remarkable period. Not so very long ago this statement would have been regarded as a rather silly paradox, and in a little while it will be looked upon as a commonplace. But as yet we are not wholly free from the beliefs of our fathers in this respect. The nineteenth century, in its lusty youth and robust middle age, adopted as part of its creed the belief that its predecessor upon the roll of time, from whose loins it sprang, deserved only the contempt and hatred of mankind. Incited thereto by the piercing invectives of the Romantic school, brimming over with genius, and just then in possession of the earth, and by the clamors of Thomas Carlyle, the nineteenth century held that the eighteenth was a period of shams and conventions, of indifference and immorality, of unspeakable oppressions and of foul miseries hidden behind a gay and glittering exterior, the heyday of a society which in a word deserved the fate of the cities of the plain.

This view was true enough, so far as it went; but it was by no means the whole story. It had the fascination of simplicity and of convenience which half-truths nearly always possess; but as Mr. Speaker Reed once said, "half-truths are simple, but the whole truth is the most complicated thing on earth." The time has now come when we may begin to approximate the whole truth. Indeed, before the nineteenth century had closed it had begun to modify its opinions and to be less sure about the total depravity of its progenitor. Under the skilful manipulations of bric-à-brac dealers the art and furniture of the eighteenth century have become and are now the fashion. It is a pretty trivial art at best, very inferior to that which the nineteenth century, in France at least, has produced; but it is always pleasant to observe the whirligig of time bring in its revenges, and it must be admitted that the eighteenth-century furniture is an indescribable improvement over the dreadful taste known as Victorian, but which really came forth like the Goths and Vandals of old time from the heart of Germany, to submerge and ruin a careless and unsuspecting world. Still, whatever their merits may be, the eighteenth century in pictures and chairs and tables is again in high fashion, and perhaps we can now begin to see also that it had its great side as well as its bad one, and that it was in reality a very wonderful time.

It is usually said as beyond dispute that it had no poetry in the nobler and more imaginative sense; and if by poetry is meant the immortal work of the Elizabethans on the one hand, and of the Romantic school on the other, we may be sure that, speaking broadly, the eighteenth century, like Audrey, was not poetical. Yet none the less this unpoetical, unimaginative century produced Gray and

Burns in Great Britain, Chénier and Gilbert in France, the first part of "Faust" — enough glory in itself for many centuries — and the "Wallenstein Trilogy" in Germany. It was, too, the century of Bach and Handel and Haydn; it gave birth to Mozart and Beethoven, — something of a record for an unimaginative century in the most imaginative of arts. Even those who decry it most admit its greatness in prose, where it developed a style which culminated in Gibbon and Burke. In pure intellect it can hardly be surpassed by any of its fellows, for it was the century of Immanuel Kant. It was likewise the century of Louis XV, perhaps the meanest thing that accident ever cast upon a throne, but it was also the century of Frederick the Great. It was illustrated in its youth by the Regent Orleans, and illuminated at its close by George Washington. It was the century of Casanova, most typical and amusing of rascals, and it was equally the century of John Wesley. It was a time when men persecuted for a religion in which they had no faith, and sneered at the doctrines of the church to which they conformed. The classes revelled in luxury, and the masses were sunk in poverty. Corruption ran riot in the public service, and the oppression of the people was without limit on the Continent, where the *lettre de cachet* of the French king flung men into prison, and wretched German princelings sold their subjects to die in foreign wars that they might build ugly palaces and maintain still more ugly mistresses. Yet in those evil days more was done to set free human thought and strike off the shackles of priestly rule than in any century which history records. More was then done to give men political liberty and build up constitutional government than in all the previous centuries, for it was the century of Montesquieu and Rousseau and the *Federalist*, of the revolt of the American Colonies and of the French Revolution. It was the century of kings and nobles, yet it gave birth to modern democracy. The spirit of revolt went side by side with the spirit of reaction and convention. There were indeed two voices in the eighteenth century. We know which one truly foretold the coming days. But which was the true voice of the time? Was it Voltaire, *antithesis* pleading the cause of the Calas family, or that of Foulon, declaring that the people might eat grass? Which was the true leader, George Washington at Valley Forge, or George III hiring Indians and Hessians to carry out his mother's injunction, "George, be a king"? It was veritably a wonderful century, full of meaning, rich in intellect, abounding in contradictions.

It produced, too, many great men, but none more fully representative than Benjamin Franklin of all that made it memorable. He reflected at once its greatness and its contradictions, although not its evil side, because in those years of change and ferment he was ranged with the children of light, and was ever reaching out for new and better things. Of pure English stock, born in a community where Puritanism was still dominant, where religion was rigid and morality austere, he was an adventurer in his youth, a liberal always, a free-thinker in religion, the moralist of common-sense, and pre-eminently the man of the world, at home in all societies and beneath every sky. He had the gift of success, and he went on and up from the narrow fortunes of a poor, hard-working family until he stood in the presence of kings and shaped the destinies of nations.

The Puritanism to which he was born fell away from him at the start, and in his qualities and his career it seems as if he reproduced the type of the men of Elizabeth's time who founded Virginia and New England; for he had all the versatility, the spirit of adventure, the enormous vitality and splendid confidence in life and in the future which characterized that great epoch. Yet he had also the calmness, the self-control, the apparent absence of enthusiasm which were the note of his own time. The restlessness of mind which marked the Elizabethans was his in a high degree, but it was masked by a cool and calculating temperament rarely found in the days of the great Queen.

Franklin was born not only a Puritan Englishman, but a colonist; yet never was there a man with less of the colonist or the provincial about him. A condition of political dependence seems for some mysterious reason to have a depressing effect upon those who remain continuously in that condition. The soil of a dependency appears to be unfavorable to the production of ability of a high type in any direction until the generation arrives which is ready to set itself free. Franklin was a colonial subject until he was seventy, and yet no more independent man than he lived in that age of independent thought. He rose to the highest distinction in four great fields of activity, any one of which would have sufficed for a life's ambition; he moved easily in the society of France and England, he appeared at the most brilliant court in Europe, and no one ever thought of calling him provincial. The atmosphere of a dependency never clung to him, nor in the heyday of aristocracy was his humble origin ever remembered. The large-mindedness, the complete independence, the entire simplicity of the man dispersed the one and destroyed the memory of the other.

Modern history contains very few examples of a man who, with such meagre opportunities and confined for many years to a province far distant from the centres of civilization, achieved so much and showed so much ability in so many different ways as Franklin. With only the education of the common school and forced to earn his living while still a boy, he became a man of wide learning, pre-eminent in science, and a writer, in the words of one of the first of English critics,[1] "of supreme literary skill." His autobiography is one of the half-dozen great autobiographies which are a perennial joy. His letters are charming, and his almanacs (was there ever a more unlikely vehicle for good literature?) were translated into many languages, delighted with their homely wisdom and easy humor thousands who thought of America only as the abode of wolves and Indians, and made the name of "Poor Richard" familiar to the civilized world. Yet literature, where he attained such a success, winning a high place in the literary history not only of his own country, but of his age and his language, was but his pastime. The intellectual ambition of his life was found in science, and he went so far in that field that the history of one of the great natural forces, which in its development has changed the world, cannot be written without giving one of the first places of pioneer and discoverer to the printer of Boston and Philadelphia.

Yet neither literature nor science, either of which is quite enough to fill most lives, sufficed for Franklin. He began almost at the very beginning to take a share in public affairs. His earliest writings when a printer at the case dealt with political questions. He then entered the politics of the city, thence he passed to the larger concerns of the great Province of Pennsylvania, and at every step he showed a capacity for organization, an

[1] Mr. Augustine Birrell, in his essay on "Old Booksellers."

ability for managing men and a power of persuasive speech
rarely equalled. He had a way of carrying measures and
securing practical and substantive results which excites
profound admiration, since nothing is more difficult than
such achievements in the whole range of public service.
This is especially true where the man who seeks results
is confronted by active opposition or by that even more
serious obstacle, the inertness or indifference of the community. Yet nothing pleased Franklin more than such a
situation as arose when in time of war he overcame the
Quaker opposition to putting the province in a state of
defence. His method was not as a rule that of direct
attack. He preferred to outwit his opponents, an operation which gratified his sense of humor; and a favorite
device of his was to defeat opposition by putting forward
anonymously arguments apparently in its behalf, which,
by their irony and extravagance, utterly discredited the
cause they professed to support. To his success in the
field of public discussion he added that of administration
when he became Postmaster-General for the colonies and
organized the service, and then again when he represented
Pennsylvania and later other provinces as their agent in
London. It was there in England that he defended the
cause of the colonies before both Parliament and Ministers
when resistance to taxation began. He came home an
old man, verging on seventy, to take his place as one of
the chief leaders in the Revolution. These leaders of
revolution were, as a rule and as is usual at such periods,
young men, and yet there was not one among them all
with greater flexibility of mind or more perfect readiness
to bring on the great change than Franklin. He returned
again to Europe to seek aid for his country in the war, and
it was chiefly due to him that the French alliance, which

turned the scale, was formed. When the war drew to a close it was he who began alone the task of making peace. He had nearly completed the work when his colleagues appeared in Paris and by incautious words broke the web so carefully spun. Patient and undisturbed, Franklin began again. Again he played one English faction against the other. Again he managed France, turning to good advantage the vigorous abilities of Adams and the caution of Jay. Finally, boldly disregarding the instructions of Congress, he emerged from all complications with a triumphant peace.

Even then his work was not done. He came back to America to govern in Pennsylvania and to share in making the Constitution of the United States, thus exhibiting the power to build up as well as to pull down, something most uncommon, for the man of revolution is rarely a constructive statesman. He closed his great career by setting his hand to the Constitution of the United States, as he had already done to the Declaration of Independence.

Yet after his achievements and services have all been recounted we still come back to that which was most remarkable, — the manner in which he at once influenced and reflected his time. The eighteenth century has for long been held up to scorn as destitute of enthusiasm, lacking in faith and ideals, indifferent and utterly worldly. Franklin was certainly devoid of enthusiasm, and yet one unbroken purpose ran strongly through his life and was pursued by him with a steadiness and force which are frequently wanting in enthusiasts. He sought unceasingly the improvement of man's condition here on earth. Whether it was the invention of a stove, the paving of Philadelphia, the founding of a library, the movement of storms, the control of electric currents, or the defence

H

of American liberty, he was always seeking to instruct and help his fellow-men and to make their lot a better and happier one. The morals he preached were indeed worldly; there never was a bit of morality more purely of the account-book kind than the familiar aphorism about honesty, and yet it may be doubted whether all the pulpits in America did more to make men honest and thrifty, and to develop good and sober citizens than the uninspired preachings of "Poor Richard." He was a sceptic, as were nearly all the great men of the century, but his honest doubt helped to free the human mind and dispel the darkness which had stayed the march of intellect. He never scoffed at religion; he did not hesitate to appeal to it at a great crisis to sway the minds of his fellows, but he suffered no dogmas to stand in the way of that opening of the mind which he believed would advance the race and soften by its discoveries the hard fate of humanity. He was conservative by nature in accordance with the habit of the time, but that which was new had no terrors for him, and he entered upon the path of revolution with entire calmness when he felt that revolution had become necessary to the welfare and happiness of his people.

There was nothing inevitable about the American Revolution at the particular time at which it came. It would have failed indeed on the field of battle had it not been for George Washington. But when the British Government, among their many blunders, insulted Franklin and rejected his counsel they cast aside the one man whose wisdom might have saved the situation, and, so far as they could, made the revolt of the colonies unavoidable. It was an indifferent, cold-blooded century, and both epithets have been applied to Franklin, no doubt with some justice. But it is never fair to judge one century or its people by the standards of another. Franklin was a man of extraordinary self-control combined with a sense of humor which never deserted him and which is easily mistaken for cold-blooded indifference. He signed the Declaration of Independence, it is said, with a jest; yet no man measured its meaning or felt its gravity more than he. He stood silent in the Cock-Pit while the coarse invective of Wedderburne beat about his head, and made no reply. The only revenge he took, the only answer he ever made, if tradition may be believed, was to wear when he signed the treaty acknowledging American independence the same coat of Manchester velvet which he wore when the pitiless abuse of England's Attorney-General was poured out upon him. He was not a man who displayed emotion — it was not the fashion of his time. He was a philosopher and a stoic. Perhaps, as Mr. Birrell says, he was neither loving nor tender-hearted, yet he manged both in his life and in the disposition of his property to do many kindnesses and much good to those to whom the battle of life was hardest. His sympathies were keen for mankind rather than for the individual, but that again was the fashion of his time — a fashion which shattered many oppressions gray with the age of centuries and redressed many wrongs.

Franklin was very human, far from perfect in more than one direction. It is easy enough to point out blemishes in his character. But as a public man he sought no private ends, and his great and versatile intellect was one of the powerful influences which in the eighteenth century wrought not only for political liberty, but for freedom of thought, and in so doing rendered services to humanity which are a blessing to mankind to-day. We accept the blessings and forget too often to whose labors in a receding past they are due. We owe a vast debt to the great men of the eighteenth century who brought out of the shams and conventions and oppressions of that time the revolutions in politics, in society, and in thought the fruits of which we of to-day now enjoy. To no one of these men is the world's debt larger than to Franklin.

THE SERIOUS PEPYS [1]

WILBUR CORTEZ ABBOTT

Much the same problem as that solved by Senator Lodge confronted
Professor Abbott. There is, however, in the latter case a large amount
of popular misunderstanding first to be cleared away. Naturally his
essay falls into three well-defined divisions. First, he states briefly
the known facts of Pepys's life. Secondly, he considers very fully the
effect upon Pepys's reputation due to the discovery of the famous "Diary."
By this means, — and he has already used half the space of the total
essay, — he has gained the reader's confidence by showing that he is
quite familiar with the usual interpretation of Pepys's character. Then
follow eloquent paragraphs in which this conception is overthrown.
Point by point a new Pepys is built up. Little by little this new figure
emerges until from the ruins of the reader's previous picture of the dissolute rake rises the conception of the great public servant.

"WHOEVER," says Montaigne, "will justly consider
and with due proportion, of what kind of men and of
what sort of actions the glory sustains itself in the records
of history, will find that there are very few actions and
very few persons of our times who can there pretend any
right." "Of so many thousands of valiant men who have
died within these fifteen hundred years in France with
their swords in their hands," he goes on, "not a hundred
have come to our knowledge. The memory not of the
commanders only, but of battles and victories is buried

[1] From *The Yale Review*, for April, 1914, by permission of the
author and of the editor of *The Yale Review*.

and gone; the fortunes of above half the world for want
of a record stir not from their place and vanish without
duration; . . . it must be some very eminent greatness
or some consequence of great importance that fortune has
added to it that signalizes" an action to make it, and the
actor, remembered.

But there is no recipe for immortality, even for the
greatest; and if fame's vagaries thus affect captains and
kings, what chance have men in lesser stations; if con-
querors are so frequently forgotten, what of the men of
peace — which has its oblivion far more profound than
war! Above all, perhaps, what hope has one who devotes
himself not to the destruction or manipulation of his
fellow men but to their service, in particular as that bul-
wark of organized society, an honest and able civil servant? Little enough, indeed. The worst of demagogues,
the most incompetent of commanders, the harshest of
tyrants, the most depraved of rakes, has far better chance
for an undying, if an undesirable, fame under present historical conditions than even the best of those "sons of
Martha." Save when preserved by other means, some
share in politics, some gift to literature, their fame is
mingled with the air. Only among the unwritten traditions of their service and its unread documents their reputations lie, safe from the praise or blame of those they
served. Of this great class, paradoxical as it may seem,
there is no better representative than the well-known
subject of this essay.

On the twenty-sixth of May, 1703, while England girded
herself for that far-spreading conflict which in a twelvemonth was to bring to her Gibraltar and the great Marl-
borough's "famous victory" of Blenheim, there died at
Clapham, near London, one Samuel Pepys, sometime a

notable figure in the world he left. Member of Parliament, Treasurer of Tangier, Surveyor General of the Victualling Office, Clerk of the Acts, and Secretary of the Admiralty, he had played no trifling part in the eventful years of the last Stuart kings. Aside from his official life, Pepys had been scarcely less well known in widely different fields. Master of Trinity House and of the Clothworkers' Company, Governor of Christ's Hospital, twice President of the Royal Society; a patron and critic of the arts, music, the drama, literature; an indefatigable collector of manuscripts and books, broadsides, ballads, music-scores, and curios; he had been no less at home in gatherings of scientists and virtuosos, in Covent Garden and in Drury Lane, or the booksellers' shops about old St. Paul's, than in the Navy Office and dockyards. He had arranged, even composed, some music, and he was no mean amateur performer on certainly one instrument; he had contributed to the Royal Society; not a few books had been dedicated to him; and he himself had published at least one. His portrait had been painted three times by Kneller, once by Lely, and again by artists of less note. Among his friends were statesmen and scientists, authors, officials, musicians, royalties: Hans Sloane, Christopher Wren, Isaac Newton, John Evelyn, John Dryden, and that "admirable Lord High Admiral but less than admirable king," James the Second, now long an exile at the court of France. Surely, if a man's achievements are to count for anything, here was a candidate for at least a moderate immortality.

"In the judgment I make of another man's life," says the old French moralist-philosopher, "I always observe how he carried himself at his death; . . . this is the day that must be the judge of all the foregoing years." This

supreme test the Secretary met bravely. "Last night,"
wrote the nonjuring clergyman, George Hickes, who was
with him at the end, "I did the last offices for Samuel
Pepys. . . . The greatness of his behaviour in his long
and sharp tryall before his death was in every respect
answerable to his great life, and in accordance with his
motto, *Mens cujusque is est quisque*," — as a man's mind
is, so is he. "This day," wrote old John Evelyn, "died
Mr. Sam. Pepys, a very worthy, industrious, and curious
person, none in England exceeding him in knowledge of
the Navy, in which he had passed thro' all the most considerable offices . . . all which he performed with great integrity. . . . He was universally beloved, hospitable,
generous, learned in many things, skilled in music, a very
greate cherisher of learned men of whom he had the
conversation ; . . . for neere 40 yeares . . . my particular friend." Such was the esteem of his contemporaries
for one who had been called successively the right hand,
the Nestor, and the father of the English navy ; reckoned
the ablest civil servant of his time, a shrewd, strict, serious
man of business, a faithful friend, a generous patron, an
accomplished gentleman, and an honest man. May none
of us have a worse epitaph.

His will bore out the character of his life and death.
The wide distribution of mourning and rings, according
to the custom of the time, witnessed his many and eminent
friendships ; his numerous bequests to his acquaintances
and servants further testified to an agreeable side of his
nature. The bestowal of his fortune on his nephew ; and
the devising of his library to Magdalene College, Cambridge, after that nephew's death ; the gift of his ship-
models to his partner and friend, William Hewer, with
recommendation "to consider how these, also together

with his own, may be preserved for publick benefit," —
gave evidence of a strong family, college, and public
spirit; which, again, often contributes somewhat to posthumous reputation.

This, for the son of a tailor, who owed small thanks to
birth or fortune, some to circumstance, most to himself,
for all the blessings he enjoyed in life, and in such unusual
and such long unsuspected degree passed on to posterity,
was no small achievement as a bid for fame. To his success his schooling at Huntingdon and St. Paul's, then at
Magdalene College, contributed somewhat; but the de-
termining factor in his career had been his connection
with his father's cousin and his own patron, Sir Edward
Montagu, the friend and relative and follower of Cromwell.
When, after a brief excursion in diplomacy, the youthful
Pepys entered the service of this capable commander,
whom the Protector had summoned from his place in the
New Model to a seat in the Council of State with charge
of naval operations against Spain, Dunkirk, and the
Northern powers; and, in particular, when, after a period
of retirement, the Convention Parliament commissioned
Montagu to bring back the exiled Charles to England and
the throne, the fortune of his secretary, Pepys, was settled
with his own. Clerk of the Acts and of the Admiralty
Board; then, by successive stages of advance, wresting
increasing reputation and authority from the catastrophes
of fire, plague, and war, Pepys had outgrown the need of
a patron long before he became the Secretary of the
Admiralty. Through twenty busy years, save for the interruption of the Popish Plot, the history of naval administration more and more became the story of his life, as he
refashioned his office on the lines it held for more than a
century. Not without color and incident, verging more

than once on tragedy as he became involved in the vicissitudes of politics, but in the main absorbed in the reform and conduct of naval affairs, until the Revolution drove him and his master James the Second from their posts, his life was one in which increasing purpose ran with vigor and success.

Such was the Pepys of the seventeenth century, the greatest Secretary of what is, in one view, England's greatest service; thus he lived and died. Thus was he not remembered; it is, indeed, amazing to find how soon he was forgotten and how completely. A dozen years after his death, his name found place in "The Continuation of Mr. Collier's Supplement to his Great Dictionary"; a dozen more, and Burnet noted his connection with the Popish Plot; while, thanks chiefly to the fact that Kneller painted and White engraved his portrait, Grainger gave him a page in his extraordinary "Biographical History of England." Another fifty years, and Hume observed that naval tradition still recalled Pepys's administration as "a model of order and economy." The rest was all but silence; among the innumerable "characters" which entertained the readers of the "Annual Register," his found no place; the long files of the "Gentleman's Magazine," save for a brief note on his library, knew him not; in its three editions in the eighteenth century not even the "Encyclopædia Britannica" recorded his name. Members or visitors of Magdalene College still observed, as now, the building which contained his books, and some even found their way inside; at least two recorded something of the treasures they discovered there; and part of the material for Percy's "Reliques of Ancient English Poetry" was drawn from that source. Frequenters of St. Olave's Church may have taken notice of the Secretary's tomb;

members of corporations or societies to which he once
belonged might now and then recall him by his gifts;
lovers of art noted his portraits as examples of the painter's
skill. Family pride, the industry of genealogist or antiquarian, might have found in parish registers the entry
of his birth, marriage, and death; or in the college books,
besides the record of his entrance and exit, that he was
once reproved for being drunk. An occasional reader may
have looked in his "Memoirs of the Royal Navy"; a
scholar or an archivist here and there have noted the
unread masses of his memoranda in the Public Records
Office or the libraries. This was the sum of Pepys's impression on the world a century after he left it — a handful
of mementos and a fast fading memory.

Of these, only his papers and his books still stood between him and oblivion. The books, indeed, had been
not seldom used; the papers were still all but unexplored.
Sometime during that eighteenth century, which concerned itself so mightily with very many things much less
worth while, a now unknown enthusiast began a catalogue
of the Pepysian collections in the Magdalene library. He
was soon, far too soon, discouraged. There lay "a vast
collection from our antient records . . . relating to our
naval affairs and those of other countries. Books of
musick, mathematicks and several other subjects all excellent in their kind." Among them were two hundred and
fifty volumes chiefly of naval manuscripts, gathered,
doubtless, as a basis for a projected history. There lay
the Lethington Collection of Scottish poetry; masses of
tracts and pamphlets; with the largest body of broadside
ballads in existence. Above all, in the mind of at least
one bibliophile, was what "he hath collected with respect
to the City of London, for the illustration of that famous

city," besides "a vast collection of heads both domestic
and foreign, beyond expression, copy-books of all the
masters of Europe," and "a large book of title-pages,
frontispieces . . . not to be paralleled," the whole crowned
with an "admirable catalogue." Besides these, fifty volumes more of Pepys's manuscripts had found their way
into the hands of the great collector, Rawlinson, and so to
the Bodleian Library at Oxford. Besides these, still, his
documents in public and in private hands, had they been
even catalogued in print, would have reared a monument
whose very size might have compelled attention and re-
vised the eighteenth century's knowledge of the past and
of Pepys.

But the exploiting of this material was reserved for later
generations, when its fulfillment became a romance of
literature and scholarship alike. It is a well-known story
how, among the masses of historical material which found
their way to print in the first quarter of the nineteenth
century, the Diary of John Evelyn, with its mention of
the Secretary, inspired the Master of Magdalene College
to put in Lord Grenville's hands six volumes of cipher
manuscript from Pepys's collections which had long puzzled curious visitors; how that accomplished nobleman,
having transcribed some pages, found them of such interest that an undergraduate, John Smith, was entrusted
with the completion of the work; and how after three
years of labor on his part there presently appeared, under
Lord Braybrooke's editorship, the "Memoirs of Samuel
Pepys, Esq. F. R. S., Secretary to the Admiralty . . .
comprising his Diary from 1659 to 1669 . . . with a
selection from his private Correspondence." It is, perhaps, scarcely so well appreciated how, with that event,
ensued a revolution in posthumous fame unparalleled in

literary history. From the obscurity of a century emerged no mere man of affairs but a Personality. What a lifetime of great endeavor could not do, a book accomplished almost in a day. By the transcriber's magic the forgotten Secretary of the Admiralty was transformed into a Prince of Diarists and set among the immortals. So complete was the triumph over oblivion that, within twenty years, even Macaulay, who had drawn largely on the Secretary's books for his History, allowed himself to write of "Samuel Pepys whose library and diary have kept his name fresh to our time"; so vivid was the book that even the great historian seems to have felt, like many since, that its author had always been well known.

It is not surprising that he was misled, nor that the first transcriber often spent fourteen hours a day upon his task, when one considers how amazingly alive the book is still, how every hour promises a fresh surprise. Read but the opening lines with their directness, reminiscent of Defoe, and you feel the charm impelling you to go on:

Blessed be God, at the end of last year I was in very good health. . . . I lived in Axe Yard, having my wife and servant Jane and no more in family than us three. . . . The condition of the State was thus, . . . the Rump after being disturbed by my Lord Lambert was lately returned to sit again. The officers of the Army all forced to yield. Lawson lies still in the river and Monk with his army in Scotland. . . . The new Common Council of the City do speak very high. . . . My own private condition very handsome and esteemed rich, but indeed very poor, besides my goods of my house and my office. . . . This morning . . . I rose, put on my suit with great skirts, . . . went to Mr. Gunning's Chapel at Exeter House. . . . Dined at home . . . where my wife dressed the remains of a turkey, . . . supt at my father's where in came Mrs. The. Turner and Madam Morrice. . . . In the morning . . . Old East brought me a dozen bottles of sack. . . . I went . . . to speak with Mr. Calthropp about the £60 due my Lord. . . [and] heard that Lambert was coming up to London.

There you have, in little, Pepys and his Diary; his house, his clothes, his wife, his food, his health, his office, his acquaintances, his amusements, his relatives, his intimate gossip of affairs. You have, indeed, much more: at once an incredibly lifelike picture of the times, and a true romance, surpassing all fiction, of the life and strange, surprising adventures of one Samuel Pepys, who lived, far from alone, for seventy years in the island of Great Britain, and whose activities are here set down with the detail that has charmed generations since in the exploits of his antithesis, Robinson Crusoe, with all the added zest of brilliant environment.

There is, indeed, some curious kinship between these two wholly unlike productions. There is the same fascination in watching Pepys rescue from the catastrophe of the Cromwellian rule the means to make his fortune as in seeing Crusoe rescue from the shipwreck the means of sustaining life; the same interest in observing the one build his career and the other build his house, the same suspense over the crises in the affairs of each; the same pleasure in their triumphs over adversity as they struggle with nature or with the world of men; the same satisfaction over their ultimate victory; there is even something curiously alike in the accumulation of minute and often apparently trivial detail by which, in truth or fancy, both authors produce their lifelike effects.

Pepys has, indeed, had full reward for all his pains. Since the appearance of his Diary in the first abbreviated form which printed scarcely half of its contents, much learned and loving labor has been spent on its elucidation. The ingenuity and industry of successive editors has enlarged our knowledge and understanding of the work; the two original volumes, what with inclusion of the parts at first

suppressed and a great bulk of comment, have increased to
ten. One editor has re-transcribed the manuscript, another has compiled a book on Pepys and the world he
lived in; the family genealogy has been unearthed and a
study made of one of its members as "a later Pepys"; so
far has the reflected glory shone. The diarist's early life
has been laid bare; his letters published, with his will;
his portraits reproduced; a whole book on Pepys as a
lover of music has appeared; an essay on the sermons
that he heard; even the medical aspects of his married
life have been explained by a physician-author. Essayists
and bookmakers still find in him an ever-fertile subject
for their pens; no biographical dictionary or encyclopædia
is without a full account of the great diarist; and, rising
finally to the full stature of a real biography, few names
to-day in English literature are better known, few classics
more widely read or more enjoyed.

If the effect on Pepys has been so great, the influence of
the Diary on seventeenth-century history has been no
less. The formal even tragic dignity which for a hundred
years enveloped that great revolutionary period was destroyed almost beyond repair of the dullest historian. "It
was as though in a musty library, slumbrous with solemn
volumes, a window had suddenly been opened, and the
spectator looked out upon the London of the mid-seven-
teenth century, full of color and movement, still breathing
the Elizabethan enchantment, . . . vehemently returned
to the lust of the eye and the pride of the flesh after the
restraints and severities of the Puritan dominion." Before the Diary appeared, the England of Charles the
Second was the England of Clarendon, Eachard, Rapin,
Hume, a dull, tangled interlude between two revolutions;
since his book it has been, for the most of us, the England

of Pepys, amusing, intimate, incredibly alive. Its obscuration has not yet been wholly cleared away, the history of the Restoration still remains to be written; but when it is, secretary-diarist will have no less a share in writing its memoirs than he had in managing its affairs. Already from his book have been evolved more than one history of seventeenth-century manners, music, drama, literature; even political historians have used it to advantage. It has been supplemented by other works, but to it we owe in greater measure than to any single book the picture of a period which, even now, makes Pepys's time nearer to us than any other decade of English history.

When one considers what the Secretary was and did, and how his reputation stood before the Diary appeared, this result seems all the more extraordinary. Eminent as he was in admiralty circles, as a patron of the arts, collector, and philanthropist; useful as his life had been and notable for honorable success in public service, it gave small promise of eminence in literature. His success, indeed, lies far outside that realm. However great the quaint attraction of his phrase; however bright the light upon his time, the Diary owes its wide appeal and deepest charm to the infusion of a wholly different quality. It is not merely trite to say that its fascination lies in its frankness; — that is a superficial, obvious, half-truth. To his Diary, Pepys confided every thought, sensation, motive, action, and desire, — good, bad, high, low, important, trivial, absurd, — with a freedom beyond mere frankness. The result is unique, not merely in literature, but almost, if not quite, in life itself. It seldom happens among myriads of human relationships that anyone knows any of his fellows, however near and dear, as well as all of us know Pepys; most of us scarcely know ourselves as well;

few of us, or none, would dare admit, even to ourselves, much less commit to paper, in whatever decent obscurity of cipher, all that the diarist records. His work is not mere frankness; it is self-revelation at its highest power — there is nothing more to tell. It is more than mere literature, it is life itself. Most of such so-called revelations are far from what they profess to be. Some are mere prurience; some, morbid psychology; some, simple vanity; some, conscious or unconscious pose; the most, mere formal record of an outer life, or merely literature. Pepys's work is the delineation of a very human being, a "natural man," stripped of the *convenances* of society, who would have been at once the terror and the pride of eighteenth-century prophets who invoked such phantoms constantly and as constantly produced imaginative figments in their place. To such vainer sophistications Pepys's Diary bears the same relation as that of frank, unashamed, and proper savage nakedness to the salacious half-revelations of a decadent stage. One has but to compare it with such outpourings from those of Rousseau to those of Marie Bashkirtseff to realize the great gulf fixed between healthy appreciation of a man's triumph over circumstances and the futile conflict with shadows.

Being Pepys, nothing human, — and very few other things which came under his observation, — were alien either to him or to his pen. First, his appearance; one reads to-day with wonder not unmixed with awe of "a velvet cloak, two new cloth suits, . . . a new shagg gowne trimmed with gold buttons and twist, with a new hat and silk tops for my legs," — all, as it were, in one mouthful. It is no wonder that his clothes cost some five times those of his wife, but it leads to serious reflection in these days.

I

Yet it was no less policy than vanity which prompted this display. "I hope I shall, with more comfort," he says, "labor to get more and with better successe than when for want of clothes I was forced to sneake like a beggar." That he got more his accounts reveal. When he went with Montagu to bring back the King, he had scarcely a penny to his name. He came back with near a hundred pounds. After seven years of office he reckoned himself worth some seven thousand pounds; prepared to set up a coach; gave his sister, Paulina, six hundred pounds as a marriage portion; and lent his cousin, Roger, five hundred; — for all of which he blessed God fervently in his Diary. When he died, the Crown owed him twenty-eight thousand pounds; yet he left a comfortable fortune. And he was neither dishonest nor niggardly. During at least the seventeenth and eighteenth centuries, few fields of human endeavor yielded such rich returns as public office; and if Pepys took his fees, like other men, unlike too many of them, he gave good service in return. Nor was he ungenerous in spending money. Books, pictures, music, objects of art, furniture, plate, hangings, he purchased with almost lavish hand. Preëminently a Londoner, he was insensible to those charms of country-seat and garden which so engrossed his friend John Evelyn; a man of weighty affairs, gambling of all kinds appealed to him even less; cautious and thrifty as became his class, no charge of penuriousness will hold against him, in the large.

His tastes, indeed, save two, were such as helped the world along. Devoted to the theatre and a good-fellowship which led him sometimes to excess, he made his frequent "vowes against wine and plays" only to break them, as men have done since. The wine at least made no inroads upon his business; the plays make his Diary the best of all guides to seventeenth-century London theatres. But at the theatre, still more in church, at home, abroad, one of his chief interests was what the eighteenth century knew as "female charms." One of his crosses was the lack of such loveliness in his own church, St. Olave's; "not one handsome face in all of them, as if, indeed, there was a curse, as Bishop Fuller heretofore said, upon our parish." What he lacked there he made up fully elsewhere. He kissed Nell Gwyn, besides uncounted others, including the face of the exhumed body of Catherine of Valois, who had been dead more than two centuries, that he might be said to have kissed a queen! His friendship with the actresses, especially Mrs. Knipp; the trials which arose when she winked at him and he had trouble to make his eyes behave as they should in his wife's presence, — are not such things and many more of like sort writ large throughout the Diary? These and the less creditable story of his relations with his wife's servant, Deb, witness something to those qualities which led the penniless youth, but two years out of college, to espouse the pretty daughter of a poverty-stricken Huguenot refugee addicted to invention and living chiefly upon charity.

All this and even more, in infinite variety of phrase, men have laid stress on since his book appeared. Largely, and no doubt naturally, this side of Pepys's nature and his Diary chiefly appealed to a world concerned for the most part with the trivial, or worse; and it might be supposed that frankness such as his would win for him a place in the esteem of those who read his book, comparable to that he occupied in his contemporaries' minds. In some degree, especially at first, thanks to the bowdlerizing of his too cautious editor, this was the case. That incomparable antiquarian, Walter Scott, hastened to welcome this "man of business, . . . of information if not learning, taste and whim as well as pleasure, statesman, virtuoso, *bel esprit*," to the world of literature, and many followed in the novelist's train. Yet, gradually, as each succeeding issue of the Diary included more and more of intimate, less decorous detail, omitted by the early editors, Pepys's reputation sank. Like Lucilius, "having dared portray himself as he found himself to be," he proved that "no man writes of himself save to his hurt." Generations smiled, frowned, shrugged, moralized, felt superior. Critics, who frequently knew nothing of him save his own revelations and the comments of his editors, often sneered. Coleridge observed he was "a pollard man," without a top, — to which Pepys might well have replied that the critic was all top. Lowell, with condescension almost worthy of a foreigner, wrote of "the unconscious blabbings of the Puritan tailor's son." Another, admitting his honesty and even a certain cleverness, laughed at his "cockney revels," and his pleasure when Lord Clarendon patted his head; others still, noted only "the strength and coarseness of the common mind," the " decomposed Puritan mind," of this "typical bourgeois, kindred to Kneller in vulgarity." A no less tolerant soul than Stevenson, following, as often, earlier lead, adduces Pepys's very appearance against him; says his face shows "no aspiration," only "an animal joy in all that comes," though he admits that "in a corrupt and idle period he played the man, toiled hard, and kept his honor bright." His severest critic elaborates at length the manifold inconsistencies of his character, forgetting the dictum expressed by Lord Rosebery that "if we accept the common and erroneous opinion that human nature is consistent with itself we find it utterly impossible to explain the character of George the Third" — to say nothing of that of other men.

Such, in general, was the judgment of the nineteenth century, hard to persuade to take the diarist seriously. Secure in its superior virtue and manners; relieved from the gay plumage of the seventeenth-century male; repressing the earlier liberties of English speech; and at least the open license of its morals; the Victorian age read, loved, despised, what seemed to it a garrulous, amusing man.   It scorned the confession of his little weaknesses perhaps even more than the weaknesses themselves — his love of company, theatre, dress, diversion, deference; looked down upon his simple vanity; above all resented what he told of his dealings with women. Some even wrote of him in terms appropriate to Sedley or Rochester — the comparison is Pepys's best defense — forgetting to read the Diary and Gramont's "Memoirs," or the Restoration drama, side by side.   Viewed thus, one may well wonder whether, after all, the Secretary would not have preferred by far the honorable obscurity of a dead lion which he enjoyed during the eighteenth century to this contemptuously affectionate regard for a living ass, which the nineteenth century has bestowed on him.

The difficulty of comprehending Pepys has arisen from two circumstances: the fact that the critics have known little or nothing of him beyond what they found in his own pages or the comment of his editors; and the fact that, most unfortunately for himself and for us, Pepys ceased to be a diarist before he became a secretary.   From the eighteenth-century historians, even had the men of literature read their books, — which there is no reason to believe they did, — little could have been gleaned, and the earlier editors, at least, were not much better.   In what spirit they began let Lord Braybrooke's own words declare.   As Pepys "was in the habit of recording the most

trifling occurrences," he wrote, "it became absolutely
necessary to curtail the manuscript materially," — and so
he omitted an entertaining *half*. Bright, daring greatly,
printed some four-fifths; Wheatley, all but about thirty
pages. It was, then, nearly seventy years before the world
saw anywhere near the whole Diary. Even so, had the
critics paid more attention to the serious element and dwelt
less on those frivolities — and worse — for whose insertion
they condemned — and read — the diarist, they might
have approximated the truth more nearly.

But, as the old philosopher has said, "The pencil of the
Holy Ghost hath labored more in describing the afflictions
of Job than the felicities of Solomon," and we ought, perhaps, to expect no more of the men of letters. Yet when
even the latest, and in some ways the best-informed of
them falls in error what can we expect? He denounces
Lowell's description of Pepys as a Philistine; he reviles
the historians of English literature for the "amazing
fallacy" that Pepys lacked enthusiasm; he blames those
who have made literary capital out of the diarist for the
small pains they have taken to correct their "childish
impressions" by the results of recent studies. And, with
all this, he permits himself to say that "the diary was the
one long deliberate effort of Pepys's life"! So hard it is
for men to realize the fundamental fact that Samuel Pepys
was not a diarist who happened to be connected with the
Navy Office, but was the greatest of all Secretaries of the
Admiralty who happened, in his earlier years, to write a
diary.

Fortunately the Diary has not been the end of the Secretary's striving against oblivion; what literature and the
literary historians have failed so signally to do for him thus
far, historical scholarship seems likely to accomplish.

When, nearly forty years ago, the English government began to print calendars of the state papers of the Restoration period, it soon became apparent that the famous diarist had played a greater part in public affairs than had previously been recognized. The development of naval history, in particular, has gradually re-created the Secretary, and the service to which he gave his life seems likely to be the final means of securing for him an appropriate immortality. His "Memoirs of the Royal Navy" has been reprinted; the naval historians have chronicled his achievements; studies have been made of his activities in many public posts; and, within a decade, the Navy Records Society has begun the publication of a catalogue of his papers preserved in Magdalene College which has already reached the proportions of three stout volumes. Hereafter we shall have even more of such material, since we are promised the "Navalia" memoranda, further memoirs and calendars, filling out the record of his manifold activities. In view of all this publication, it is not too much to say that, had Pepys's Diary never seen the light, we should in time have had adequate knowledge of the Secretary's work, however little we should have known of the man.

The result of all this is that we have another and a better Pepys than the amusing figure which did duty for him throughout the greater part of the nineteenth century. Though even to-day few readers of the Diary will be likely to delve into this mass of calendars, inaccessible to a previous generation, and any alteration in opinion will, therefore, probably be slow, it is high time to begin to realize what the true Pepys was like, to do him the justice which he has, in a sense, denied himself.

For we are too apt to forget that to his own generation

there was no such person as the diarist. Amid the silks
and paduasoy of the Diary, its days of cheer and its nights
at the play, its family secrets and its personal details, men
have lost sight of the more serious side of him who found
comfort in pouring out those things which he concealed
from all the world beside into the safe cipher of his only
confidant. As we go through the mass of correspondence;
as we read the endless list of orders and memoranda,
catalogues of ships, reports, recommendations, statements
of accounts, and observe the operation and results of his
administration, we perceive the petty, childish, simple
figure, evoked by literary critics from the Diary, transformed into the truer character of the historian — a man
shrewd, cautious, able, conscientious, honest, brave,
wholly devoted to his service and his government.

The story of naval administration and reform between
the revolutions whence emerged the modern system of
the admiralty is, indeed, no glittering chronicle. The
"building of our ships more burdensome"; construction
by the state rather than contractors; reform in victualling
and sailors' pay; the manning and the officering of the
fleet and the re-rating of its vessels; the reorganization of
the ordnance; long experiment in sailing and in fighting
qualities; elaborate calculations of speed, strength, and
sea-worthiness; investigations in the source and quality
of all supplies; accounting, storage; — this infinite variety
of detail, much now of but an antiquarian interest even
to the most technical of experts, is not easy reading and
provides little enough material for epigram. But it does
give us what is far more to the purpose, and that is a correct
view of Samuel Pepys.

Here is the civil servant at his best. "Æquiponderous,"
to his colleagues, "in moral, and much superior in philo-

sophical knowledge of the œconomy of the navy," as he appeared to the men of his own day, his latest critics declare that the principles of his naval statesmanship may even now be lessons to a "sea economy as valid as they were two centuries ago." It is, indeed, almost incredible how acute and diligent he was. The single holiday of a busy life he spent in looking over Dutch and French naval establishments. Upon his first and only visit to Tangier, he found out in an hour's walk about the town what twenty years of costly statesmanship and military occupation had scarcely learned, — that it was no fit place for English occupation. It would be too long even to enumerate here all the changes which he made in admiralty administration; it is perhaps enough to say that a century and a quarter after he left office, in the midst of England's struggle with Napoleon, a naval commission found in his system scarcely a thing to change or blame. Nor was he, through all of this, a man of "sweet, uncritical mind," much less the time-server he has often been pictured. Under the transparent guise of a report to his chief, the Duke of York, which set the wheels of reform in motion, he criticised with frank courage Comptroller, Treasurer, Surveyor, Navy Board, colleagues, courtiers, contractors, every powerful interest of his service, whose alienation might well have meant ruin to him. He was, in Marvel's phrase, one of that "handful of salt, a sparkle of soul that . . . preserved this gross body from putrification, . . . constant, invariable, indeed, Englishmen." It is with high appropriateness that, in the two-hundredth year after his death, the editor of the "Catalogue of Pepysian Manuscripts" dedicates his work "To the memory of Samuel Pepys, a great public servant." After so long an interval, and through such great vicissitudes, the Secretary of the seventeenth century takes on his proper guise in the beginning of the twentieth, and appears again in something like the form he doubtless would have chosen for himself.

We must then, in this view, re-read the Diary and revise our estimate of Pepys. As long presented, he has unquestionably antagonized many persons of highly moral minds or highly cultivated taste; — and even more of those inclined merely to prudishness. The spectacle of a man who dared to set down the acts and thoughts common to many men, is so unusual in human affairs, so contrary to all those instincts of pride and shame which drive us to conceal or to condone our weaknesses not only from our fellows but from ourselves, that it has done Pepys's reputation great damage. One who so far out-Boswelled Boswell as to paint not his friend's portrait but his own, has suffered accordingly. That he was garrulous the very Diary, on which the accusation rests, disproves. The confidence reposed in him by men of every rank; his rapid rise to high responsibilities; his reputation as a safe man of affairs; the fact that only once, and then by accident, did he reveal the secret of his book, — bear out his character as one not given to betrayal of his trust. That, with all his dallyings and philanderings, he was as licentious as most men of his own day, no one familiar with the period will assert. That Pepys was dishonest no one believes, or if he does, let him read the editor's informing paragraph prefacing his papers which declares: "There is no trace of anything of the kind in the official correspondence," and "even official letters, when they are numbered by thousands may be witnesses to character, for by an infinite number of delicate strokes they at length produce a portrait of the writer." Tested by this there is "no evidence of corruption."

In Pepys's case it certainly has not been true that actions speak louder than words. Bacon's saying more nearly hits the mark, that "Fame is like a river which bears up things light and swollen, but drowns things heavy and solid." Of all the charges brought against the Secretary, one of the worst is that he was not brave. Let the great crises of his life attest. A young man, new in office and affairs, dependent on the favor of Montagu, he yet ventured to remonstrate with his powerful patron for improprieties unworthy of his station and himself, in a reproof which is a model of its kind. "I judge it," he writes, "very unbecoming the duty which every bit of bread I eat tells me I owe your Lordship to expose your honor to the uncertainty of my return . . . but, sir, your Lordship's honor being such as I ought to value it to be, and finding both in city and court that discourses pass to your prejudice, . . . I shall, my Lord, without the least greatening or lessening the matter, do my duty in laying it shortly before you." When the Plague fell on London and all who could had fled — Court and Society, as usual, the first, — among the few bold spirits who remained to carry on the business of the state — the brave, bigoted Bishop of London, Sheldon; the "best justice of the peace in England," Godfrey; the grim Duke of Albemarle, old General Monk, — amid this courageous company of picked men, the Clerk of the Acts stuck to his post in daily peril of his life. Read his letter to Coventry if you would have a measure of the man. "The sickness in general thickens round us," thus he writes, "particularly upon our neighborhood. You, sir, took your turn of the sword; I must not, therefore, grudge to take mine of the pestilence." When, following the Plague, the Great Fire of London threatened to consume the entire

city, he hastened to have workmen brought from the dockyards, to suggest destroying houses in the path of the
conflagration, and planned, worked, commanded, till
the Navy Offices were saved. When the Dutch fleet
sailed up the Medway and the Thames, burning and sinking helpless, laid-up English men-of-war, and threatening
the capital itself; while Monk rallied forces to resist,
threw up entrenchments, mounted guns, and sank vessels
to oppose further advance; — Pepys labored no less
manfully to meet the clamorous demands for adequate
supplies by day and night, "alone at the office . . . yet
doing the king good service." When a hostile House,
hungry for vengeance, seeking a scapegoat for a mis-
managed war, fell on the Navy; when "the whole world
was at work blaming one another," and even the Duke
advised his friends to save themselves, Pepys, unused to
public speech, alone before the Commons, defended his
service, his colleagues, and himself with such conspicuous
ability and success "as gave great satisfaction to every
one." Amid the revelations of corruption and maladministration which followed the war, he dared to beard
even Prince Rupert before the Navy Board — and to
prove his point. Ten years thereafter he was accused, by
no less dangerous an enemy than Shaftesbury, of being a
Catholic and possibly involved in Popish plots. He lost
his office and his liberty, he stood to lose his life; but he
did not lose his courage or resource, and, in the Tower,
prepared defense so ample as to make the absurd charge
fall of its own weight.

Through all he was, he tells us, horribly afraid — but
he was never too frightened to do his duty; incredible as
it seems in view of the conception of the man with which
we have been instilled, his conscience was continually

too much for him. Over and over again he resolves to follow the dictates of prudence and not involve himself in Montagu's affairs — but finally he does. "I was fearful of going to any house," he writes in the Plague year — but he went. "I do see everybody is on his own defense and spare not to blame another, and the same course I shall take" — but he did not. "I was afraid," he writes at another crisis in affairs, "but I did not shew it." Amid the difficulties which confronted him in the naval investigation he even found time to advise a persecuted colleague, "poor weak brother," in his defense. Proud as he was of his success in life, his house, his clothes, his coach, his dignities, his place, — not all his vanity nor all his fears prevented his risking them for what he thought was right. If this be cowardice, then make the most of it.

If, finally, you would have a fairer measure of the man, compare Pepys with Gibbon, the historian, who most nearly occupies an eminence in one department of historical literature commensurate with that of the Secretary in another. Not merely does each owe his present reputation to his literary skill in that field, but the outlines of their lives show certain similarities. Both were of middle class; both rose through their abilities from relative obscurity to distinction; both were members of Parliament; both held public office; and the private life of the historian has been approved by sober folk almost as much as that of the diarist has been condemned. Gibbon, accustomed to inherited means, refrained from marriage with one of the most attractive women on the Continent from prudent fear of his father's displeasure, "sighed as a lover but obeyed as a son"; the penniless Pepys, with a rash unworldliness the more remarkable in a man conspicuous above his fellows for his sound judgment, married in defiance of every prudent consideration. The one, financially independent of his place, gave silent votes against his conscience for a policy which led to England's quarrel with America; the other, owing his living to his place, dared oppose the Commons' anger and his superiors' ill will wherever he believed his cause was right. One slumbered with his colleagues of the Board of Trade over the duties of a pleasant sinecure, while the imperial policy went down to ruin; the other spent his days and, not infrequently, his nights in furthering the interests of his government. "I have entered Parliament," wrote the historian, "without patriotism and without ambition; . . . all my views are bounded by the comfortable and modest position of a Lord of Trade." "My great design," wrote Pepys, "is to get myself to be a Parliament man . . . both for the King's and Service's sake and for the Duke of York's." Reverse Gibbon, and you get Pepys.

Neither could have succeeded in the other's field: Pepys failed as much at history as Gibbon in affairs. From the desert of family and official life which the historian created and called peace, there rose, indeed, a splendid history: from the varied and fertile plain of everyday affairs the Secretary brought a no less immortal Diary. Like character, like book; the style was in each case the man himself. "The manner of the 'Decline and Fall,'" says Bagehot, "is not a style in which you can tell the truth. . . . Truth is of various kinds; grave, solemn, dignified, — petty, low, ordinary: and a historian who has to tell the truth must be able to tell what is little as well as what is amazing. Gibbon is at fault here: he *cannot* mention Asia *Minor*. The petty order of sublunary matters, the common existence of ordinary people, the necessary littlenesses of necessary life are little suited to his sublime narrative." One may not venture to declare what the ideal style of diaries should be; but, by whatever chance, all men agree that Pepys has hit upon it; and, whatever charges may be brought against him, none can say he was not competent to tell the truth in whatever form it showed itself to him, that he failed to find an apt expression for every emotion or experience he had, or that his book does not conform to the "necessary littlenesses of necessary life." One cannot imagine writing of Pepys that "the way to reverence him is not to read him at all, but look at him from the outside . . . and think how much there is within." Rather his book is "actually read, a man is glad to take it up and slow to lay it down; . . . once having had it in his library he would miss it from its shelves," the more so that it was not the product of "a life-time of horrid industry." Least of all did the diarist, with the peculiar vanity of the historian, identify himself with the world's greatness. Gibbon, it has been said, confused himself with the Roman Empire; describing his pilgrimages from Buriton to London and London to Buriton in the same majestic periods that record the fall of states and empires; his amateur experiences with the English yeomanry in phrases that recall the tramp of Roman legions; his voiceless and insignificant presence in the House of Commons in a manner suited to an account of the deliberations of the Roman senators. Whatever form the diarist's egotism took, he realized his place within the universe. Nor can we well believe that the great work of the historian would have suffered from some infusion of the Secretary's qualities.

Comparisons, however invidious, are in this case at least illuminating; for to many minds the smug, impeccable career of the historian has seemed far to surpass the garrulous, inconsequent, vain pursuits of the gossipy diarist in all those enviable qualities which make for virtue and true success; in particular it has seemed to stand for the accomplishment of a great purpose nobly planned, idealistic, admirable, as opposed to Pepys's selfish strivings after the pleasures and profits of a worldly existence. Nothing could be much farther from the truth. If the one made a success of intellect, the other made a success of life; if the historian did much for the past and the future, the Secretary did no less for his own day and for posterity. We would not willingly give up the work of either; but, if one should fail, we could more easily replace the work of Gibbon than the work of Pepys; if we should have to choose between selfish ascetic and hard-working hedonist — let each man make his choice.

That one shall ask more of life than life can give, that is the great tragedy. From it, save in perhaps a single particular, Pepys was spared. But that a man may reasonably expect of posterity an honorable remembrance for eminent service well performed, and receive instead a familiar, half-contemptuous regard as a light-minded, evil-mannered, amusing babbler, that height of fame's tragi-comic irony has been his fate too long. In the records of his service, and in the Diary read by their light, there resides the quality which the critics have found wanting and blamed him for lacking — devotion to high purpose and ideals, and a sense of duty which served at once as lofty patriotism or sustaining belief in a great cause might have to another type of mind. This does not mean that he was a perfect character, only a very human man, eminent in more than one field of human endeavor and of great service to his fellow men. To the appreciation of this world's goods and pleasures, to intellectual and philanthropic tastes, to the doctrines of Franklin and Polonius, he added a sense of public duty and an unremitting industry, with talents which lift him far above the level of his present reputation, as they raised him above the generality of his own times.

He was, in short, an admirable representative of a class not uncommon during the Restoration yet not typical of it, the left-over Puritans, bred in the sterner, more efficient school of the Protectorate; on whom, amid the corruption and extravagance of shifty politicians and dissolute courtiers, rested the burden of the state. What he said of another applies no less to himself: "It is pretty to see that they are fain to find out an old-fashioned man of Cromwell's time to do their business for them." "If it comes to fighting," observed one of his acquaintances when dangers thickened about Charles the Second's path, "the King must rely on the old party"; and this proved, throughout, scarcely less true of administration. With all its faults, the Cromwellian régime had one virtue which was clearly revealed under its successor — it bred strong men. They were not seldom far from immaculate, and the most made of their failings was by their royalist rivals; but in morals they were, at worst, below the level of their generation, and in efficiency they rose far above it. Among these worthies Pepys holds high place. Admitting all the frailties, and the inconsistencies of this Puritan in Restoration garb, his manners and his morals not untouched with something of the weakness of his day, there yet remains a man whom it is next to impossible to dislike, and whom it would be wholly impossible, in the light of adequate knowledge of his career,

K

not to respect. His motto, which in the half-light of his Diary has long seemed so appropriate *Mens cujusque is est quisque* — "as a man's mind is, so is he," — may, in this view, well be replaced by one far more appropriate to his life, "Seest thou a man diligent in his business, he shall stand before kings."

WHAT THE TEN-YEAR SERGEANT OF POLICE TELLS [1]

BY

HENRY HASTINGS CURRAN

Mr. Curran has some very real suggestions to make regarding the conditions of the police force of New York City. The difficulty in regard to the police there is that (a) criminals enter the police force, (b) that the policeman is untrained, (c) that he is inadequately paid, (d) that promotion may be bought, etc. Similar criticisms individually and collectively have been made so often that the public has lost interest. Therefore logically he introduces his main essay by a narrative section in which he tells about the dramatic murder of the gambler Rosenthal and how the subject came to have a particular appropriateness at present. Having by this means gained both the reader's interest and his confidence, he proceeds to enumerate his proposed criticisms.

In his yearning for other lands and other days, Kipling's Tommy Atkins laments that he is "learnin' 'ere in London what the ten-year soldier tells." New Yorkers have been learning through the last winter something of what the ten-year sergeant of police tells. Their equanimity is not increased by the fact that this veteran's recital holds true of many another American city.

The school was set in motion by the latest accident in government by investigation. One Herman Rosenthal, a professional gambler, who had fallen out with his police

[1] From *The Yale Review,* for July, 1913, by permission of the author and of the editor of *The Yale Review.*

protector, had agreed to call on the District Attorney on a July morning and tell what he knew. The appointment was not kept. Rosenthal stepped out of the Hotel Metropole at two o'clock that morning in response to a message that a friend wished to see him, and was shot to death the moment he set foot upon the sidewalk. The murderers made their escape from this brilliantly lighted spot in the Tenderloin with ridiculous ease. If a bystander had not caught the number of the fleeing automobile, the efforts of the District Attorney to call these gunmen to account might well have failed. As events turned out, not only were the four gunmen caught, tried, and convicted, but the police lieutenant involved was convicted of complicity in the affair, and all five are in Sing Sing Prison, sentenced to death.

Meanwhile, the horrified amazement of the people of the city had turned into fiery indignation as the revelations following the shots became more and more sinister in their indications of police complicity in the murder itself. The idea that a lieutenant of police could turn to organized murder to protect his "graft" from exposure was enough to shake the complacency of the blindest. In less than a week from that early morning's work, a movement was on foot in the Board of Aldermen to investigate the police department.

When the investigating committee began its work there was many a wiseacre to predict that "a little graft would be dug up — enough to satisfy the public — then it would all blow over, and the game would go on as before." Others scented a political move and speculated upon the chance of elevating a moral spasm into a "moral issue." And still others, while greedy of the sensations to come, fell back upon the folly of attempting to improve conditions without changing the substantive law on gambling, excise, and prostitution. "The people want to gamble," argued these last doubters, "and laws against gambling cannot be enforced; the people want the saloons open on Sunday, and you cannot keep them shut by law; and no law for the prohibition of prostitution has been possible of enforcement since the beginning of time. These are State-made laws, and the legislators from the rural districts, who are still in the majority at Albany, have imposed their own more rigorous ideas of morality upon a liberty-loving metropolis that systematically sets the imposition at naught. Until the law represents the will of the people of this city, policemen will profit by its non-enforcement; and all the investigations in the world will not cut out the cancer." With a vigorous plea for home rule for the city in these matters, this school of critics usually dismissed the subject as exhausted and settled, on that basis.

The language of the city's charter with respect to aldermanic investigations is simple indeed:

The Board of Aldermen shall have power and it shall be its duty to see to the faithful execution of the laws and ordinances of the city; and it may appoint from time to time a special committee to inquire whether the laws and ordinances of the city relating to any subject or to any department of the city government are being faithfully observed, and the duties of the officers of such department are being faithfully discharged. . . .

The charter framers took it for granted that law is made to be enforced. They decreed further that it be the "duty," as well as the power, of the Board of Aldermen "to see to the faithful execution of the laws . . . of the city"; and nowhere do the fathers countenance such deceitful sacrifices to a distorted conception of personal liberty as "partial" or "proportionate" or "reasonable" enforcement of law. There is no hint in the books of a twilight zone between what is and is not crime, save as the law prescribes.

The committee therefore, in obedience to its charter mandate, held aloof from that engaging field of "when is a crime not a crime," and went in straight pursuit of an answer to the question, "Is the law enforced and are the officers of the police department faithfully discharging their duties?" In other words, New York for the first time studied its police department as a problem of administration. Committees have come and gone, startling the city with the depth of their revelations and revolting their audiences to the point of satiety. They operated, but they took no steps to heal the disease uncovered; the surgeon dropped his work with his knife, and, after calling his clinic to witness what the gash revealed, left the patient to recover as he might. This committee had a different conception of its task.

The police problem is one of character, and the key to a policeman's character is the kind of administration under which he lives. A police career should be as honorable as an army career, with its incentive to ambition and its reward for merit. Is it aided, then, or hindered, by the way in which the department is managed? Is the policeman fortified by his environment and handling to resist temptation, or is the fortitude he brings into the department with him sapped and buffeted to exhaustion by bad management? Let the ten-year sergeant — one of the honest majority — give a few glimpses of his experience, as seen through the lens of this latest investigation, and perhaps even this fragmentary kaleidoscope will reveal something of the intense directness of the pressure which administration brings to bear upon the character of the "cop."

When a square-jawed, well-framed young fellow leaves his truck or workshop and "makes the cops" in New York, he does so by way of a civil service examination, mental and physical. He may be of very ordinary mental calibre, but must be physically without a flaw. In his application he must give his previous history and employment, and answer under oath whether he has been arrested, indicted, or convicted, giving the circumstances. Then he is looked up. New York recruits its police force at the rate of thirty men a month, and the Civil Service Commission confesses to having to look up the character of this human stream with the aid of just two investigators. Prior to the present police administration, an effective character investigation bureau was maintained at police headquarters, under the capable direction of Lieutenant John Stanton, to supplement the absurdly inadequate staff of the Civil Service Commission. This bureau delved into such refinements as the detection, by watermarks, of bogus Irish county birth-certificates, whereby many an intending "copper" was caught swearing falsely as to his age and promptly prevented from beginning a police career with a successful lie upon his lips. But this bureau was abolished by the present administration, and the ten-year sergeant has seen thirty-eight men appointed by the present commissioner who were known by him to have sworn falsely that they had never been arrested. How many more of this ilk have come in since, the public will never know, for the machinery of detection has been thrown into the scrap heap. One of these men had been acquitted of murder (shooting), and of felonious assault (stabbing), after arrest, in addition to having

been sued by his wife for non-support and brutal treatment.
Letters against his character were on file in the department, and the boy he had stabbed, in his barber shop in
Brooklyn, had protested both to the Mayor and the commissioner against making the man a policeman.   When
the boy told his story before the committee, the deep
red of the scar he bore from the stabbing, running from
the ear to the point of the jaw, was visible across the whole
space of the aldermanic chamber.   A present deputy
commissioner accounted, on the witness stand, for the
assailant's appointment as follows :

Q. Then if anybody can escape going to jail, he is a good enough
policeman for you — is that right ?

A. Yes, sir ; he is a good enough policeman for me.

And the commissioner thus explained :

I am stating that, in my opinion, when a man has been tried for a
crime and has been acquitted, it is not incumbent upon any public official
to condemn him or conduct any further prosecution of him. . . . Any
man who, after indictment, has been acquitted, is good enough for me.

The commissioner did not seem to perceive that it was
not a question of prosecuting or condemning a man, but
of clothing him in blue, giving him a gun and a club,
and making him a guardian of the peace and the State's
witness for twenty-five years to come.   Another applicant-
perjurer had been arrested for seduction, discharged upon
agreeing to marry, had then cruelly beaten his wife and
abandoned her, and, finally, had struck a bargain with his
mother-in-law to pay her five dollars a month if she would
keep those incidents from the knowledge of the department.   They came to the present commissioner's knowledge and he promptly made the man a policeman.   Still
another man, appointed a few years ago and escaping

even the vigilance of the department's character investigation, had served a year in the King's County Penitentiary for burglary. Thus the ten-year sergeant, standing at the gate of the citadel of police headquarters, has seen this band of liars enter and made welcome in the place where truth should be the first quality; and many a truth-telling young fellow he has seen left standing without, because the liars spelled or punctuated a little better. He has also seen the dismissal from the force of that Lieutenant Stanton who testified to the committee, under subpœna, of his character investigation work, before the present commissioner did away with it. Following his testimony, came a charge of attempted extortion, suddenly remembered after three years by the commissioner's former policeman-chauffeur; then Stanton's trial and dismissal, though his record in the department was clean for seventeen years back. This extraordinary charge was, immediately after the police trial, thoroughly sifted and exploded before the aldermanic committee, but Stanton remains the sacrifice of the investigation.

When the new policeman has run the preliminary gauntlet and is finally appointed to be one of "the finest," he is corralled for thirty days in the school of recruits to be "halter-broken." Here he receives competent instruction in pistol practice, drilling, and humane handling of prisoners, with many a sharp fall from the wrestling teacher who shows the different grips. In the old days, there was also fruitful schooling in the law of crime, gathering of evidence, and presentation of the State's case in court, with an active moot court in session to demonstrate indelibly this vital part of a policeman's work. The mental training, however, has fallen into decay, and its old vigor is now replaced by hours of monologue from a captain to a score of perspiring truckmen who neither ask nor are asked questions. With no running stimulus to independent thinking, there is also no test at the end, in which respect the police probationer may wake a chord of envy in the collegiate heart. London schools its police neophytes for six weeks, and Düsseldorf, supplying schooled recruits to the Rhine provinces, for eleven weeks, while a German policeman must first have been a "non-com" in the German Army, with at least six years of army experience. That New York, without the extra safeguards of the British and the Germans, should turn its policemen out on the street equipped with thirty days of mental malnutrition, serves to show another of the honest policeman's initial handicaps.

A more serious instance of starting a man on his race with a hobble about his knees is encountered in the rate of pay of the first and second year patrolmen, and this is a matter that the ten-year sergeant has been through himself. The $800 of the first year becomes $900 in the second, and then ranges upward by degrees until it reaches the patrolman's maximum of $1400 at the end of the fifth year. The $800 is quite fictitious. It is in fact only $556.64, as the city takes back the balance by compelling the new patrolman to buy his entire equipment out of his own pocket. Summer and winter uniforms, raincoat, boots, billet, locust night-stick, whistle, nippers, revolver and cartridges, rawhide straps, cap-devices — these and a thousand and one other expenses must be footed by the patrolman. He must even pay for his bedding at the station-house, where he is required to be when asleep on reserve; and his pension and benevolent association dues complete the rebate that he thus furnishes the city. The wives of 175 patrolmen picked at random have told the committee their experience, with figures of household budgets. They pass muster in thrift and frugality, but their little savings cannot bridge the gap between a salary of $556.64 and an average budget for family purposes of $848.71. It is only debt that finds room in this gap, with the tradesman and the doctor vying for the monthly pay cheque, and the loan shark ever at the door. One of these parasites finally collected $60 from a patrolman for a loan of $30. It needs only a slight dereliction of duty to bring down a fine upon the patrolman's head, and then it is the wife and babies who are punished. Fines are deducted from the offender's pay, and there has been much thoughtful condemnation of this instrument of discipline. The New York policeman thus begins his career in debt, and if he yields before some of the graft that is thrust at him, must the condemnation be blind to all causes? One has little patience with those sympathetic souls who would excuse a policeman from wrong-doing because he is peculiarly tempted; the town is thoroughly sated with this maudlin fashion of talk. But has the city done its part when it fastens the shield with the city's seal on the breast of the new "cop" with one hand, and with a niggardly clutch of the other pulls him aside into unavoidable debt?

The old saying, "You must take 'em young," applies to the policeman. Let him "get away" with a fraud at his entrance, and he will try another before he has long been in. The next step is promotion, and on this point a police captain, of years gone by, has testified to the following miniature of high finance:

A. I was not three months on the police before somebody came to me and wanted $300 to have me detailed to the Harbor Squad.

Q. Did you pay it?

A. No, sir.

Q. Were you detailed?

A. No, sir. Five or six months after that my grandmother died, and she left a little money to my mother, and the scouts heard about that, and they came around and wanted to make me a roundsman for $600.

This captain was under examination concerning a story that he had done some negotiating for the payment of $10,000 to a politician for his promotion to his captaincy. The colloquy over this reveals a refreshing degree of frankness.

Q. Would you be willing to pay $10,000 for your promotion?

A. If somebody else paid it for me. I would not have paid it.

Q. You would have consented to have had it paid?

A. Most assuredly I would. I wanted to get promoted.

Q. How would you get the $10,000 back?

A. I do not know (*laughter*). There is a legacy coming to me, and I would be able to pay it back some day.

Q. How would you get the $10,000 back that you had to put up for a captaincy?

A. Why the job was worth it (*laughter*).

Q. How?

A. For the simple reason that you do not have to work nights. You can sleep all night (*laughter*).

If ever a department of city government should have its drawbridge up and gates bolted against politicians, however well-intentioned, the police department is that one. The insidious plague that has suddenly destroyed the chestnut trees of a continent is no more potent in its blight than is the devastation of discipline that political access can work in a police department. The police commissioners who have come and gone are a unit on this point. Is anyone yet so simple as to think that a policeman who benefits in his calling by political favor will not some day have to repay that favor by winking at an infraction of the law? And that is quite apart from many a cash payment made in bygone days, if rumor be true.

Ten years ago, Captain Miles O'Reilly, who bears the distinctive appellation of "Honest Miles O'Reilly," was in command of the Oak Street precinct and on the look-out for malingerers. So, when at three o'clock one morning, four of his men were discovered "shooting craps" in the back room of a saloon when they were supposed to be on duty, there was trouble ahead. O'Reilly was a good deal of a disciplinarian in his day, and the particular "crap-shooter" who figures in this drama was promptly dismissed from the force. With an ambition to return to the fold, the dismissed patrolman went to court; he was rejected with equal promptness by two courts, the second being the court of last resort of the State. He then accomplished the passage, by the legislature of the State of New York, of a special Act reinstating him as a policeman, which was vetoed by Mayor McClellan. Then came a general Act, with a retroactive clause to admit the "crap-shooter," but General Bingham, then commissioner, used the discretion given him by turning this bad penny down again. The fifth attempt, made upon the present commissioner, succeeded, and "Honest Miles O'Reilly's" tarrier is back again after nine years of lobbying, with a new uniform and a service stripe, as lively as a cricket, while the passing decade has seen the honorable retirement of his old commander. The slang phrase that "they never come back" boasts two notable exceptions in Rip Van Winkle and this peripatetic patrolman. The ten-year sergeant knows this as "a reinstatement," and he has seen more than one man justly dismissed by the last administration but cheerfully reinstated under the present régime, with rank still equal to that of his comrade who had escaped this vacation by steadily doing his duty.

When the aldermanic investigation began, the ten-year sergeant had not only seen a dismissed patrolman come back after nine years of lobbying, but he had also seen eight police commissioners come and go in eleven years. Birds of passage, a former deputy commissioner has testified that "the force gets a glimpse of them flying over and hardly has time to determine their species." Commissioners come and go, but the policeman goes on forever. And with this tradition, has come about a sort of police peerage, a group of powerful barons in the department who, holding the higher offices, can make and unmake a commissioner. If the barons become disaffected, the commissioner's days are numbered. Judge McAdoo, a former commissioner, has testified that in November, 1905, standing odds of two to one were posted in every gambling house in town that "McAdoo would not last beyond the year." There were no takers, and McAdoo went when the clock struck twelve on New Year's Eve. The police barons manufacture "crime waves," bring pressure upon a mayor vested with power to remove the commissioner, stir up political sorties by the "outs" against the "ins" of police officialdom, and never yet have they failed to get the head of the ruler. That these Igorrotes administer the lair of such "crooks" as the department harbors, might well be believed, even in the absence of the recent conviction of four inspectors now in stripes on Blackwell's Island. The young policeman is under the command of these higher officers, and he has his own existence to look to, with always the chance of a "frame-up" if he displeases the barons by unwelcome zeal in protected fields of law-breaking. This is the "system." The presence of a number of higher officers of sterling uprightness only emphasizes the "gait" of the others. With these men so difficult to dislodge that some have, uncannily enough, been honorably retired on pension just to get them out of the department, the barons command respect in the ranks when the commissioner cannot. General Bingham has testified that when the peerage carried its power into the legislature, he was compelled, to his military amazement, to take the defensive before the legislative committee and, in trying to defeat their legislation, to face a volley of questions from spokesmen of his own subordinates. In other words, the head of the house was called sharply to account for opposing a bill emanating from his own *entourage!* That each of these commissioners who succeeded each other so rapidly has different ideas from those of his predecessor, which he invariably puts into effect, only increases the confusion of the policeman who must do his work in such a remarkable household.

There are few young policemen who do not cherish an ambition to serve in the detective bureau. The plain clothes of the "bull" are a magnet of envy that never fails to draw. With a sense of romance and responsibility begotten of boyhood, the chance of a high *esprit de corps* here would seem second to none. That opportunity is now in abeyance. Maladministration has emptied headquarters of detectives and scattered them to the precincts, with the inevitable disappearance of cohesion, team work, and conference. The "Italian Squad," a famous set of men who under the valiant Petrosino proved the first effective check to bomb-throwing, kidnapping, and the "Black Hand," has been abolished. The pickpocket squad, specialists in capturing these disciples of Fagin, is gone. Captain Carey's homicide squad has been scattered, and his human bloodhounds are more likely now to be found on the trail of Saturday-night street brawls than of murder. In short, specialization, the main support of detective efficiency, has received its death blow. Abolished also is the "morning line-up," the daily array of crooks at headquarters for inspection and identification by detectives under mask. Worst of all, 8,400 pictures in the "Rogues' Gallery" have been burned up in the furnace at headquarters, by official order, together with the accompanying Bertillon records, and this invaluable aid to criminal justice in all parts of the country is a thing of the past. The number of arrested persons now "mugged" is so paltry as to be negligible — O personal liberty, "what crimes are committed in thy name!" With the temple thus pulled down over the departmental head, and the detectives searching for tools to work with, the rotation of members of the bureau has proceeded so fast that in fifteen months 254 men went in and 290 went out and back to patrol duty, out of an average complement of 500 in the bureau. The prophet has not yet appeared who will essay to prove that detectives may thus be made overnight.

The ten-year sergeant found the detective's climax capped when he heard of the ostrich feather exploit of a June night last year. The detective bureau, with a laudable ambition to put three known "loft burglars" behind the bars, engaged the services of a "stool-pigeon," that is to say, another "crook," who cheerfully agreed to lead his comrades into a police trap for the price. Twenty-five dollars of the city's money was spent for a kit of burglar tools, and further funds for wining and dining the three "crooks," the vouchers for all of which now lie in state in the comptroller's office. The plan was prettily set for a midnight melodrama opposite old Grace Church on Broadway, and the appointed time and place found the three burglars and their obliging "stool-pigeon" friend busily blowing a hole into the loft building which contained the goal of their hopes, the dynamite being also a municipal investment. The trio being engaged in the loft, their automobile and chauffeur accomplice waiting in Union Square, a few blocks away, for the signal, and the department's detectives planted in adjacent doorways, the little drama came to its climax upon the collision of these three expeditions. The burglars were on the sidewalk with bags stuffed with several thousand dollars' worth of ostrich feathers, the automobile speeding to the rescue had slowed up at the curb to take aboard the thieves and their loot, when at the proper moment a swarm of detectives swept down upon the adventurers and captured the entire outfit, without a shot or a struggle. This constitutes the official burglary, but the unofficial burglary came to light the next morning when the merchant who had unwittingly provided the scenery for the drama counted up his losses and then, in the station-house of the precinct, whither the feathers had been taken, made an inventory of the capture. As the value of the feathers in the hands of the police was $1,500 less than that of the feathers taken from the loft, and a hard-hearted burglar insurance company had felt certain enough of the loss to pay over the $1,500 to the merchant, the disappearing difference in the feathers survived as the greater mystery. Although no one but the detectives and the crooks had been on the spot, and the detectives had captured the crooks, they vouchsafed no answer to the mystery of who

L

had captured the missing feathers. The play became still more a burlesque when the lieutenant of detectives a few days later demanded and received from the merchant $175 as a reward for personal bravery.

Mary Goode's testimony marked the beginning of the committee's inquiry into the department's methods of handling vice. Self-confessed proprietress of a disorderly house, she passed across the stage with a modesty of demeanor and modulated gentility of speech that well-nigh gave the lie to her vocation. When attacked by a hostile member of the committee, her discerning retort, complete in its answer, was delivered so quietly and with such evident sincerity that her story has never since been questioned. Her tale is worn threadbare in private knowledge but seldom told in public under oath. The shifting of zones of prostitution, the dreariness of the trade, the cupidity of police officials, and the incessant payment of "protection" money to their collectors were only a few of the familiar incidents related. The ten-year sergeant knows this story by heart. It concerns more than him. He could not, however, know her estimate of the number of prostitutes, showing a total of 35,000 fallen women in New York City. One need not stand aghast when he compares this figure with that of the 10,000 similarly unfortunate women that an aldermanic committee found domiciled in the town seventy years ago. There were some 500,000 people in the present city area in 1843, where there are now 5,250,000. So the old proportion was one prostitute to every fifty of population, where now it is only one to every one hundred and fifty. Hope may lie there.

George A. Sipp, who had kept a "hotel" in Harlem, followed the Goode story within a week, and his unadorned tale of consistent payment for police protection was equally convincing. He served the additionally useful purpose of introducing the committee to the "friendly collar," a species of arrest that is visited from time to time upon protected law breakers, to keep the precinct record straight. The difference between an ordinary "collar" and a "friendly collar" is that the arresting officers suffer a lapse of memory when they appear in court against the victim of the latter, so that the case fails and is "turned out"; but the record of arrests shows a fine degree of activity, *pro bono publico*, on the part of the profiting police protectors.

The ten-year sergeant knows Sipp's story as well as he knows Mary Goode's, for the police barons rule more by fear than by secrecy. But he knows more. He is aware that citizens constantly write to the commissioner accusing police officers of "grafting" from gambling and disorderly houses, and has learned to his amazement that the practice of the present commissioner is to refer all such complaints to the officers accused for investigation. In a test period of fourteen months, in the present administration, out of 301 such complaints, 270 are found to have been politely forwarded to the accused policemen, or their immediate superiors involved by inference in the accusation, with a request to investigate themselves. As many as 190 were referred to the officers in question merely for their "information." When these Spartan policemen investigated, they invariably found themselves not guilty and solemnly so reported to the commissioner, who must have been immensely relieved to find his officers so sure of themselves. One letter, addressed to the Mayor and forwarded to the commissioner, ran as follows:

March 27, 1912.

Hon. W. J. Gaynor:

I would like to have you investigate quietly Lieut. Becker. He is now collecting more money than Devery, and it is well known to everyone at Police Headquarters. Please do this and you will be surprised at the result.

Yours,

HENRY WILLIAMS.

This was "respectfully referred to Lieutenant Becker for investigation and report," and the Lieutenant himself, in this case, respectfully suggested in his report that someone else might better do the investigating. The Lieutenant is now in prison for the murder of Rosenthal. A complaint that one of Inspector Sweeney's "wardmen" was "grafting" was referred to the Inspector for investigation and report, and the latter promptly absolved himself. He is now confined in the penitentiary for conspiracy. With no system of informing himself of conditions, to check the reassurances of his lying subordinates, the present commissioner has coupled an honest effort to enforce the gambling law with a studied indifference to Sunday liquor-selling and to the heyday of disorderly house activity that has reigned; and his idea of "auto-investigation" by accused policemen has led straight into the Rosenthal murder. The ten-year sergeant wonders that the explosion did not come before.

When the agitation for this investigation was begun, the sensation-loving portion of the public found its food in the committee's struggle for permission to exist. With high city officials of every persuasion offering obstacle after obstacle to a police inquiry of any kind, there was presented a steeplechase of such stiffness and variety that all New York took a sporting interest in the running. The jumps all taken and the course to the arena run, there followed the period of "great expectations." The audience clamored for blood. "Show us the graft! Give us the 'man higher up.' Produce or get off!" Thus the cry of the crowd, the yearning for a human sacrifice, with its opportunity for the turning down of thumbs. Meanwhile the committee had been going about its business seeking the answer to the question, "Is the law of the city faithfully observed and are the duties of its officers faithfully discharged?" The administration of the department was and is the problem, and the driest details received their due notice in the scheme. In December the inquiry was pointing up, in its logical course, to the department's method of handling gambling and prostitution, and its machinery was working smoothly, and fruitfully, with every promise of the beneficial results that must accrue from careful study as distinguished from sensation seeking. From the point of view of the sensation lovers, however, the affair was quite in the doldrums, and was becoming generally labelled as a humdrum, sewing-machine matter, soon to die and best forgotten. Most serious of all, the modest appropriation was nearly exhausted, and those hostile to the inquiry could prevent the granting of another dollar unless there were a public demand that would not brook denial. That a great number of thinking people wanted the inquiry completed along its proper lines did not lessen the opportunity of the hostile.

At this point of peril, Mary Goode's story came to the rescue with the spectacular suddenness of lightning. Back came the special writers of the newspapers who had "featured" the inquiry in the beginning but had long since fled to more exciting fields. Back came the audience, which had dwindled to a dozen when Mary Goode took the stand, but now thronged the chamber at every hearing.

Back came public interest, with three-column headlines in the papers and animated discussion wherever in the town one man might meet with another. The chasm was crossed, the extra appropriation granted with eulogies from friend and foe alike, and the street-corner comment changed to, "Now you're *doing* something — keep it up!"

Sipp's story a week later settled all uncertainty, and history records the punitive aftermath of that revelation of revenge: A score of policemen indicted, two patrolmen convicted and in Sing Sing, a captain and another patrolman who have confessed, awaiting sentence. And, finally, for the first time in its history, New York has witnessed the spectacle of four inspectors of police — the highest rank in the uniformed force — in stripes, with heads shaved, making brooms and mending shoes within the gray walls of a penitentiary. That the story of one man before an aldermanic committee should give the District Attorney an opportunity to carry his masterly pursuit of crooked policemen to the point already reached, was a chance by-product of an administrative investigation that looms larger and larger in its educational benefit to the police and the community. Having set the Sipp saturnalia in motion, the committee returned to its patient, closed its ears to the clamor of the clinic, and quietly finished its work.

Will the analysis be followed by synthesis? Will the public remember long enough to see that punitive destruction is followed by administrative construction? Preventive hygiene will be required to follow convalescence. If the call is not heeded, the consequences will come in the shape of another police explosion and another police investigation. The ten-year sergeant knows this.

He will well know, too, whether the events of 1913 have

helped to give the police the administrative backbone of a
"career." If they have not, the adage that "the policeman's lot is not a happy one," will still apply to him, for
he is of the honest and preponderant portion of an army
that New York honors to a man for its courage, and wants
to honor to a man for its uprightness. But if they have,
the ten-year sergeant may translate Tommy Atkins for a
new toast to the spirit of the corps:

> When you've 'eard your city callin',
> W'y you won't 'eed nothin' else.

THE POWERS OF THE PRESIDENT [1]

BY

WILLIAM HOWARD TAFT

To every American the exact extent and the exact limitation of the powers of the President of the United States is of necessity interesting. Still more interesting does it become when the subject is treated by one who himself has been President. He rightfully speaks with authority. Consequently the first paragraph simply states the question, but states is in a very personal way. There are six *I*'s in that first paragraph. The succeeding paragraphs treat each function, defining and limiting it. Then the final paragraph returns to the comparison between the king of England and the President with which the essay opened. Therefore as a whole the structure is severely simple. The development within the paragraph, the precision of phrase, the accuracy of definition, and the clarity of exposition, make it a model of legal acuteness.

IT has been said that the President of the United States has more real power than most monarchs of Europe. I do not know that I am able to institute an intelligent comparison, because to do that one ought to be quite familiar with the extent of the royal or imperial power to be measured with that of our President; and I have not sufficient knowledge on the subject. I know something with respect to the real governing power of the King of England, and, except in an indirect way, the President's power far exceeds that of King George; and I think it is very considerably more than that of the President of France. When,

[1] From *The Yale Review*, for October, 1914, by permission of the author and of the editor of *The Yale Review*.

however, one examines the imperial power in governments like Germany, Austria, Italy, and Spain, the question is much more difficult; and I presume no one would say that the President's power was equal to that of the Czar of Russia.

With us, a President is elected for four years, and nothing can get him out of office except his death, or his resignation — which never comes, — or his impeachment. The certainty of his tenure for four years makes our executive administration a little more rigid and less subject to quick changes of public opinion than in the parliamentary countries. I am inclined to think that our system is a good thing for our country, however much parliamentary government may suit the countries where it is in use. Of course, it has this disadvantage. In a parliamentary government there is a union between the executive and the legislative branches, and they, therefore, work together, because those who constitute the executive lead and direct the legislation; whereas in the separation of the great branches of the government with us, the President represents the executive, Congress the legislative, and the courts the judicial branch; and the plan of the men who framed the Constitution was to preserve these branches separate. The President is able to recommend legislation to Congress, and he may go in person to argue the wisdom of it if he chooses. Mr. Wilson has restored an old custom of that sort, which was abandoned by President Jefferson, and I think he was right in doing so. It emphasizes his recommendations and focusses the eyes of the people on that which he regards as important to the public welfare, and it puts a greater responsibility on Congress to give attention to his suggestions.

The British constitution gives the power of veto to the

King; but it has not been exercised for more than two centuries, and were it attempted, it would shake the throne. The exercise of the President's veto always rouses eloquence on the part of those who are much disappointed at the defeat of the measure, and the walls of Congress not infrequently resound with denunciation of his tyrannical exercise of a kingly prerogative. But the fact is it has come to be a more frequent characteristic of a republic than of a modern monarchy. For a king or an emperor to interpose a veto to an Act of the popular legislature is really to obstruct the people's will, because he was not chosen by their votes but inherited his royal power. He must, indeed, be careful in exercising a veto lest he incur a protest and arouse a feeling dangerous to his dynasty. The case of the President is very different. The Constitution established by the people requires the President to withhold his signature from a bill if he disapprove it, and return it with his objections to the House in which it originated. For the President is quite as much the representative of the people as are the members of the two Houses. Indeed, the whole people of the United States is his constituency, and he therefore speaks and acts for them quite as certainly as the members elected from congressional districts or the Senators from the States. He is not exercising a kingly power in a veto. He is acting in a representative capacity for the whole people, and is preventing a law that he thinks would work to the detriment of the whole country. On this account, the roar of the young lions of Congress against a veto never frightens the occupant of the White House. He is not obstructing popular will; he is only seeking to express it in his veto, as he has the duty and power to do. It is much more to the point for those who hurl their burning words into the Congressional Record to gather votes enough to pass the bill over the veto. If they fail in this, they are not likely to disturb anybody's equanimity by trying to establish an analogy between the royal prerogative and a power given the President by the people for their own protection.

Again, the President is, by the Constitution, the commander-in-chief of the army and navy. That gives him the constitutional right to issue orders to the army and navy to do what he wishes them to do within the law and the restrictions of the Constitution. He can send them to any place in the country, can change their stations, can mass them where he will, and he can call upon them to help him in the execution of the laws. Ordinarily, of course, the law is enforced, so far as the United States is concerned, by the civil executive officers, like United States marshals, post-office employees, collectors of internal revenue and of customs, public land officers, and forestry agents. But wherever the United States law is resisted by violence, wherever the decrees of a United States court are so resisted, and the court calls upon the President to enforce its decree, it is the business of the President to see that this is done; and if his United States marshals are unable to do it, he may call upon the army to do so. In the Debs strike, or "rebellion," as it was called, when an association, known as the "American Railway Union," sought to boycott all the railways, to prevent by violence their operation, and to stop the mail cars in transportation of the United States mail, the federal courts issued injunctions against the leaders; but the enforcement of these was forcibly resisted. Then President Cleveland called out the army, and the law was enforced. In a subsequent case, involving the validity of Mr. Cleveland's action, the Supreme Court of the United States fully sustained him.

There was a time when under the Constitution the Republican party sought to make possible the legitimate negro vote in the South, and elaborate laws were passed, called "force laws," to subject congressional elections to the supervision of United States election officers, and the army was used to protect them in the discharge of their duty. The Democratic party came into power with a Republican President, Mr. Hayes, and insisted upon imposing a rider upon the army appropriation bill, forbidding the use of the army to help in the enforcement of the election laws. Mr. Hayes vetoed the army appropriation bill because it contained such a rider, and the army went without money for one year. Subsequently, however, it was passed. The question never arose as to whether such a restriction upon the executive power was valid. I think it was not. It is a constitutional duty on the part of the President to execute the laws; and as long as he has an army, and the Constitution contemplates his having an army under his command, he cannot be deprived of the power to use that army to execute all the laws.

But the President's constitutional function as commander-in-chief of the army and navy gives him a very great scope in the exercise of much wider power than merely issuing military orders to generals for the use of troops. The President was, of course, commander-in-chief in the Spanish War, and as such, under the declaration of war that Congress made, he sent troops to Cuba, and subsequently to the Philippines. After the war was over, we continued in occupation of Cuba, Porto Rico, and the Philippines; and until Congress intervened by legislation, President McKinley carried on the military government in these three important dependencies. There were a million people in Porto Rico. There were two and one-half million people in Cuba, and there were upwards of eight millions in the Philippines; and he exercised not only executive power but legislative power over those twelve millions of people. His executive orders were law. There were some restrictions upon the character of laws he could make, where the question involved the customs laws of the United States; but all laws that had force in the dependencies themselves, he was able to make and enforce. The protocol which stopped hostilities in the Spanish War was signed in August of 1898, and the Treaty of Paris that ended the war and transferred to us Porto Rico, the Philippines, and the control of Cuba, was signed late in the same year. From that time on, the President created courts, enacted criminal and civil laws, collected taxes, and administered the government through his power as commander-in-chief of the army and the navy, and he did not need to use military agents to accomplish this purpose.

In 1900 he sent to the Philippines a Commission of five men to institute a government in the islands. It was called civil government, and it was in fact civil government, and yet it was established under his military power. At first he retained in the Philippines a military governor, and a major-general of the army was the executive, while the Commission enacted such civil legislation as was needed there and established such municipal and provincial governments as the condition of the country permitted. The President, through the Secretary of War, who acted for him, appointed in July, 1901, a civil governor in the Philippines, under his military power. That civil governor assumed office on the fourth of July, 1901, and it was not until June, 1902, nearly four years after we acquired possession of the Philippines, that Congress took a hand at all. It was a very wise arrangement, because through the ease with which the President and the Secretary of War could mould the government to suit the conditions, the character of the people, and the exigencies of the campaign to tranquillize the islands, by executive orders and Acts of the Commission, a government was created that fitted the country as a suit would be fitted to a man by a tailor. And then after it was all done, after the work was seen to be good, Congress took up the matter and confirmed what had been done, and established the present government there, on the exact lines of the government that the President had built up under his power as commander-in-chief. The same thing is more or less true of Cuba and Porto Rico, though we did not retain Cuba but turned the island over to the Cubans, in accordance with our promise made when we began the war, and although the government of Porto Rico was not fitted to the necessities of Porto Rico, by experimental administration, as fully and as successfully as in the case of the Philippines. The second intervention in Cuba in 1906 was by order of the President, without special congressional action or authority. He acted under his power to see that the laws are executed, and by virtue of his power as commander-in-chief of the army and navy.

The President has no right to declare war. That rests by the Constitution with Congress. While he cannot declare war, he can direct the action of the army and the navy, and so he could direct an invasion of a foreign country, but that would be an act of war which would necessarily bring on war. There have been cases where the President has used the marine force and landed men to protect American property, but such landing is not to be regarded as an invasion. Certainly a President would violate his duty if he directed such an invasion without the consent of the constituted authority in a foreign country, and thus brought on war. But in the case of Cuba and the intervention to which I have referred, Cuba had consented in the treaty which she made with the United States, and had provided in her own constitution that the United States might intervene at its discretion for the purpose of maintaining law and order. So far as the President was concerned, this put Cuba within the jurisdiction of the United States to that extent, and so it became the President's duty to see that the laws were executed in Cuba, without receiving special congressional authority. And he did it with the army and the navy, because he was their commander-in-chief.

Another instance. The Canal Zone on the Isthmus of Panama is a territory belonging to the United States, in which we exercise authority equal to absolute dominion. Congress passed a law authorizing the President to establish a government there, and to appoint officers to exercise governmental authority; but the law, by its own terms, expired within a year after its enactment. Meantime we were on the Isthmus building the canal. Congress had given the President authority to build the canal, indeed had made it his duty to do so, but there was absolutely no authority expressly given to him to continue a government after the expiration of the law to which I have referred. But the President went right on exercising the same authority that he had been exercising; and he did so under his constitutional authority to see that the laws of the United States are executed. In the absence of congressional action, when there is a piece of United

States territory without a government, he has to take charge of it, and govern it as best he can. Congress knows the conditions and does not act, and so the President is compelled to do so. Judges may be appointed, laws administered, men imprisoned and executed for crime, and all by direction of the executive power.

Another power of the President, and one of his greatest powers, is expressed in a very innocent and simple sentence: "He shall receive all Ambassadors and public Ministers." He can make treaties, but he cannot do that without the ratification, or, as it is called in the Constitution, without "the advice and consent of the Senate," by a vote of two-thirds of those present. He cannot declare war, because that is a power that Congress exercises under the Constitution. Except for these specific limitations, he controls entirely our international relations. In the first place, no treaty can be made unless he initiates it. The Senate may pass a resolution suggesting his making a treaty, and so might the House, and so might Congress, but he is not obliged to follow their recommendation. All our intercourse, except the formal making of treaties with foreign countries, is carried on by the President through the State Department. Now that involves the presentation of claims and complaints by our citizens against foreign countries, and the presentation by us of petitions for all sorts of action by foreign governments. It involves a correspondence as to the complaints by foreign citizens or subjects against our government. It involves a constant reference to treaties made and their construction by our government, which construction after a while practically fixes our attitude. The President recognizes foreign governments. Thus we see in Mexico, which fell into a state of revolution and almost anarchy,

President Wilson declined to recognize Huerta as provisional president. He had the right to do so. He had the right to recognize him if he chose; and the resulting crisis made it evident what a very important and responsible power that is.

Take the case of the fur seals. Congress passed a law, punishing anyone who resorted to pelagic sealing in the Bering Sea. The government owned the Pribilof Islands, upon which was a herd of seals. The destruction of the female seals out at sea was very injurious to the herd. That was the occasion for the enactment of the congressional law to which I referred. Now under the construction that international law would ordinarily put upon such a statute, it could only apply to sealing within three miles of United States land, or else in some way or other we would have to establish ownership in the seals themselves. Mr. Blaine, who was then Secretary of State, took the position that the grant of Alaska to the United States in 1867 carried with it dominion over the Bering Sea for the purpose of preserving these seals, and he went back into the records to show that Russia had claimed such dominion and attempted to prove that it had been acquiesced in by the Powers. Following that view, the United States Court of Alaska sustained the seizure of certain Canadian fishing vessels that had been caught in pelagic sealing by one of our revenue cutters, forfeited them under the congressional Act and sold them. The British government, through Canadian agents, brought a suit in the Supreme Court of the United States to secure a writ of prohibition against the Alaska court to prevent that court from carrying out its decree, on the ground that there was no jurisdiction over the Bering Sea which Congress could assert or which the President could maintain. The

M

Supreme Court dismissed the application, on the main ground that the question of the dominion of the United States was a political question, to be determined by the President or Congress; and because the President had asserted the claim through the Secretary of State that we had dominion over the Alaskan waters beyond the three-mile limit, the court would be bound by it. Then we had an international arbitration in which the court considered the question and held that the Secretary of State was wrong. For the purposes of my present discussion, it is a good illustration of the very great power that the President can exercise in his control over foreign relations.

By the Constitution, the President has the right to appoint all ambassadors, ministers, consuls, and judges of the Supreme Court, subject to confirmation by the Senate of the United States. Congress may place the appointment of all other officers, with the consent of the Senate, in the President alone, or in the heads of departments, or in the courts. Practically, the general power of appointment of all officers, except very inferior and unimportant officers, is in the President, and generally confirmation is required by the Senate. This, of course, is a great power. It is a power, so far as the great offices are concerned, that the President must have in order that he may have his policies carried out. That is, he must appoint his Cabinet, because, as the Supreme Court has said, they are the fingers of his hand, and they must do his will and exercise his discretion. Therefore, if there is to be uniformity, if there is to be consistency, if there is to be solidarity of movement and force in the executive branches of the government, the President must appoint the men who act at the heads of departments and form his Cabinet.

In respect to all the other executive offices, however, a different rule should obtain. With the exception of the judges of the courts, of the ambassadors and ministers, of the members of his Cabinet, and the appointment of the general officers of the army, I think that the action of the President ought practically to be nothing more than a formal acquiescence in a system which prevails in other well-governed countries, by which the selection and promotion of all officers is by examination, and their tenure is for life. The President should not be bothered, as he is now, with having to exercise an arbitrary discretion enabling him, if he choose, to use the offices for political purposes, and involving him in controversies that interfere with his effectiveness as the chief executive officer of the nation and do not help the public weal. It is entirely possible to put all these offices, except the ones I have named, under the system called the classified civil service. If popular government is to be a success, the success will be measured by the ability of the government to use the services of experts in carrying it on. The selection of other than the highest officers on political grounds will not result in the use of experts to carry on the various functions that the government performs.

We are acquiescing now, all of us, in the view that the government can accomplish and ought to accomplish much more benefit for the people than Mr. Jefferson and his school of political thinkers admitted. Mr. Jefferson contended that the least government was the best government; that the function of government should be confined, as nearly as possible, to the administration of justice through the courts, and the maintenance of law and order through the police. But we now take a different view, and hold that there are many things the government can do well and better than private contractors. For instance, we have always run the post office, and now we run the parcels post. We have built the Panama Canal; and the state governments are discharging many functions that it was formerly thought would be better performed by private agency. But such functions for their successful performance require the highest experts. If we are to change such officers every four years with the political complexion of the administration, then we lose the benefit of experience, we lose the benefit of the disinterested devotion to the public service that a life-tenure brings about, and we take away from the public service its attractiveness for the many whose service would be valuable, but who because of the uncertainty of tenure in the government service decline to accept positions of responsibility in it. I speak whereof I know when I say it injures the dignity and the usefulness of a President to be bothered about the preference to be given to candidates for post offices, for collectors of customs, collectors of internal revenue all over this country. Under the present law, the Senate is required to confirm them. That necessity gives to the Senators an opportunity to use duress, for that is what it amounts to, upon the President to establish a custom by which he shall consult their political views as to who shall be appointed to those local offices.

The office of President is one of the greatest responsibility. No one knows the burden he has to carry in the Presidency until he has laid it down and realizes the exhaustion of his mental and nervous energy which unconsciously was going on while he attempted to discharge his duties. One of the most aggravating features of his present duties is this constant attention that he has to pay to the visits of Congressmen and Senators in regard to the local patronage. He ought not to have to do with such offices at all. Thus far the Senate has not been willing to give up its power in this regard. While I was in the White House I recommended it every year. I believe it is coming. We have made great progress in this matter. We have now a civil service law that covers many of the inferior offices, but what we ought to have is a permanent machinery of the government reaching up to include the assistant secretaries in the various departments. It will make for efficiency; it will make for economy; it will make for saving of the time and energy of the President and Senators and Congressmen. It will take away opportunities for political machines; it will tend towards purity in politics and effectiveness of government; and, therefore, it will make for the weal of the people of the United States; and it can all be accomplished by an Act of Congress, and a President who will approve the Act and carry out its spirit. It is coming. The Lord is on that side, but sometimes He moves more slowly than we impatient mortals think necessary.

The other great power which the President has, in addition to being commander-in-chief of the army and navy, conducting the foreign relations of the government, making treaties and declaring war, and the power of appointment and the power to see the law executed, is in the granting of reprieves and pardons to those suffering punishment for violating laws of the United States. This is a very wide power. The President may exercise it after a crime is committed and before any trial begins; may exercise it before the man is arrested; may issue an amnesty — that is, a pardon of a number of people by a class description. The power of pardon in States has been greatly abused by some governors, but I never heard that any President had called down on himself just criticism for his use of this great and merciful instrument. In the exercise of the pardoning power, there is no certain line to guide the executive to a safe conclusion. He has to balance in his mind the considerations for which punishment is provided. The aim of punishment of a criminal is, first, to furnish an example to induce others who are about to commit similar crimes to avoid them; second, to reform the criminal, if possible, that is, to chasten him and then treat him in such a way as to bring him back into the law-abiding classes of the community. If one takes up an individual case there are always circumstances that suggest, and appeal for, mercy because it happens so frequently that the imprisonment of the criminal inflicts a heavier punishment on those who are related to him by blood or kinship, than upon himself, and the pardoning power is deeply moved to save them from undeserved suffering. But the interests of society require that such a consideration should be rejected in order that the example of punishment may be effective and persuasive. It is a most dangerous power to entrust to the executive with a big heart and a little head, or a man with a big heart and very little power over his feelings. By such governors, criminals will be let loose on society and the whole effort of those who are conducting the machinery of assistance will be paralyzed. One never knows until he has been in the Presidency the amount of pressure that is brought in one way and another to stay the prosecutions and to pardon criminals. I had two cases once before me, in which it was represented to me that both the convicts were near death, and I instituted an investigation to find out the truth through the Army Medical Corps. Examinations were made, watches were established over the sick men, and it was reported to me that they were both in the last stages of a fatal disease. One of them died soon after he was released from the penitentiary. The other is apparently in excellent health and seeking to reëstablish himself in the field in which he committed a penitentiary offense. This shakes one's faith in expert examinations. Then there are many applications in advance of prosecutions to prevent indictments and prevent trials. The influences brought are insidious, and usually the very fact of seeking such influences is an indication that the person charged is guilty.

I have referred to the duty and the power of the President to see that the laws are executed. This is stated in the Constitution, but it involves considerably more than seeing that the letter of the law is carried out. It involves the construction of the law by the President and his subordinates, because he cannot execute it until he finds out what it means, and frequently laws are very blind and the interpretation of the law covers so much that it involves the exercise of an important function. Of course, courts in litigated cases are called upon to consider laws, but there are many laws of the national government that can never be brought before courts of law — acts of appropriation, for instance, as to what the appropriation includes and how to be expended. These questions are settled by the Attorney-General, by the Comptroller of the Currency, appointees of the President, and sometimes by the President himself. Then there are a great many projects to be carried out by the government, and Congress naturally vests the control of them in the President. That is what it did in the case of the Panama Canal. The Spooner Act in 1902 directed the President to construct the canal. It required him to do it through a commission, but the commission was subject to his appointment and removal.

However, "money makes the mare go." You cannot have a government unless you have a treasury full of funds with which to run it, and all these executive functions of the President are to be performed by agents who must be paid in order that they shall serve. In other words, while these powers that I have pointed out are very broad, Congress retains very great restraining power in that clause of the Constitution which provides that no money shall be paid out of the Treasury except upon appropriation of Congress; and if the President is left without money, he is well-nigh helpless. By refusal to vote supply bills, the Commons of England brought the Stuarts and kings before them to a realization of the power of the people, and this same power still exists in our Congress to restrain any executive who may seek to exceed his constitutional limitations.

Of course, I am speaking now of the legal powers of the President. I am not speaking of those powers that naturally come to him through our political system, and because he is the head of the party. He can thus actually exercise very considerable influence, sometimes a controlling influence, in the securing of legislation by his personal intervention with the members of his party who are in control in each House. I think he ought to have very great influence, because he is made responsible to the people for what the party does; and if the party is wise, it will bend to his leadership as long as it is tolerable, and especially where it is in performance of promises that the party has made in its platform and on the faith of which it must be assumed to have obtained its power. But such power as he exercises in this way is not within the letter of the law and probably does not come within the legitimate bounds of such an article as this.

The functions of the President which I have enumerated seem very broad; but when many speak of the enormous power of a President, they have in mind that what the President does goes like kissing, by favor. Now the Presidency offers but few opportunities for discretion of that sort. The responsibility of the office is so heavy, the earnest desire of every man who fills the place to deserve the approval of his countrymen by doing the thing that is best for the country so strong, and the fear of just popular criticism so controlling, that it is difficult for one who has been brought through four years of it to remember any personal favor that he was able to confer. There are certain political obligations that the custom of a party requires the President to discharge on the recommendation of Senators and Congressmen, and of the men who have had the conduct of the political campaign in which he was successful. I think, as I have already said, that this kind of obligation should be reduced to its lowest terms by a change of the law, and that the custom which has been maintained since the beginning of government, and which has not been in the interest of good government, ought to be minimized to a point where it will cease to be harmful. But I refer now to that kind of power that imagination clothes the President and all rulers with, to gratify one man and humiliate another and punish a third, in order to satisfy the whim or the vengeance of the man in power. That does not exist, and the truth is that great as these powers are, when a President comes to exercise them, he is much more concerned with the limitations upon them to see that he does not exceed them, than he is affected by personal gratification over the big things he can do.

The President is given $25,000 a year for travelling
expenses; and this enables him to travel in a private car,
and it is wise that it should be so. Were he to travel in a
Pullman car, where the public could approach him, the
ordinarily commendable curiosity of the American people
to see their President close at hand would subject to such
annoyances both him and the travelling public with whom
he might happen to be that both he and they would be
made most uncomfortable. There is an impression that
the President cannot leave the country and that the law
forbids. This is not true. The only provision of law
which bears on the subject at all is that which provides
that the Vice-President shall take his place when the
President is disabled from performing his duties. Now if
he is out of the country at a point where he cannot discharge the necessary functions that are imposed on him,
such disability might arise; but the communication by
telegraph, wireless, and telephone are now so good that
it would be difficult for a President to go anywhere and
not be able to keep his subordinates in constant information as to his whereabouts and his wishes. As a matter
of fact, Presidents do not leave the country very often.
Occasionally it seems in the public interest that they
should. President Roosevelt visited the Canal Zone for
the purpose of seeing what work was being done on the
canal and giving zest to that work by personal contact
with those who were engaged in it. I did the same thing
later on, travelling, as he did, on the deck of a government
vessel which is technically the soil of the United States.
The Zone is the soil of the United States. He was not
out of the jurisdiction of the United States except for a
few hours. He went into the city of Panama, as I did,
and dined with the President of the Panamanian Republic.

So, too, I dined with President Diaz at Juarez, in Mexico, just across the border from El Paso, but nobody was heard to say that in any of these visits we had disabled ourselves from performing our constitutional and statutory functions.

The assassination of three Presidents has led Congress to provide that the chief of the Secret Service shall furnish protection to the President as he moves about, either in Washington or in the country at large. I presume that experience shows this to be necessary. While President, I never was conscious of any personal anxiety while in large crowds, and I have been in many of them. Yet the record of assaults upon Presidents is such that Congress would be quite derelict if it disregarded it. The necessary precautions are a great burden on the President. He never can go anywhere that he does not have to inflict upon those whom he wishes to see the burden of the presence of a body guard, and it is a little difficult to get away from the feeling that one is under surveillance himself rather than being protected from somebody else. The Civil Service men are level-headed, experienced, and of good manners, and they are wise in their methods and most expert in detecting those from whom danger is most to be expected. I mean the partially demented and "cranks." If a person is determined to kill a President and is willing to give up his life for it, no such protection will save his victim. But such persons are very rare. The worst danger is from those who have lost part or all of their reason, and whom the presence of a President in the community excites. I may be mistaken, but it seems to me that with the experts that we now have and the system that is now pursued, the assassination of President McKinley at Buffalo might possibly have been avoided. The presence of the assassin with a revolver under his handkerchief would now be detected long before he could get within range of the object of his perverted purpose.

The President is in office for only four years or at most eight, and the social influence that he and his family can exercise is quite limited. It is sufficient for our democratic purposes; but it does not compare with the social influence that is exercised by the head of the state in a country like Great Britain. The truth is that the chief and almost the only power that the King of Britain has, except in an advisory way, is as the social head of the kingdom. The moral influence that he exercises over his court may thus be made strong. It always permeates to those who do not come directly within the court circles. There is, too, a political influence that the King and the royal family can exert in this way, not affirmative and direct, but conserving, softening, and conciliatory, alleviating party bitterness and moderating extreme views. The ancient and still living respect for royalty is strong in itself to discourage violent methods, to compel good manners. In this respect, of course, because the King is permanent during his life and the members of the royal family likewise, this social rule is vastly stronger than that of the President. But in every other respect as between the King of England and the President of the United States, the President really rules within the limit of the functions entrusted to him by the Constitution, while the King has lost much of his former power in the progress of democracy to complete control in Great Britain, and merely reigns as the titular and social head of the state.

JOHN GREENLEAF WHITTIER [1]

BY

GEORGE EDWARD WOODBERRY

The death of Whittier in 1889 furnished the occasion for Professor
Woodberry's essay. It opens logically with two paragraphs giving the
immediate reason for writing; although Whittier was local to New England, he is really national so far as the spirit of New England has passed
into the nation at large; and, the New England of Whittier has become
historical. The next paragraph defines the subject, that Whittier will
be treated as a poet. The following paragraphs, therefore, take up in
succession various phases and characteristics of his poetic activity.
The whole is bound together by the concluding thought, that among the
honored names of the New England past his place is secure. There is
no biographical introduction, and there is little more than an occasional
trenchant sentence of biographical detail. The assumption is made that
the reader is both familiar with the subject and already sufficiently interested in it to desire a succinct presentation of literary judgment
free from the introduction of irrelevant detail. Thus this is a good
example of a clean-cut critical essay. On the other hand, there is no
appeal to the casual reader.

THE time has come to pay tribute of farewell upon the
occasion of the death of Whittier. The popular instinct
which long ago adopted him as the poet of New England
is one of those sure arbiters, superior to all academic
judgments upon the literary works of a man, which confer a rightful fame in life, and justify the expectation
of a long remembrance. Whittier was distinctly a local

[1] From "Makers of Literature," by permission of The Macmillan
Co.

poet, a New Englander; but to acknowledge this does not diminish his honor, nor is he thereby set in a secondary place. His locality, if one may use the expression, was a country by itself; its inhabitants were a peculiar people, with a strongly marked social and moral character, with a landscape and an atmosphere, with historical traditions, legends often romantic, and with strong vitalizing ideas. There was something more than a literary fancy in the naturalness with which Whittier sought a kind of fellowship with Burns; there was a true resemblance in their situation as the poets of their own kin and soil, in their reliance upon the strength of the people of whom they were born, and in their cherished attachment to the places and scenes where they grew. New England, moreover, had this advantage, that it was destined to set the stamp of its character upon the larger nation in which it was an element; so that if Whittier be regarded, as he sometimes is, as a representative American poet, it is not without justice. He is really national so far as the spirit of New England has passed into the nation at large; and that vast body of Western settlers who bore New England to the frontier, and yet look back to the old homestead, find in him the sentiment of their past. There can be little question, too, that he is representative of a far larger portion of the American people than any other of the elder poets. His lack of the culture of the schools has here been in his favor, and has brought him closer to the common life; he is more democratic than he otherwise might have been; and the people, recognizing in him their own strain, have accepted him with a judgment as valid as that with which cultivated critics accept the work of the man of genius who is also an artist. One calls him a local poet rather to define his qualities than to characterize his range.

The New England which Whittier represents has now become historical. The length of his life carried him beyond his times. It is plainer now than it was at an earlier day that his poems are one of the living records of a past which will be of perennial interest and ever held in honor. That his early poetic career fell in with the anti-slavery movement was not a misfortune for his Muse; the man fed upon it, and drew therefrom an iron strength for the moral nature which was the better half of his endowment. He was, too, one who was destined to develop, to reach his powers, more by exercising than by cultivating his poetic gift; and in the events of the agitation for the abolition of slavery he had subjects that drew out his moral emotions with most eloquent heat, and exalted his spirit to its utmost of sympathy, indignation, and heroic trust. The anti-slavery movement was his education, — in a true sense, the gymnastic of his genius; but in the whole body of his work it was no more than an incident, although the most stirring and most noble, in his literary career, just as it was no more in the career of New England.

The great events with which a man deals, and part of which he is, obscure the other portions of his life; but it should not be forgotten that Whittier began as a poet, and not as a reformer, and it may be added that the poet in him was, in the long run, more than the reformer. He did not resort to verse as an expedient in propagandism; rather, wearing the laurel, — to use the good old phrase, — he descended into the field just as he was. He had begun with those old Indian legends in lines which still echoed with Byron's tales, and he had with them much the same success that attended other aboriginal poetry. It seems, as one reads the hundred weary epics, from which Whittier's are hardly to be distinguished, that the curse of extinction resting on the doomed race clung also to the Muse that so vainly attempted to recompense it with immortality in the white man's verse. These were Whittier's juvenile trials. He came early, nevertheless, to his mature form in the ballad and the occasional piece; his versification was fixed, his manner determined, and thenceforth there was no radical change.

This is less remarkable inasmuch as it is a commonplace to say that he owed nothing to art; the strength of his native genius was all his secret, and when he had freed a way for its expression the task of his novitiate was done. He had now a mould in which to run his metal, and it satisfied him because he was not exacting of perfect form or high finish; probably he had no sense for them. This indifference to the artistic workmanship, which a later day prizes so much as to require it, allowed him to indulge his natural facility, and the very simplicity of his metres was in itself a temptation to diffuseness. The consequence was that he wrote much, and not always well, unevenness being usually characteristic of poets who rely on the energy of their genius for the excellence of their work. To the artist his art serves often as a conscience, and forces him to a standard below which he is not content to fall. Whittier, however, experienced the compensations which are everywhere to be found in life, and gained in fullness, perhaps, more than he lost in other ways. The free flow of his thought, the simplicity of his structure, the willingness not to select with too nice a sense, but to tell the whole, all helped to that frankness of the man which is the great charm of his works, taken together, and assisted him in making his expression of old New England life complete. No man could have written

Snow-Bound who remembered Theocritus. In Whittier, Nature reminds us, as she is wont to do from time to time, that the die which she casts exceeds the diploma of the school. Art may lift an inferior talent to higher estimation, but genius makes a very little art go a long way. This was Whittier's case. The poetic spark was inborn in him, living in his life; and when academic criticism has said its last word, he remains a poet, removed by a broad and not doubtful line from all stringers of couplets and filers of verses.

Whittier had, in addition to this clear native genius, character; his subject, too, New England, had character; and the worth of the man blending with the worth of the life he portrayed, independent of all considerations of art, has won for him the admiration and affection of the common people, who know the substance of virtue, and always see it shining with its own light. They felt that Whittier wrote as they would have written, had they been gifted with the miraculous tongues; and this feeling is a true criterion to discover whether a poet has expressed the people rather than himself. They might choose to write like the great artists of letters; they know they never could do so; but Whittier is one of themselves.

The secret of his vogue with the plain people is his own plainness. He appeals directly to the heart, as much in his lesser poems as in those which touch the sense of right and wrong in men with stinging keenness, or in those which warm faith to its ardor. He has the popular love of a story, and tells it more nearly in the way of the old ballad-makers. He does not require a tragedy, or a plot, or any unusual action. An incident, if it only have some glamour of fancy, or a touch of pathos, or the likeness of old romance, is enough for him; he will take it and sing it merely as

N

something that happened. He was familiar with the legendary lore and historical anecdote of his own county of Essex, and he enjoyed these traditions less as history than as poetry; he came to them on their picturesque and human side, and cared for them because of the emotions they could still awake. It is to be acknowledged, too, that the material for these romances was just such as delights the popular imagination. The tales of the witches, notwithstanding the melancholy of the delusion, have something of the eeriness that is inseparable from the thought of the supernatural, and stir the dormant sense of some evil fascination; and the legends of spectral shapes that haunted every seacoast in old times, and of which New England had its share, have a similar quality. Whether they are told by credulous Mather or the make-believing poet, they have the same power to cast a spell. When to this sort of interest Whittier adds, as he often does, the sights of religious persecution, or some Lochinvar love-making, or the expression of his faith in heaven, his success as a story-teller is assured. In reality, he has managed the ballad form with more skill than other measures; but it is because he loves a story and tells it for its own sake, with the ease of one who sits by the fireside, and with a childish confidence that it will interest, that he succeeds so well in pleasing. In his sea-stories, and generally in what he writes about the ocean, it is observable that he shows himself to be an inland-dweller, whose acquaintance with the waves is by distant glimpses and vacation days. He is not a poet of the sea, but this does not invalidate the human truth of his tales of voyaging, which is the element he cared for. Perhaps the poetic quality of his genius is most clear in these ballads; there is a freer fancy; there are often verses about woman's eyes and hair and cheeks, all with similes from sky and gold and roses, in the old fashion, but not with less naturalness on that account; there is a more absorbing appeal to the imagination both in the characters and the incidents. If these cannot be called his most vigorous work, they are at least most attractive to the purely poetic taste.

In the ballads, nevertheless, one feels the strong undertow of the moral sense dragging the mind back to serious realities. It is probably true of all the English stock, as it certainly is of New England people, that they do not object to a moral, in a poem or anywhere else. Whittier's moral hold upon his readers is doubtless greater than his poetic hold. He appeals habitually to that capacity for moral feeling which is the genius of New England in its public life, and the explanation of its extraordinary influence. No one ever appeals to it in vain; and with such a cause as Whittier took up to champion, he could ring out a challenge that was sure to rank the conscience of his people upon his side. His Quaker blood, of which he was proud, pleaded strongly in his own veins. He was the inheritor of suffering for conscience' sake; he was bred in the faith of equality, of the right of every man to private judgment, and the duty of every man to follow it in public action; and he was well grounded in the doctrines of political liberty which are the foundation of the commonwealth. It is more likely, however, that his enthusiasm for the slave did not proceed from that love of freedom which is the breath of New England. It arose from his humanity, in the broad sense; from his belief, sincerely held and practiced, in the brotherhood of men; from the strong conviction that slavery was wrong. It was a matter of conscience more than of reason, of compassion and sympathy more than of theoretical ideas. These

were the sources of his moral feeling; his attitude was the
same whether he was dealing with Quaker outrages in
the past or with negro wrongs in the present. In expressing
himself upon the great topic of his time, he was thus able
to make the same direct appeal to the heart that was
natural to his temperament. The people either felt as
he did, or were so circumstanced that they would respond
from the same springs which had been touched in him,
if a way could be found to them. Outside of the reserves of
political expediency, the movement for abolition was
harmonious with the moral nature of New England. Yet
Whittier's occasional verses upon this theme made him
only the poet of his party. In themselves they have
great vigor of feeling, and frequently force of language;
they have necessarily the defects, judged from the artistic
standpoint, of poems upon a painful subject, in which it
was desirable not to soften, but to bring out the tragedy
most harshly. The pain, however, is entirely in the
facts presented; the poetry lies in the indignation, the
eloquence, the fine appeal. These verses, indeed, are
nearer to a prose level than the rest of his work, in the
sense of partaking of the character of eloquence rather
than of poetry. Their method is less through the imagination than by rhetoric. They are declamatory. But
rhetoric of the balanced and concise kind natural to short
metrical stanzas is especially well adapted to arrest
popular attention and to hold it. Just as he told a
story in the ballad with a true popular feeling, so he
pleaded the cause of the abolitionists in a rhetoric most
effective with the popular taste. In the war time, he rose,
under the stress of the great struggle, to finer poetic work;
the softer feelings of pity, together with a solemn religious
trust, made the verses of those battle-summers different

in quality from those of the literary conflict of the earlier years. He never surpassed, on the lower level of rhetoric, the lines which bade farewell to Webster's greatness, nor did he ever equal in intensity those rallying-cries of defiance to the South, in which the free spirit of the North seemed to speak before its time. In these he is urging on to the conflict, — a moral and peaceful one, he thought, but not less real and hard; in the war pieces, he seems rather to be waiting for the decision of Providence, while the fight has rolled on far in the van of where he stands. The power of all these poems, their reality to those times, is undeniable. Their fitness for declamation perhaps spread his reputation. Longfellow is distinctly the children's poet; but Whittier had a part of their suffrages, and it was by such stirring occasional verses that he gained them. In those years of patriotism he was to many of them, as he was to me, the first poet whom they knew. At that time his reputation in ways like these became established. If he had not then done his best work, he had at times reached the highest level he was to attain, and he had already given full expression to his nature. His place as the poet of the anti-slavery movement was fixed. It is observable that he did not champion other causes after that of abolition was won, and in this he differed from most of his companions. The only other cause that roused him to the point of poetic expression was that of the Italian patriots. Some of his most indignant and sharpest invective was directed against Pope Pius IX., who stood to Whittier as the very type of that Christian obstructiveness to the work of Christ which in a lesser degree he had seen in his own country, and had seen always only to express the heartfelt scorn which descended to him with his Quaker birthright.

It would be unfitting to leave this part of the subject without reference to the numerous personal tributes, often full of grace, of tender feeling, and of true honor paid to the humble, which he was accustomed to lay as his votive wreath on the graves of his companions. One is struck once more by the reflection how large a part those who are now forgotten had in advancing the cause, how many modest but earnest lives entered into the work, and what a feeling of comradery there was among those engaged in philanthropic service in all lands. The verses to Garrison and Sumner naturally stand first in fervor and range as well as in interest, but nearly all these mementos of the dead have some touch of nobility.

The victory of the Northern ideas left to Whittier a freer field for the later exercise of his talent. It was natural that he should have been among the first to speak words of conciliation to the defeated South, and to offer to forget. He was a man of peace, of pardons, of all kinds of catholic inclusions; and in this temperament with regard to the future of the whole country, fortunately, the people agreed with him. With the coming of the years of reconciliation his reputation steadily gained. His representative quality as a New Englander was recognized. It was seen that from the beginning the real spirit of New England had been truly with him, and, the cause being now won and the past a great one, his countrymen were proud of him for having been a part of it. At this happy moment he produced a work free from any entanglement with things disputed, remarkable for its truth to life, and exemplifying the character of New England at its fireside in the way which comes home to all men. It is not without perfect justice that Snow-Bound takes rank with The Cotter's Saturday Night and The

Deserted Village; it belongs in this group as a faithful picture of humble life. It is perfect in its conception and complete in its execution; it is the New England home, entire, with its characteristic scene, its incidents of household life, its Christian virtues. Perhaps many of us look back to it as Horace did to the Sabine farm; but there are more who can still remember it as a reality, and to them this winter idyl is the poetry of their own lives. It is, in a peculiar sense, the one poem of New England, — so completely indigenous that the soil has fairly created it, so genuine as to be better than history. It is by virtue of this poem that Whittier must be most highly rated, because he is here most impersonal, and has succeeded in expressing the common life with most directness. All his affection for the soil on which he was born went into it; and no one ever felt more deeply that attachment to the region of his birth which is the great spring of patriotism. In his other poems he had told the legends of the country, and winnowed its history for what was most heroic or romantic; he had often dwelt, with a reiteration which emphasized his fondness, upon its scenery in every season, by all its mountains and capes and lakes and rivers, as if fearful lest he should offend by omission some local divinity of the field or flood; he had shared in the great moral passion of his people in peace and war, and had become its voice and been adopted as one of its memorable leaders; but here he came to the heart of the matter, and by describing the homestead, which was the unit and centre of New England life, he set the seal upon his work, and entered into all New England homes as a perpetual guest.

There remains one part of his work, and that, in some respects, the loftiest, which is in no sense local. The

Christian faith which he expressed is not to be limited as
distinctly characteristic of New England. No one would
make the claim. It was descended from the Quaker faith
only as Emerson's was derived from that of the Puritan.
Whittier belongs with those few who arise in all parts of
the Christian world and out of the bosom of all sects,
who are lovers of the spirit. They illustrate the purest
teachings of Christ, they express the simplest aspirations
of man; and this is their religious life. They do not
trouble themselves except to do good, to be sincere, to
walk in the sight of the higher powers with humbleness,
and if not without doubt, yet with undiminished trust.
The optimism of Whittier is one with theirs. It is in-
dissolubly connected with his humanity to men. In his
religious as in his moral nature there was the same simplicity, the same entire coherency. His expression of the
religious feeling is always noble and impressive. He is
one of the very few whose poems, under the fervor of
religious emotion, have taken a higher range and become
true hymns. Several of these are already adopted into
the books of praise. But independently of these few most
complete expressions of trust and worship, wherever
Whittier touches upon the problems of the spiritual life
he evinces the qualities of a great and liberal nature;
indeed, the traits which are most deeply impressed upon
us, in his character, are those which are seen most clearly
in his religious verse. It is impossible to think of him and
forget that he is a Christian. It is not rash to say that it
is probable that his religious poems have reached many
more hearts than his anti-slavery pieces, and have had a
profounder influence to quiet, to console, and to refine.
Yet he was not distinctly a poet of religion, as Herbert
was. He was a man in whom religion was vital, just as

affection for his home and indignation at wrongdoing were
vital. He gave expression to his manhood, and consequently to the religious life he led. There are in these
revelations of his nature the same frankness and the same
reality as in his most heated polemics with the oppressors
of the weak; one cannot avoid feeling that it is less the
poet than the man who is speaking, and that in his words
he is giving himself to his fellow-men. This sense that
Whittier belongs to that class of writers in whom the man
is larger than his work is a just one. Over and above his
natural genius was his character. At every step of the
analysis, it is not with art, but with matter, not with the
literature of taste, but with that of life, not with a poet's
skill, but with a man's soul, that we find ourselves dealing;
in a word, it is with character almost solely: and it is this
which has made him the poet of his people, as the highest
art might have failed to do, because he has put his New
England birth and breeding, the common inheritance of
her freedom-loving, humane, and religious people which
he shared, into plain living, yet on such a level of distinction that his virtues have honored the land.

The simplicity and dignity of Whittier's later years,
and his fine modesty in respect to his literary work, have
fitly closed his career. He has received in the fullest
measure from the younger generation the rewards of honor
which belong to such a life. In his retirement these un-
sought tributes of an almost affectionate veneration have
followed him; and in the struggle about us for other
prizes than those he aimed at, in the crush for wealth and
notoriety, men have been pleased to remember him, the
plain citizen, uncheapened by riches and unsolicitous for
fame, ending his life with the same habits with which he
began it, in the same spirit in which he led it, without any

compromise with the world. The Quaker aloofness which has always seemed to characterize him, his difference from other men, has never been sufficient to break the bonds which unite him with the people, but it has helped to secure for him the feeling with which the poet is always regarded as a man apart; the religious element in his nature has had the same effect to win for him a peculiar regard akin to that which was felt in old times for the sacred office; to the imagination he has been, especially in the years of his age, a man of peace and of God. No one of his contemporaries has been more silently beloved and more sincerely honored. If it be true that in him the man was more than the poet, it is happily not true, as in such cases it too often is, that the life was less than it should have been. The life of Whittier affects us rather as singularly fortunate in the completeness with which he was able to do his whole duty, to possess his soul, and to keep himself unspotted from the world. He was fortunate in his humble birth and the virtues which were about his cradle; he was fortunate in the great cause for which he suffered and labored in his prime, exactly fitted as it was to develop his nature to its highest moral reach, and lift him to real greatness of soul; he was fortunate in his old age, in the mellowness of his humanity, the repose of his faith, the fame which, more truly than can usually be said, was "love disguised." Lovers of New England will cherish his memory as that of a man in whom the virtues of this soil, both for public and for private life, shine most purely. On the roll of American poets we know not how he may be ranked hereafter, but among the honored names of the New England past his place is secure.

THACKERAY'S CENTENARY [1]

BY

HENRY AUGUSTINE BEERS

In this very delightful and acutely critical essay by Professor Beers the use of the catalogue should be noted, — and equally how that use is concealed. The first paragraph frankly states the two objects of the paper : first, to enquire what changes, in our way of looking at him, have come about in the half century since Thackeray's death; secondly, to give Professor Beers' own personal experience as a reader of Thackeray. But the first question is dismissed in two short paragraphs. The rest of the essay discusses the critical aspect of Thackeray's work in the guise of personal reminiscence. Thackeray is a satirist, is imperfectly realistic, detested sham heroics, has a mixture of humor and pensiveness, etc. But, by means of the device of the personal experience, this criticism is kept from disagreeable dogmatic assertion. And the whole is unified by the charm of a single personality.

AFTER all that has been written about Thackeray, it would be flat for me to present here another estimate of his work, or try to settle the relative value of his books. In this paper I shall endeavor only two things : First to enquire what changes, in our way of looking at him, have come about in the half century since his death. Secondly to give my own personal experience as a reader of Thackeray, in the hope that it may represent, in some degree, the experience of others.

What is left of Thackeray in this hundredth year since his birth; and how much of him has been eaten away by destructive criticism; or rather by time, that far more

[1] From *The Yale Review* for October, 1911, by permission of the author and of the editor of *The Yale Review*.

corrosive acid, whose silent operation criticism does but record? As the nineteenth century recedes, four names in the English fiction of that century stand out ever more clearly, as the great names: Scott, Dickens, Thackeray, and George Eliot. I know what may be said — what has been said — for others: Jane Austen and the Brontë sisters, Charles Reade, Trollope, Meredith, Stevenson, Hardy. I believe that these will endure, but will endure as writers of a secondary importance. Others are already fading, Bulwer is all gone, and Kingsley is going fast.

The order in which I have named the four great novelists is usually, I think, the order in which the reader comes to them. It is also the order of their publication. For although Thackeray was a year older than Dickens, his first novels were later in date, and he was much later in securing his public. But the chronological reason is not the real reason why we read them in that order. It is because of their different appeal. Scott was a romancer, Dickens a humorist, Thackeray a satirist, and George Eliot a moralist. Each was much more than that; but that was what they were, reduced to the lowest term. Romance, humor, satire, and moral philosophy respectively were their starting point, their strongest impelling force, and their besetting sin. Whenever they fell below themselves, Walter Scott lapsed into sheer romantic unreality, Dickens into extravagant caricature, Thackeray into burlesque, George Eliot into psychology and ethical reflection.

I wonder whether your experience here is the same as mine. By the time that I was fourteen, as nearly as I can remember, I had read all the Waverley novels. Then I got hold of Dickens, and for two or three years I lived in Dickens's world, though perhaps he and Scott somewhat overlapped at the edge — I cannot quite remember-

I was sixteen when Thackeray died, and I heard my elders mourning over the loss. "Dear old Thackeray is gone," they told each other, and proceeded to re-read all his books, with infinite laughter. So I picked up "Vanity Fair" and tried to enjoy it. But fresh from Scott's picturesque page and Dickens's sympathetic extravagances, how dull, insipid, repellent, disgusting were George Osborne, and fat Joseph Sedley, and Amelia and Becky! What sillies they were and how trivial their doings! "It's just about a lot of old girls," I said to my uncle, who laughed in a provokingly superior manner and replied, "My boy, those old girls are life." I will confess that even to this day, something of that shock of disillusion, that first cold plunge into "Vanity Fair," hangs about the book. I understand what Mr. Howells means when he calls it "the poorest of Thackeray's novels — crude, heavy-handed, caricatured." I ought to have begun, as he did, with "Pendennis," of which he writes: "I am still not sure but it is the author's greatest book." I don't know about that, but I know that it is the novel of Thackeray's that I have read most often and like the best, better than "Henry Esmond" or "Vanity Fair"; just as I prefer "The Mill on the Floss" to "Adam Bede," and "The House of the Seven Gables" to "The Scarlet Letter" (as Hawthorne did himself, by the way); or as I agree with Dickens that "Bleak House" was his best novel, though the public never thought so. We may concede to the critics that, objectively considered, and by all the rules of judgment, this or that work is its author's masterpiece and we *ought* to like it best — only we don't. We have our private preferences which we cannot explain and do not seek to defend. As for "Esmond," my comparative indifference to it is only, I suppose, a part of my dislike of the *genre*.

I know the grounds on which the historical novel is recommended, and I know how intimately Thackeray's imagination was at home in the eighteenth century. Historically
that is what he stands for: he was a Queen Anne man —
like Austin Dobson: he passed over the great romantic
generation altogether and joined on to Fielding and Gold-
smith and their predecessors. Still no man knows the past
as he does the present. I will take Thackeray's report
of the London of his day; but I do not care very much
about his reproduction of the London of 1745. Let me
whisper to you that since early youth I have not been able
to take much pleasure in the Waverley novels, except those
parts of them in which the author presents Scotch life and
character as he knew them.

I think it was not till I was seventeen or eighteen, and a
Freshman in College, that I really got hold of Thackeray;
but when once I had done so, the result was to drive
Dickens out of my mind, as one nail drives out another. I
never could go back to him after that. His sentiment
seemed tawdry, his humor, buffoonery. Hung side by
side, the one picture killed the other. "Dickens knows,"
said Thackeray, "that my books are a protest against
him: that, if the one set are true, the other must be false."
There is a species of ingratitude, of disloyalty, in thus
turning one's back upon an old favorite who has furnished
one so intense a pleasure and has had so large a share in
one's education. But it is the cruel condition of all
growth.

> "The heavens that now draw him with sweetness untold,
> Once found, for new heavens he spurneth the old."

But when I advanced to George Eliot, as I did a year or
two later, I did not find that her fiction and Thackeray's
destroyed each other. I have continued to re-read them

both ever since and with undiminished satisfaction. And yet it was, in some sense, an advance. I would not say that George Eliot was a greater novelist than Thackeray, nor even so great. But her message is more gravely intellectual: the psychology of her characters more deeply studied: the problems of life and mind more thoughtfully confronted. Thought, indeed, thought in itself and apart from the story, which is only a chosen illustration of a thesis, seems her principal concern. Thackeray is always concrete, never speculative or abstract. The mimetic instinct was strong in him, but weak in his great contemporary, to the damage and the final ruin of her art. His method was observation, hers analysis. Mr. Brownell says that Thackeray's characters are "delineated rather than dissected." There is little analysis, indeed hardly any literary criticism in his "English Humorists": only personal impressions. He deals with the men, not with the books. The same is true of his art criticisms. He is concerned with the sentiment of the picture, seldom with its technique, or even with its imaginative or expressional power.

In saying that Dickens was essentially a humorist and Thackeray a satirist, I do not mean, of course, that the terms are mutually exclusive. Thackeray was a great humorist as well as a satirist, but Dickens was hardly a satirist at all. I know that Mr. Chesterton says he was, but I cannot believe it. He cites "Martin Chuzzlewit." Is "Martin Chuzzlewit" a satire on the Americans? It is a caricature — a very gross caricature — a piece of *bouffe*. But it lacks the true likeness which is the sting of satire. Dickens and Thackeray had, in common, a quick sense of the ridiculous, but they employed it differently. Dickens was a humorist almost in the Ben Jonsonian sense: his field was the odd, the eccentric,

the grotesque — sometimes the monstrous; his books,
and especially his later books, are full of queer people,
frequently as incredible as Jonson's *dramatis personæ*.
In other words, he was a caricaturist.   Mr. Howells says
that Thackeray was a caricaturist, but I do not think he
was so except incidentally; while Dickens was constantly
so.   When satire identifies itself with its object, it takes
the form of parody.   Thackeray was a parodist, a travesty
writer, an artist in burlesque.   What is the difference
between caricature and parody?   I take it to be this, that
caricature is the ludicrous *exaggeration* of character for
purely comic effect, while parody is its ludicrous *imitation*
for the purpose of mockery.   Now there is plenty of invention in Dickens, but little imitation.   He began with
broad *facetiæ* — "Sketches by Boz" and the "Pickwick
Papers"; while Thackeray began with travesty and kept
up the habit more or less all his life.   At the Charterhouse
he spent his time in drawing burlesque representations
of Shakespeare, and composing parodies on L. E. L. and
other lady poets.   At Cambridge he wrote a mock heroic
"Timbuctoo," the subject for the prize poem of the year —
a prize which Tennyson captured.   Later he wrote those
capital travesties, "Rebecca and Rowena" and "Novels by
Eminent Hands."   In "Fitzboodle's Confessions" he
wrote a sentimental ballad, "The Willow Tree," and
straightway a parody of the same.   You remember Lady
Jane Sheepshanks who composed those lines comparing
her youth to

> "A violet shrinking meanly
>   Where blow the March winds[1] keenly —
>   A timid fawn on wildwood lawn
>   Where oak-boughs rustle greenly."

[1] Unquestionably Lady Jane pronounced it wīnds.

I cannot describe the gleeful astonishment with which I discovered that Thackeray was even aware of our own excellent Mrs. Sigourney, whose house in Hartford I once inhabited (*et nos in Arcadia*). The passage is in "Blue-Beard's Ghost."

> "As Mrs. Sigourney sweetly sings,
> O the heart is a soft and delicate thing,
> O the heart is a lute with a thrilling string,
> A spirit that floats on a gossamer's wing,
> Such was Fatima's heart."

Do not try to find these lines in Mrs. Sigourney's complete poems: they are not there. Thackeray's humor always had this satirical edge to it. Look at any engraving of the bust by Deville (the replica of which is in the National Portrait Gallery) which was taken when its subject was fourteen years old. There is a quizzical look about the mouth, prophetic and unmistakable. That boy is a tease: I would not like to be his little sister. And this boyish sense of fun never deserted the mature Thackeray. I like to turn sometimes from his big novels, to those delightful "Roundabout Papers" and the like where he gives a free rein to his frolic: "Memorials of Gormandizing," the "Ballads of Policeman X," "Mrs. Perkins' Ball," where the Mulligan of Ballymulligan, disdaining the waltz step of the Saxon, whoops around the room with his terrified partner in one of the dances of his own green land. Or that paper which describes how the author took the children to the zoölogical gardens, and how

> "First he saw the white bear, then he saw the black,
> Then he saw the camel with a hump upon his back.
> *Chorus of Children:*
> Then he saw the camel with the HUMP upon his back."

o

Of course in all comic art there is a touch of caricature, i.e.,
of exaggeration. The Rev. Charles Honeyman in "The
Newcomes," e.g., has been denounced as a caricature.
But compare him with any of Dickens's clerical characters,
such as Stiggins or Chadband, and say which is the fine
art and which the coarse. And this brings me to the first of
those particulars in which we do not view Thackeray
quite as his contemporaries viewed him. In his own time
he was regarded as the greatest of English realists. "I
have no head above my eyes," he said. "I describe what
I see." It is thus that Anthony Trollope regarded him,
whose life of Thackeray was published in 1879. And of
his dialogue, in special, Trollope writes: "The ear is never
wounded by a tone that is false." It is not quite the same
to-day. Zola and the *roman naturaliste* of the French
and Russian novelists have accustomed us to forms of
realism so much more drastic, that Thackeray's realism
seems, by comparison, reticent and partial. Not that he
tells falsehoods, but that he does not and will not tell the
whole truth. He was quite conscious, himself, of the limits
which convention and propriety imposed upon him and
he submitted to them willingly. "Since the author of
'Tom Jones' was buried," he wrote, "no writer of fiction
has been permitted to depict, to his utmost power, a Man."
Thackeray's latest biographer, Mr. Whibley, notes in
him certain early Victorian prejudices. He wanted to
hang a curtain over Etty's nudities. Goethe's "Wahlver-
wandtschaften" scandalized him. He found the drama
of Victor Hugo and Dumas "profoundly immoral and
absurd"; and had no use for Balzac, his own closest
parallel in French fiction. Mr. G. B. Shaw, the blas-
phemer of Shakespeare, speaks of Thackeray's "enslaved
mind," yet admits that he tells the truth in spite of him-

self. "He exhausts all his feeble pathos in trying to make you sorry for the death of Col. Newcome, imploring you to regard him as a noble-hearted gentleman, instead of an insufferable old fool . . . but he gives you the facts about him faithfully." But the denial of Thackeray's realism goes farther than this and attacks in some instances the truthfulness of his character portrayal. Thus Mr. Whibley, who acknowledges, in general, that Thackeray was "a true naturalist," finds that the personages in several of his novels are "drawn in varying planes." Charles Honeyman and Fred Bayham, e.g., are frank caricatures; Helen and Laura Pendennis, and "Stunning" Warrington are somewhat unreal; Col. Newcome is overdrawn — "the travesty of a man"; and even Beatrix Esmond, whom Mr. Brownell pronounces her creator's masterpiece, is a "picturesque apparition rather than a real woman." And finally comes Mr. Howells and affirms that Thackeray is no realist but a caricaturist: Jane Austen and Trollope are the true realists.

Well, let it be granted that Thackeray is imperfectly realistic. I am not concerned to defend him. Nor shall I enter into this wearisome discussion of what realism is or is not, further than to say that I don't believe the thing exists; that is, I don't believe that photographic fiction — the "mirror up to nature" fiction — exists or can exist. A mirror reflects, a photograph reproduces its object without selection or rejection. Does any artist do this? Try to write the history of one day: everything — literally everything — that you have done, said, thought: and everything that you have seen, done, or heard said during twenty-four hours. That would be realism, but, suppose it possible, what kind of reading would it make? The artist must select, reject, combine, and he does it differently from every other artist : he mixes his personality with his art, colors his art with it. The point of view from which he works is personal to himself : satire is a point of view, humor is a point of view, so is religion, so is morality, so is optimism or pessimism, or any philosophy, temper, or mood. In speaking of the great Russians Mr. Howells praises their "transparency of style, unclouded by any mist of the personality which we mistakenly value in style, and which ought no more to be there than the artist's personality should be in a portrait." This seems to me true; though it was said long ago, the style is the man. Yet if this transparency, this impersonality is measurably attainable in the style, it is not so in the substance of the novel. If an impersonal report of life is the ideal of naturalistic or realistic fiction — and I don't say it is — then it is an impossible ideal. People are saying now that Zola is a romantic writer. Why? Because, however well documented, his facts are *selected* to make a particular impression. I suppose the reason why Thackeray's work seemed so much more realistic to his generation than it does to ours was that his particular point of view was that of the satirist, and his satire was largely directed to the exposure of cant, humbug, affectation and other forms of unreality. Disillusion was his trade. He had no heroes, and he saw all things in their unheroic and unromantic aspect. You all know his famous caricature of Ludovicus Rex inside and outside of his court clothes : a most majestic, bewigged and beruffled *grand monarque:* and then a spindle-shanked, potbellied, bald little man — a good illustration for a chapter in "Sartor Resartus." The ship in which Thackeray was sent home from India, a boy of six, touched at St. Helena and he saw Napoleon. He always remembered him as a little fat man in a suit of white duck and a palm leaf hat.

Thackeray detested pose and strut and sham heroics. He called Byron "a big sulky dandy." "Lord Byron," he said, "wrote more cant . . . than any poet I know of. Think of the 'peasant girls with dark blue eyes' of the Rhine — the brown-faced, flat-nosed, thick-lipped, dirty wenches! Think of 'filling high a cup of Samian wine': . . . Byron himself always drank gin." The captain in "The White Squall" does not pace the deck like a dark-browed Corsair, but calls "George, some brandy and water!"

And this reminds me of Thackeray's poetry. Of course one who held this attitude toward the romantic and the heroic could not be a poet in the usual sense. Poetry holds the quintessential truth, but, as Bacon says, it "subdues the shows of things to the desires of the mind"; while realism clings to the shows of things, and satire disenchants, ravels the magic web which the imagination weaves. Heine was both satirist and poet, but he was each by turns, and he had the touch of ideality which Thackeray lacked. Yet Thackeray wrote poetry and good poetry of a sort. But it has beauty purely of sentiment, never of the imagination that transcends the fact. Take the famous lines with which this same "White Squall" closes:

> "And when, its force expended,
> The harmless storm was ended,
> And as the sunrise splendid
>   Came blushing o'er the sea;
> I thought, as day was breaking,
> My little girls were waking
> And smiling and making
>   A prayer at home for me."

And such is the quality of all his best things in verse —
"The Mahogany Tree," "The Ballad of Bouillebaisse,"
"The End of the Play"; a mixture of humor and pensive-
ness, homely fact and sincere feeling.

Another modern criticism of Thackeray is that he is
always interrupting his story with reflections. This fault,
if it is a fault, is at its worst in "The Newcomes," from
which a whole volume of essays might be gathered. The
art of fiction is a progressive art and we have learned a
great deal from the objective method of masters like
Turgenev, Flaubert, and Maupassant. I am free to confess, that, while I still enjoy many of the passages in which
the novelist appears as chorus and showman, I do find
myself more impatient of them than I used to be. I find
myself skipping a good deal. I wonder if this is also your
experience. I am not sure, however, but there are signs
of a reaction against the slender, episodic, short-story
kind of fiction, and a return to the old-fashioned, biographical novel. Mr. Brownell discusses this point and
says that "when Thackeray is reproached with 'bad art'
for intruding upon his scene, the reproach is chiefly the
recommendation of a different technique. And each
man's technique is his own." The question, he acutely
observes, is whether Thackeray's subjectivity destroys
illusion or deepens it. He thinks that the latter is true.
I will not argue the point further than to say that, whether
clumsy or not, Thackeray's method is a thoroughly English
method and has its roots in the history of English fiction.
He is not alone in it. George Eliot, Hawthorne, and
Trollope and many others practice it; and he learned it
from his master, Fielding.

Fifty years ago it was quite common to describe
Thackeray as a cynic, a charge from which Shirley

Brooks defended him in the well known verses contributed to "Punch" after the great novelist's death. Strange that such a mistake should ever have been made about one whose kindness is as manifest in his books as in his life: "a big, fierce, weeping man," as Carlyle grotesquely describes him: a writer in whom we find to-day even an excess of sentiment and a persistent geniality which sometimes irritates. But the source of the misapprehension is not far to seek. His satiric and disenchanting eye saw, with merciless clairvoyance, the disfigurements of human nature, and dwelt upon them perhaps unduly. He saw

> "How very weak the very wise,
> How very small the very great are."

Moreover, as with many other humorists, with Thomas Hood and Mark Twain and Abraham Lincoln (who is one of the foremost American humorists), a deep melancholy underlay his fun. *Vanitas Vanitatum* is the last word of his philosophy. Evil seemed to him stronger than good and death better than life. But he was never bitter: his pen was driven by love, not hate. Swift was the true cynic, the true misanthrope; and Thackeray's dislike of him has led him into some injustice in his chapter on Swift in "The English Humorists." And therefore I have never been able to enjoy "The Luck of Barry Lyndon" which has the almost unanimous praises of the critics. The hard, artificial irony of the book; maintained, of course, with superb consistency; seems to me uncharacteristic of its author. It repels and wearies me, as does its model, "Jonathan Wild." Swift's irony I enjoy because it is the natural expression of his character. With Thackeray it is a mask.

Lastly I come to a point often urged against Thackeray.

The favorite target of his satire was the snob. His lash
was always being laid across flunkeyism, tuft hunting, the
"mean admiration of mean things," such as wealth, rank,
fashion, title, birth. Now, it is said, his constant ob-
session with this subject, his acute consciousness of
social distinctions, prove that he is himself one of the class
that he is ridiculing. "Letters four do form his name,"
to use a phrase of Dr. Holmes, who is accused of the same
weakness, and, I think, with more reason. Well,
Thackeray owned that he was a snob, and said that we
are all of us snobs in a greater or less degree. Snobbery
is the fat weed of a complex civilization, where grades are
unfixed, where some families are going down and others
rising in the world, with the consequent jealousies, heart
burnings, and social struggles. In India, I take it, where
a rigid caste system prevails, there are no snobs. A
Brahmin may refuse to eat with a lower caste man, whose
touch is contamination, but he does not despise him as
the gentleman despises the cad, as the man who eats with
a fork despises the man who eats with a knife, or as the
educated Englishman despises the Cockney who drops
his h's, or the Boston Brahmin the Yankee provincial
who says *häow*, the woman who *callates*, and the gent
who wears *pants*. In feudal ages the lord might treat
the serf like a beast of the field. The modern swell does
not oppress his social inferior : he only calls him a bounder.
In primitive states of society differences in riches, station,
power are accepted quite simply : they do not form ground
for envy or contempt. I used to be puzzled by the conventional epithet applied by Homer to Eumaeus — "the
godlike swineherd" — which is much as though one should
say, nowadays, the godlike garbage collector. But when
Pope writes

"Honor and fame from no condition rise"

he writes a lying platitude. In the eighteenth century, and in the twentieth, honor and fame do rise from conditions. Now in the presence of the supreme tragic emotions, of death, of suffering, all men are equal. But this social inequality is the region of the comedy of manners, and that is the region in which Thackeray's comedy moves — the *comédie mondaine*, if not the full *comédie humaine*. It is a world of convention, and he is at home in it, in the world and a citizen of the world. Of course it is not primitively human. Manners are a convention: but so are morals, laws, society, the state, the church. I suppose it is because Thackeray dwelt contentedly in these conventions and rather liked them although he laughed at them, that Shaw calls him an enslaved mind. At any rate, this is what Mr. Howells means when he writes: "When he made a mock of snobbishness, I did not know but snobbishness was something that might be reached and cured by ridicule. Now I know that so long as we have social inequality we shall have snobs: we shall have men who bully and truckle, and women who snub and crawl. I know that it is futile to spurn them, or lash them for trying to get on in the world, and that the world is what it must be from the selfish motives which underlie our economic life. . . . This is the toxic property of all Thackeray's writing. . . . He rails at the order of things, but he imagines nothing different." In other words, Thackeray was not a socialist, as Mr. Shaw is, and Mr. Howells, and as we are all coming measurably to be. Meanwhile, however, equality is a dream.

All his biographers are agreed that Thackeray was honestly fond of mundane advantages. He liked the conversation of clever, well mannered gentlemen, and the society of agreeable, handsome, well dressed women. He liked to go to fine houses: liked his club, and was gratified when asked to dine with Sir Robert Peel or the Duke of Devonshire. Speaking of the South and of slavery, he confessed that he found it impossible to think ill of people who gave you such good claret.

This explains his love of Horace. Venables reports that he would not study his Latin at school. But he certainly brought away with him from the Charterhouse, or from Trinity, a knowledge of Horace. You recall what delightful, punning use he makes of the lyric Roman at every turn. It is *solvuntur rupes* when Col. Newcome's Indian fortune melts away; and *Rosa sera moratur* when little Rose is slow to go off in the matrimonial market. Now Horace was eminently a man of the world, a man about town, a club man, a gentle satirist, with a cheerful, mundane philosophy of life, just touched with sadness and regret. He was the poet of an Augustan age, like that English Augustan age which was Thackeray's favorite; social, gregarious, urban.

I never saw Thackeray. I was a boy of eight when he made his second visit to America, in the winter of 1855–56. But Arthur Hollister, who graduated at Yale in 1858, told me that he once saw Thackeray walking up Chapel Street, a colossal figure, six feet four inches in height, peering through his big glasses with that expression which is familiar to you in his portraits and in his charming caricatures of his own face. This seemed to bring him rather near. But I think the nearest that I ever felt to his bodily presence was once when Mr. Evarts showed me a copy of Horace, with inserted engravings, which Thackeray had given to Sam Ward and Ward had given to Evarts. It was a copy which Thackeray had used and which has his autograph on the fly leaf.

And this mention of his Latin scholarship induces me to close with an anecdote that I find in Melville's "Life." He says himself that it is almost too good to be true, but it illustrates so delightfully certain academic attitudes, that I must give it, authentic or not. The novelist was to lecture at Oxford and had to obtain the license of the Vice-Chancellor. He called on him for the necessary permission and this was the dialogue that ensued:

V. C. Pray, sir, what can I do for you?

T. My name is Thackeray.

V. C. So I see by this card.

T. I seek permission to lecture within your precincts.

V. C. Ah! You are a lecturer: what subjects do you undertake, religious or political?

T. Neither. I am a literary man.

V. C. Have you written anything?

T. Yes, I am the author of "Vanity Fair."

V. C. I presume, a dissenter — has that anything to do with Jno. Bunyan's book?

T. Not exactly: I have also written "Pendennis."

V. C. Never heard of these works, but no doubt they are proper books.

T. I have also contributed to "Punch."

V. C. "Punch." I have heard of that. Is it not a ribald publication?

formal - By hard work made it easy reading

TENNYSON[1]

BY

Paul Elmer More

In the treatment of an author such as Tennyson, the first assumption is that every reader already knows and has thought about the subject. There is, then, none of the attraction of novelty. Logically, therefore, as Mr. More conceived the solution, the appeal should be made, not by a number of observations, but by a few carefully expanded. His thought divides into the main positions: (*a*) Tennyson represented his age, (*b*) he was the poet of compromise, and (*c*) he was the poet of insight. Each of these in turn is very carefully and elaborately defined and explained. For example, to bring out the first, Tennyson is shown in his relation to the men of the time. This is done by anecdote, by quotation from the poet himself, by quotation from the work of others, by citations from diaries, etc. The result is that not only is the essay delightful reading itself, but one lays it aside with a feeling of conviction. By this very elaboration, the writer shows himself impartial, sensitive both to Tennyson's faults as well as his virtues. By his abundant citations from other poets he both explains his own conceptions and gives the reader a standard of judgment. Consequently one feels implicit confidence in his final decision.

WHATEVER changes may occur in the fame of Tennyson — and undoubtedly at the present hour it is passing into a kind of obscuration — he can never be deprived of the honour of representing, more almost than any other single poet of England, unless it be Dryden, a whole period of national life. Tennyson is the Victorian age. His *Poems,*

[1] From "The Shelburne Essays" (seventh series), by permission of the author and of the publishers, G. P. Putnam's Sons.

Chiefly Lyrical had been published only seven years when the Queen came to the throne in 1837; he succeeded Wordsworth as poet-laureate in 1850; and from that time to his death in 1892 he was the official voice of the Court and the acknowledged spokesman of those who were leading the people through that long period of transition. There was something typical of the heart of England in his birth and childhood. For what better nursery can be imagined for such a poet than one of those village rectories where the ancient traditions of the land are preserved with religious reverence and the pride of station is unaccompanied by the vanity of wealth? And what scenery could be more appropriate than the country of Lincolnshire, rolling up from the salt marshes of the sea and from the low dunes, "where the long breakers fall with a heavy clap and spread in a curdling blanket of seething foam over the level sands"? Tennyson never forgot those sights and sounds of his childhood; their shadows and echoes are in all his later verse.

And the surroundings of his early manhood were equally characteristic. In 1828 he went to Cambridge and was matriculated at Trinity College, leaving in 1831 without a degree. Those were years when the spirit stirred in many lands. In France the romantic movement, with Victor Hugo as prophet and Sainte-Beuve as interpreter, was beginning its career of high-handed victory. In England it was a time of reform, felt at the two universities as powerfully as in Parliament. At Oxford, Newman and Keble and Hurrell Froude were preparing the great reintegration of religion and the imagination which runs through the century parallel and hostile to the main current of ideas. In Tennyson's university a group of young men were brooding over strange and lofty liberties, and were dreaming vaguely of a new guide born of the union of idealism and science. A few of these more ardent minds had banded together as the Apostles, a secret debating society which afterwards became famous from the achievement of its members. Among the strongest of the brotherhood was Arthur Henry Hallam, whose sudden death at Vienna caused grief to many friends, and to Tennyson the long sorrow which, with the vexatious problems of human mortality, winds in and out through the cantos of *In Memoriam*. The meaning of this loss cannot be measured by the scanty remains of Hallam's own writings. He stands with John Sterling and Hurrell Froude among the inheritors of unfulfilled renown — young men, whose confidence in life was, in those aspiring days, accounted as achievement, and whose early death, before the inevitable sordor of wordly concession touched their faces, crowned them with imperishable glory. So the memory of his friend became to Tennyson in a few years a symbol of hopes for him and for the world frustrate. He revisits college and goes to see the rooms where Hallam dwelt; but, hearing only the clapping of hands and the crashing of glass, thinks of the days when he and his circle held debate, and would listen to Hallam's master words:

> . . . Who, but hung to hear
> The rapt oration flowing free
>
> From point to point, with power and grace
>   And music in the bounds of law,
>   To those conclusions when we saw
> The God within him light his face,
>
> And seem to lift the form, and glow
>   In azure orbits heavenly wise;
>   And over those ethereal eyes
> The bar of Michael Angelo.

Those who at college have felt the power of such a guiding friendship will tell you it is the fairest and most enduring part of education. I myself know.

To Tennyson that high comradeship of youth and those generous ideals lasted as one of the forces that made him the typical poet of the age. You may read through the memoirs of the period, and almost always you will meet him somewhere moving among other men with the mark of the Muses upon him, as a bard in the old days stood amid lords and warriors with the visible insignia of his calling in his hands and on his brow — *sacra ferens*. Whether in his free-footed and wandering earlier years, or as the prosperous householder in his beautiful homes at Farringford on the Isle of Wight and at Aldworth on Blackdown, Surrey, "overlooking the vast expanses of light and shadow, golden cornfields, blue distances" — wherever you see him, he is the same bearer of conscious inspiration. Now we have a glimpse of him with Fitz-Gerald, visiting James Spedding in his home in the Lake country — Spedding who devoted a lifetime to the white-washing of Chancellor Bacon, he of the "venerable fore-head"; "No wonder," said his waggish friend, "that no hair can grow at such an altitude; no wonder his view of Bacon's virtue is so rarefied that the common consciences of men cannot endure it." The three young men, we know, discoursed endlessly and enthusiastically about the canons of poetry, while the elder Spedding, a staunch squire of the land who "had seen enough of the trade of poets not to like them" — Shelley and Coleridge and Southey and Wordsworth — listened with ill-concealed impatience. It was at this time, probably, that Tennyson and FitzGerald held a contest as to which could produce the worst Words-worthian line, with the terrible example claimed by both of them: "A Mr. Wilkinson, a clergyman." Again Tennyson is seen with the same friends in London, "very droll, and very awkward; and much sitting up of nights till two or three in the morning with pipes in our mouths: at which good hour we would get Alfred to give us some of his magic music, which he does between growling and smoking; and so to bed." Or he is at Carlyle's house at Chelsea, with "Jack and a friend named Darwin, both admirers of Alfred's," still talking and interminably smoking — "one of the powerfullest *smokers* I have ever worked along with in that department," writes the experienced host. Or in the Isle of Wight, he is wandering one stormy night with Moncure Daniel Conway, while "his deep bass voice came through the congenial darkness like mirthful thunder."

With another guest, perhaps, we go up-stairs to the poet's den on the top-story at Farringford, where in safe seclusion he can pour out his stores of deep questioning and Rabelaisian anecdote; or climb still higher, up a ladder to the leads, where he was wont to go to contemplate the heavens, and whence one night, like Plato's luckless philosopher, he fell down the hatch; whereat a brother bard quoted to him: "A certain star shot madly from his sphere." Such stories could be multiplied endlessly. The best of all pictures of him is that written down in the diary of the Rev. R. S. Hawker, the strange vicar of Morwenstow, near Tintagel, the birthplace of the legendary Arthur, whither Tennyson had come in 1848 to make himself familiar with the country of the *Idylls.*

It is observable in all these accounts that the great personality of Tennyson, with his contempt for little conventions, impressed those who lived with him as if he possessed some extraordinary dæmonic power not granted to lesser men. And his conversation was like his figure. It is agreeable, when we consider certain finical over-nice quali-ties of his verse, to know that his talk was racy with strong, downright Saxon words; that, like our Lincoln, he could give and take deep draughts of Pantagruelian mirth. I confess that it does not displease me to touch this vein of earthy coarseness in the man. But I like also to hear that his mind rose more habitually from the soil to the finer regions of poetry and religion. In a hundred recorded conversations you will find him at close grips with the great giants of doubt and materialism, which then, as in the caverns and fastnesses of old fable, were breeding in every scientific workshop and stalking thence over the land. How often you will find him, when these questions are discussed, facing them calmly, and then ending all with an expression of unalterable faith in the spirit-forces that blow like one of his mystic winds about the solid earth; speaking words which sound common-place enough in print but which, with his manner and voice, seem to have affected his hearers as if they had been surprised by a tongue of revelation.

Still oftener his talk was of the poets and their work. Sometimes it was long discourse and rich comparison. Other times it was a flashing comment on the proper emphasis or cadence of a line, as on that day when he visited Lyme Regis with William Allingham, and, sitting on the wall of the Cobb, listened to the passage out of *Persuasion* where Louisa Mulgrave hurts her ankle. And then, continues Allingham, we

. . . take a field-path that brings us to Devonshire Hedge and past that boundry into Devon. Lovely fields, an undercliff with tumbled heaps of verdure, honeysuckle, hawthorns, and higher trees. Rocks

P

peeping through the sward, in which I peculiarly delight, reminding me of the West of Ireland. I quote —

"Bowery hollows crowned with summer sea."

T. (as usual), "You don't say it properly " — and repeats it in his own sonorous manner, lingering with solemn sweetness on every vowel sound, — a peculiar *incomplete* cadence at the end.

It is but one example among a thousand of Tennyson's supreme care for the sound of a word and for the true melody of a verse. "When Tennyson finds anything in poetry that touches him," says Coventry Patmore, "not pathos, but a happy line or epithet — the tears come into his eyes."

But it was as reciter of his own poems that he maintained in our modern prosaic society the conscious office of bard. He read on all occasions and to all sorts of people, frankly and seriously, rolling out his verses with the rhythm and magnificent emphasis that poets love to bestow on their own works. Nor can I recall a single instance in which the listener was troubled by our tedious sense of humour — not even when, on the celebrated voyage to Copenhagen with Gladstone and a party of royalties, Tennyson patted time to one of his poems on the shoulder of an unknown lady, whom he afterwards discovered to be the Empress of all the Russias. Best of all these accounts is that of Mrs. J. H. Shorthouse, who, with her husband, the novelist, visited the poet at Farringford :

Then the moon rose, and through the great cedar on the lawn we saw its light approach and fill the room, and when the gentlemen came in, and Lady Tennyson returned to her sofa, we had the great pleasure of hearing Lord Tennyson read three of his favourite poems — the *Ode to the Duke of Wellington, Blow, Bugle, Blow,* and *Maud.* Only the candles by his side lit up the book of poems from which he read ; the rest of the room was flooded by moonlight. . . . Many of Lord Tennyson's visitors have described his reading of poetry, varying of course, with their own tastes and sympathies. To me, as we sat in the moonlight listening to the words we loved, I seemed to realise the scenes of very olden days when the bards improvised their own lays in great baronial halls to en-raptured listeners.

Nothing could better characterise the position of Tennyson as the official voice of the land, turning its hard affairs and shrewd debates into the glamour of music before flattered eyes and ears. He was beloved of the Queen and the Prince Consort. Men of science like Huxley were "impressed with the Doric beauty" of his dialect poems; or, like Herschel, Owen, and Tyndall, admired him "for the eagerness with which he welcomed all the latest scientific discoveries, and for his trust in truth." Serious judges cited him on the bench, as did Lord Bowen when, being compelled to preside over an admiralty case, he ended an apology to counsel for his inexperience with the punning quotation:

> And may there be no moaning at the Bar,
> When I put out to sea.

In all this chorus of acceptance there is a single strangely significant discord. Edward FitzGerald, as we have seen, was one of Tennyson's warmest friends; of all the great men of his acquaintance, and he knew the greatest, Tennyson alone overawed him. "I must, however, say further," he once writes, after visiting with Tennyson, "that I felt what Charles Lamb describes, a sense of depression at times from the overshadowing of a so much more lofty intellect than my own: this (though it may seem vain to say so) I never experienced before, though I have often been with much greater intellects: but I could not be mistaken in the universality of his mind." FitzGerald was one of those who first recognized Tennyson's poetic genius; but after a while there comes a change in the tone of his comment. *In Memoriam*, which he read in manuscript before it was published, he cannot away with; it has to him the "air of being evolved by a Poetical Machine of the highest order"; and from that time his letters contain frequent hints of dissatisfaction. It was not that Tennyson's later works were inferior to his earlier, but that somehow he seems to have felt, as we to-day are likely to feel, a disparity between the imposing genius of the man himself and these rather nerveless elegies and rather vapid tales like *The Princess*. He cries out once upon "the cursed inactivity" of the nineteenth century for spoiling his poet, coming close to, but not quite touching, the real reason of his discontent. That determined recluse of Little Grange, who, in the silent night hours, loved to walk about the flat Suffolk lanes, among the shadows of the windmills that reminded him of his beloved Don Quixote; who, as the years passed, could scarcely be got to visit his friends at all, but wrote to them letters of quaint and wistful tenderness — he alone among the busy, anxious Victorians, so far as I know them, stood entirely aloof from the currents of the hour, judging men and things from the larger circles of time; he alone was completely emancipated from the illusions of the present, and this is the secret of the grave, pathetic wisdom that so fascinates us in his correspondence. And so the very fact that Tennyson was the mouthpiece of his generation, with the limitations that such a character implies, cooled the praise of our disillusioned philosopher, just as it warmed the enthusiasm of more engaged minds.

One is impressed by this quality of Tennyson's talent as one goes through his works anew in the Eversley

edition[1] that has just been published, with notes by the
poet and by the poet's son. It is useless to deny that to a
later taste much of this writing seems an insubstantial
fabric; that it has many of the qualities that stamp the
distinctly Victorian creations as provincial and ephemeral.
There is upon it, first of all, the mark of prettiness, that
prettiness which has been, and still is, the bane of British
art. Look through collections of the work of Landseer
and Birket Foster and Sir John Everett Millais, and
others of that group, and observe its quality of "guileless
beauty," as Holman Hunt calls it, or innocuous sentimentality as it seems to us. These scenes of meek love-
making, of tender home-partings and reconciliations, of
children floating down a stream in their cradle with perhaps
a kitten peering into the water — it is not their morality
that offends us, far from that, but their deliberate blinking
of what makes life real and, in the higher sense of the word,
beautiful. You will find this same prettiness in many of
Tennyson's early productions, such as *The May Queen* and
Dora and *The Miller's Daughter*. Or take a more preten-
tious poem, such as *Enoch Arden*, and compare it with a
similar tale from Crabbe; set Tennyson's picture of the
three children, "Annie Lee, the prettiest little damsel in
the port," etc., beside one of the coast scenes of the earlier
poet's Aldworth, and you will be struck by the difference
between the beribboned daintiness of the one and the
naked strength, as of a Dutch *genre* painting, of the other.
Or go still higher, and consider some of the scenes of the
Idylls. In its own kind *Launcelot and Elaine* is certainly
a noble work, yet somehow to all its charm there still

[1] *The Works of Alfred Lord Tennyson.* In six volumes. The Eversley
Edition. Annotated by Alfred Lord Tennyson, edited by Hallam Lord
Tennyson. New York: The Macmillan Company, 1908.

clings that taint of prettiness, which is a different thing
altogether.   I read the words of Gawain to the lily maid
of Astolat :

> "Nay, by mine head," said he,
> "I lose it, as we lose the lark in heaven,
> O, damsel, in the light of your blue eyes."

'Tis a sweet compliment, but I remember the same metaphor in an old play :

> Once a young lark
> Sat on thy hand, and gazing on thine eyes
> Mounted and sung, thinking them moving skies, —

and by comparison I seem again to note in Tennyson's lines
the something false we designate as Victorian.   There is in
the same poem another scene, one of the most picturesque
in all the *Idylls*, where Launcelot and Elaine's brother
ride away from the ancient castle and the lily maid to
join the tournament :

> She stay'd a minute,
> Then made a sudden step to the gate, and there —
> Her bright hair blown about the serious face
> Yet rosy-kindled with her brother's kiss —
> Paused by the gateway, standing near the shield
> In silence, while she watch'd their arms far-off
> Sparkle, until they dipt below the downs.

One sees it all — the sentimental maiden at the arch,
gazing with shaded eyes after the two departing knights,
while some flowering vine of an English summer droops
from the stones about her slender form ; one sees it, but
again it is a painting on the walls of the Burlington House
rather than the reality of a more virile art.

There is not a little of this effeminate grace in the long

elegy *In Memoriam*, which above any other single poem, I think, seemed to the men of the Victorian age to express the melancholy and the beauty of life. I find a trace of it even in the more exquisite sections, in the nineteenth for instance:

> The Danube to the Severn gave
>   The darken'd heart that beat no more;
>   They laid him by the pleasant shore,
> And in the hearing of the wave.
>
> There twice a day the Severn fills;
>   The salt sea-water passes by,
>   And hushes half the babbling Wye,
> And makes a silence in the hills.

The imagery of grief's home could not be more melodiously uttered, and it is close to the facts. "From the Graveyard," writes the editor of the Eversley edition, "you can hear the music of the tide as it washes against the low cliffs not a hundred yards away "; and the poet himself adds in the note: "Taken from my own observation — the rapids of the Wye are stilled by the incoming sea." The application is like the image:

> The Wye is hush'd nor moved along,
>   And hush'd my deepest grief of all,
>   When fill'd with tears that cannot fall,
> I brim with sorrow drowning song.
>
> The tide flows down, the wave again
>   Is vocal in its wooded walls;
>   My deeper anguish also falls,
> And I can speak a little then.

Such was the music that Tennyson learned from the Wye at Tintern Abbey, where, as the editor tells us, the verses were actually composed. Exquisitely refined and curious, no doubt; but the editor's note sets us involuntarily to thinking of other *Lines Composed a Few Miles Above Tintern Abbey*, where Wordsworth heard "These waters, rolling from their inland springs, with a sweet inland murmur," and from that sound conjectured "the still, sad music of humanity." It is not a question here of philosophy but of art, and no one can fail to note the thinness of Tennyson's style compared with the larger harmonies of Wordsworth.

But however much the prettiness of *In Memoriam* caught the ears of the sentimental, it was another quality which won the applause of the greater Victorians. There is an interesting letter given among the editor's notes, showing how the men who were leading English thought in those days felt toward the new poem, and in particular toward one of its religious sections:

> If e'er when faith had fall'n asleep,
>   I heard a voice "believe no more"
>   And heard an ever-breaking shore
> And tumbled in the Godless deep;
>
> A warmth within the breast would melt
>   The freezing reason's colder part,
>   And like a man in wrath the heart
> Stood up and answer'd "I have felt."
>
> No, like a child in doubt and fear:
>   But that blind clamour made me wise;
>   Then was I as a child that cries,
> But, crying, knows his father near.

"These lines," writes Prof. Henry Sidgwick in the letter referred to — "these lines I can never read without tears. I feel in them the indestructible and inalienable minimum of faith which humanity cannot give up because it is necessary for life ; and which I know that I, at least so far as the man in me is deeper than the methodical thinker, cannot give up." Now Sidgwick was no ordinary man. He was in fact one of the keenest and hardest-headed thinkers of those days, one of the leaders in the philosophical and economical revolution then taking place ; and these tears of his were no cheap contribution of sentiment, but rose from the deepest wells of trouble. Many men still living can remember the dismay and the sense of homelessness that fell upon the trusting mind of England when it became aware of a growing hostility between the new school of science and the established creed. When Arthur Hallam died in 1833, Darwin was making his memorable voyage of investigation on the *Beagle*, and while Tennyson was elaborating his grief in long-linked sweetness, Darwin was writing that "first note-book of Transmutation of Species" which was developed into the *Origin of Species* of 1859. The alarm of the Church over this assimilation of man and monkey, the bitter fight between Huxley and Wilberforce and between Huxley and Gladstone — all this is well known, though the tumult of the fray begins to sound in younger ears as distant as the battles about Troy. Meanwhile within the Church itself the scientific criticism of sources was working a havoc no less dreaded than the attacks from without. This breach within the walls, though long a-making, first became generally visible by the publication of the famous *Essays and Reviews* in 1860, which, harmless as the book now seems, kept two of its principal contributors, Jowett and Mark Pattison, for years from university promotion.

To these currents of thought Tennyson was quickly responsive. Without hesitation he accepted the new point of view for his *In Memoriam*, and those who were leading the revolution felt this and welcomed enthusiastically a recruit from the writers of the imagination who were commonly against them. "Wordsworth's Attitude towards Nature," says Professor Sidgwick, in the same letter to Tennyson's son, "was one that, so to say, left Science unregarded: the Nature for which Wordsworth stirred our feelings was Nature as known by simple observation and interpreted by religious and sympathetic intuition. But for your father the physical world is always the world as known to us through physical science; the scientific view of it dominates his thoughts about it." And Professor Sidgwick is perfectly right. It is unnecessary to point out the many passages of *In Memoriam* in which the law of evolution, the survival of the fittest, and man's kinship to the ape, were clearly hinted before Darwin had definitely formulated them in his epoch-making book. What more impressed men like Sidgwick was the fact that Tennyson felt with them the terrifying doubts awakened by this conception of man as part of a vast, unfeeling, blind mechanism, but still clung to "the indestructible and inalienable minimum of faith which humanity cannot give up because it is necessary for life." And Tennyson, and this is the view to be emphasised, found this minimum of faith, not outside of the new science but at its very heart. He does, indeed, cry out at times against the harsher hypothesis, declaring that we are not "magnetic mockeries" —

> Not only cunning casts in clay:
>   Let Science prove we are, and then
>   What matters Science unto men,
> At least to me? I would not stay.

> Let him, the wiser man who springs
>   Hereafter, up from childhood shape
>   His action like the greater ape,
> But I was *born* to other things.

That note is heard in *In Memoriam*, but the gist of Tennyson's faith, and what made him the spokesman of the age, was in a bold completion of evolution by the theory of indefinite progress and by a vision of some magnificent consummation wherein the sacrifices and the waste and the pain of the present were to be compensated somehow, somewhere, somewhen — who shall say?

> Oh yet we trust that somehow good
>> Will be the final goal of ill,
>> To pangs of nature, sins of will,
> Defects of doubt, and taints of blood;

> That nothing walks with aimless feet;
>> That not one life shall be destroy'd,
>> Or cast as rubbish to the void,
> When God hath made the pile complete;

> That not a worm is cloven in vain;
>> That not a moth with vain desire
>> Is shrivell'd in a fruitless fire,
> Or but subserves another's gain.

And the end of the poem is the climax of this comfortable belief:

> That God, which ever lives and loves,
>> One God, one law, one element,
>> And one far-off divine event,
> To which the whole creation moves.

That reconcilation of faith and science, this discovery of a father near at hand within the inexorable law of evolution, this vision of an eternal state to be reached in the progress of time — all this is what we call the Victorian compromise. The prettiness which we found so characteristic of Victorian painting and of Tennyson's non-religious verse was indeed only another phase of the same compromise. The imperious sense of beauty, which has led the great visionaries out of the world and which Tennyson portrayed tremblingly in his *Palace of Art*, was felt by the Victorians to be dangerous to the British sentiment of the home, and motherhood, and girlish innocence, and so they rested in the middle ground of prettiness where beauty and innocent sentiment might meet. Here also they held to that "indestructible and inalienable minimum of faith which humanity" — British humanity at least in those years — could not give up. And men like Professor Sidgwick were stirred to the heart by this compromise, and wept.

Undoubtedly the fame of Tennyson in his own day was due largely to his expression of what may be called the official philosophy, but it is a question whether this very trait has not weakened his hold upon a later generation; whether, for instance, the stoic resolve and self-determination of Matthew Arnold, whom Professor Sidgwick in one of the most scathing essays of the century denounced as a trifling "prophet of culture," have not really expressed the higher meaning of that age — though not the highest meaning of all — better than any official and comfortable compromise; whether the profounder significance of that time of doubt was not rather in Matthew Arnold's brave disease :

> And we are here as on a darkling plain
> Swept with confused alarms of struggle and flight,
> Where ignorant armies clash by night.

I am confirmed in this view by one of the present editor's observations. I read the stanza of *In Memoriam* which describes the reception of the poet's dead friend into the heavenly host :

> The great Intelligences fair
>   That range above our mortal state,
>   In circle round the blessed gate,
> Received and gave him welcome there; —

and then in the editor's note I read the lines of Milton's
Lycidas which Tennyson imitated :

> There entertain him all the Saints above
> In solemn troops, and sweet societies,
> That sing, and singing, in their glory move,
> And wipe the tears for ever from his eyes.

Why is it that Tennyson here leaves us so cold, whereas
at the sound of Milton's words the heart still leaps as at
a bugle call ? Why are these fair Intelligences so meaningless and so frigid? Is not the cause just the spirit of
compromise between religion and science that has entered
into Tennyson's image, leaving it neither the simple objective faith of Milton nor the honest questioning of Matthew
Arnold ?

It may seem that I have dwelt over-much on this weaker
side of an admired writer who has so much noble work to
his credit, but it was these compromises that gave him his
historic position, and, also, it is only by bringing out
clearly this aspect of his work that we are enabled to discern the full force of another and contrasted phase, which
was not of the age but was the unfettered voice of the poet
himself. As we hear of the impression made by the man
Tennyson upon his contemporaries, and then consider the
sleeker qualities of his verse, we find it difficult to associate
the two together ; there was no prettiness or convention in
his character, but a certain elusive wildness of beauty and
a noble, almost defiant, independence. To distinguish between the two poets in the one writer is the only way
rightly to understand and wisely to enjoy him. Now if
we examine the spirit of compromise, which made the
official poet in Tennyson, we shall see that it rests finally
on a denial of religious dualism, on a denial, that is, of the

Poet of Compromise

consciousness, which no reasoning of philosophy and no noise of the world can ever quite obliterate, of two opposite principles within us, one bespeaking unity and peace and infinite life, the other calling us to endless change and division and discord. Just this cleft within our nature the Victorians attempted to gloss over. Because they could not discover the rational bond between the world of time and evolution and the idea of eternity and change-lessness, they would deny that these two can exist side by side as totally distinct spheres, and by raising the former and lowering the latter would seek the truth in some middle ground of compromise. Thus instead of saying, as Michael Angelo said, "Happy the soul where time no longer courses," they placed the faith of religion in some far-off event of time, as if eternity were a kind of enchant-ment lent by distance.

Such was the official message of Tennyson. But by the side of this there comes up here and there through his works an utterly different vein of mysticism, which is scarcely English and certainly not Victorian. It was a sense of estrangement from time and personality which took possession of him at intervals from youth to age. In a well-known passage he tries to analyse this state :

A kind of waking trance I have frequently had, quite up from boyhood, when I have been all alone. This has generally come upon me thro' re-peating my own name two or three times to myself silently, till all at once, as it were out of the intensity of the consciousness of individuality, the individuality itself seemed to dissolve away into boundless being, and this not a confused state, but the clearest of the clearest, the surest of the surest, the weirdest of the weirdest, utterly beyond words, where death was almost a laughable impossibility, the loss of personality (if so it were) seeming no extinction but the only true life.

This was not a reading into youth of a later knowledge gained from Oriental sources. In the notes to the Eversley volumes, the editor gives an unpublished juvenile poem, *The Mystic*, in which the same feeling is expressed, if not so clearly, at least with a self-knowledge every way remarkable for a boy:

> Ye could not read the marvel in his eye,
> The still serene abstraction; he hath felt
> The vanities of after and before.
>
> *　　*　　*　　*　　*　　*
>
> He often lying broad awake, and yet
> Remaining from the body, and apart
> In intellect and power and will, hath heard
> Time flowing in the middle of the night,
> And all things creeping to a day of doom.

The point to note is how Tennyson in such passages feels himself an entity set apart from the flowing of time, whereas in the official compromise of *In Memoriam* he — not only he, but God Himself — is one with the sum of things in their vague temporal progress. In that difference, if rightly understood, lies, I think, the distinction between faith and naturalism.

This sense of himself as a being set apart from change strengthened, if anything, as he grew old. Its most philosophic expression is in *The Ancient Sage*, which was first published in 1885 and was regarded by him as one of his best later poems; it is rebellious in *Vastness*, lyrical in *Break, Break, Break*, purely melodic in *Far — Far — Away*, dramatic in *Ulysses*, autobiographical in *The Gleam*. Always it is the man himself speaking his own innermost religious experience, and no mere "minimum of faith" needed for the preservation of society.

For the fullest and most artistic utterance of this faith we must go to the *Idylls of the King*. I will confess to being no unreserved lover of that mangled epic as a whole; it seems to me that in most of its parts the Victorian prettiness is made doubly, and at times offensively, conspicuous by the contrast between Tennyson's limpid sentimentality and the sturdier fibre of Malory's *Morte Darthur* from which he drew his themes. But it is true that here and there, in a line or a musically haunting passage, he has in the *Idylls* spoken from the depth of his heart, as he has spoken nowhere else, and that one of them, *The Holy Grail*, has an insight into things spiritual and a precision it would be hard to match in any other English poem. The mystic cup, which had been brought to England by Joseph of Arimathea and had vanished away for the sinfulness of the people, was first seen in vision by a holy sister of Sir Percivale, and by her Galahad was incited to go on the sacred quest. Meanwhile, one day, when the knights were gathered at the Round Table in the absence of the King, Galahad sits in Merlin's magic seat, which, as Tennyson explains, is a symbol of the spiritual imagination, the siege perilous, wherein "no man could sit but he should lose himself":

> And all at once, as there we sat, we heard
> A crackling and a riving of the roofs,
> And rending, and a blast, and overhead
> Thunder, and in the thunder was a cry.
> And in the blast there smote along the hall
> A beam of light seven times more clear than day:
> And down the long beam stole the Holy Grail
> All over cover'd with a luminous cloud,
> And none might see who bare it, and it past.
> But every knight beheld his fellow's face
> As in a glory, and all the knights arose,
> And staring each at other like dumb men
> Stood, till I found a voice and sware a vow.

The vision, in other words, is nothing else but a sudden
and blinding sense of that dualism of the world and of
the human soul beneath which the solid-seeming earth
reels and dissolves away, overwhelming with terror and
uncomprehended impulses all but those purely spiritual
to whom the earth is already an unreal thing. Then
enters the King and perceives the perturbation among
his knights. It is characteristic of England and of the
age, although it has, too, its universal significance, that
Tennyson's Arthur should deplore the search for the Grail
as a wild aberration, which is to bring impossible hopes
and desolate disappointments to those whose business was
to do battle among very material forces. "Go," he
says —

> Go, since your vows are sacred, being made :
> Yet — for ye know the cries of all my realm
> Pass thro' this hall — how often, O my knights,
> Your places being vacant at my side,
> This chance of noble deeds will come and go
> Unchallenged, while ye follow wandering fires
> Lost in the quagmire !

Only Sir Galahad, in whom is no taint of sin or selfishness,
and who was bold to find himself by losing himself, had
beheld clearly the vision of the cup as it smote across the
hall. I do not know how it may be with others, but to
me the answer of Galahad to the King has a mystical
throb and exultation almost beyond any other words of
English :

> But I, Sir Arthur, saw the Holy Grail,
> I saw the Holy Grail and heard a cry —
> "O Galahad," and "O Galahad, follow me."

That is the cry and the voice, now poetry and philosophy,
which Tennyson had in mind when he wrote of hearing

Q

"the word that is the symbol of myself." He who has once heard it and heard the responding echo within his own breast, can never again close his ears to its sound. To Galahad it meant the vanishing of the world altogether, and there is nothing more magnificent in Tennyson, scarcely in English verse, I think, than Sir Percivale's sight of Galahad fleeing over the bridges out into the far horizon, and disappearing into the splendours of the sky, while —

> . . . thrice above him all the heavens
> Open'd and blazed with thunder such as seem'd
> Shoutings of all the sons of God : and first
> At once I saw him far on the great Sea,
> In silver-shining armour starry-clear;
> And o'er his head the Holy Vessel hung
> Clothed in white samite or a luminous cloud.

There, in the inspiration from Tennyson's own visionary faith and from no secular compromise, we find the lift and the joy and the assurance that Milton knew and sang in *Lycidas* and that was so sadly missed in the "great Intelligences fair" of *In Memoriam*.

But to Sir Percivale himself the vision brought no such divine transfiguration. He is the one who sees, indeed, and understands, yet cannot lose himself. Because the Holy Grail signifies a dualism which sets the eternal world not at the end of the temporal, but utterly apart from it, he who knows the higher while lacking the courage to renounce the lower, wanders comfortless with neither the ecstatic joy of the one nor the homely satisfactions of the other. So the world and all that it contains turn into dust at his touch, leaving him alone and wearying, in a land of sand and thorns. Another, Sir Bors, the simple, trustful gentleman, who goes out on the word of others,

following duty only and trusting in the honour or the act
as it comes to him, sees in adversity the Holy Cup shining
through a rift in his prison, and abides content that the
will of God should reserve these high things as a reward
for whomsoever it chooses. Still another, Sir Gawain,
finding the vision is not for him, and having turned his
eyes from the simple rule of duty, sinks into sensual
pleasures, and declares his twelvemonth and a day a
merry jaunt. Most fatal of all is the experience of Launcelot, he, the greatest of all, who brought the sin into the
court, who cannot disentangle the warring impulses of
good and evil within himself. He, too, rides out of Came-
lot on the Quest, and then:

> My madness came upon me as of old
> And whipt me into waste fields far away.

>   *   *   *   *   *   *

> But such a blast, my King, began to blow,
> So loud a blast along the shore and sea,
> Ye could not hear the waters for the blast,
> Tho' heapt in mounds and ridges all the sea
> Drove like a cataract, and all the sand
> Swept like a river, and the clouded heavens
> Were shaken with the motion and the sound.

This is an application to the smaller field of wind and
earth and water of that dizzy tempestuous motion which
in Tennyson's earlier poem of *Lucretius* surged through
the Epicurean's atomic universe. To the eye of the
spirit, Tennyson would seem to say, the material world is
a flux and endless, purposeless mutation — leaving the
self-possessed soul to its own inviolable peace, or, upon
one that perceives yet is still enmeshed in evil desires,
thronging in visions and terrors of madness. One need
not be a confessed mystic to feel the power of these pas-

sages, any more than one need be a Puritan (standing, that is, at the opposite pole of religion from mystic) to appreciate Milton. To the genuine conviction of these poets our human nature responds as it can never respond to the insincerity of the world's "minimum of faith." With Tennyson, unfortunately, the task is always to separate the poet of insight from the poet of compromise.

REALISM AND REALITY IN FICTION [1]

BY

William Lyon Phelps

Discussion of literary theory is difficult because of lack of definition. In his paper, read before the American Academy, Professor Phelps brings out his thought by means of concrete illustration. He opens with an anecdote in which the two ideas, Realism and Reality, are brought sharply into contrast. Then follow three paragraphs of general discussion in which the difference is fully explained. Then seven paragraphs in catalogue form of the predicates of Reality. Each of these paragraphs by illustration, anecdote, dialogue, is made very clear, — so clear that the author feels no need for a summary at the end. And by this omission, the reader is scarcely conscious of the catalogue nature of the essay as a whole.

During those early years of his youth at Paris, which the melancholy but unrepentant George Moore insists he spent in riotous living, he was on one memorable occasion making a night of it at a ball in Montmartre. In the midst of the revelry a grey giant came placidly striding across the crowded room, looking, I suppose, something like Gulliver in Lilliput. It was the Russian novelist Turgenev. For a moment the young Irishman forgot the girls, and plunged into eager talk with the man from the North. Emile Zola had just astonished Paris with *L'Assommoir*. In response to a leading question, Turgenev shook his head gravely and said: "What difference

word a
word of
genius

[1] From "Essays on Books," by permission of the author and of The Macmillan Co.

does it make whether a woman sweats in the middle of her back or under her arms? I want to know how she thinks, not how she feels."

In this statement the great master of diagnosis indicated the true distinction between realism and reality. A work of art may be conscientiously realistic, — few men have had a more importunate conscience than Zola, — and yet be untrue to life, or, at all events, untrue to life as a whole. Realism may degenerate into emphasis on sensational but relatively unimportant detail: reality deals with that mystery of mysteries, the human heart. Realism may degenerate into a creed; and a formal creed in art is as unsatisfactory as a formal creed in religion, for it is an attempt to confine what by its very nature is boundless and infinite into a narrow and prescribed space. Your microscope may be accurate and powerful, but its strong regard is turned on only one thing at a time; and no matter how enormously this thing may be enlarged, it remains only one thing out of the infinite variety of God's universe. To describe one part of life by means of a perfectly accurate microscope is not to describe life any more than one can measure the Atlantic Ocean by means of a perfectly accurate yardstick. Zola was an artist of extraordinary energy, sincerity, and honesty; but, after all, when he gazed upon a dunghill, he saw and described a dunghill. Rostand looked steadfastly at the same object, and beheld the vision of *Chanticler*.

Suppose some foreign champion of realism should arrive in New York at dusk, spend the whole night visiting the various circles of our metropolitan hell, and depart for Europe in the dawn. Suppose that he should make a strictly accurate narrative of all that he had seen. Well and good; it would be realistic, it would be true. But suppose he should call his narrative *America*.   Then we should assuredly protest.

"You have not described America.   Your picture lacks the most essential features."

He would reply :

"But isn't what I have said all true?   I defy you to deny its truth.   I defy you to point out errors or exaggerations.   Everything that I described I saw with my own eyes."

All this we admit, but we refuse to accept it as a picture of America.   Here is the cardinal error of realism.   It selects one aspect of life, — usually a physical aspect, for it is easy to arouse strained attention by physical detail, — and then insists that it has made a picture of life.   The modern Parisian society drama, for example, cannot possibly be a true representation of French family and social life.   Life is not only better than that; it is surely less monotonous, more complex.   You cannot play a great symphony on one instrument, least of all on the triangle.   The plays of Bernstein, Bataille, Hervieu, Donnay, Capus, Guinon, and others, brilliant in technical execution as they often are, really follow a monotonous convention of theatrical art rather than life itself.   As an English critic has said, "The Parisian dramatists are living in an atmosphere of half-truths and shams, grubbing in the divorce courts and living upon the maintenance of social intrigue just as comfortably as any bully upon the earnings of a prostitute."   An admirable French critic, M. Henry Bordeaux, says of his contemporary playwrights, that they have ceased to represent men and women as they really are.   This is not realism, he declares; it is a new style of false romanticism, where men and women are represented as though they possessed no moral sense — a romanticism sensual, worldly, and savage. Life is pictured as though there were no such things as daily tasks and daily duties.

Shakespeare was an incorrigible romantic; yet there is more reality in his compositions than in all the realism of his great contemporary, Ben Jonson. Confidently and defiantly, Jonson set forth his play *Every Man in His Humour* as a model of what other plays should be; for, said he, it contains deeds and language such as men do use. So it does: but it falls far short of the reality reached by Shakespeare in that impossible tissue of absurd events which he carelessly called *As You Like It*. In his erudite and praiseworthy attempt to bring back the days of ancient Rome on the Elizabethan stage Jonson achieved a resurrection of the dead: Shakespeare, unembarrassed by learning and unhampered by a creed, achieved a resurrection of the living. Catiline and Sejanus talk like an old text; Brutus and Cassius talk like living men. For the letter killeth, but the spirit giveth life.

The form, the style, the setting, and the scenery of a work of art may determine whether it belongs to realism or romanticism; for realism and romanticism are affairs of time and space. Reality, however, by its very essence, is spiritual, and may be accompanied by a background that is contemporary, ancient, or purely mythical. An opera of the Italian school, where, after a tragic scene, the tenor and soprano hold hands, trip together to the footlights, and produce fluent roulades, may be set in a drawing-room, with contemporary, realistic furniture. Compare *La Traviata* with the first act of *Die Walküre*, and see the difference between realism and reality. In the wildly romantic and mythical setting, the passion of love is intensely real; and as the storm ceases, the portal swings open, and the soft air of the moonlit spring night enters the room, the eternal reality of love makes its eternal appeal in a scene of almost intolerable beauty. Even so carefully realistic an opera as *Louise* does not seem for the moment any more real than these lovers in the spring moonlight, deep in the heart of the whispering forest.

A fixed creed, whether it be a creed of optimism, pessimism, realism, or romanticism, is a positive nuisance to an artist.   Joseph Conrad, all of whose novels have the unmistakable air of reality, declares that the novelist should have no programme of any kind and no set rules. In a memorable phrase he cries, "Liberty of the imagination should be the most precious possession of a novelist." Optimism may be an insult to the sufferings of humanity, but, says Mr. Conrad, pessimism is intellectual arrogance. He will have it that while the ultimate meaning of life — if there be one — is hidden from us, at all events this is a *spectacular* universe; and a man who has doubled the Horn and sailed through a typhoon on what was unintentionally a submarine vessel may be pardoned for insisting on this point of view.   It is indeed a spectacular universe, which has resisted all the attempts of realistic novelists to make it dull.   However sad or gay life may be, it affords an interesting spectacle.   Perhaps this is one reason why all works of art that possess reality never fail to draw and hold attention.

Every critic ought to have a hospitable mind.   His attitude toward art in general should be like that of an old-fashioned host at the door of a country inn, ready to welcome all guests except criminals.   It is impossible to judge with any fairness a new poem, a new opera, a new picture, a new novel, if the critic have preconceived opinions as to what poetry, music, painting, and fiction should be.   We are all such creatures of convention that the first impression made by reality in any form of art is sometimes a distinct shock, and we close the windows of our intelligence and draw the blinds that the fresh air and the new light may not enter in. Just as no form of art is so strange as life, so it may be the strangeness of reality in books, in pictures, and in music that makes our attitude one of resistance rather than of welcome.

Shortly after the appearance of Wordsworth's *Resolution and Independence,*

> "There was a roaring in the wind all night,
> The rain came heavily and fell in floods,"

some one read aloud the poem to an intelligent woman. She burst into tears, but, recovering herself, said shamefacedly, "After all, it isn't poetry." When Pushkin, striking off the shackles of eighteenth-century conventions, published his first work, a Russian critic exclaimed, "For God's sake don't call this thing a poem!" These two poems seemed strange because they were so natural, so real, so true, just as a sincere person who speaks his mind in social intercourse is regarded as an eccentric. We follow conventions and not life. In operas the lover must be a tenor, as though the love of a man for a woman were something soft, something delicate, something emasculate, instead of being what it really is, the very essence of masculine virility. I suppose that on the operatic stage a lover with a bass voice would shock a good many people in the auditorium, but I should like to see the experiment tried. In Haydn's *Creation,* our first parents sing a bass and soprano duet very sweetly. But Verdi gave that seasoned old soldier Otello a tenor rôle, and even the fearless Wagner made his leading lovers all sing tenor except the Flying Dutchman, who can hardly be called human. In society dramas we have become so accustomed to conventional inflections, conventional gestures, conventional grimaces, that when an actor speaks and behaves exactly as he would were the situation real, instead of assumed, the effect is startling.   Virgin snow often looks blue, but it took courage to paint it blue, because people judge not by eyesight, but by convention, and snow conventionally is assuredly white.   In reading works of fiction we have become so accustomed to conventions that we hardly notice how often they contradict reality.   In many novels I have read I have been introduced to respectable women with scarlet lips, whereas in life I never saw a really good woman with such labial curiosities.   Conversations are conventionally unnatural.   A trivial illustration will suffice. Some one in a group makes an attractive proposition. "Agreed!" cried they all.   Did you ever hear any one say "Agreed"?

I suppose that all novels, no matter how ostensibly objective, must really be subjective.   Out of the abundance of the heart the mouth speaketh.   Every artist feels the imperative need of self-expression.   Milton used to sit in his arm-chair, waiting impatiently for his amanuensis, and cry, "I want to be milked."   Even so dignified, so reticent, and so sober-minded a novelist as Joseph Conrad says, "The novelist does not describe the world : he simply describes his own world."   Sidney's advice, "Look in thy heart, and write," is as applicable to the realistic novelist as it is to the lyric poet.   We know now that the greatest novelist of our time, Tolstoi, wrote his autobiography in every one of his so-called works of fiction. The astonishing air of reality that they possess is owing largely to the fact not merely that they are true to life, but that they are the living truth. When an artist succeeds in getting the secrets of his inmost heart on the printed page, the book lives. This accounts for the extraordinary power of Dostoevski, who simply turned himself inside out every time he wrote a novel.

The only reality that we can consistently demand of a novel is that its characters and scenes shall make a permanent impression on our imagination. The object of all forms of art is to produce an illusion, and the illusion cannot be successful with experienced readers unless it have the air of reality. The longer we live, the more difficult it is to deceive us: we smile at the scenes that used to draw our tears, we are left cold by the declamation that we once thought was passion, and we have supped so full with horrors that we are not easily frightened. We are simply bored as we see the novelist get out his little bag of tricks. But we never weary of the great figures in Fielding, in Jane Austen, in Dickens, in Thackeray, in Balzac, in Turgenev, for they have become an actual part of our mental life. And it is interesting to remember that while the ingenious situations and boisterous swashbucklers of most romances fade like the flowers of the field, Cooper and Dumas are read by generation after generation. Their heroes cannot die, because they have what Mrs. Browning called the "principle of life."

The truly great novelist is not only in harmony with life; his characters seem to move with the stars in their courses. "To be," said the philosopher Lotze, "is to be in relations." The moment a work of art ceases to be in relation with life, it ceases to be. All the great novelists are what I like to call *sidereal* novelists. They belong to the earth, like the procession of the seasons; they are universal, like the stars. A commonplace producer of novels for the market describes a group of people that remains nothing but a group of people; they interest us perhaps momentarily, like an item in a newspaper; but they do not interest us deeply, any more than we are really interested at this moment in what Brown and Jones are doing in Rochester or Louisville. They may be interesting to their author, for children are always interesting to their parents; but to the ordinary reader they begin and end their fictional life as an isolated group. On the contrary, when we read a story like *The Return of the Native*, the book seems as inevitable as the approach of winter, as the setting of the sun. All its characters seem to share in the diurnal revolution of the earth, to have a fixed place in the order of the universe. We are considering only the fortunes of a little group of people living in a little corner of England, but they seem to be in intimate and necessary relation with the movement of the forces of the universe.

The recent revival of the historical romance, which shot up in the nineties, flourished mightily at the end of the century, and has already faded, was a protest not against reality, but against realism. Realism in the eighties had become a doctrine, and we know how its fetters cramped Stevenson. He joyously and resolutely burst them, and gave us romance after romance, all of which except the *Black Arrow* showed a reality superior to realism. The year of his death, 1894, ushered in the romantic revival. Romanticism suddenly became a fashion that forced many new writers and some experts to mould their work in its form. A few specific illustrations must be given to prove this statement. Mr. Stanley Weyman really wanted to write a realistic novel, and actually wrote one, but the public would none of it: he therefore fed the mob with *The House of the Wolf*, with *A Gentleman from France*, with *Under the Red Robe*. Enormously successful were these stirring tales. The air became full of obsolete oaths and the clash of steel — "God's bodikins! man, I will spit you like a lark!" To use a scholar's phrase, we began to revel in the glamour of a bogus antiquity. For want of a better term, I call all these romances the "Gramercy" books. Mr. Winston Churchill, now a popular disciple of the novel of manners, gained his reputation by *Richard Carvel* with a picture of a duel facing the title-page. Perhaps the extent of the romantic craze is shown most clearly in the success attained by the thoroughly sophisticated Anthony Hope with *The Prisoner of Zenda*, by the author of *Peter Sterling* with *Janice Meredith*, and most of all by the strange *Adventures of Captain Horn*, a bloody story of buried treasure, actually written by our beloved humorist, Frank Stockton. Mr. Stockton had the temperament most fatal to romance, the bright gift of humorous burlesque; the real Frank Stockton is seen in that original and joyful work, *The Casting Away of Mrs. Lecks and Mrs. Aleshine*. Yet the fact that he felt the necessity of writing *Captain Horn*, is good evidence of the tide. This romantic wave engulfed Europe as well as America, but so far as I can discover, the only work after the death of Stevenson that seems destined to remain, appeared in the epical historical romances of the Pole Sienkiewicz. Hundreds of the romances that the world was eagerly reading in 1900 are now forgotten like last year's almanac; but they served a good purpose apart from temporary amusement to invalids, overtired business men, and the young. There was the sound of a mighty wind, and the close chambers of modern realism were cleansed by the fresh air.

A new kind of realism, more closely related to reality, has taken the place of the receding romance. We now behold the "life" novel, the success of which is a curious demonstration of the falseness of recent prophets. We were told a short time ago that the long novel was extinct. The three-volume novel seemed very dead indeed, and the fickle public would read nothing but a short novel, and would not read that unless some one was swindled, seduced, or stabbed on the first page. Then suddenly appeared *Joseph Vance*, which its author called an ill-written autobiography, and it contained 280,000 words. It was devoured by a vast army of readers, who clamoured for more. Mr. Arnold Bennett, who had made a number of short flights without attracting much attention, produced *The Old Wives' Tale*, giving the complete life-history of two sisters. Emboldened by the great and well-deserved success of this history, he launched a trilogy, of which two huge sections are already in the hands of a wide public. No details are omitted in these vast structures; even a cold in the head is elaborately described. But thousands and thousands of people seem to have the time and the patience to read these volumes. Why? Because the story is in intimate relation with life. A gifted Frenchman appears on the scene with a novel in ten volumes, *Jean Christophe*, dealing with the life of this hero from the cradle to the grave. This is being translated into all the languages of Europe, so intense is the curiosity of the world regarding a particular book of life. Some may ask, Why should the world be burdened with this enormous mass of trivial detail in rather uneventful lives? The answer may be found in Fra Lippo Lippi's spirited defence of his art, which differed from the art of Fra Angelico in sticking close to reality :

> "For, don't you mark ? we're made so that we love
> First when we see them painted, things we have passed
> Perhaps a hundred times nor cared to see."

I find in the contemporary "life" novel a sincere, dignified, and successful effort to substitute reality for the former rather narrow realism ; for it is an attempt to represent life as a whole.

TEACHING ENGLISH [1]

BY

Henry Seidel Canby

To arouse the interest of the ordinary reader in what is after all a technical problem, Professor Canby begins his essay with a careful statement of the difficulty. He then propounds his solution, that the aim of the teacher of English literature should be to teach the pupils to read literature. As this is the main position, he explains and illustrates it through the body of the essay. This is followed by a brief catalogue of the four possible types of teachers, each in its own paragraph. The essay, then, returns to emphasize the main thought in the paragraph, "I have already answered the question according to my own beliefs." Try the effect of omitting the catalogue altogether, of omitting the paragraphs beginning "Thus the effects of English teaching are sometimes hidden" to the paragraph beginning "What *is* teaching literature?" The continuity of the thought remains unbroken. Exactly what is gained by the insertion of those intervening paragraphs?

THE so-called new professions have been given abundant space of late in the Sunday newspaper; but among them I do not find numbered the teaching of English. Nevertheless, with such exceptions as advertising, social service, and efficiency-engineering, it is one of the newest as well as one of the largest. I do not mean the teaching of English writing. Directly or indirectly that has been taught since the heavenly grace instructed Cædmon in his

[1] From *The Yale Review* for October, 1914, by permission of the author and of the editor of *The Yale Review*.

stable. I mean English literature, which has been made a subject of formal instruction in our schools and colleges only since the mid-nineteenth century. Yet already the colleges complain that the popularity of this comparatively recent addition to the curriculum is so great that harder, colder, more disciplinary subjects are pushed to the wall (and this in practical America!); and in the schools only the so-called vocational courses are as much talked about and argued over by the educational powers. An army of men and women are teaching or trying to teach us English — which includes American — literature.

The results of this new profession — as even those who earn their bread thereby are willing to confess — are sometimes humorous. The comicality of scholarship — as when the sweaty hack work of some hanger-on of the great Elizabethans is subjected to elaborate study and published in two volumes — belongs rather to the satire of research than to teaching. But there are many ludicrous sequels to the compulsory study of literature. Poor Hawthorne, shyest and rarest of spirit among our men of letters, becomes a text-book for the million. Dick Steele, who dashed off his cheerful trifles between sprees, is raised to a dreary immortality of comparison with the style and humor of Addison; their reputations — like a new torture in the Inferno — seesawing with the changing opinions of critics who edit "The Spectator" for the schools. And Shakespeare, who shares the weaknesses of all mortal workmen, is made a literary god (since this new profession must have its divinity), before whom all tastes bow down. Then in our classes we proceed to paraphrase, to annotate, to question, and cross-question the books these great men have left behind them, until their tortured spirits must envy the current unpopularity of Latin and Greek. As one of my undergraduates wrote at the end of an examination:

> Shakespeare, this prosy paper makes me blush,
> Your finest fancies we have turned to — mush!

Nevertheless, it is the dillettante, the connoisseur, and the æsthete who sneer at the results of teaching English. The practical man will not usually be scornful, even when he is unsympathetic; and the wise many, who know that power over good books is better than a legacy, are too thankful for benefits received to judge a profession by its failures. In truth, the finer minds, the richer lives which must be made possible if our democracy is not to become a welter of vulgar commercialism, are best composted by literature. And therefore the teacher of English, provided he can really teach, has a just claim upon the attention of every American parent. But what is teaching literature?

There is a function borrowed from Germany for our graduate schools, in which a group of professors have at their mercy for an hour of oral examination a much-to-be-pitied candidate for the degree of doctor of philosophy. They may ask him any question in their field which appears on previous reflection to be sufficiently difficult; and as the more one knows the more difficulty a given subject presents, and they are specialists, the ordeal is infernal. If I were brought before a like tribunal, composed of parents of our undergraduates, and asked to justify this new profession, I should probably begin by asserting that the purpose of teaching English is to give light for the mind and solace for the heart.

The function of the teacher of English as a shedder of light is perhaps more familiar to himself than to the world;

but it assuredly exists, and has even been forced upon him. The teacher of pure science utterly repudiates the notion that *he* is to shed light upon the meaning of life. His business is to teach the observed processes of nature, and he is too busy exploding old theories of how she works, and creating new ones, to concern himself with the spiritual welfare of this generation. Perhaps it is just as well. As for the philosophers, in spite of the efforts of William James, they have not yet consented to elucidate their subjects for the benefit of the democracy; — with this result, that the average undergraduate learns the little philosophy that is taught him, in his class in English literature. Indeed, as if by a conspiracy in a practical world anxious to save time for the study of facts, not only the attributes of culture, but even ethics, morality, and the implications of science are left to the English department.

The burden is heavy. The temptation to throw it off, or to make use of the opportunity for a course in things-in-general and an easy reputation, is great. And yet all the world of thought does form a part of a course in English, for all that has matured in human experience finds its way into literature. And since good books are the emanations of radiant minds, the teacher of English must in the long run teach light.

But even if literature did not mean light for the mind, it would still be worth while to try to teach it, if only to prepare that solace for the weary soul in reading which the most active must some day crave. The undergraduate puts on a solemn face when told that he may need the stimulus of books as an incentive to life, or the relaxation of books as a relief from it; but he remains inwardly unimpressed. And yet one does not have to be a philosopher to know that in this age of hurry and strain and sudden depressions, the power to fall back on other minds and other times is above price. Therefore we teach literature in the hope that to the poets and the essayists, the playwrights and the novelists, men may be helped to bring slack or weary minds for cure.

All essays upon literature discourse upon the light and sweetness which flow from it. But this is not an essay upon literature; and that is why I have dismissed these hoped-for results so summarily, although profoundly believing that they are the ultimate purpose, indeed the *raison d'être* of teaching English. My business is rather with the immediate aim of these English courses to which you are sending your sons and daughters by the tens of thousands. I wish to discuss frankly, not so much the why, as the how, of teaching English. Fine words cannot accomplish it. When I first began to teach, I met my Freshman classes with rich and glowing words, — which I have repeated with more sobriety in the preceding paragraphs. Literature, I said, is the criticism of life; it is the spur of the noble mind, and the comfort of the depressed. My ardent descriptions fell flat. They were too true; the Freshmen had heard them before. Now I begin bluntly with the assertion that the average young American does not know how to read; and proceed to prove it. To read out the meaning of a book; to interpret literature as it in turn interprets life, — whatever may be our ultimate purpose, that I take to be the most immediate aim of teaching English.

I do not intend to slight the knowledge to be gained. Facts are well worth picking up on the way, but unless they are used they remain just facts — and usually forgotten ones. Where are your college note-books, crammed with the facts of English lectures? How much does the graduate remember of dates of editions, of "tendencies," and "sources"? What can he say (as the examination paper has it) of Vaughan, of Cynewulf, of the Gothic novel, and Pantisocracy? Something, somewhere, I hope, for if the onward sweep of English literature is not familiar to him, if the great writers have no local habitation and a name, and Milton must be read in terms of twentieth-century England, and Poe as if he wrote for a Sunday newspaper syndicate, his English courses were dismally unsuccessful. And yet to have heard of Beowulf and Tess of the D'Urbervilles and Fair Rosamond, is not to know English literature.

The undergraduate (and his parent) must be able to read literature in order to know it, and to read he must have the power of interpretation. It is easy to read the story in the Sunday supplement, where thoughts of one syllable are clothed in obvious symbols supposed to represent life. It is harder to read contemporary writing that contains real thought and real observation, for the mind and the imagination have to be stretched a little to take in the text. It is still more difficult to enjoy with due comprehension the vast treasure of our inherited literature, which must always outweigh in value our current gains. There the boy you send us to teach will be perplexed by the peculiarities of language, set astray by his lack of background, and confused by the operations of a time-spirit radically different from his own. A few trivialities of diction or reference may hide from him the life which some great genius has kept burning in the printed page. And even if the unfamiliar and the unexplained do not discourage him, even if he reads Shakespeare, or Milton, or Gray with his ardor unchilled, nevertheless, if he does not interpret, he gets but half. Here is the chief need for teaching English.

Hotspur, for example, in the first part of Shakespeare's "Henry IV," bursts into enthusiastic speech:

> By heaven, methinks it were an easy leap,
> To pluck bright honor from the pale-faced moon,
> Or dive into the bottom of the deep,
> Where fathom line could never touch the ground,
> And pluck up drowned honor by the locks.

Can the Freshman read it? Not unless he knows what "honor" meant for Hotspur and for Shakespeare. Not unless he comprehends the ardent exuberance of the Renaissance that inspires the extravagance of the verse. Or Milton's famous portrait of Satan:

> Darkened so, yet shone
> Above them all the Archangel: but his face
> Deep scars of thunder had intrenched, and care
> Sat on his faded cheek, but under brows
> Of dauntless courage, and considerate pride
> Waiting revenge.

Do you see him? Not unless, like Milton, you remember Jove and his lightnings, not unless the austere imagery of the Old Testament is present in your imagination, not unless "considerate" means more to you than an accent in the verse. In truth, the undergraduate cannot read Stevenson's "Markheim," Tennyson's "Lotos-Eaters," Kipling's "Recessional," or an essay by Emerson — to gather scattered instances — without background, without an interpretative insight, and without an exact understanding of the thought behind the words. Without them, he must be content, at best, with a fifty-per-cent efficiency of comprehension. And fifty per cent is below the margin of enjoyment, and below the point where real profit begins.

But even fifty per cent is a higher figure than some undergraduates attain at the beginning of their college careers. Old Justice Shallow, for instance, pompous, boastful, tedious, Justice Shallow with his ridiculous attempts to prove himself as wicked as Falstaff, and his empty sententiousness is certainly as well-defined a comic character as Shakespeare presents, and yet it is astonishing how much of him is missed by the reader who cannot yet interpret.

"Justice Shallow," writes a Freshman, "seems to be a jolly old man who loves company, and who would do anything to please his guests." "Justice Shallow," says another, "was an easy-going man; that is, he did not allow things to worry him. At times he was very mean." "Justice Shallow," a third proposes, "is kind-hearted. . . . He means well, but things do not come out as he had planned them."

Shallow jolly! Shallow kind-hearted! Perhaps occasionally, — for the benefit of gentlemen from the court. But to describe him thus is as if one should define an elephant as an animal with four legs and a fondness for hay. They missed the flavor of Shallow, these boys, not because it was elusive, but because they had not learned to read.

All good books, whether new or old, present such difficulties of interpretation, — difficulties often small in themselves but great when they prevent that instant flush of appreciation which literature demands. And therefore, if one cannot read lightly, easily, intelligently, — why the storehouse is locked; the golden books may be purchased and perused, but they will be little better than so much paper and print. Two-thirds of an English course must be learning to search out the meaning of the written word; must be just learning how to read.

This is the English teacher's programme. Does he carry it out? In truth, it is depressing to sit in a recitation room, estimating, while someone recites, and your voice is resting, the volume and the flow of the streams of literary instruction washing over the undergraduates; — and then to see them bob up to the surface at the end of the hour, seemingly as impervious as when their heads went under. We teachers of English propose, as I have said above, to ennoble the mind by showing it how to feed upon the thoughts of the great, to save the state by sweetness and light; while our students sell their Miltons and Tennysons to the second-hand bookstore, and buy the machine-made, please-the-million magazines! The pessimist will assert that there is a screw out somewhere in our intellectual platform.

Not out, but loose. My picture of the undergraduate, like Hamlet's picture of Claudius, is a likeness but not a faithful portrait. The college English course certainly carries with it no guarantee of solid literary taste, no certainty that the average bachelor of arts will take a stand against the current cheapening of literature. He may have a row of leather-bound pocket Shakespeares in the living-room book-case, but that is sometimes the only outward evidence of his baptism into the kingdom of English books. Further than that you cannot be sure of what teaching English has done for him. But neither can you be certain that this is all it has done for him. The evidence of his parents is not always to be trusted, for the undergraduate feels that grown-up America does not approve of bookishness, and so, if he has any literary culture, keeps it to himself. Men of letters, editorial writers, and other professional critics of our intellectual accomplishments are not good judges, for they are inclined to apply to a recent graduate the standards of an elegant and allusive brand of culture which is certainly not American, though in its way admirable enough. I am doubtful myself, but this much my experience has taught me, that, disappointing as the apparent results of teaching English may be, the actual results are far more considerable than pessimists suppose — as great perhaps as we can expect.

The mind of the undergraduate is like a slab of coarse-grained wood, upon which the cabinet-maker lavishes his stain. Its empty pores soak in the polishing mixture, no matter how richly it may be applied, and in many instances we fail to get the expected gloss. Much English teaching, in fact, is (to change the figure) subterranean in its effects. You may remember no Tennyson, and yet have gained a sensitiveness to moral beauty, and an ear for the glory of words. Your Shakespeare may have gathered dust for a decade, and yet still be quickening your sympathy with human nature. That glow in the presence of a soaring pine or towering mountain; that warmth of the imagination as some modern struggle recalls an ancient protagonist; the feeling that life is always interesting somehow, somewhere, — how much of this is due to Wordsworth, Shelley, Stevenson, Browning, or Keats, dim in the memory perhaps, but potent in the sub-consciousness, no one can ever determine. The psychologist will answer, much. The layman must consider the spring, the recuperative power, the quantity and quality of happiness among the well-read in comparison with the unread, for his reply. The results of my own observation enable me to view even the *débris* of lectures and study in a "flunker's" examination paper with dejection to be sure, but not with despair. The undergraduate, I admit sorrowfully, is usually superficial in his reading, and sometimes merely barbarous in the use he makes of it; but there is more gained from his training in literature than meets the sight.

Thus the effects of English teaching are sometimes hidden. But English teachers are so common nowadays that of them everyone may form his own opinion. And, indeed, the rain of criticism falls upon just and unjust alike.

The undergraduate, if he takes the trouble to classify his teachers of English otherwise than as "hard" or "easy," would probably divide the species into two types: the highly polished variety with somewhat erratic clothes and an artistic temperament; and the cold scholar who moves in a world of sources, editions, and dates. I would be content with this classification, superficial as it is, were it not that the parent of the undergraduate, who is footing the bills, has made no classification at all, and deserves, if he wants it, a more accurate description of the profession he is patronizing. English teachers, I may say to him, are of at least four different kinds. For convenience, I shall name them the gossips, the inspirationists, the scientists, and the middle-of-the-road men whose ambition it is to teach neither anecdote, nor things in general, nor mere facts, but literature.

The literary gossip is the most engaging, and not the least useful of them all. As the horse's hoofs beat "proputty, proputty, proputty" for Tennyson's greedy farmer, so "personality" rings forever in his brain, and constantly mingles in his speech. "The man behind the book," is his worthy motto; and his lectures are stuffed with biographical anecdote until the good stories spill over. No humorous weakness of the Olympians is left without its jest, and the student learns more of Carlyle's indigestion, Coleridge's absent-mindedness, or the deformity of Pope, than of their immortal works.

The literary gossip is an artist. He can raise dead authors to life, and give students of little imagination an interest in the books of the past which they never would have gained from mere printed texts. But he has the faults of the artistic temperament. He will sacrifice everything in order to impress his hearers. Hence he is never dull; and when he combines his skill in anecdote with real literary criticism, he becomes a teacher of such power that college presidents compete for his services. But when his talents do not rise above the ordinary, his courses are better designated vaudeville than the teaching of English. As the old song has it, when he is good he is very, very good, for he ploughs up the unresponsive mind so that appreciation may grow there. But when he is bad, he is horrid.

The inspirationists held the whole field of English teaching until the scientists attacked them in the rear, found their ammunition wagons lacking in facts, and put them upon their defense. The inspirationist was — no is, — for he has been sobered but not routed by the onslaughts of German methodologies, — a fighter in the cause of "uplift" in America. In 1814 he would have been a minister of the gospel, or an apostle of political freedom. In 1914 he uses Shakespeare, Milton, the novelists, the essayists, indifferently to preach ideas — moral, political, æsthetic, philosophical, scientific — to his undergraduates. At the club table after hours, he orates at imaginary Freshmen. "Make 'em think!" he shouts. "Make 'em feel! Give them ideas — and their literary training will take care of itself!" And the course he offers is like those famous mediæval ones, where the whole duty of man, here and hereafter, was to be obtained from a single professor. Indeed, since the field of teaching began to be recruited from predestined pastors who found the pulpit too narrow for their activities, it is simply astonishing how much ethics, spirituality, and inspiration generally has been freed in the classroom. Ask the undergraduates.

I mean no flippancy. I thoroughly believe that it is far more important to teach literature than the facts about literature. And all these things are among the ingredients of literature. I am merely pointing out the extremes of extra-literary endeavor into which the remoteness of the philosophers, the slackening of religious training in the home, and the absence of æsthetic influences in American life, have driven some among us. A friend of mine begins his course in Carlyle with a lecture on the unreality of matter, Browning with a discussion of the immortality of the soul, and Ruskin with an exhibition of pictures. He is responding to the needs of the age. Like most of the inspirationists, he does not fail to teach something; like many of them, he has little time left for literature.

The day does not differ from the night more sharply than the scientist in teaching English from the inspirationist. The literary scientist sprang into being when the scientific activity of the nineteenth century reached æsthetics and began to lay bare our inaccuracies and our ignorance. Chaucer, Spenser, Milton, Defoe — we knew all too little about their lives, and of what we knew a disgraceful part was wrong. Our knowledge of the writers of the Anglo-Saxon period, and of the thirteenth and fifteenth centuries, of the minor Elizabethan dramatists and the lyricists of the seventeenth century, consisted chiefly of ill-assorted facts or unproved generalizations.

Our catalogue of errors was a long one. The response to this crying need for scholarship, for science, was slow, — but when it came, it came with a rush. Nowadays, the great majority of university teachers of English are specialists in some form of literary research.

As far as the teacher is concerned, the result has doubtless been good. There have been broader backgrounds, more accuracy in statement, less "bluffing" — in a word, more thoroughness; and the out-and-out scientists have set a pace in this respect which other teachers of English have had to follow. But curiously enough, while the teacher of English, and especially the professed scientist, has become more thorough, the students are said to be less so. How to account for so distressing a phenomenon!

The truth seems to be that science in English literature has become so minute in its investigation of details, so scrupulous in the accuracy of even the most trivial statement, that the teacher who specializes in this direction despairs of dragging his classes after him. Scholarship for this scientist has become esoteric. Neither the big world outside, nor his little world of the classroom, can comprehend his passion for date, and source, and text; and, like the Mormon who keeps his wives at home, he has come to practice his faith without imposing it upon others. The situation is not entirely unfortunate. Until scientific scholarship has ended its mad scurryings for the unconsidered trifles still left uninvestigated, and begun upon the broader problems of criticism and of teaching which will remain when all the dates are gathered and all the sources hunted home, it is questionable whether it has anything but facts to contribute to the elementary teaching of English.

At present, the scientist's best position is in the upper

branches of a college education. There he is doing good work, — except when an emotional, sensitive Junior or Senior, eager to be thrilled by literature, and to understand it, is provided with nothing but "scientific" courses. For studying about literature — and this is the scientist's programme — can in no possible sense be regarded as a satisfactory alternative to studying the thing itself, no matter how great may be its auxiliary value. And many a recent graduate of many a college who reads these lines, will recognize his own plight in that of the youth who, finding only gossips who amused him, inspirationists who sermoned him, and scientists who reduced glowing poetry to a skeleton of fact, decided that in spite of the catalogue, literature itself was not taught in his university.

What *is* teaching literature? But I have already answered that question according to my own beliefs, in the earlier part of this paper. It must be — at least for the undergraduate — instruction in the interpretation of literature; it must be teaching how to read. For if the boy is once taught how to turn the key, only such forces of heredity and environment as no teaching will utterly overcome, can prevent him from entering the door. It is this that all wise teachers of English realize; it is this that the middle-of-the-road men try to put in practice. I give them this title because they do keep to the middle of the literary road, — because they understand that the teacher of English should avoid the extremes I have depicted in the preceding paragraphs, without despising them. He should master his facts as the scientist does, because it is too late in the day to impose unverified facts or shaky generalizations even upon hearers as uncritical as the usual run of undergraduates. He should try to inspire his classes with the ideas and emotions of the text, for to teach the form of a book and neglect its contents, is as if your grocer should send you an empty barrel. He should not neglect the life and color which literary biography brings into his field. And yet the aim of the right kind of instructor is no one of these things. He uses them all, but merely as steps in the attempt to teach his students how to read.

This it is to follow the golden mean and make it actually golden in our profession. And indeed, when one considers that throughout America there are hundreds of thousands calling themselves educated who cannot read Shakespeare, or the Bible, or even a good magazine, with justice to the text; when one considers the treasures of literature, new as well as old, waiting to be used for the increase of happiness, intelligence, and power, what else can be called teaching English?

EDWARD GIBBON [1]

BY

JAMES FORD RHODES

Gibbon is a man of one book, but that book is a masterpiece. In 1776, the birth-year of our country, he began writing his "Decline and Fall of the Roman Empire," — and to-day at any bookstore, you can find copies in endless editions. How wonderful that is! That a drama or romance should persist through centuries is easily explainable, since the subject matter of them is human nature, and human nature has changed but slightly. But why a history, written much too long after the events it describes to have contemporaneous value, should survive all more recent studies based on modern research and archeological investigation, — that is the question. And it is this question that our greatest living historian here attempts to answer. The problem is presented in two paragraphs. The answer is then sought in his life, in his intellectual training, in his attitude of mind, and in his own point of view regarding his work. Notice the care with which each phase of the subject is proved by citations, quotations, and references. The aim then is to make the reader intellectually comprehend the writer of the book. And as the essay was first delivered as a lecture at Harvard University, for such an audience Dr. Rhodes rightfully emphasizes the intellectual nature of the appeal.

No English or American lover of history visits Rome without bending reverent footsteps to the Church of Santa Maria in Ara Cœli. Two visits are necessary, as on the first you are at once seized by the sacristan, who can con-

[1] Lecture read at Harvard University, April 6, 1908, and printed in *Scribner's Magazine*, June, 1909. Reprinted from "Historical Essays," by permission of the author and of The Macmillan Co.

ceive of no other motive for entering this church on the Capitol Hill than to see the miraculous Bambino — the painted doll swaddled in gold and silver tissue and "crusted over with magnificent diamonds, emeralds, and rubies." When you have heard the tale of what has been called "the oldest medical practitioner in Rome," of his miraculous cures, of these votive offerings, the imaginary picture you had conjured up is effaced; and it is better to go away and come a second time when the sacristan will recognize you and leave you to yourself. Then you may open your Gibbon's Autobiography and read that it was the subtle influence of Italy and Rome that determined the choice, from amongst many contemplated subjects of historical writing, of "The Decline and Fall of the Roman Empire." "In my Journal," wrote Gibbon, "the place and moment of conception are recorded; the 15th of October, 1764, in the close of the evening, as I sat musing in the Church of the Franciscan friars while they were singing vespers in the Temple of Jupiter on the ruins of the Capitol." [1] Gibbon was twenty-seven when he made this fruitful visit of eighteen weeks to Rome, and his first impression, though often quoted, never loses interest, showing, as it does, the enthusiasm of an unemotional man. "At the distance of twenty-five years," he wrote, "I can neither forget nor express the strong emotions which agitated my mind as I first approached and entered the *Eternal City*. After a sleepless night, I trod with a lofty step the ruins of the Forum; each memorable spot where Romulus *stood* or Cicero spoke or Cæsar fell was at once present to my eye."

The admirer of Gibbon as he travels northward will stop at Lausanne and visit the hotel which bears the historian's

[1] Autobiography, 270.

name. Twice have I taken luncheon in the garden where he wrote the last words of his history; and on a third visit, after lunching at another inn, I could not fail to admire the penetration of the Swiss concierge. As I alighted, he seemed to divine at once the object of my visit, and before I had half the words of explanation out of my mouth, he said, " Oh, yes. It is this way. But I cannot show you anything but a spot." I have quoted from Gibbon's Autobiography the expression of his inspiration of twenty-seven; a fitting companion-piece is the reflection of the man of fifty. "I have presumed to mark the moment of conception," he wrote; "I shall now commemorate the hour of my final deliverance. It was on the day, or rather the night, of the 27th of June, 1787, between the hours of eleven and twelve, that I wrote the last lines of the last page in a summer-house in my garden. . . . I will not dissemble the first emotions of joy on the recovery of my freedom and perhaps the establishment of my fame. But my pride was soon humbled, and a sober melancholy was spread over my mind by the idea that I had taken my everlasting leave of an old and agreeable companion." [1]

Although the idea was conceived when Gibbon was twenty-seven, he was thirty-one before he set himself seriously at work to study his material. At thirty-six he began the composition, and he was thirty-nine, when, in February, 1776, the first quarto volume was published. The history had an immediate success. "My book," he wrote, "was on every table and almost on every toilette; the historian was crowned by the taste or fashion of the day." [2] The first edition was exhausted in a few days, a second was printed in 1776, and next year a third.

[1] Autobiography, 333.　　　　[2] *Ibid.*, 311.

The second and third volumes, which ended the history of the Western empire, were published in 1781, and seven years later the three volumes devoted to the Eastern empire saw the light. The last sentence of the work, written in the summer-house at Lausanne, is, "It was among the ruins of the Capitol that I first conceived the idea of a work which has amused and exercised near twenty years of my life, and which, however inadequate to my own wishes, I finally deliver to the curiosity and candor of the public."

This is a brief account of one of the greatest historical works, if indeed it is not the greatest, ever written. Let us imagine an assemblage of English, German, and American historical scholars called upon to answer the question, Who is the greatest modern historian? No doubt can exist that Gibbon would have a large majority of the voices; and I think a like meeting of French and Italian scholars would indorse the verdict. "Gibbon's work will never be excelled," declared Niebuhr.[1] "That great master of us all," said Freeman, "whose immortal tale none of us can hope to displace." [2] Bury, the latest editor of Gibbon, who has acutely criticised and carefully weighed "The Decline and Fall," concludes "that Gibbon is behind date in many details. But in the main things he is still our master, above and beyond date." [3] His work wins plaudits from those who believe that history in its highest form should be literature and from those who hold that it should be nothing more than a scientific narrative. The disciples of Macaulay and Carlyle, of Stubbs and Gardiner, would be found voting in unison in my imaginary

[1] Lectures, 763.
[2] Chief Periods European Hist., 75.
[3] Introduction, lxvii.

Congress. Gibbon, writes Bury, is "the historian and
the man of letters," thus ranking with Thucydides and
Tacitus.   These three are put in the highest class, exemplifying that "brilliance of style and accuracy of statement
are perfectly compatible in an historian." [1] Accepting
this authoritative classification it is well worth while to
point out the salient differences between the ancient
historians and the modern.   From Thucydides we have
twenty-four years of contemporary history of his own
country.   If the whole of the Annals and History of
Tacitus had come down to us, we should have had eighty-
three years; as it is, we actually have forty-one of nearly
contemporary history of the Roman Empire.   Gibbon's
tale covers 1240 years.   He went far beyond his own
country for his subject, and the date of his termination
is three centuries before he was born.   Milman spoke of
"the amplitude, the magnificence, and the harmony of
Gibbon's design," [2] and Bury writes, "If we take into
account the vast range of his work, his accuracy is amazing." [3]   Men have wondered and will long wonder at the
brain with such a grasp and with the power to execute
skillfully so mighty a conception.   "The public is seldom
wrong" in their judgment of a book, wrote Gibbon in his
Autobiography,[4] and, if that be true at the time of actual
publication to which Gibbon intended to apply the remark,
how much truer it is in the long run of years.   "The
Decline and Fall of the Roman Empire" has had a life of
over one hundred and thirty years, and there is no indication that it will not endure as long as any interest
is taken in the study of history.   "I have never presumed
to accept a place in the triumvirate of British historians,"

[1] Introduction, xxxi.   [3] Introduction, xli.
[2] Preface, ix.   [4] p. 324.

said Gibbon, referring to Hume and Robertson. But in our day Hume and Robertson gather dust on the shelf, while Gibbon is continually studied by students and read by serious men.

A work covering Gibbon's vast range of time would have been impossible for Thucydides or Tacitus. Historical skepticism had not been fully enough developed. There had not been a sufficient sifting and criticism of historical materials for a master's work of synthesis. And it is probable that Thucydides lacked a model. Tacitus could indeed have drawn inspiration from the Greek, while Gibbon had lessons from both, showing a profound study of Tacitus and a thorough acquaintance with Thucydides.

If circumstances then made it impossible for the Greek or the Roman to attempt history on the grand scale of Gibbon, could Gibbon have written contemporary history with accuracy and impartiality equal to his great predecessors? This is one of those delightful questions that may be ever discussed and never resolved. When twenty-three years old, arguing against the desire of his father that he should go into Parliament, Gibbon assigned, as one of the reasons, that he lacked "necessary prejudices of party and of nation"; [1] and when in middle life he embraced the fortunate opportunity of becoming a member of the House of Commons, he thus summed up his experience, "The eight sessions that I sat in Parliament were a school of civil prudence, the first and most essential virtue of an historian." [2] At the end of this political career, Gibbon, in a private letter to an intimate Swiss friend, gave the reason why he had embraced it. "I entered Parliament," he said, "without patriotism, and without ambition, and

[1] Letters, I, 23.   [2] Autobiography, 310.

I had no other aim than to secure the comfortable and honest place of a *Lord of Trade*. I obtained this place at last. I held it for three years, from 1779 to 1782, and the net annual product of it, being £750 sterling, increased my revenue to the level of my wants and desires." [1] His retirement from Parliament was followed by ten years' residence at Lausanne, in the first four of which he completed his history. A year and a half after his removal to Lausanne, he referred, in a letter to his closest friend, Lord Sheffield, to the "abyss of your cursed politics," and added: "I never was a very warm patriot and I grow every day a citizen of the world. The scramble for power and profit at Westminster or St. James's, and the names of Pitt and Fox become less interesting to me than those of Cæsar and Pompey." [2]

These expressions would seem to indicate that Gibbon might have written contemporary history well and that the candor displayed in "The Decline and Fall" might not have been lacking had he written of England in his own time. But that subject he never contemplated. When twenty-four years old he had however considered a number of English periods and finally fixed upon Sir Walter Raleigh for his hero; but a year later, he wrote in his journal: "I shrink with terror from the modern history of England, where every character is a problem, and every reader a friend or an enemy; where a writer is supposed to hoist a flag of party and is devoted to damnation by the adverse faction. . . . I must embrace a safer and more extensive theme." [3]

How well Gibbon knew himself! Despite his coolness and candor, war and revolution revealed his strong Tory prejudices, which he undoubtedly feared might color any

[1] Letters, II, 36.   [2] *Ibid.*, 127.   [3] Autobiography, 196.

history of England that he might undertake. "I took my seat," in the House of Commons, he wrote, "at the beginning of the memorable contest between Great Britain and America; and supported with many a sincere and *silent* vote the rights though perhaps not the interests of the mother country." [1] In 1782 he recorded the conclusion: "The American war had once been the favorite of the country, the pride of England was irritated by the resistance of her colonies, and the executive power was driven by national clamor into the most vigorous and coercive measures." But it was a fruitless contest. Armies were lost; the debt and taxes were increased; the hostile confederacy of France, Spain and Holland was disquieting. As a result the war became unpopular and Lord North's ministry fell. Dr. Johnson thought that no nation not absolutely conquered had declined so much in so short a time. "We seem to be sinking," he said. "I am afraid of a civil war." Dr. Franklin, according to Horace Walpole, said "he would furnish Mr. Gibbon with materials for writing the History of the Decline of the British Empire." With his country tottering, the self-centered but truthful Gibbon could not avoid mention of his personal loss, due to the fall of his patron, Lord North. "I was stripped of a convenient salary," he said, "after having enjoyed it about three years." [2]

The outbreak of the French Revolution intensified his conservatism. He was then at Lausanne, the tranquillity of which was broken up by the dissolution of the neighboring kingdom. Many Lausanne families were terrified by the menace of bankruptcy. "This town and country,"

---

[1] Autobiography, 310. "I am more and more convinced that we have both the right and power on our side." Letters, I, 248.

[2] Hill's ed. Gibbon Autobiography, 212, 213, 314.

Gibbon wrote, "are crowded with noble exiles, and we sometimes count in an assembly a dozen princesses and duchesses."[1] Bitter disputes between them and the triumphant Democrats disturbed the harmony of social circles. Gibbon espoused the cause of the royalists. "I beg leave to subscribe my assent to Mr. Burke's creed on the Revolution of France," he wrote. "I admire his eloquence, I approve his politics, I adore his chivalry, and I can almost excuse his reverence for Church establishments."[2] Thirteen days after the massacre of the Swiss guard in the attack on the Tuileries in August, 1792, Gibbon wrote to Lord Sheffield, "The last revolution of Paris appears to have convinced almost everybody of the fatal consequences of Democratical principles which lead by a path of flowers into the abyss of hell."[3] Gibbon, who was astonished by so few things in history, wrote Sainte-Beuve, was amazed by the French Revolution.[4] Nothing could be more natural. The historian in his study may consider the fall of dynasties, social upheavals, violent revolutions, and the destruction of order without a tremor. The things have passed away. The events furnish food for his reflections and subjects for his pen, while sanguine uprisings at home or in a neighboring country in his own time inspire him with terror lest the oft-prophesied dissolution of society is at hand. It is the difference between the earthquake in your own city and the one 3000 miles away. As Gibbon's pocket-nerve was sensitive, it may be he was also thinking of the £1300 he had invested in 1784 in the new loan of the King of France, deeming the French funds as solid as the English.[5]

It is well now to repeat our dictum that Gibbon is the

[1] Letters, II, 249.   [2] Autobiography, 342.   [3] Letters, II, 310.
[4] Causeries du Lundi, viii, 469.   [5] Letters, II, 98.

greatest modern historian, but, in reasserting this, it is no more than fair to cite the opinions of two dissentients — the great literary historians of the nineteenth century, Macaulay and Carlyle. "The truth is," wrote Macaulay in his diary, "that I admire no historians much except Herodotus, Thucydides, and Tacitus. . . . There is merit no doubt in Hume, Robertson, Voltaire, and Gibbon. Yet it is not the thing. I have a conception of history more just, I am confident, than theirs." [1] "Gibbon," said Carlyle in a public lecture, is "a greater historian than Robertson but not so great as Hume. With all his swagger and bombast no man ever gave a more futile account of human things than he has done of the decline and fall of the Roman Empire; assigning no profound cause for these phenomena, nothing but diseased nerves, and all sorts of miserable motives, to the actors in them." [2] Carlyle's statement shows envious criticism as well as a prejudice in favor of his brother Scotchman. It was made in 1838, since when opinion has raised Gibbon to the top, for he actually lives while Hume is read perfunctorily, if at all. Moreover among the three — Gibbon, Macaulay, and Carlyle — whose works are literature as well as history, modern criticism has no hesitation in awarding the palm to Gibbon.

Before finally deciding upon his subject Gibbon thought of "The History of the Liberty of the Swiss" and "The History of the Republic of Florence under the House of Medicis," [3] but in the end, as we have seen, he settled on the later history of the Roman Empire, showing, as Lowell said of Parkman, his genius in the choice of his

---

[1] Trevelyan, II, 232.

[2] Lectures on the Hist. of Literature, 185.

[3] Autobiography, 196.

subject. His history really begins with the death of Marcus Aurelius, 180 A.D., but the main narrative is preceded by three excellent introductory chapters, covering in Bury's edition eighty-two pages. After the completion of his work, he regretted that he had not begun it at an earlier period. On the first page of his own printed copy of his book where he announces his design, he has entered this marginal note: "Should I not have given the *history* of that fortunate period which was interposed between two iron ages? Should I not have deduced the decline of the Empire from the Civil Wars that ensued after the Fall of Nero or even from the tyranny which succeeded the reign of Augustus? Alas! I should; but of what avail is this tardy knowledge?"[1] We may echo Gibbon's regret that he had not commenced his history with the reign of Tiberius, as, in his necessary use of Tacitus, we should have had the running comment of one great historian on another, of which we have a significant example in Gibbon's famous sixteenth chapter wherein he discusses Tacitus's account of the persecution of the Christians by Nero. With his power of historic divination, he would have so absorbed Tacitus and his time that the history would almost have seemed a collaboration between two great and sympathetic minds. "Tacitus," he wrote, "very frequently trusts to the curiosity or reflection of his readers to supply those intermediate circumstances and ideas, which, in his extreme conciseness, he has thought proper to suppress."[2] How Gibbon would have filled those gaps! Though he was seldom swayed by enthusiasm, his admiration of the Roman historian fell little short of idolatry. His references in "The Decline and Fall" are many, and some of them

[1] Bury's ed., xxxv.   [2] Decline and Fall, Smith's ed., 236.

are here worth recalling to mind. "In their primitive state of simplicity and independence," he wrote, "the Germans were surveyed by the discerning eye and delineated by the masterly pencil of Tacitus, the first of historians who applied the science of philosophy to the study of facts." [1] Again he speaks of him as "the philosophic historian whose writings will instruct the last generation of mankind." [2] And in Chapter XVI he devoted five pages to citation from, and comment on, Tacitus, and paid him one of the most splendid tributes one historian ever paid another. "To collect, to dispose, and to adorn a series of fourscore years in an immortal work, every sentence of which is pregnant with the deepest observations and the most lively images, was an undertaking sufficient to exercise the genius of Tacitus himself during the greatest part of his life." [3] So much for admiration. That, nevertheless, Gibbon could wield the critical pen at the expense of the historian he rated so highly, is shown by a marginal note in his own printed copy of "The Decline and Fall." It will be remembered that Tacitus published his History and wrote his Annals during the reign of Trajan, whom he undoubtedly respected and admired. He referred to the reigns of Nerva and Trajan in suggested contrast to that of Domitian as "times when men were blessed with the rare privilege of thinking with freedom, and uttering what they thought." [4] It fell to both Tacitus and Gibbon to speak of the testament of Augustus which, after his death, was read in the Senate: and Tacitus wrote, Augustus "added a recommendation to keep the empire within fixed limits," on which he thus commented, "but whether from appre-

---

[1] Decline and Fall, Smith's ed., I, 349. [2] *Ibid.*, II, 35.
[3] II, 235. [4] History, I, 1.

hension for its safety, or jealousy of future rivals, is uncertain." [1] Gibbon thus criticised this comment: "Why must rational advice be imputed to a base or foolish motive? To what cause, error, malevolence, or flattery, shall I ascribe the unworthy alternative? Was the historian dazzled by Trajan's conquests?" [2]

The intellectual training of the greatest modern historian is a matter of great interest. "From my early youth," wrote Gibbon in his Autobiography, "I aspired to the character of an historian." [3] He had "an early and invincible love of reading" which he said he "would not exchange for the treasures of India" and which led him to a "vague and multifarious" perusal of books. Before he reached the age of fifteen he matriculated at Magdalen College, giving this account of his preparation. "I arrived at Oxford," he said, "with a stock of erudition that might have puzzled a Doctor and a degree of ignorance of which a schoolboy would have been ashamed." [4] He did not adapt himself to the life or the method of Oxford, and from them apparently derived no benefit. "I spent fourteen months at Magdalen College," he wrote; "they proved the fourteen months the most idle and unprofitable of my whole life." [5] He became a Roman Catholic. It was quite characteristic of this bookish man that his conversion was effected, not by the emotional influence of some proselytizer, but by the reading of books. English translations of two famous works of Bossuet fell into his hands. "I read," he said, "I applauded, I believed . . . and I surely fell by a noble hand." Before a priest in London, on June 8, 1753, he privately "abjured the errors of heresy" and was admitted into the "pale of the church."

[1] Annals, I, 11.   [2] Bury's introduction, xxxv.
[3] Autobiography, 193.   [4] *Ibid.*, 48, 59.   [5] *Ibid.*, 67.

But at that time this was a serious business for both priest and proselyte. For the rule laid down by Blackstone was this, "Where a person is reconciled to the see of Rome, or procures others to be reconciled, the offence amounts to High-Treason." This severe rule was not enforced, but there were milder laws under which a priest might suffer perpetual imprisonment and the proselyte's estate be transferred to his nearest relations. Under such laws prosecutions were had and convictions obtained. Little wonder was it when Gibbon apprised his father in an "elaborate controversial epistle" of the serious step which he had taken, that the elder Gibbon should be astonished and indignant. In his passion he divulged the secret which effectually closed the gates of Magdalen College to his son,[1] who was packed off to Lausanne and "settled under the roof and tuition" of a Calvinist minister.[2] Edward Gibbon passed nearly five years at Lausanne, from the age of sixteen to that of twenty-one, and they were fruitful years for his education. It was almost entirely an affair of self-training, as his tutor soon perceived that the student had gone beyond the teacher and allowed him to pursue his own special bent. After his history was published and his fame won, he recorded this opinion : "In the life of every man of letters there is an æra, from a level, from whence he soars with his own wings to his proper height, and the most important part of his education is that which he bestows on himself." [3] This was certainly true in Gibbon's case. On his arrival at Lausanne he hardly knew any French, but before he returned to England he thought spontaneously in French and understood, spoke, and wrote it better than he did his mother

---

[1] Autobiography, 86 *et seq.;* Hill's ed., 69, 291.
[2] *Ibid.,* 131. [3] *Ibid.,* 137.

tongue.[1] He read Montesquieu frequently and was struck with his "energy of style and boldness of hypothesis." Among the books which "may have remotely contributed to form the historian of the Roman Empire" were the Provincial Letters of Pascal, which he read "with a new pleasure" almost every year. From them he said, "I learned to manage the weapon of grave and temperate irony, even on subjects of ecclesiastical solemnity." As one thinks of his chapters in "The Decline and Fall" on Julian, one is interested to know that during this period he was introduced to the life and times of this Roman emperor by a book written by a French abbé. He read Locke, Grotius, and Puffendorf, but unquestionably his greatest knowledge, mental discipline, and peculiar mastery of his own tongue came from his diligent and systematic study of the Latin classics. He read nearly all of the historians, poets, orators, and philosophers, going over for a second or even a third time Terence, Virgil, Horace, and Tacitus. He mastered Cicero's Orations and Letters so that they became ingrained in his mental fiber, and he termed these and his other works, "a library of eloquence and reason." "As I read Cicero," he wrote, "I applauded the observation of Quintilian, that every student may judge of his own proficiency by the satisfaction which he receives from the Roman orator." And again, "Cicero's epistles may in particular afford the models of every form of correspondence from the careless effusions of tenderness and friendship to the well-guarded declaration of discreet and dignified resentment."[2] Gibbon never mastered Greek as he did Latin; and Dr. Smith, one of his editors, points out where he has fallen into three errors from the use of the French or Latin

---

[1] *Ibid.*, 134.　　　　　　　[2] *Ibid.*, 139–142.

translation of Procopius instead of consulting the original.
Indeed he himself has disclosed one defect of self-training.
Referring to his youthful residence at Lausanne, he wrote :
"I worked my way through about half the Iliad, and afterwards interpreted alone a large portion of Xenophon and
Herodotus.   But my ardor, destitute of aid and emulation,
was gradually cooled and, from the barren task of searching
words in a lexicon, I withdrew to the free and familiar
conversation of Virgil and Tacitus." [2]

All things considered, however, it was an excellent training for a historian of the Roman Empire.   But all except
the living knowledge of French he might have had in his
"elegant apartment in Magdalen College" just as well as
in his "ill-contrived and ill-furnished small chamber"
in "an old inconvenient house," situated in a "narrow
gloomy street, the most unfrequented of an unhandsome
town" ; [3] and in Oxford he would have had the "aid and
emulation" of which at Lausanne he sadly felt the lack.

The Calvinist minister, his tutor, was a more useful
guide for Gibbon in the matter of religion than in his intellectual training.   Through his efforts and Gibbon's
"private reflections," Christmas Day, 1754, one year
and a half after his arrival at Lausanne, was witness to
his reconversion, as he then received the sacrament in
the Calvinistic Church.   "The articles of the Romish
creed," he said, had "disappeared like a dream" ; and
he wrote home to his aunt, "I am now a good Protestant
and am extremely glad of it." [4]

An intellectual and social experience of value was his
meeting with Voltaire, who had set up a theater in the
neighborhood of Lausanne for the performance mainly

---

[1] Smith's ed., V, 108, 130, 231.   [3] Ibid., 132.
[2] Autobiography, 141.   [4] Hill's ed., 89, 293.

of his own plays. Gibbon seldom failed to procure a ticket to these representations. Voltaire played the parts suited to his years; his declamation, Gibbon thought, was old-fashioned, and "he expressed the enthusiasm of poetry rather than the feelings of nature." "The parts of the young and fair," he said, "were distorted by Voltaire's fat and ugly niece." Despite this criticism, these performances fostered a taste for the French theater, to the abatement of his idolatry for Shakespeare, which seemed to him to be "inculcated from our infancy as the first duty of an Englishman." [1] Personally, Voltaire and Gibbon did not get on well together. Dr. Hill suggests that Voltaire may have slighted the " English youth," and if this is correct, Gibbon was somewhat spiteful to carry the feeling more than thirty years. Besides the criticism of the acting, he called Voltaire "the envious bard" because it was only with much reluctance and ill-humor that he permitted the performance of Iphigenie of Racine. Nevertheless, Gibbon is impressed with the social influence of the great Frenchman. "The wit and philosophy of Voltaire, his table and theatre," he wrote, "refined in a visible degree the manners of Lausanne, and however addicted to study, I enjoyed my share of the amusements of society. After the theatrical representations, I sometimes supped with the actors : I was now familiar in some, and acquainted in many, houses; and my evenings were generally devoted to cards and conversation, either in private parties or numerous assemblies." [2]

Gibbon was twenty-one when he returned to England. Dividing his time between London and the country, he continued his self-culture. He read English, French, and Latin, and took up the study of Greek. "Every day,

[1] Autobiography, 149.   [2] Ibid., 149.

T

every hour," he wrote, "was agreeably filled"; and "I was never less alone than when by myself." [1] He read repeatedly Robertson and Hume, and has in the words of Sainte-Beuve left a testimony so spirited and so delicately expressed as could have come only from a man of taste who appreciated Xenophon.[2] "The perfect composition, the nervous language," wrote Gibbon, "the well-turned periods of Dr. Robertson inflamed me to the ambitious hope that I might one day tread in his footsteps; the calm philosophy, the careless inimitable beauties of his friend and rival, often forced me to close the volume with a mixed sensation of delight and despair." [3] He made little progress in London society and his solitary evenings were passed with his books, but he consoled himself by thinking that he lost nothing by a withdrawal from a "noisy and expensive scene of crowds without company, and dissipation without pleasure." At twenty-four he published his "Essay on the Study of Literature," begun at Lausanne and written entirely in French. This possesses no interest for the historical student except to know the bare fact of the writing and publication as a step in the intellectual development of the historian. Sainte-Beuve in his two essays on Gibbon devoted three pages to an abstract and criticism of it, perhaps because it had a greater success in France than in England; and his opinion of Gibbon's language is interesting. "The French," Sainte-Beuve wrote, "is that of one who has read Montesquieu much and imitates him; it is correct, but artificial French." [4]

Then followed two and a half years' service in the Hampshire militia. But he did not neglect his reading. He

[1] Autobiography, 161. [2] Causeries du Lundi, VIII, 445.
[3] Autobiography, 167. [4] Ibid., 446.

mastered Homer, whom he termed "the Bible of the ancients," and in the militia he acquired "a just and indelible knowledge" of what he called "the first of languages." And his love for Latin abided also: "On every march, in every journey, Horace was always in my pocket and often in my hand." [1] Practical knowledge he absorbed almost insensibly. "The daily occupations of the militia," he wrote, "introduced me to the science of Tactics" and led to the study of "the precepts of Polybius and Cæsar." In this connection occurs the remark which admirers of Gibbon will never tire of citing: "A familiar view of the discipline and evolutions of a modern battalion gave me a clearer notion of the Phalanx and the Legion; and the Captain of the Hampshire Grenadiers (the reader may smile) has not been useless to the historian of the decline and fall of the Roman Empire." [2] The grand tour followed his militia service. Three and a half months in Paris, and a revisit to Lausanne preceded the year that he passed in Italy. Of the conception of the History of the Decline and Fall, during his stay in Rome, I have already spoken.

On his return to England, contemplating "the decline and fall of Rome at an awful distance," he began, in collaboration with the Swiss Deyverdun, his bosom friend, a history of Switzerland written in French. During the winter of 1767, the first book of it was submitted to a literary society of foreigners in London. As the author was unknown the strictures were free and the verdict unfavorable. Gibbon was present at the meeting and related that "the momentary sensation was painful," but, on cooler reflection, he agreed with his judges and intended to consign his manuscript to the flames. But this, as Lord Sheffield, his literary executor and first editor, shows con-

---

[1] Autobiography, Hill's ed., 142.   [2] Ibid., 258.

clusively, he neglected to do.[1] This essay of Gibbon's possesses interest for us, inasmuch as David Hume read it, and wrote to Gibbon a friendly letter, in which he said: "I have perused your manuscript with great pleasure and satisfaction. I have only one objection, derived from the language in which it is written. Why do you compose in French, and carry faggots into the wood, as Horace says with regard to Romans who wrote in Greek?"[2] This critical query of Hume must have profoundly influenced Gibbon. Next year he began to work seriously on "The Decline and Fall" and five years later began the composition of it in English. It does not appear that he had any idea of writing his magnum opus in French.

In this rambling discourse, in which I have purposely avoided relating the life of Gibbon in anything like a chronological order, we return again and again to the great History. And it could not well be otherwise. For if Edward Gibbon could not have proudly said, I am the author of "six volumes in quartos"[3] he would have had no interest for us. Dr. Hill writes, "For one reader who has read his 'Decline and Fall,' there are at least a score who have read his Autobiography, and who know him, not as the great historian, but as a man of a most original and interesting nature."[4] But these twenty people would never have looked into the Autobiography had it not been the life of a great historian; indeed the Autobiography would never have been written except to give an account of a great life work. "The Decline and Fall," therefore, is the thing about which all the other incidents of his life revolve. The longer this history is read and studied, the greater is the appreciation of it. Dean Milman followed Gibbon's track through many portions of his work,

<hr />

[1] Autobiography, 277.   [2] Ibid.   [3] Letters, II, 279.   [4] Preface, x.

and read his authorities, ending with a deliberate judgment in favor of his "general accuracy." "Many of his seeming errors," he wrote, "are almost inevitable from the close condensation of his matter." [1] Guizot had three different opinions based on three various readings. After the first rapid perusal, the dominant feeling was one of interest in a narrative, always animated in spite of its extent, always clear and limpid in spite of the variety of objects. During the second reading, when he examined particularly certain points, he was somewhat disappointed; he encountered some errors either in the citations or in the facts and especially shades and strokes of partiality which led him to a comparatively rigorous judgment. In the ensuing complete third reading, the first impression, doubtless corrected by the second, but not destroyed, survived and was maintained; and with some restrictions and reservations, Guizot declared that, concerning that vast and able work, there remained with him an appreciation of the immensity of research, the variety of knowledge, the sagacious breadth and especially that truly philosophical rectitude of a mind which judges the past as it would judge the present.[2] Mommsen said in 1894: "Amid all the changes that have come over the study of the history of the Roman Empire, in spite of all the rush of the new evidence that has poured in upon us and almost overwhelmed us, in spite of changes which must be made, in spite of alterations of view, or alterations even in the aspect of great characters, no one would in the future be able to read the history of the Roman Empire unless he read, possibly with a fuller knowledge, but with the broad views, the clear insight, the strong grasp of Edward Gibbon." [3]

[1] Smith's ed., I, xi. [2] Causeries du Lundi, VIII, 453.
[3] *London Times*, November 16, 1894.

It is difficult for an admirer of Gibbon to refrain from
quoting some of his favorite passages. The opinion of a
great historian on history always possesses interest. History, wrote Gibbon, is "little more than the register of
the crimes, follies, and misfortunes of mankind." Again,
"Wars and the administration of public affairs are the
principal subjects of history." And the following cannot
fail to recall a similar thought in Tacitus, "History undertakes to record the transactions of the past for the instruction of future ages." [1] Two references to religion under
the Pagan empire are always worth repeating. "The
various modes of worship which prevailed in the Roman
world," he wrote, "were all considered by the people as
equally true; by the philosopher as equally false; and by
the magistrate as equally useful." "The fashion of in-
credulity was communicated from the philosopher to
the man of pleasure or business, from the noble to the
plebeian, and from the master to the menial slave who
waited at his table and who equally listened to the freedom
of his conversation." [2] Gibbon's idea of the happiest
period of mankind is interesting and characteristic. "If,"
he wrote, "a man were called to fix the period in the history
of the world during which the condition of the human
race was most happy and prosperous, he would, without
hesitation, name that which elapsed from the death of
Domitian to the accession of Commodus." [3] This period
was from A.D. 96 to 180, covering the reigns of Nerva,
Trajan, Hadrian, Antoninus Pius, and Marcus Aurelius.
Professor Carter, in a lecture in Rome in 1907, drew, by a
modern comparison, a characterization of the first three
named. When we were studying in Germany, he said,

[1] Smith's ed., I, 215, 371; II, 230.
[2] Ibid., I, 165; II, 205.   [3] Ibid., I, 216.

we were accustomed to sum up the three emperors, William I, Frederick III, and William II, as der greise Kaiser, der weise Kaiser, und der reise Kaiser. The characterizations will fit well Nerva, Trajan, and Hadrian. Gibbon speaks of the "restless activity" of Hadrian, whose life "was almost a perpetual journey," and who during his reign visited every province of his empire.[1]

A casual remark of Gibbon's, "Corruption [is] the most infallible symptom of constitutional liberty," [2] shows the sentiment of the eighteenth century. The generality of the history becomes specific in a letter to his father, who has given him hopes of a seat in Parliament. "This seat," so Edward Gibbon wrote, "according to the custom of our venal country was to be bought, and fifteen hundred pounds were mentioned as the price of purchase." [3]

Gibbon anticipated Captain Mahan. In speaking of a naval battle between the fleet of Justinian and that of the Goths in which the galleys of the Eastern empire gained a signal victory, he wrote, "The Goths affected to depreciate an element in which they were unskilled; but their own experience confirmed the truth of a maxim, that the master of the sea will always acquire the dominion of the land." [4] But Gibbon's anticipation was one of the frequent cases where the same idea has occurred to a number of men of genius, as doubtless Captain Mahan was not aware of this sentence any more than he was of Bacon's and Raleigh's epitomes of the theme which he has so originally and brilliantly treated.[5]

No modern historian has been the subject of so much critical comment as Gibbon. I do not know how it will

[1] Smith's ed., I, 144.   [3] Letters, I, 23.
[2] *Ibid.*, III, 78.   [4] Smith's ed., V, 230.
[5] See Mahan's From Sail to Steam, 276.

compare in volume with either of the similar examinations of Thucydides and Tacitus; but the criticism is of
a different sort. The only guarantee of the honesty of
Tacitus, wrote Sainte-Beuve, is Tacitus himself; [1] and a
like remark will apply to Thucydides. But a fierce light
beats on Gibbon. His voluminous notes furnish the
critics the materials on which he built his history, which,
in the case of the ancient historians, must be largely a
matter of conjecture. With all the searching examination of "The Decline and Fall," it is surprising how few
errors have been found and, of the errors which have been
noted, how few are really important. Guizot, Milman,
Dr. Smith, Cotter Morison, Bury, and a number of lesser
lights have raked his text and his notes with few momen-
tous results. We have, writes Bury, improved methods
over Gibbon and "much new material of various kinds,"
but "Gibbon's historical sense kept him constantly right
in dealing with his sources"; and "in the main things he
is still our master." [2] The man is generally reflected in
his book. That Gibbon has been weighed and not found
wanting is because he was as honest and truthful as any
man who ever wrote history. The autobiographies and
letters exhibit to us a transparent man, which indeed
some of the personal allusions in the history might have
foreshadowed. "I have often fluctuated and shall *tamely*
follow the Colbert Ms.," he wrote, where the authenticity
of a book was in question.[3] In another case "the scarcity
of facts and the uncertainty of dates" opposed his attempt
to describe the first invasion of Italy by Alaric.[4] In the
beginning of the famous Chapter XLIV which is "admired
by jurists as a brief and brilliant exposition of the principles

---

[1] Causeries du Lundi, I, 153.
[2] Introduction, xlv, l, lxvii.
[3] Smith's ed., III, 14.
[4] *Ibid.*, IV, 31.

of Roman law," [1] Gibbon wrote, "Attached to no party, interested only for the truth and candor of history, and directed by the most temperate and skillful guides, I enter with just diffidence on the subject of civil law." [2] In speaking of the state of Britain between 409 and 449, he said, "I owe it to myself and to historic truth to declare that some *circumstances* in this paragraph are founded only on conjecture and analogy." [3] Throughout his whole work the scarcity of materials forces Gibbon to the frequent use of conjecture, but I believe that for the most part his conjectures seem reasonable to the critics. Impressed with the correctness of his account of the Eastern empire a student of the subject once told me that Gibbon certainly possessed the power of wise divination.

Gibbon's striving after precision and accuracy is shown in some marginal corrections he made in his own printed copy of "The Decline and Fall." On the first page in his first printed edition and as it now stands, he said, "To deduce the most important circumstances of its decline and fall: a revolution which will ever be remembered and is still felt by the nations of the earth." For this the following is substituted: "To prosecute the decline and fall of the empire of Rome: of whose language, religions and laws the impression will be long preserved in our own and the neighboring countries of Europe." He thus explains the change: "Mr. Hume told me that, in correcting his history, he always labored to reduce superlatives and soften positives. Have Asia and Africa, from Japan to Morocco, any feeling or memory of the Roman Empire?"

On page 6, Bury's edition, the text is, "The praises of Alexander, transmitted by a succession of poets and his-

[1] Bury, lii.   [2] Smith's ed., V, 258.   [3] *Ibid.*, IV, 132 n.

torians, had kindled a dangerous emulation in the mind of Trajan." We can imagine that Gibbon reflected, What evidence have I that Trajan had read these poets and historians? Therefore he made this change: "Late generations and far distant climates may impute their calamities to the immortal author of the Iliad. The spirit of Alexander was inflamed by the praises of Achilles; and succeeding heroes have been ambitious to tread in the footsteps of Alexander. Like him, the Emperor Trajan aspired to the conquest of the East."[1]

The "advertisement" to the first octavo edition published in 1783 is an instance of Gibbon's truthfulness. He wrote, "Some alterations and improvements had presented themselves to my mind, but I was unwilling to injure or offend the purchasers of the preceding editions." Then he seems to reflect that this is not quite the whole truth, and adds, "Perhaps I may stand excused if, amidst the avocations of a busy winter, I have preferred the pleasures of composition and study to the minute diligence of revising a former publication."[2]

The severest criticism that Gibbon has received is on his famous chapters XV and XVI which conclude his first volume in the original quarto edition of 1776. We may disregard the flood of contemporary criticism from certain people who were excited by what they deemed an attack on the Christian religion. Dean Milman, who objected seriously to much in these chapters, consulted these various answers to Gibbon on the first appearance of his work with, according to his own confession, little profit.[3] "Against his celebrated fifteenth and sixteenth chapters," wrote Buckle, "all the devices of controversy have been

[1] Bury's ed., xxxv, xxxvi.   [2] Smith's ed., I, xxi.
[3] *Ibid.*, I, xvii.

exhausted; but the only result has been, that while the
fame of the historian is untarnished, the attacks of his
enemies are falling into complete oblivion. The work of
Gibbon remains; but who is there who feels any interest
in what was written against him?" [1] During the last
generation, however, criticism has taken another form
and scientific men now do not exactly share Buckle's
gleeful opinion. Both Bury and Cotter Morison state or
imply that well-grounded exceptions may be taken to
Gibbon's treatment of the early Christian church. He
ignored some facts; his combination of others, his in-
ferences, his opinions are not fair and unprejudiced. A
further grave objection may be made to the tone of these
two chapters: sarcasm pervades them and the Gibbon
sneer has become an apt characterization.

Francis Parkman admitted that he was a reverent ag-
nostic, and if Gibbon had been a reverent free-thinker,
these two chapters would have been far different in tone.
Lecky regarded the Christian church as a great institution worthy of reverence and respect although he stated
the central thesis of Gibbon with emphasis just as great.
Of the conversion of the Roman Empire to Christianity,
Lecky wrote, "it may be boldly asserted that the assumption of a moral or intellectual miracle is utterly gratuitous.
Never before was a religious transformation so manifestly
inevitable." [2] Gibbon's sneering tone was a characteristic
of his time. There existed during the latter part of the
eighteenth century, wrote Sir James Mackintosh, "an
unphilosophical and indeed fanatical animosity against
Christianity." But Gibbon's private defense is entitled
to consideration as placing him in a better light. "The
primitive church, which I have treated with some free-

[1] History of Civilization, II, 308 n.　　　　[2] Morals, I, 419.

dom," he wrote to Lord Sheffield in 1791, "was itself at that time an innovation, and I was attached to the old Pagan establishment." [1] "Had I believed," he said in his Autobiography, "that the majority of English readers were so fondly attached to the name and shadow of Christianity, had I foreseen that the pious, the timid, and the prudent would feel, or affect to feel, with such exquisite sensibility, I might perhaps have softened the two invidious chapters." [2]

On the other hand Gibbon's treatment of Julian the Apostate is in accordance with the best modern standard. It might have been supposed that a quasi-Pagan, as he avowed himself, would have emphasized Julian's virtues and ignored his weaknesses as did Voltaire, who invested him with all the good qualities of Trajan, Cato, and Julius Cæsar, without their defects.[3] Robertson indeed feared that he might fail in this part of the history; [4] but Gibbon weighed Julian in the balance, duly estimating his strength and his weakness, with the result that he has given a clear and just account in his best and most dignified style.[5]

Gibbon's treatment of Theodora, the wife of Justinian, is certainly open to objection. Without proper sifting and a reasonable skepticism, he has incorporated into his narrative the questionable account with all its salacious details which Procopius gives in his Secret History, Gibbon's love of a scandalous tale getting the better of his historical criticism. He has not neglected to urge a defense. "I am justified," he wrote, "in painting the manners of the times; the vices of Theodora form an essential feature in the reign and character of Justinian.

---

[1] Letters, II, 237. [2] Autobiography, 316. [3] Cotter Morison, 118
[4] Sainte-Beuve, 458. [5] Cotter Morison, 120.

. . . My English text is chaste, and all licentious passages are left in the obscurity of a learned language." [1] This explanation satisfies neither Cotter Morison nor Bury, nor would it hold for a moment as a justification of a historian of our own day. Gibbon is really so scientific, so much like a late nineteenth-century man, that we do right to subject him to our present-day rigid tests.

There has been much discussion about Gibbon's style, which we all know is pompous and Latinized. On a long reading his rounded and sonorous periods become wearisome, and one wishes that occasionally a sentence would terminate with a small word, even a preposition. One feels as did Dickens after walking for an hour or two about the handsome but "distractingly regular" city of Philadelphia. "I felt," he wrote, "that I would have given the world for a crooked street." [2] Despite the pomposity, Gibbon's style is correct, and the exact use of words is a marvel. It is rare, I think, that any substitution or change of words will improve upon the precision of the text. His compression and selection of salient points are remarkable. Amid some commonplace philosophy he frequently rises to a generalization as brilliant as it is truthful. Then, too, one is impressed with the dignity of history; one feels that Gibbon looked upon his work as very serious, and thought with Thucydides, "My history is an everlasting possession, not a prize composition which is heard and forgotten."

To a writer of history few things are more interesting than a great historian's autobiographical remarks which relate to the composition of his work. "Had I been more indigent or more wealthy," wrote Gibbon in his Autobiography, "I should not have possessed the leisure or

---

[1] Autobiography, 337 n.　　　[2] American Notes, Chap. VII.

the perseverance to prepare and execute my voluminous history." [1] "Notwithstanding the hurry of business and pleasure," he wrote from London in 1778, "I steal some moments for the Roman Empire." [2] Between the writing of the first three and the last three volumes, he took a rest of "near a twelvemonth" and gave expression to a thought which may be echoed by every studious writer, "Yet in the luxury of freedom, I began to wish for the daily task, the active pursuit which gave a value to every book and an object to every inquiry." [3] Every one who has written a historical book will sympathize with the following expression of personal experience as he approached the completion of "The Decline and Fall": "Let no man who builds a house or writes a book presume to say when he will have finished. When he imagines that he is drawing near to his journey's end, Alps rise on Alps, and he continually finds something to add and something to correct." [4]

Plain truthful tales are Gibbon's autobiographies. The style is that of the history, and he writes of himself as frankly as he does of any of his historical characters. His failings — what he has somewhere termed "the amiable weaknesses of human nature" — are disclosed with the openness of a Frenchman. All but one of the ten years between 1783 and 1793, between the ages of 46 and 56, he passed at Lausanne. There he completed "The Decline and Fall," and of that period he spent from August, 1787, to July, 1788, in England to look after the publication of the last three volumes. His life in Lausanne was one of study, writing, and agreeable society, of which his correspondence with his English friends gives an animated ac-

[1] p. 155.
[2] Letters, I, 331.

[3] Autobiography, 325.
[4] Letters, II, 143.

count. The two things one is most impressed with are his love for books and his love for Madeira. "Though a lover of society," he wrote, "my library is the room to which I am most attached." [1] While getting settled at Lausanne, he complains that his boxes of books "loiter on the road." [2] And then he harps on another string. "Good Madeira," he writes, "is now become essential to my health and reputation;" [3] yet again, "If I do not receive a supply of Madeira in the course of the summer, I shall be in great shame and distress." [4] His good friend in England, Lord Sheffield, regarded his prayer and sent him a hogshead of "best old Madeira" and a tierce, containing six dozen bottles of "finest Malmsey," and at the same time wrote: "You will remember that a hogshead is on his travels through the torrid zone for you. . . . No wine is meliorated to a greater degree by keeping than Madeira, and you latterly appeared so ravenous for it, that I must conceive you wish to have a stock." [5] Gibbon's devotion to Madeira bore its penalty. At the age of forty-eight he sent this account to his step-mother: "I was in hopes that my old Enemy the Gout had given over the attack, but the Villain, with his ally the winter, convinced me of my error, and about the latter end of March I found myself a prisoner in my library and my great chair. I attempted twice to rise, he twice knocked me down again and kept possession of both my feet and knees longer (I must confess) than he ever had done before." [6] Eager to finish his history, he lamented that his "long gout" lost him "three months in the spring." Thus as you go through his correspondence, you find that orders for Madeira and attacks of gout alternate with regularity.

[1] Letters, II, 130.   [2] Ibid., II, 89.   [3] Ibid., II, 211.
[4] Ibid., II, 217.   [5] Ibid., II, 232.   [6] Ibid., II, 129.

Gibbon apparently did not connect the two as cause and effect, as in his autobiography he charged his malady to his service in the Hampshire militia, when "the daily practice of hard and even excessive drinking" had sown in his constitution "the seeds of the gout." [1]

Gibbon has never been a favorite with women, owing largely to his account of his early love affair. While at Lausanne, he had heard much of "the wit and beauty and erudition of Mademoiselle Curchod" and when he first met her, he had reached the age of twenty. "I saw and loved," he wrote. "I found her learned without pedantry, lively in conversation, pure in sentiment, and elegant in manners. . . . She listened to the voice of truth and passion. . . . At Lausanne I indulged my dream of felicity"; and indeed he appeared to be an ardent lover. "He was seen," said a contemporary, "stopping country people near Lausanne and demanding at the point of a naked dagger whether a more adorable creature existed than Suzanne Curchod." [2] On his return to England, however, he soon discovered that his father would not hear of this alliance, and he thus related the sequence : "After a painful struggle, I yielded to my fate. . . . I sighed as a lover, I obeyed as a son." [3] From England he wrote to Mademoiselle Curchod breaking off the engagement. Perhaps it is because of feminine criticism that Cotter Morison indulges in an elaborate defense of Gibbon, which indeed hardly seems necessary. Rousseau, who was privy to the love affair, said that "Gibbon was too cold-blooded a young man for his taste or for Mademoiselle Curchod's happiness." [4] Mademoiselle Curchod a few years later married Necker, a rich Paris

[1] Letters, II, 189.   [2] Ibid., I, 40.
[3] Autobiography, pp. 151, 239.   [4] Letters, I, 41.

banker, who under Louis XVI held the office of director-general of the finances. She was the mother of Madame de Staël, was a leader of the literary society in Paris and, despite the troublous times, must have led a happy life. One delightful aspect of the story is the warm friendship that existed between Madame Necker and Edward Gibbon. This began less than a year after her marriage. "The Curchod (Madame Necker) I saw at Paris," he wrote to his friend Holroyd. "She was very fond of me and the husband particularly civil. Could they insult me more cruelly? Ask me every evening to supper; go to bed, and leave me alone with his wife — what an impertinent security!" [1]

If women read the Correspondence as they do the Autobiography, I think that their aversion to the great historian would be increased by these confiding words to his stepmother, written when he was forty-nine: "The habits of female conversation have sometimes tempted me to acquire the piece of furniture, a wife, and could I unite in a single Woman the virtues and accomplishments of half a dozen of my acquaintance, I would instantly pay my addresses to the Constellation." [2]

I have always been impressed with Gibbon's pride at being the author of "six volumes in quartos"; but as nearly all histories now are published in octavo, I had not a distinct idea of the appearance of a quarto volume until the preparation of this essay led me to look at different

[1] *Ibid.*, I, 81. In 1790 Madame de Staël, then at Coppet, wrote: "Nous possédons dans ce château M. Gibbon, l'ancien amoreux de ma mère, celui qui voulait l'épouser. Quand je le vois, je me demande si je serais née de son union avec ma mère : je me reponds que non et qu'il suffisait de mon père seul pour que je vinsse au monde." — Hill's ed. 107, n. 2.

[2] Letters, II, 143.

U

editions of Gibbon in the Boston Athenæum. There I found the quartos, the first volume of which is the third edition, published in 1777 [it will be remembered that the original publication of the first volume was in February, 1776]. The volume is $11\frac{1}{4}$ inches long by 9 inches wide and is much heavier than our very heavy octavo volumes. With this volume in my hand I could appreciate the remark of the Duke of Gloucester when Gibbon brought him the second volume of the "Decline and Fall." Laying the quarto on the table he said, "Another d—d thick square book! Always scribble, scribble, scribble! Eh! Mr. Gibbon?" [1]

During my researches at the Athenæum, I found an octavo edition, the first volume of which was published in 1791, and on the cover was written, "Given to the Athenæum by Charles Cabot. Received December 10, 1807." This was the year of the foundation of the Athenæum. On the quarto of 1777 there was no indication, but the scholarly cataloguer informed me that it was probably also received in 1807. Three later editions than these two are in this library, the last of which is Bury's of 1900 to which I have constantly referred. Meditating in the quiet alcove, with the two early editions of Gibbon before me, I found an answer to the comment of H. G. Wells in his book "The Future in America" which I confess had somewhat irritated me. Thus wrote Wells: "Frankly I grieve over Boston as a great waste of leisure and energy, as a frittering away of moral and intellectual possibilities. We give too much to the past. . . . We are obsessed by the scholastic prestige of mere knowledge and genteel remoteness." [2] Pondering this iconoclastic utterance, how delightful it is to light upon evidence in

[1] Birkbeck Hill's ed., 127.   [2] p. 235.

the way of well-worn volumes that, since 1807, men and women here have been carefully reading Gibbon, who, as Dean Milman said, "has bridged the abyss between ancient and modern times and connected together the two worlds of history." [1] A knowledge of "The Decline and Fall" is a basis for the study of all other history; it is a mental discipline, and a training for the problems of modern life. These Athenæum readers did not waste their leisure, did not give too much to the past. They were supremely right to take account of the scholastic prestige of Gibbon, and to endeavor to make part of their mental fiber this greatest history of modern times.

I will close with a quotation from the Autobiography which in its sincerity and absolute freedom from literary cant will be cherished by all whose desire is to behold "the bright countenance of truth in the quiet and still air of delightful studies." "I have drawn a high prize in the lottery of life," wrote Gibbon. "I am disgusted with the affectation of men of letters, who complain that they have renounced a substance for a shadow and that their fame affords a poor compensation for envy, censure, and persecution. My own experience at least has taught me a very different lesson: twenty happy years have been animated by the labor of my history; and its success has given me a name, a rank, a character in the world, to which I should not otherwise have been entitled. . . . D'Alembert relates that as he was walking in the gardens of Sanssouci with the King of Prussia, Frederick said to him, 'Do you see that old woman, a poor weeder, asleep on that sunny bank? She is probably a more happy Being than either of us.'" Now the comment of Gibbon: "The King and the Philosopher may speak for themselves; for my part I do not envy the old woman." [2]

[1] Smith's ed., I, vii.   [2] Autobiography, 343, 346.

THE MILDNESS OF THE YELLOW PRESS [1]

BY

GILBERT K. CHESTERTON

Obviously the danger in the catalogue form lies in the even distribution of emphasis. Since the reader may at any moment lay the essay aside with the thought complete up to that point, it often happens that he does so before finishing the essay. Therefore an author is apt to try to conceal the catalogue. This is done most successfully by Mr. Chesterton in his attack upon the "yellow" type of journalism. He wishes to tell us that in his opinion "yellow" journalism is mediocre, timid, infantile, and unrepresentative. To attract attention, however, he begins with the paradox that such journalism is not sufficiently sensational. This thought, when developed, leads naturally to a discussion of other weaknesses. The whole is flooded by concrete illustration. As such illustration is chosen with a desire to make the object of the attack ridiculous, and as it serves as almost the only support for statements made authoritatively, the essay is clever rather than profound. Yet it is so clever that the reader, without thinking, tends to accept his conclusion.

THERE is a great deal of protest made from one quarter or another nowadays against the influence of that new journalism which is associated with the names of Sir Alfred Harmsworth and Mr. Pearson. But almost everybody who attacks it attacks on the ground that it is very sensational, very violent and vulgar and startling. I am speaking in no affected contrariety, but in the simplicity of a genuine personal impression, when I say that this journalism offends as being not sensational or violent

[1] From "Heretics," by permission of the publishers, John Lane Co.

enough. The real vice is not that it is startling, but that
it is quite insupportably tame. The whole object is to
keep carefully along a certain level of the expected and the
commonplace; it may be low, but it must take care also
to be flat. Never by any chance in it is there any of that
real plebeian pungency which can be heard from the ordinary cabman in the ordinary street. We have heard of
a certain standard of decorum which demands that things
should be funny without being vulgar, but the standard of
this decorum demands that if things are vulgar they shall
be vulgar without being funny. This journalism does not
merely fail to exaggerate life — it positively underrates
it; and it has to do so because it is intended for the faint
and languid recreation of men whom the fierceness of
modern life has fatigued. This press is not the yellow
press at all; it is the drab press. Sir Alfred Harmsworth
must not address to the tired clerk any observation more
witty than the tired clerk might be able to address to Sir
Alfred Harmsworth. It must not expose anybody (anybody who is powerful, that is), it must not offend anybody,
it must not even please anybody, too much. A general
vague idea that in spite of all this, our yellow press is
sensational, arises from such external accidents as large
type or lurid headlines. It is quite true that these editors
print everything they possibly can in large capital letters.
But they do this, not because it is startling, but because
it is soothing. To people wholly weary or partly drunk in
a dimly lighted train, it is a simplification and a comfort
to have things presented in this vast and obvious manner.
The editors use this gigantic alphabet in dealing with their
readers, for exactly the same reason that parents and gov-
ernesses use a similar gigantic alphabet in teaching children
to spell. The nursery authorities do not use an A as big as

a horseshoe in order to make the child jump; on the contrary, they use it to put the child at his ease, to make things smoother and more evident. Of the same character is the dim and quiet dame school which Sir Alfred Harmsworth and Mr. Pearson keep. All their sentiments are spelling-book sentiments — that is to say, they are sentiments with which the pupil is already respectfully familiar. All their wildest posters are leaves torn from a copy-book.

Of real sensational journalism, as it exists in France, in Ireland, and in America, we have no trace in this country. When a journalist in Ireland wishes to create a thrill, he creates a thrill worth talking about. He denounces a leading Irish member for corruption, or he charges the whole police system with a wicked and definite conspiracy. When a French journalist desires a *frisson* there is a *frisson;* he discovers, let us say, that the President of the Republic has murdered three wives. Our yellow journalists invent quite as unscrupulously as this; their moral condition is, as regards careful veracity, about the same. But it is their mental calibre which happens to be such that they can only invent calm and even reassuring things. The fictitious version of the massacre of the envoys of Pekin was mendacious, but it was not interesting, except to those who had private reasons for terror or sorrow. It was not connected with any bold and suggestive view of the Chinese situation. It revealed only a vague idea that nothing could be impressive except a great deal of blood. Real sensationalism, of which I happen to be very fond, may be either moral or immoral. But even when it is most immoral, it requires moral courage. For it is one of the most dangerous things on earth genuinely to surprise anybody. If you make any sentient creature jump, you render it by no means improbable that it will jump on you. But the leaders of this movement have no moral courage or immoral courage; their whole method consists in saying, with large and elaborate emphasis, the things which everybody else says casually, and without remembering what they have said. When they brace themselves up to attack anything, they never reach the point of attacking anything which is large and real, and would resound with the shock. They do not attack the army as men do in France, or the judges as men do in Ireland, or the democracy itself as men did in England a hundred years ago. They attack something like the War Office — something, that is, which everybody attacks and nobody bothers to defend, something which is an old joke in fourth-rate comic papers. Just as a man shows he has a weak voice by straining it to shout, so they show the hopelessly unsensational nature of their minds when they really try to be sensational. With the whole world full of big and dubious institutions, with the whole wickedness of civilization staring them in the face, their idea of being bold and bright is to attack the War Office. They might as well start a campaign against the weather, or form a secret society in order to make jokes about mothers-in-law. Nor is it only from the point of view of particular amateurs of the sensational such as myself, that it is permissible to say, in the words of Cowper's Alexander Selkirk, that "their tameness is shocking to me." The whole modern world is pining for a genuinely sensational journalism. This has been discovered by that very able and honest journalist, Mr. Blatchford, who started his campaign against Christianity, warned on all sides, I believe, that it would ruin his paper, but who continued from an honourable sense of intellectual responsibility. He discovered, however, that while he had undoubtedly shocked his readers, he had also greatly advanced his newspaper. It was bought — first, by all the people who agreed with him and wanted to read it; and secondly, by all the people who disagreed with him, and wanted to write him letters. Those letters were voluminous (I helped, I am glad to say, to swell their volume), and they were generally inserted with a generous fulness. Thus was accidentally discovered (like the steam engine) the great journalistic maxim — that if an editor can only make people angry enough, they will write half his newspaper for him for nothing.

Some hold that such papers as these are scarcely the proper objects of so serious a consideration; but that can scarcely be maintained from a political or ethical point of view. In this problem of the mildness and tameness of the Harmsworth mind there is mirrored the outlines of a much larger problem which is akin to it.

The Harmsworthian journalist begins with a worship of success and violence, and ends in sheer timidity and mediocrity. But he is not alone in this, nor does he come by this fate merely because he happens personally to be stupid. Every man, however brave, who begins by worshipping violence, must end in mere timidity. Every man, however wise, who begins by worshipping success, must end in mere mediocrity. This strange and paradoxical fate is involved, not in the individual, but in the philosophy, in the point of view. It is not the folly of the man which brings about this necessary fall; it is his wisdom. The worship of success is the only one out of all possible worships of which this is true, that its followers are foredoomed to become slaves and cowards. A man may be a hero for the sake of Mrs. Gallup's ciphers or for the sake of human sacrifice, but not for the sake of success. For obviously a man may choose to fail because he loves

Mrs. Gallup or human sacrifice; but he cannot choose to fail because he loves success. When the test of triumph is men's test of everything, they never endure long enough to triumph at all. As long as matters are really hopeful, hope is a mere flattery or platitude; it is only when everything is hopeless that hope begins to be a strength at all. Like all the Christian virtues, it is as unreasonable as it is indispensable.

It was through this fatal paradox in the nature of things that all these modern adventurers come at last to a sort of tedium and acquiescence. They desired strength; and to them to desire strength was to admire strength; to admire strength was simply to admire the *statu quo*. They thought that he who wished to be strong ought to respect the strong. They did not realize the obvious verity that he who wishes to be strong must despise the strong. They sought to be everything, to have the whole force of the cosmos behind them, to have an energy that would drive the stars. But they did not realize the two great facts — first, that in the attempt to be everything the first and most difficult step is to be something; second, that the moment a man is something, he is essentially defying everything. The lower animals, say the men of science, fought their way up with a blind selfishness. If this be so, the only real moral of it is that our unselfishness, if it is to triumph, must be equally blind. The mammoth did not put his head on one side and wonder whether mammoths were a little out of date. Mammoths were at least as much up to date as that individual mammoth could make them. The great elk did not say, "Cloven hoofs are very much worn now." He polished his own weapons for his own use. But in the reasoning animal there has arisen a more horrible danger, that he may fail through perceiving his own failure. When modern sociologists talk of the necessity of accommodating one's self to the trend of the time, they forget that the trend of the time at its best consists entirely of people who will not accommodate themselves to anything. At its worst it consists of many millions of frightened creatures all accommodating themselves to a trend that is not there. And that is becoming more and more the situation of modern England. Every man speaks of public opinion, and means by public opinion, public opinion minus his opinion. Every man makes his contribution negative under the erroneous impression that the next man's contribution is positive. Every man surrenders his fancy to a general tone which is itself a surrender. And over all the heartless and fatuous unity spreads this new and wearisome and platitudinous press, incapable of invention, incapable of audacity, capable only of a servility all the more contemptible because it is not even a servility to the strong. But all who begin with force and conquest will end in this.

The chief characteristic of the "New Journalism" is simply that it is bad journalism. It is beyond all comparison the most shapeless, careless, and colourless work done in our day.

I read yesterday a sentence which should be written in letters of gold and adamant; it is the very motto of the new philosophy of Empire. I found it (as the reader has already eagerly guessed) in *Pearson's Magazine*, while I was communing (soul to soul) with Mr. C. Arthur Pearson, whose first and suppressed name I am afraid is Chilperic. It occurred in an article on the American Presidential Election. This is the sentence, and every one should read it carefully, and roll it on the tongue, till all the honey be tasted.

"A little sound common sense often goes further with an audience of American working-men than much high-flown argument. A speaker who, as he brought forward his points, hammered nails into a board, won hundreds of votes for his side at the last Presidential Election."

I do not wish to soil this perfect thing with comment; the words of Mercury are harsh after the songs of Apollo. But just think for a moment of the mind, the strange inscrutable mind, of the man who wrote that, of the editor who approved it, of the people who are probably impressed by it, of the incredible American working-man, of whom, for all I know, it may be true. Think what their notion of "common sense" must be! It is delightful to realize that you and I are now able to win thousands of votes should we ever be engaged in a Presidential Election, by doing something of this kind. For I suppose the nails and the board are not essential to the exhibition of "common sense"; there may be variations. We may read —

"A little common sense impresses American working-men more than high-flown argument. A speaker who, as he made his points, pulled buttons off his waistcoat, won thousands of votes for his side."

Or,

"Sound common sense tells better in America than high-flown argument. Thus Senator Budge, who threw his false teeth in the air every time he made an epigram, won the solid approval of American working-men."

Or again,

"The sound common sense of a gentleman from Earlswood, who stuck straws in his hair during the progress of his speech, assured the victory of Mr. Roosevelt."

There are many other elements in this article on which I should love to linger. But the matter which I wish to point out is that in that sentence is perfectly revealed the

whole truth of what our Chamberlainites, hustlers, bus-
tlers, Empire builders, and strong, silent men, really mean
by "common sense." They mean knocking, with deafen-
ing noise and dramatic effect, meaningless bits of iron into
a useless bit of wood.

A man who goes on to an American platform and
behaves like a mountebank fool with a board and a hammer; well, I do not blame him; I might even admire
him. He may be a dashing and quite decent strategist.
He may be a fine romantic actor, like Burke flinging the
dagger on the floor. He may even (for all I know) be a
sublime mystic, profoundly impressed with the ancient
meaning of the divine trade of the Carpenter, and offering
to the people a parable in the form of a ceremony. All I
wish to indicate is the abyss of mental confusion in which
such wild ritualism can be called "sound common sense."
And it is in that abyss of mental confusion, and in that
alone, that the new Imperialism lives and moves and has
its being. The whole glory and greatness of Mr. Chamberlain consists in this: that if a man hits the right nail
on the head nobody cares where he hits it to or what it
does. They care about the noise of the hammer, not
about the silent grip of the nail. Before and throughout
the African war, Mr. Chamberlain was always knocking
in nails, with ringing decisiveness. But when we ask,
"But what have these nails held together? Where is
your carpentry? Where are your contented Outlanders?
Where is your free South Africa? Where is your British
prestige? What have your nails done?" then what
answer is there? We must go back (with an affectionate
sigh) to our Pearson for the answer to the question of
what the nails have done: "The speaker who hammered
nails into a board won thousands of votes."

Now the whole of this passage is admirably characteristic of the new journalism which Mr. Pearson represents, the new journalism which has just purchased the *Standard*. To take one instance out of hundreds, the incomparable man with the board and nails is described in the *Pearson's* article as calling out (as he smote the symbolic nail), "Lie number one. Nailed to the Mast! Nailed to the Mast!" In the whole office there was apparently no compositor or office-boy to point out that we speak of lies being nailed to the counter, and not to the mast. Nobody in the office knew that *Pearson's Magazine* was falling into a stale Irish bull, which must be as old as St. Patrick. This is the real and essential tragedy of the sale of the *Standard*. It is not merely that journalism is victorious over good literature. It is that bad journalism is victorious over good journalism.

It is not that one article which we consider costly and beautiful is being ousted by another kind of article which we consider common or unclean. It is that of the same article a worse quality is preferred to a better. If you like popular journalism (as I do), you will know that *Pearson's Magazine* is poor and weak popular journalism. You will know it as certainly as you know bad butter. You will know as certainly that it is poor popular journalism as you know that the *Strand*, in the great days of Sherlock Holmes, was good popular journalism. Mr. Pearson has been a monument of this enormous banality. About everything he says and does there is something infinitely weak-minded. He clamours for home trades and employs foreign ones to print his paper. When this glaring fact is pointed out, he does not say that the thing was an oversight, like a sane man. He cuts it off with scissors, like a child of three. His very cunning is infantile. And like a child of three, he does not cut it quite off. In all human records I doubt if there is such an example of a profound simplicity in deception. This is the sort of intelligence which now sits in the seat of the sane and honourable old Tory journalism. If it were really the triumph of the tropical exuberance of the Yankee press, it would be vulgar, but still tropical. But it is not. We are delivered over to the bramble, and from the meanest of the shrubs comes the fire upon the cedars of Lebanon.

The only question now is how much longer the fiction will endure that journalists of this order represent public opinion. It may be doubted whether any honest and serious Tariff Reformer would for a moment maintain that there was any majority for Tariff Reform in the country comparable to the ludicrous preponderance which money has given it among the great dailies. The only inference is that for purposes of real public opinion the press is now a mere plutocratic oligarchy. Doubtless the public buys the wares of these men, for one reason or another. But there is no more reason to suppose that the public admires their politics than that the public admires the delicate philosophy of Mr. Crosse or the darker and sterner creed of Mr. Blackwell. If these men are merely tradesmen, there is nothing to say except that there are plenty like them in the Battersea Park Road, and many much better. But if they make any sort of attempt to be politicians, we can only point out to them that they are not as yet even good journalists.

WHAT IS EDUCATION?[1]

BY

CHARLES MACOMB FLANDRAU

A curious, and clever, modification of the catalogue appears in Mr. Flandrau's essay. By a series of eliminations he shows what education is *not*, tying it all together with the negative that knowledge is not wisdom. This he does by a continued use of the interrogation. And the answers to his questions show no thoroughfare. Notice also the extreme use of the device of the writer speaking in the first person. This enables him to illustrate his points by his personal experiences. The result is that he has written a sparklingly delightful essay upon one of the most dreary subjects in the world, — and incidentally charged a number of educational windmills.

BOOKS, the titles of which are interrogatory, always have a fascination for me. "What is Ibsenism?" "Can You Forgive Her?" "What Shall We Do With Our Girls?" for instance. Of course, they are invariably unsatisfactory and, sometimes, exasperating. They never really answer the questions they propound, and they leave one somewhat more muddled than one was before. Tolstoi's "What is Art?" is a most bigoted and tedious performance. In it one of the greatest artists of modern times elaborately tells one nothing whatever about art, and leaves one with the impression that his claim on immortality is something of which he has become very much ashamed. But, crafty old person though I be, I succumb to them all, and read them because I can't resist a title in the form of a question.

[1] From "Prejudices," by permission of D. Appleton & Co.

303

At present, I am longing for someone to write a book and call it "What is Education?" What, as a matter of fact, *is* education? Every few days someone, in endeavoring to describe and sum up someone else, ends with the clinching statement : "And the strange part of it was that he was a man, or she was a woman, of education." This is supposed to settle the matter — to arouse in one's mind a definite image. "He was a man of education," apparently means something, but what? To me it has come to mean nothing at all. A short time ago I read in the morning paper of a dead body that had been found in the river and taken to the county morgue. "All means of identification had been removed," wrote the reporter, in commenting on the incident, "but," he added, "the body was evidently that of a man of education." And, to me, the remarkable part of this was that the reporter, without doubt, had a hazy idea of what he was trying to express. In the poor, dead, unidentified thing he had discovered and recognized something that, to him, implied "education," but how he did it, and what it was, I don't know, because he did not explain.

There are in this connection all sorts of questions I hope the author of the book, to which I look forward, will answer. Is, for instance, "a man of education" the same as "an educated man"? Or is one, perhaps, somewhat more — well, more educated than the other? At times both these phrases sound to me as if they meant precisely the same thing, and then again they suddenly, through no wish of mine, develop subtle but important differences that cause first the one and then the other to seem expressive of a higher, a more comprehensive, form of education. Then, too, is there any particular point at which education leaves off and "cultivation" begins?

And can a person be "cultivated" without being educated? The words education and cultivation are constantly upon the American tongue, but what do they mean? Or, do they mean something entirely different to everyone who employs them? Every American girl who flirts her way through the high school is "educated," and it would be indeed a brave man who dared to suggest that she wasn't. But is she? (Heaven forbid that *I* should suggest anything; I merely crave information.) And here let me hasten to add that a friend of mine has always maintained, quite seriously, that he likes me in spite of the fact that I am, as he expresses it, "one of the most illiterate persons" of his acquaintance. His acquaintance, it is some slight comfort to remember, is not large, and he is a doctor of philosophy who lectures at one of the great English universities. Not only has he read and studied much, his memory is appalling; he has never forgotten anything. From his point of view I am not "an educated person." But then, in the opinion of Macaulay, Addison was sadly lacking in cultivation! "He does not appear to have attained more than an ordinary acquaintance with the political and moral writers of Rome; nor was his own Latin prose by any means equal to his Latin verse," Macaulay complains in the *Edinburgh Review* in 1843. And while Macaulay admits that "Great praise is due to the notes which Addison appended to his version of the second and third books of the Metamorphoses," and confesses them to be "rich in apposite references to Virgil, Statius and Claudian," he cannot understand anyone's failing to allude to Euripides and Theocritus, waxes indignant over the fact that Addison quoted more from Ausonius and Manilius than from Cicero, and feels positively hurt at his having cited "the languid hexameters of Silius Italicus," rather than the "authentic narrative of Polybius." In Rome and Florence — Macaulay continues, more in sorrow than in anger — Addison saw all the best ancient works of art, "without recalling one single verse of Pindar, of Callimachus, or of the Attic dramatists."

Of course all this is very sad and leaves us quite cross with Addison for having deluded us into believing him to be a person of considerable erudition. How *could* anybody in the presence of a statue be so absent-minded as not to recall a single verse of Pindar or Callimachus? And how hopelessly superficial must be the mind that actually prefers the languid hexameters of Silius Italicus to the authentic narrative of Polybius! Yet, on the other hand, if we casually referred to Polybius while conversing with most of our educated and even so-called cultivated acquaintances, how many of them, I wonder, would know whether we were talking about a Greek historian or a patent medicine. Macaulay would have considered them hopeless; we (and they) are in the habit (perhaps it is a very bad habit — I don't know) of regarding them as educated.

Another question that my suppositious author must devote a chapter to, is the difference between just an education and a "liberal" education. We used to hear much more about a "liberal" education than we do now, although Prexy Eliot has of late endeavored to restore the phrase as well as the thing itself. When does an education leave off being penurious, so to speak, and become liberal? According to Mr. Eliot, Milton's "Areopagitica" helps a lot. I once read Milton's "Areopagitica" ("but not for love") with great care, and when I had finished it I had to procure at much trouble and expense another book (written some hundreds of years later) that told me what it was all about. The next day I passed an examination in the subject — and to-day I couldn't, if my life were at stake, recall the nature or the purpose of the work in question or even explain the meaning of the title. It is possible, of course, that this is more my fault than Milton's, but whoever is to blame, I can truthfully say that never before or since have I read anything so completely uninteresting or that contributed so little to the liberality of my education. In Mr. Eliot's opinion, however, and no one more firmly believes in the soundness of Mr. Eliot's opinions than I do, this ghastly, unintelligible, jaw-breaking relic of the seventeenth century is, if not absolutely essential to a liberal education, at least highly conducive to one. What on earth does it all signify?

Some persons pin their entire faith to a correct use of the pronouns *I* and *me*. They cheerfully commit every other form of linguistic violence, but as long as they can preserve sufficient presence of mind boldly to say once in so often something like, "He left James and me behind," instead of resorting to the cowardly "James and myself." or the elegantly ungrammatical "James and I," they feel that their educational integrity has been preserved. Others believe that education and true refinement begin and end with always saying, "You would better," instead of "You had better," while Mr. Eliot, in musing on the career cf Mr. Roosevelt, no doubt remarks to himself, "An estimable, even an interesting man, but is he, after all, conversant with the 'Areopagitica'?" (I hate to admit it, but I think it highly probable that he is.) And Macaulay, in the book review from which I have quoted, disposes once and for all of a certain scholar named

Blackmore — rips open his intellectual back, in fact, by stating with dignified disgust: "Of Blackmore's attainments in the ancient tongues, it may be sufficient to say that, in his prose, he has confounded an aphorism with an apothegm." Isn't it all wonderful? And doesn't it make you wish that someone would write a work called, "What is Education?" so you could find out whether you were educated or not?

Of late I have begun to have an ineradicable conviction that I am not — and this, not because I have a perverse fondness for the "languid" vocabulary of Silius Italicus (of whom, of course, I never had heard) but because I apparently know so little about the idiom that, by inheritance and environment, I am privileged to call my own. Not long ago, in reading a passage of excellent English prose, I came across a word that suddenly, as words have a devilish way of doing, stood out from the page and challenged me. The word was "nadir." "At this period he was at the nadir of his fortunes," was, I think, the sentence in which it occurred, and from the context I was able to divine not the exact meaning of the term, but the general idea it expressed. It meant, I could see, that the person in question had experienced a run of bad luck, that his affairs, for the time being, were in anything but a prosperous condition. But this was very far from knowing the specific meaning of the word "nadir." It was obviously a noun, and a simple-looking little creature at that, yet I neither knew how to pronounce it nor what it meant. So I made a note of it, intending, later, to inform myself. Further on, I came to the word "apogee," a familiar combination of letters that suddenly appeared to be perfectly absurd. The gentlemen referred to was now no longer at the nadir of his fortunes — he was at the "apo-

gee" of them, and, of course, I was able to guess that
something agreeable had happened to him of late. But
what, after all, was an apogee? I had often read the
word before, and I feel sure that it may be found here and
there among my "complete works," employed with an
air of authority. But, upon my soul, I didn't know what
it meant, and, therefore, virtuously made another little
note.

Once started upon this mad career of disillusionment,
there seemed to be absolutely no end to it, and I read on
and on, no longer for the pleasure of reading, but more
because the book had become like one of those electric
machines with metal handles, where, after turning on the
current with a cent, you hang on in interesting agony
because you can't let go. "Not one jot nor tittle!" I
groaned as I wrote it down. "Jot" as a verb, conveyed
something to me, but what was it when it became a noun?
And what sort of a thing, for heaven's sake, was a "tittle"?
It sounded more like a kitchen utensil than anything else.
(Polly, put the tittle on — No, that wouldn't do.) And
why, also, were jots and tittles such inseparable companions? In all my life I had never met a solitary
tittle — a tittle walking about alone, so to speak, unaccompanied by a devoted jot. Why was it that when
I did meet them, hand in hand, as usual, I didn't know
what they were?

By this time I was beginning to be verbally groggy.
What, I wondered, was — or, rather, wasn't — "a scintilla of evidence"? (For, oddly enough, one is never
informed that there *is* a scintilla of evidence, but merely
that there isn't.) And just how did it happen, in the
first place, that a lack of evidence should have been called
a "scintilla," whereas a certain kind of expensive gray

fur was called a "chinchilla." Scintilla chinchilla, scintilla chinchilla — the jury was unable to find a chinchilla of evidence, although Mrs. Vasterbolt was present
at the trial in a handsome coat of the costliest scintilla.
Why not? But as madness seemed to be lurking in that
direction, I hastened feverishly on to "adamant." Oh,
yes, I know it's something very hard and unyielding and,
in the kind of novels that no one reads any more, someone
is, at a critical moment, always "as" it — never "like"
it. But what is it? It might be some sort of a mytho-
logical cliff against which people were supposed ineffect-
ually to have hurled themselves; it might be a kind of
metal, or a particularly durable precious stone, or a satisfactory species of paving material. It might be any old
thing; I don't know. What in the dickens does it mean
to "dree your own weird"? For, as I almost tore off a
page in my anxiety to turn it, my eyes caught sight of:
"'Everyone must dree his own weird,' she answered, senten-
tiously." Early in life it had dawned on me that to be
told you must "dree your own weird" was merely a more
obscure and delicate fashion of telling you that you must
"skin your own skunk"; and yet I very much doubt if
the verb "to dree" means to skin, or if "weird," used as
a noun, has much connection with the fragrant little
denizen of our forests whom we all, I trust, are accustomed
to refer to as the *mephitis Americana*.

On and on I toiled for another hour, at the end of which
time I had a formidable list of ordinary words belonging
to my own language, as to whose real meaning I was
completely in the dark. To-day I intended to look them
all up and write a charming little paper on them, primarily
designed, of course, to make dear reader gasp at the scope
and thoroughness of my education. But the day is

indescribably hot, and, as I have been away, my dictionary, unfortunately, is gritty with dust. To get up and
slap at the corpulent thing with a damp towel would be
most repulsive. I shan't do it. Instead I shall recall
that the most intellectual nation in the world has a saying
to the effect that, "*On peut être fort instruit sans avoir
d'éducation.*"

WHY A CLASSIC IS A CLASSIC [1]

BY

ARNOLD BENNETT

In one section of his handbook on *Literary Taste*, Mr. Arnold Bennett wishes his readers to realize that the first essential to literary taste is an enjoyment of literature. That conception is his objective point. Therefore as in an argument, he starts with the generalization that the majority of people are indifferent to literature. This he assumes. But if this be true, the reputation of a great author must depend not upon the majority but upon the passionate minority. This is the case also with the posthumous reputation. But the minority are thus passionate because of the intensity of their enjoyment. Therefore, the first essential to literary taste is an enjoyment of literature. From this very brief analysis it is clear that the essay is conceived as a whole, and that each paragraph is a step to a predetermined end. Contrast this method with that used in the essay on *Tact* by Lord Avebury. Here, having granted the first premise, the reader is carried irresistibly to the final conclusion. Clearly this type of essay is more difficult to write and requires careful thought before composition is begun, but it is equally clear that it is more convincing.

THE large majority of our fellow-citizens care as much about literature as they care about aeroplanes or the programme of the Legislature. They do not ignore it; they are not quite indifferent to it. But their interest in it is faint and perfunctory; or, if their interest happens to be violent, it is spasmodic. Ask the two hundred thousand persons whose enthusiasm made the vogue of

[1] From "Literary Taste; How to Form It," by permission of George H. Doran Co.

a popular novel ten years ago what they think of that novel now, and you will gather that they have utterly forgotten it, and that they would no more dream of reading it again than of reading Bishop Stubbs's *Select Charters*. Probably if they did read it again they would not enjoy it — not because the said novel is a whit worse now than it was ten years ago; not because their taste has improved — but because they have not had sufficient practice to be able to rely on their taste as a means of permanent pleasure. They simply don't know from one day to the next what will please them.

*　　*　　*　　*　　*　　*　　*

In the face of this one may ask: Why does the great and universal fame of classical authors continue? The answer is that the fame of classical authors is entirely independent of the majority. Do you suppose that if the fame of Shakespeare depended on the man in the street it would survive a fortnight? The fame of classical authors is orginally made, and it is maintained, by a passionate few. Even when a first-class author has enjoyed immense success during his lifetime, the majority have never appreciated him so sincerely as they have appreciated second-rate men. He has always been reënforced by the ardour of the passionate few. And in the case of an author who has emerged into glory after his death the happy sequel has been due solely to the obstinate perseverance of the few. They could not leave him alone; they would not. They kept on savouring him, and talking about him, and buying him, and they generally behaved with such eager zeal, and they were so authoritative and sure of themselves, that at last the majority grew accustomed to the sound of his name and placidly agreed to the proposition that he was a genius; the majority really did not care very much either way.

*   *   *   *   *   *   *

And it is by the passionate few that the renown of genius is kept alive from one generation to another. These few are always at work. They are always rediscovering genius. Their curiosity and enthusiasm are exhaustless, so that there is little chance of genius being ignored. And, moreover, they are always working either for or against the verdicts of the majority. The majority can make a reputation, but it is too careless to maintain it. If, by accident, the passionate few agree with the majority in a particular instance, they will frequently remind the majority that such and such a reputation has been made, and the majority will idly concur: "Ah, yes. By the way, we must not forget that such and such a reputation exists." Without that persistent memory-jogging the reputation would quickly fall into the oblivion which is death. The passionate few only have their way by reason of the fact that they are genuinely interested in literature, that literature matters to them. They conquer by their obstinacy alone, by their eternal repetition of the same statements. Do you suppose they could prove to the man in the street that Shakespeare was a great artist? The said man would not even understand the terms they employed. But when he is told ten thousand times, and generation after generation, that Shakespeare was a great artist, the said man believes — not by reason, but by faith. And he too repeats that Shakespeare was a great artist, and he buys the complete works of Shakespeare and puts them on his shelves, and he goes to see the marvellous stage-effects which accompany *King Lear* or *Hamlet*, and comes back religiously convinced that Shakespeare was a great artist. All because the passionate few could not keep their admiration of Shakespeare to themselves. This is not cynicism; but truth. And it is important that those who wish to form their literary taste should grasp it.

* * * * * * *

What causes the passionate few to make such a fuss about literature? There can be only one reply. They find a keen and lasting pleasure in literature. They enjoy literature as some men enjoy beer. The recurrence of this pleasure naturally keeps their interest in literature very much alive. They are for ever making new researches, for ever practising on themselves. They learn to understand themselves. They learn to know what they want. Their taste becomes surer and surer as their experience lengthens. They do not enjoy to-day what will seem tedious to them to-morrow. When they find a book tedious, no amount of popular clatter will persuade them that it is pleasurable; and when they find it pleasurable no chill silence of the street-crowds will affect their conviction that the book is good and permanent. They have faith in themselves. What are the qualities in a book which give keen and lasting pleasure to the passionate few? This is a question so difficult that it has never yet been completely answered. You may talk lightly about truth, insight, knowledge, wisdom, humour, and beauty. But these comfortable words do not really carry you very far, for each of them has to be defined, especially the first and last. It is all very well for Keats in his airy manner to assert that beauty is truth, truth beauty, and that that is all he knows or needs to know. I, for one, need to know a lot more. And I never shall know. Nobody,

not even Hazlitt nor Sainte-Beuve, has ever finally ex‹
plained why he thought a book beautiful. I take the
first fine lines that come to hand —

> The woods of Arcady are dead,
> And over is their antique joy —

and I say that those lines are beautiful because they give
me pleasure. But why? No answer! I only know that
the passionate few will, broadly, agree with me in deriving
this mysterious pleasure from those lines.   I am only convinced that the liveliness of our pleasure in those and many
other lines by the same author will ultimately cause the
majority to believe, by faith, that W. B. Yeats is a genius.
The one reassuring aspect of the literary affair is that the
passionate few are passionate about the same things.   A
continuance of interest does, in actual practice, lead ultimately to the same judgments.   There is only the difference in width of interest.   Some of the passionate few
lack catholicity, or, rather, the whole of their interest is
confined to one narrow channel; they have none left
over.   These men help specially to vitalise the reputations of the narrower geniuses: such as Crashaw.   But
their active predilections never contradict the general
verdict of the passionate few; rather they reinforce it.

    *   *   *   *   *   *   *

A classic is a work which gives pleasure to the minority
which is intensely and permanently interested in literature.
It lives on because the minority, eager to renew the sensation of pleasure, is eternally curious and is therefore engaged
in an eternal process of rediscovery.   A classic does not
survive for any ethical reason.   It does not survive because it conforms to certain canons, or because neglect

would not kill it. It survives because it is a source of pleasure, and because the passionate few can no more neglect it than a bee can neglect a flower. The passionate few do not read "the right things" because they are right. That is to put the cart before the horse. "The right things" are the right things solely because the passionate few *like* reading them. Hence — and I now arrive at my point — the one primary essential to literary taste is a hot interest in literature. If you have that, all the rest will come. It matters nothing that at present you fail to find pleasure in certain classics. The driving impulse of your interest will force you to acquire experience, and experience will teach you the use of the means of pleasure. You do not know the secret ways of yourself : that is all. A continuance of interest must inevitably bring you to the keenest joys. But, of course, experience may be acquired judiciously or injudiciously, just as Putney may be reached *via* Walham Green or *via* St. Petersburg.

HOMER AND THE STUDY OF GREEK [1]

ANDREW LANG

Andrew Lang wishes to argue in defense of the study of Greek. In brief, the argument may be stated: although the study of Greek has fallen into disfavor, some boys will profit greatly from the study; they will profit from it, because they will read Homer; and Homer must be read in the original because the poems are not capable of translation. As the essay is avowedly written for those that do not believe in the study of Greek, he takes two paragraphs to an exposition of that side. But granting that for the many perhaps it is a waste of time, he argues for the few. Here he frankly drops into autobiography. He gives his personal testimony. This leads easily to his appreciation of Homer. Then to illustrate the untranslatable nature of Homer, he gives parodies of translations by various types of authors. On one hand, in so far as the parodies are clever, he gains by concrete illustration. On the other, since the verses are for the most part his imitations of what the authors might have written, does not this leave a suspicion of unfairness? Actually from the reading of these imaginary translations, would the student be impelled to study Greek? Moreover, is there not an element of pedantry in his references to the various authors? Surely the reader familiar with the difference in style between the translations of Chapman and Cowper would have already decided for himself the question at issue.

THE Greek language is being ousted from education, here, in France, and in America. The speech of the earliest democracies is not democratic enough for modern anarchy. There is nothing to be gained, it is said, by a

[1] From "Essays in Little," by permission of Charles Scribner's Sons.

318

meets reader on own level

knowledge of Greek. We have not to fight the battle of
life with Hellenic waiters; and, even if we had, Romaic,
or modern Greek, is much more easily learned than the
old classical tongue. The reason of this comparative ease
will be plain to any one who, retaining a vague memory of
his Greek grammar, takes up a modern Greek newspaper.
He will find that the idioms of the modern newspaper are the
idioms of all newspapers, that the grammar is the grammar
of modern languages, that the opinions are expressed in
barbarous translations of barbarous French and English
journalistic *clichés* or commonplaces. This ugly and un-
dignified mixture of the ancient Greek characters, and of
ancient Greek words with modern grammar and idioms,
and stereotyped phrases, is extremely distasteful to the
scholar. Modern Greek, as it is at present printed, is
not the natural spoken language of the peasants. You
can read a Greek leading article, though you can hardly
make sense of a Greek rural ballad. The peasant speech
is a thing of slow development; there is a basis of ancient
Greek in it, with large elements of Slavonic, Turkish,
Italian, and other imposed or imported languages. Modern literary Greek is a hybrid of revived classical words,
blended with the idioms of the speeches which have arisen
since the fall of the Roman Empire. Thus, thanks to the
modern and familiar element in it, modern Greek "as
she is writ" is much more easily learned than ancient
Greek. Consequently, if any one has need for the speech
in business or travel, he can acquire as much of it as most of
us have of French, with considerable ease. People therefore argue that ancient Greek is particularly superfluous
in schools. Why waste time on it, they ask, which could
be expended on science, on modern languages, or any other
branch of education? There is a great deal of justice in

this position. The generation of men who are now middle-aged bestowed much time and labour on Greek; and in what, it may be asked, are they better for it? Very few of them "keep up their Greek." Say, for example, that one was in a form of fifty boys who began the study, it is odds against five of the survivors still reading Greek books. The worldly advantages of the study are slight: it may lead three of the fifty to a good degree, and one to a fellowship; but good degrees may be taken in other subjects, and fellowships may be abolished, or "nationalised," with all other forms of property.

Then, why maintain Greek in schools? Only a very minute percentage of the boys who are tormented with it really learn it. Only a still smaller percentage can read it after they are thirty. Only one or two gain any material advantage by it. In very truth, most minds are not framed by nature to excel and to delight in literature, and only to such minds and to schoolmasters is Greek valuable.

This is the case against Greek put as powerfully as one can state it. On the other side, we may say, though the remark may seem absurd at first sight, that to have mastered Greek, even if you forget it, is not to have wasted time. It really is an educational and mental discipline. The study is so severe that it needs the earnest application of the mind. The study is averse to indolent intellectual ways; it will not put up with a "there or thereabouts," any more than mathematical ideas admit of being made to seem "extremely plausible." He who writes, and who may venture to offer himself as an example, is naturally of a most slovenly and slatternly mental habit. It is his constant temptation to "scamp" every kind of work, and to say "it will do well enough."

He hates taking trouble and verifying references. And he can honestly confess that nothing in his experience has so helped, in a certain degree, to counteract those tendencies — as the labour of thoroughly learning certain Greek texts — the dramatists, Thucydides, some of the books of Aristotle. Experience has satisfied him that Greek is of real educational value, and, apart from the acknowledged and unsurpassed merit of its literature, is a severe and logical training of the mind. The mental constitution is strengthened and braced by the labour, even if the language is forgotten in later life.

It is manifest, however, that this part of education is not for everybody. The real educational problem is to discover what boys Greek will be good for, and what boys will only waste time and dawdle over it. Certainly to men of a literary turn (a very minute percentage), Greek is of an inestimable value. Great poets, even, may be ignorant of it, as Shakespeare probably was, as Keats and Scott certainly were, as Alexandre Dumas was. But Dumas regretted his ignorance; Scott regretted it. We know not how much Scott's admitted laxity of style and hurried careless habit might have been modified by a knowledge of Greek; how much of grace, permanence, and generally of art, his genius might have gained from the language and literature of Hellas. The most Homeric of modern men could not read Homer. As for Keats, he was born a Greek, it has been said; but had he been born with a knowledge of Greek, he never, probably, would have been guilty of his chief literary faults. This is not certain, for some modern men of letters deeply read in Greek, have all the qualities of fustian and effusiveness which Longinus most despised. / Greek will not make a luxuriously Asiatic mind Hellenic, it is certain; but it may,

Y

at least, help to restrain effusive and rhetorical gabble. Our Asiatic rhetoricians might perhaps be even more barbarous than they are if Greek were a sealed book to them. However this may be, it is, at least, well to find out in a school what boys are worth instructing in the Greek language. Now, of their worthiness, of their chances of success in the study, Homer seems the best touchstone; and he is certainly the most attractive guide to the study.

At present boys are introduced to the language of the Muses by pedantically written grammars, full of the queerest and most arid metaphysical and philological verbiage. The very English in which these deplorable books are composed may be scientific, may be comprehensible by and useful to philologists, but is utterly heart-breaking to boys.

Philology might be made fascinating; the history of a word, and of the processes by which its different forms, in different senses, were developed, might be made as interesting as any other story of events. But grammar is not taught thus: boys are introduced to a jargon about matters meaningless, and they are naturally as much enchanted as if they were listening to a *chimæra bombinans in vacuo*. The grammar, to them, is a mere buzz in a chaos of nonsense. They have to learn the buzz by rote; and a pleasant process that is — a seductive initiation into the mysteries. When they struggle so far as to be allowed to try to read a piece of Greek prose, they are only like the Marchioness in her experience of beer: she once had a sip of it. Ten lines of Xenophon, narrating how he marched so many parasangs and took breakfast, do not amount to more than a very unrefreshing sip of Greek. Nobody even tells the boys who Xenophon was, what he did there, and what it was all about. Nobody gives a brief and interesting sketch of the great march, of its history and objects. The boys straggle along with Xenophon, knowing not whence or whither:

> "They stray through a desolate region,
> And often are faint on the march."

One by one they fall out of the ranks; they mutiny against Xenophon; they murmur against that commander; they desert his flag. They determine that anything is better than Greek, that nothing can be worse than Greek, and they move the tender hearts of their parents. They are put to learn German; which they do not learn, unluckily, but which they find it comparatively easy to shirk. In brief, they leave school without having learned anything whatever.

Up to a certain age my experiences at school were precisely those which I have described. Our grammar was not so philological, abstruse and arid as the instruments of torture employed at present. But I hated Greek with a deadly and sickening hatred; I hated it like a bully and a thief of time. The verbs in $\mu\iota$ completed my intellectual discomfiture, and Xenophon routed me with horrible carnage. I could have run away to sea, but for a strong impression that a life on the ocean wave "did not set my genius," as Alan Breck says. Then we began to read Homer; and from the very first words, in which the Muse is asked to sing the wrath of Achilles, Peleus' son, my mind was altered, and I was the devoted friend of Greek. Here was something worth reading about; here one knew where one was; here was the music of words, here were poetry, pleasure, and life. We fortunately had a teacher (Dr. Hodson) who was not wildly enthusiastic about grammar.

He would set us long pieces of the Iliad or Odyssey to learn, and, when the day's task was done, would make us read on, adventuring ourselves in "the unseen," and construing as gallantly as we might, without grammar or dictionary. On the following day we surveyed more carefully the ground we had pioneered or skirmished over, and then advanced again. Thus, to change the metaphor, we took Homer in large draughts, not in sips: in sips no epic can be enjoyed. We now revelled in Homer like Keats in Spenser, like young horses let loose in a pasture. The result was not the making of many accurate scholars, though a few were made; others got nothing better than enjoyment in their work, and the firm belief, opposed to that of most schoolboys, that the ancients did not write nonsense. To love Homer, as Steele said about loving a fair lady of quality, "is a liberal education."

Judging from this example, I venture very humbly to think that any one who, even at the age of Cato, wants to learn Greek, should begin where Greek literature, where all profane literature begins — with Homer himself. It was thus, not with grammars *in vacuo*, that the great scholars of the Renaissance began. It was thus that Ascham and Rabelais began, by jumping into Greek and splashing about till they learned to swim. First, of course, a person must learn the Greek characters. Then his or her tutor may make him read a dozen lines of Homer, marking the cadence, the surge and thunder of the hexameters — a music which, like that of the Sirens, few can hear without being lured to the seas and isles of song. Then the tutor might translate a passage of moving interest, like Priam's appeal to Achilles; first, of course, explaining the situation. Then the teacher might go over some lines, minutely pointing out how the Greek

words are etymologically connected with many words in
English. Next, he might take a substantive and a verb,
showing roughly how their inflections arose and were
developed, and how they retain forms in Homer which
do not occur in later Greek. There is no reason why
even this part of the lesson should be uninteresting. By
this time a pupil would know, more or less, where he was,
what Greek is, and what the Homeric poems are like. He
might thus believe from the first that there are good reasons
for knowing Greek; that it is the key to many worlds of
life, of action, of beauty, of contemplation, of knowledge.
Then, after a few more exercises in Homer, the grammar
being judiciously worked in along with the literature of
the epic, a teacher might discern whether it was worth
while for his pupils to continue in the study of Greek.
Homer would be their guide into the "realms of gold."

It is clear enough that Homer is the best guide. His is
the oldest extant Greek, his matter is the most various
and delightful, and most appeals to the young, who are
wearied by scraps of Xenophon, and who cannot be
expected to understand the Tragedians. But Homer is a
poet for all ages, all races, and all moods. To the Greeks
the epics were not only the best of romances, the richest
of poetry; not only their oldest documents about their
own history, — they were also their Bible, their treasury
of religious traditions and moral teaching. With the Bible
and Shakespeare, the Homeric poems are the best training
for life. There is no good quality that they lack : manli-
ness, courage, reverence for old age and for the hospitable
hearth; justice, piety, pity, a brave attitude towards life
and death, are all conspicuous in Homer. He has to write
of battles; and he delights in the joy of battle, and in all
the movement of war. Yet he delights not less, but more,

in peace : in prosperous cities, hearths secure, in the tender beauty of children, in the love of wedded wives, in the frank nobility of maidens, in the beauty of earth and sky and sea, and seaward murmuring river, in sun and snow, frost and mist and rain, in the whispered talk of boy and girl beneath oak and pine tree.

Living in an age where every man was a warrior, where every city might know the worst of sack and fire, where the noblest ladies might be led away for slaves, to light the fire and make the bed of a foreign master, Homer inevitably regards life as a battle. To each man on earth comes "the wicked day of destiny," as Malory unconsciously translates it, and each man must face it as hardily as he may.

Homer encourages them by all the maxims of chivalry and honour. His heart is with the brave of either side — with Glaucus and Sarpedon of Lycia no less than with Achilles and Patroclus. "Ah, friend," cries Sarpedon, "if once escaped from this battle we were for ever to be ageless and immortal, neither would I myself fight now in the foremost ranks, neither would I urge thee into the wars that give renown; but now — for assuredly ten thousand fates of death on every side beset us, and these may no man shun, nor none avoid — forward now let us go, whether we are to give glory or to win it!" And forth they go, to give and take renown and death, all the shields and helms of Lycia shining behind them, through the dust of battle, the singing of the arrows, the hurtling of spears, the rain of stones from the Locrian slings. And shields are smitten, and chariot horses run wild with no man to drive them, and Sarpedon drags down a portion of the Achæan battlement, and Aias leaps into the trench with his deadly spear, and the whole battle shifts and shines be-

neath the sun.   Yet he who sings of the war, and sees it
with his sightless eyes, sees also the Trojan women working at the loom, cheating their anxious hearts with broidery
work of gold and scarlet, or raising the song to Athene, or
heating the bath for Hector, who never again may pass
within the gates of Troy.   He sees the poor weaving
woman, weighing the wool, that she may not defraud her
employers, and yet may win bread for her children.   He
sees the children, the golden head of Astyanax, his shrink-
ing from the splendour of the hero's helm.   He sees the
child Odysseus, going with his father through the orchard,
and choosing out some apple trees "for his very own."   It
is in the mouth of the ruthless Achilles, the fatal, the fated,
the swift-footed hero with the hands of death, that Homer
places the tenderest of his similes.   "Wherefore weepest
thou, Patroclus, like a fond little maid, that runs by her
mother's side, praying her mother to take her up, snatch-
ing at her gown, and hindering her as she walks, and tear-
fully looking at her till her mother takes her up? — like
her, Patroclus, dost thou softly weep."

This is what Chesterfield calls "the porter-like language
of Homer's heroes."   Such are the moods of Homer, so
full of love of life and all things living, so rich in all human
sympathies, so readily moved when the great hound Argus
welcomes his master, whom none knew after twenty years,
but the hound knew him, and died in that welcome.   With
all this love of the real, which makes him dwell so fondly
on every detail of armour, of implement, of art; on the
divers-coloured gold-work of the shield, on the making
of tires for chariot-wheels, on the forging of iron, on the
rose-tinted ivory of the Sidonians, on cooking and eating
and sacrificing, on pet dogs, on wasps and their ways,
on fishing, on the boar hunt, on scenes in baths where fair

maidens lave water over the heroes, on undiscovered
isles with good harbours and rich land, on ploughing,
mowing, and sowing, on the furniture of houses, on the
golden vases wherein the white dust of the dead is laid, —
with all this delight in the real, Homer is the most romantic
of poets. He walks with the surest foot in the darkling
realm of dread Persephone, beneath the poplars on the
solemn last beach of Ocean. He has heard the Siren's
music, and the song of Circe, chanting as she walks to
and fro, casting the golden shuttle through the loom of
gold. He enters the cave of the Man Eater; he knows
the unsunned land of the Cimmerians; in the summer of
the North he has looked, from the fiord of the Læstrygons,
on the Midnight Sun. He has dwelt on the floating isle of
Æolus, with its wall of bronze unbroken, and has sailed
on those Phæacian barks that need no help of helm or
oar, that fear no stress either of wind or tide, that come
and go and return obedient to a thought and silent as a
dream. He has seen the four maidens of Circe, daughters
of wells and woods, and of sacred streams. He is the
second-sighted man, and beholds the shroud that wraps
the living who are doomed, and the mystic dripping from
the walls of blood yet unshed. He has walked in the garden
closes of Phæacia, and looked on the face of gods who fare
thither, and watch the weaving of the dance. He has
eaten the honey-sweet fruit of the lotus, and from the
hand of Helen he brings us that Egyptian nepenthe which
puts all sorrow out of mind. His real world is as real
as that in *Henry V.*, his enchanted isles are charmed
with the magic of the *Tempest*. His young wooers
are as insolent as Claudio, as flushed with youth; his
beggar-men are brethren of Edie Ochiltree; his Nausicaa is
sister to Rosalind, with a different charm of stately purity

in love. His enchantresses hold us yet with their sorceries; his Helen is very Beauty : she has all the sweetness of ideal womanhood, and her repentance is without remorse. His Achilles is youth itself, glorious, cruel, pitiful, splendid, and sad, ardent and loving, and conscious of its doom. Homer, in truth, is to be matched only with Shakespeare, and of Shakespeare he has not the occasional wilfulness, freakishness, and modish obscurity. He is a poet all of gold, universal as humanity, simple as childhood, musical now as the flow of his own rivers, now as the heavy plunging wave of his own Ocean.

Such, then, as far as weak words can speak of him, is the first and greatest of poets. This is he whom English boys are to be ignorant of, if Greek be ousted from our schools, or are to know only in the distorting mirror of a versified, or in the pale shadow of a prose translation. Translations are good only as teachers to bring men to Homer. English verse has no measure which even remotely suggests the various flow of the hexameter. Translators who employ verse give us a feeble Homer, dashed with their own conceits, and moulded to their own style. Translators who employ prose "tell the story without the song," but, at least, they add no twopenny "beauties" and cheap conceits of their own.

I venture to offer a few examples of original translation, in which the mannerisms of poets who have, or have not, translated Homer, are parodied, and, of course (except in the case of Pope), exaggerated. The passage is the speech of the Second-sighted Man, before the slaying of the wooers in the hall : —

"Ah! wretched men, what ill is this ye suffer? In night are swathed your heads, your faces, your knees; and the voice of wailing is kindled, and cheeks are wet with tears, and with blood drip the walls, and the fair main beams of the roof, and the porch is full of shadows, and full is the courtyard, of ghosts that hasten hellward below the darkness, and the sun has perished out of heaven, and an evil mist sweeps up over all."

So much for Homer. The first attempt at metrical translation here given is meant to be in the manner of Pope:

> "Caitiffs!" he cried, "what heaven-directed blight
> Involves each countenance with clouds of night!
> What pearly drop the ashen cheek bedews!
> Why do the walls with gouts ensanguined ooze?
> The court is thronged with ghosts that 'neath the gloom
> Seek Pluto's realm, and Dis's awful doom;
> In ebon curtains Phœbus hides his head,
> And sable mist creeps upward from the dead."

This appears pretty bad, and nearly as un-Homeric as a translation could possibly be. But Pope, aided by Broome and Fenton, managed to be much less Homeric, much more absurd, and infinitely more "classical" in the sense in which Pope is classical:

> "O race to death devote! with Stygian shade
> Each destined peer impending fates invade;
> With tears your wan distorted cheeks are drowned;
> With sanguine drops the walls are rubied round:
> Thick swarms the spacious hall with howling ghosts,
> To people Orcus and the burning coasts!
> Nor gives the sun his golden orb to roll,
> But universal night usurps the pole."

Who could have conjectured that even Pope would wander away so far from his matchless original? "Wretches!" cried Theoclymenus, the seer; and that becomes, "O race to death devote!" "Your heads are swathed in night," turns into "With Stygian shade each destined peer" (peer is good!) "impending fates invade," where Homer says nothing about Styx nor peers. The

Latin Orcus takes the place of Erebus, and "the burning coasts" are derived from modern popular theology. The very grammar detains or defies the reader; is it the sun that does not give his golden orb to roll, or who, or what?

The only place where the latter-day Broome or Fenton can flatter himself that he rivals Pope at his own game is —

"What pearly drop the ashen cheek bedews!"

This is, if possible, *more* classical than Pope's own —

"With tears your wan distorted cheeks are drowned."

But Pope nobly revindicates his unparalleled power of translating funnily, when, in place of "the walls drip with blood," he writes —

"With sanguine drops the walls are rubied round."

Homer does not appear to have been acquainted with rubies; but what of that? And how noble, how eminently worthy of Pope it is to add that the ghosts "howl"! I tried to make them gibber, but ghosts *do* gibber in Homer (thought not in this passage), so Pope, Fenton, Broome, and Co., make them howl.

No, Pope is not lightly to be rivalled by a modern translator. The following example, a far-off following of a noted contemporary poet, may be left unsigned —

"Wretches, the bane hath befallen, the night and the blight of your sin
Sweeps like a shroud o'er the faces and limbs that were gladsome therein;
And the dirge of the dead breaketh forth, and the faces of all men are
   wet,
And the walls are besprinkled with blood, and the ghosts in the gateway
   are met,
Ghosts in the court and the gateway are gathered, Hell opens her lips,
And the sun in his splendour is shrouded, and sickens in spasm of eclipse."

Color hurts the argument.

The next is longer and slower : the poet has a difficulty in telling his story :

Tennyson)

> "Wretches," he cried, "what doom is this? what night
> Clings like a face-cloth to the face of each, —
> Sweeps like a shroud o'er knees and head? for lo!
> The windy wail of death is up, and tears
> On every cheek are wet; each shining wall
> And beauteous interspace of beam and beam
> Weeps tears of blood, and shadows in the door
> Flicker, and fill the portals and the court —
> Shadows of men that hellwards yearn — and now
> The sun himself hath perished out of heaven,
> And all the land is darkened with a mist."

That could never be mistaken for a version by the Laureate, as perhaps any contemporary hack's works might have been taken for Pope's. The difficulty, perhaps, lies here : any one knows where to have Pope, any one knows that he will evade the *mot propre*, though the precise evasion he may select is hard to guess. But the Laureate would keep close to his text, and yet would write like himself, very beautifully, but not with an Homeric swiftness and strength. Who is to imitate him? As to Mr. William Morris, he might be fabled to render Ἀ δειλοί "niddering wights," but beyond that, conjecture is baffled.[1] Or is *this* the kind of thing? —

"Niddering wights, what a bane do ye bear, for your knees in the night,
And your heads and your faces, are shrouded, and clamour that knows not delight
Rings, and your cheeks are begrutten, and blood is besprent on the walls,
Blood on the tapestry fair woven, and barrow-wights walk in the halls.
Fetches and wraiths of the chosen of the Norns, and the sun from the lift
Shudders, and over the midgarth and swan's bath the cloud-shadows drift."

[1] Conjecture may cease, as Mr. Morris has translated the Odyssey.

It may be argued that, though this is perhaps a translation, it is not English, never was, and never will be. But it is quite as like Homer as the performance of Pope.

Such as these, or not so very much better than these as might be wished, are our efforts to translate Homer. From Chapman to Avia, or Mr. William Morris, they are all eminently conscientious, and erroneous, and futile. Chapman makes Homer a fanciful, euphuistic, obscure, and garrulous Elizabethan, but Chapman has fire. Pope makes him a wit, spirited, occasionally noble, full of points, and epigrams, and queer rococo conventionalisms. Cowper makes him slow, lumbering, a Milton without the music. Maginn makes him pipe an Irish jig : —

> "Scarcely had she begun to wash
> When she was aware of the grisly gash!"

Lord Derby makes him respectable and ponderous. Lord Tennyson makes him not less, but certainly not more, than Tennysonian. Homer, in the Laureate's few fragments of experiment, is still a poet, but he is not Homer. Mr. Morris, and Avia, make him Icelandic, and archaistic, and hard to scan, though vigorous in his fetters for all that. Bohn makes him a crib; and of other translators in prose it has been said with a humour which one of them appreciates, that they render Homer into a likeness of the Book of Mormon.

Homer is untranslatable. None of us can bend the bow of Eurytus, and make the bow-string "ring sweetly at the touch, like the swallow's song." The adventure is never to be achieved; and, if Greek is to be dismissed from education, not the least of the sorrows that will ensue is English ignorance of Homer.

HOMER AND HUMBUG [1]

An Academic Discussion

BY

STEPHEN LEACOCK

Curiously similar in treatment, is Mr. Leacock's essay, as compared with Lang's, but utterly different in content and in style. His thought is as follows: although he has had the advantage of a classical training, he regards it as useless; to illustrate this uselessness, he writes two burlesque translations; his conclusion is that the classics are only primitive literature. Not only do both essayists use parodies as illustrations, they also illustrate from their own individual experience. But whereas Lang is serious and a trifle heavy, Mr. Leacock is humorous and consciously popular. If Lang limits his audience by his pedantry, does not Mr. Leacock limit his by his obviousness? Is Mr. Leacock's attack stronger than Lang's defense?

THE following discussion is of course only of interest to scholars. But, as the public schools returns show that in the United States there are now over a million coloured scholars alone, the appeal is wide enough.

I do not mind confessing that for a long time past I have been very sceptical about the classics. I was myself trained as a classical scholar. It seemed the only thing to do with me. I acquired such a singular facility in handling Latin and Greek that I could take a page of either of them, distinguish which it was by merely glancing at it, and, with the help of a dictionary and a pair of compasses, whip off a translation of it in less than three hours.

[1] From "Behind the Beyond," by permission of John Lane Co.

But I never got any pleasure from it. I lied about it. At first, perhaps, I lied through vanity. Any coloured scholar will understand the feeling. Later on I lied through habit; later still because, after all, the classics were all that I had and so I valued them. I have seen thus a deceived dog value a pup with a broken leg, and a pauper child nurse a dead doll with the sawdust out of it. So I nursed my dead Homer and my broken Demosthenes though I knew in my heart that there was more sawdust in the stomach of one modern author than in the whole lot of them. Observe, I am not saying which it is that has it full of it.

So, as I say, I began to lie about the classics. I said to people who knew no Greek that there was a sublimity, a majesty about Homer which they could never hope to grasp. I said it was like the sound of the sea beating against the granite cliffs of the Ionian Esophagus: or words to that effect. As for the truth of it, I might as well have said that it was like the sound of a rum distillery running a night shift on half time. At any rate this is what I said about Homer, and when I spoke of Pindar, — the dainty grace of his strophes, — and Aristophanes, the delicious sallies of his wit, sally after sally, each sally explained in a note calling it a sally — I managed to suffuse my face with an animation which made it almost beautiful.

I admitted of course that Virgil in spite of his genius had a hardness and a cold glitter which resembled rather the brilliance of a cut diamond than the soft grace of a flower. Certainly I admitted this: the mere admission of it would knock the breath out of anyone who was arguing.

From such talks my friends went away sad. The conclusion was too cruel. It had all the cold logic of a syllogism (like that almost brutal form of argument so much admired in the Paraphernalia of Socrates). For if : —

Virgil and Homer and Pindar had all this grace, and pith and these sallies, —
And if I read Virgil and Homer and Pindar,
And if they only read Mrs. Wharton and Mrs. Humphrey Ward
Then where were they?

So continued lying brought its own reward in the sense of superiority and I lied more.

When I reflect that I have openly expressed regret, as a personal matter, even in the presence of women, for the missing books of Tacitus, and the entire loss of the Abacadabra of Polyphemus of Syracuse, I can find no words in which to beg for pardon. In reality I was just as much worried over the loss of the ichthyosaurus. More, indeed : I'd like to have seen it : but if the books Tacitus lost were like those he didn't, I wouldn't.

I believe all scholars lie like this. An ancient friend of mine, a clergyman, tells me that in Hesiod he finds a peculiar grace that he doesn't find elsewhere. He's a liar. That's all. Another man, in politics and in the legislature, tells me that every night before going to bed he reads over a page or two of Thucydides to keep his mind fresh. Either he never goes to bed or he's a liar. Doubly so : no one could read Greek at that frantic rate : and anyway his mind isn't fresh. How could it be, he's in the legislature. I don't object to this man talking freely of the classics, but he ought to keep it for the voters. My own opinion is that before he goes to bed he takes whiskey : why call it Thucydides?

I know there are solid arguments advanced in favour of the classics. I often hear them from my colleagues. My friend the professor of Greek tells me that he truly believes the classics have made him what he is. This is a very grave statement, if well founded. Indeed I have heard the same argument from a great many Latin and Greek scholars. They all claim, with some heat, that Latin and Greek have practically made them what they are. This damaging charge against the classics should not be too readily accepted. In my opinion some of these men would have been what they are, no matter what they were.

Be this as it may, I for my part bitterly regret the lies I have told about my appreciation of Latin and Greek literature. I am anxious to do what I can to set things right. I am therefore engaged on, indeed have nearly completed, a work which will enable all readers to judge the matter for themselves. What I have done is a translation of all the great classics, not in the usual literal way but on a design that brings them into harmony with modern life. I will explain what I mean in a minute.

The translation is intended to be within reach of everybody. It is so designed that the entire set of volumes can go on a shelf twenty-seven feet long, or even longer. The first edition will be an *édition de luxe* bound in vellum, or perhaps in buckskin, and sold at five hundred dollars. It will be limited to five hundred copies and, of course, sold only to the feeble minded. The next edition will be the Literary Edition, sold to artists, authors, actors, and contractors. After that will come the Boarding House Edition, bound in board and paid for in the same way.

My plan is to so transpose the classical writers as to give, not the literal translation word for word, but what is really the modern equivalent. Let me give an odd sample or two to show what I mean. Take the passage in the First Book of Homer that describes Ajax the Greek dashing

z

into the battle in front of Troy. Here is the way it runs (as nearly as I remember), in the usual word for word translation of the classroom, as done by the very best professor, his spectacles glittering with the literary rapture of it.

"Then he too Ajax on the one hand leaped (or possibly jumped) into the fight wearing on the other hand, yes certainly a steel corselet (or possibly a bronze under tunic) and on his head of course, yes without doubt he had a helmet with a tossing plume taken from the mane (or perhaps extracted from the tail) of some horse which once fed along the banks of the Scamander (and it sees the herd and raises its head and paws the ground) and in his hand a shield worth a hundred oxen and on his knees too especially in particular greaves made by some cunning artificer (or perhaps blacksmith) and he blows the fire and it is hot. Thus Ajax leapt (or, better, was propelled from behind), into the fight."

Now that's grand stuff. There is no doubt of it. There's a wonderful movement and force to it. You can almost see it move, it goes so fast. But the modern reader can't get it. It won't mean to him what it meant to the early Greek. The setting, the costume, the scene has all got to be changed in order to let the reader have a real equivalent to judge just how good the Greek verse is. In my translation I alter it just a little, not much but just enough to give the passage a form that reproduces the proper literary value of the verses, without losing anything of the majesty. It describes, I may say, the Directors of the American Industrial Stocks rushing into the Balkan War Cloud. —

Then there came rushing to the shock of war
Mr. McNicoll of the C. P. R.
He wore suspenders and about his throat
High rose the collar of a sealskin coat.
He had on gaiters and he wore a tie,
He had his trousers buttoned good and high;

> About his waist a woollen undervest
> Bought from a sad-eyed farmer of the West.
> (And every time he clips a sheep he sees
> Some bloated plutocrat who ought to freeze),
> Thus in the Stock Exchange he burst to view,
> Leaped to the post, and shouted, "Ninety-two!"

There! That's Homer, the real thing! Just as it sounded to the rude crowd of Greek peasants who sat in a ring and guffawed at the rhymes and watched the minstrel stamp it out into "feet" as he recited it!

Or let me take another example from the so-called Catalogue of the Ships that fills up nearly an entire book of Homer. This famous passage names all the ships, one by one, and names the chiefs who sailed on them, and names the particular town or hill or valley that they came from. It has been much admired. It has that same majesty of style that has been brought to an even loftier pitch in the New York Business Directory and the City Telephone Book. It runs along, as I recall it, something like this, —

"And first, indeed, oh yes, was the ship of Homistogetes the Spartan, long and swift, having both its masts covered with cowhide and two rows of oars. And he, Homistogetes, was born of Hermogenes and Ophthalmia and was at home in Syncope beside the fast flowing Paresis. And after him came the ship of Preposterus the Eurasian, son of Oasis and Hysteria," . . .

and so on endlessly.

Instead of this I substitute, with the permission of the New York Central Railway, the official catalogue of their locomotives taken almost word for word from the list compiled by their superintendent of works. I admit that he wrote in hot weather. Part of it runs: —

> Out in the yard and steaming in the sun
> Stands locomotive engine number forty-one;
> Seated beside the windows of the cab

G

Are Pat McGaw and Peter James McNab.
Pat comes from Troy and Peter from Cohoes,
And when they pull the throttle off she goes;
And as she vanishes there comes to view
Steam locomotive engine number forty-two.
Observe her mighty wheels, her easy roll,
With William J. Macarthy in control.
They say her engineer some time ago
Lived on a farm outside of Buffalo
Whereas his fireman, Henry Edward Foy,
Attended School in Springfield, Illinois.
Thus does the race of man decay or rot —
Some men can hold their jobs and some can not.

Please observe that if Homer had actually written that last line it would have been quoted for a thousand years as one of the deepest sayings ever said. Orators would have rounded out their speeches with the majestic phrase, quoted in sonorous and unintelligible Greek verse, "some men can hold their jobs and some can not": essayists would have begun their most scholarly dissertations with the words, — "It has been finely said by Homer that (in Greek) 'some men can hold their jobs'": and the clergy in mid-pathos of a funeral sermon would have raised their eyes aloft and echoed "Some men can not"!

This is what I should like to do. I'd like to take a large stone and write on it in very plain writing, —

"The classics are only primitive literature. They belong in the same class as primitive machinery and primitive music and primitive medicine," — and then throw it through the windows of a University and hide behind a fence to see the professors buzz!!

ON THE CASE OF A CERTAIN MAN WHO IS NEVER THOUGHT OF [1]

BY

WILLIAM GRAHAM SUMNER

This brilliant essay by Professor Sumner illustrates the effective use of the deductive structure. In two paragraphs defining who is the Forgotten Man, the general principle is stated so fully that the reader unconsciously accepts it. But once the reader has accepted this principle, it is applied to the consideration of trades unions and temperance legislation, with startling results. The essay, then, consists in the statement of a general principle, followed by two illustrations. Just as the form resolves itself into a simple arrangement, so the style is simple. There is no attempt at rhetorical exaggeration, no appeal to the emotions. It does read, and it is intended to read, as an ordinary exercise of the logical faculty. This mathematical effect is gained by the device of using the A and B that are associated in the mind with school problems. And the brilliance of the essay lies in the apparent inevitability with which the author reaches conclusions widely differing from conventional views. Since the importance of the essay lies exactly in these applications, actually the structure approaches the deductive type.

THE type and formula of most schemes of philanthropy or humanitarianism is this: A and B put their heads together to decide what C shall be made to do for D. The radical vice of all these schemes, from a sociological point of view, is that C is not allowed a voice in the matter,

[1] From "What Social Classes Owe to Each Other." Copyright, 1883, by Harper and Brothers. Copyright, 1911, by Jeannie W. Sumner. Also by permission of the Sumner Estate and of The Yale University Press.

and his position, character, and interests, as well as the ultimate effects on society through C's interests, are entirely overlooked. I call C the Forgotten Man. For once let us look him up and consider his case, for the characteristic of all social doctors is, that they fix their minds on some man or group of men whose case appeals to the sympathies and the imagination, and they plan remedies addressed to the particular trouble; they do not understand that all the parts of society hold together, and that forces which are set in action act and react throughout the whole organism, until an equilibrium is produced by a re-adjustment of all interests and rights. They therefore ignore entirely the source from which they must draw all the energy which they employ in their remedies, and they ignore all the effects on other members of society than the ones they have in view. They are always under the dominion of the superstition of government, and, forgetting that a government produces nothing at all, they leave out of sight the first fact to be remembered in all social discussion — that the State cannot get a cent for any man without taking it from some other man, and this latter must be a man who has produced and saved it. This latter is the Forgotten Man.

The friends of humanity start out with certain benevolent feelings toward "the poor," "the weak," "the laborers," and others of whom they make pets. They generalize these classes, and render them impersonal, and so constitute the classes into social pets. They turn to other classes and appeal to sympathy and generosity, and to all the other noble sentiments of the human heart. Action in the line proposed consists in a transfer of capital from the better off to the worse off. Capital, however, as we have seen, is the force by which civilization is maintained and carried on.   The same piece of capital cannot be used in two ways.   Every bit of capital, therefore, which is given to a shiftless and inefficient member of society, who makes no return for it, is diverted from a reproductive use; but if it was put to reproductive use, it would have to be granted in wages to an efficient and productive laborer.   Hence the real sufferer by that kind of benevolence which consists in an expenditure of capital to protect the good-for-nothing is the industrious laborer. The latter, however, is never thought of in this connection. It is assumed that he is provided for and out of the account. Such a notion only shows how little true notions of political economy have as yet become popularized.   There is an almost invincible prejudice that a man who gives a dollar to a beggar is generous and kind-hearted, but that a man who refuses the beggar and puts the dollar in a savings bank is stingy and mean.   The former is putting capital where it is very sure to be wasted, and where it will be a kind of seed for a long succession of future dollars, which must be wasted to ward off a greater strain on the sympathies than would have been occasioned by a refusal in the first place.   Inasmuch as the dollar might have been turned into capital and given to a laborer who, while earning it, would have reproduced it, it must be regarded as taken from the latter.   When a millionnaire gives a dollar to a beggar the gain of utility to the beggar is enormous, and the loss of utility to the millionnaire is insignificant.   Generally the discussion is allowed to rest there. But if the millionnaire makes capital of the dollar, it must go upon the labor market, as a demand for productive services.   Hence there is another party in interest — the person who supplies productive services. There always are two parties.   The second one is always the Forgotten Man, and any one who wants to truly understand the matter in question must go and search for the Forgotten Man. He will be found to be worthy, industrious, independent, and self-supporting. He is not, technically, "poor" or "weak"; he minds his own business, and makes no complaint. Consequently the philanthropists never think of him, and trample on him.

We hear a great deal of schemes for "improving the condition of the working-man." In the United States the farther down we go in the grade of labor, the greater is the advantage which the laborer has over the higher classes. A hod-carrier or digger here can, by one day's labor, command many times more days' labor of a carpenter, surveyor, book-keeper, or doctor than an unskilled laborer in Europe could command by one day's labor. The same is true, in a less degree, of the carpenter, as compared with the book-keeper, surveyor, and doctor. This is why the United States is the great country for the unskilled laborer. The economic conditions all favor that class. There is a great continent to be subdued, and there is a fertile soil available to labor, with scarcely any need of capital. Hence the people who have the strong arms have what is most needed, and, if it were not for social consideration, higher education would not pay. Such being the case, the working-man needs no improvement in his condition except to be freed from the parasites who are living on him. All schemes for patronizing "the working classes" savor of condescension. They are impertinent and out of place in this free democracy. There is not, in fact, any such state of things or any such relation as would make projects of this kind appropriate. Such projects demoralize both parties, flattering the vanity of one and undermining the self-respect of the other.

For our present purpose it is most important to notice that if we lift any man up we must have a fulcrum, or point of reaction. In society that means that to lift one man up we push another down. The schemes for improving the condition of the working classes interfere in the competition of workmen with each other. The beneficiaries are selected by favoritism, and are apt to be those who have recommended themselves to the friends of humanity by language or conduct which does not betoken independence and energy. Those who suffer a corresponding depression by the interference are the independent and self-reliant, who once more are forgotten or passed over; and the friends of humanity once more appear, in their zeal to help somebody, to be trampling on those who are trying to help themselves.

Trades-unions adopt various devices for raising wages, and those who give their time to philanthropy are interested in these devices, and wish them success. They fix their minds entirely on the workmen for the time being *in* the trade, and do not take note of any other *workmen* as interested in the matter. It is supposed that the fight is between the workmen and their employers, and it is believed that one can give sympathy in that contest to the workmen without feeling responsibility for anything farther. It is soon seen, however, that the employer adds the trades-union and strike risk to the other risks of his business, and settles down to it philosophically. If, now, we go farther, we see that he takes it philosophically because he has passed the loss along on the public. It then appears that the public wealth has been diminished, and that the danger of a trade war, like the danger of a revolution, is a constant reduction of the well-being of all. So far, however, we have seen only things which could *lower* wages — nothing which could raise them. The employer is worried, but that does not raise wages. The public loses, but the loss goes to cover extra risk, and that does not raise wages.

A trades-union raises wages (aside from the legitimate and economic means noticed in Chapter VI) by restricting the number of apprentices who may be taken into the trade. This device acts directly on the supply of laborers, and that produces effects on wages. If, however, the number of apprentices is limited, some are kept out who want to get in. Those who are in have, therefore, made a monopoly, and constituted themselves a privileged class on a basis exactly analogous to that of the old privileged aristocracies. But whatever is gained by this arrangement for those who are in is won at a greater loss to those who are kept out. Hence it is not upon the masters nor upon the public that trades-unions exert the pressure by which they raise wages; it is upon other persons of the labor class who want to get into the trades, but, not being able to do so, are pushed down into the unskilled labor class. These persons, however, are passed by entirely without notice in all the discussions about trades-unions. They are the Forgotten Men. But, since they want to get into the trade and win their living in it, it is fair to suppose that they are fit for it, would succeed at it, would do well for themselves and society in it; that is to say, that, of all persons interested or concerned, they most deserve our sympathy and attention.

The cases already mentioned involve no legislation. Society, however, maintains police, sheriffs, and various institutions, the object of which is to protect people against themselves — that is, against their own vices. Almost all legislative effort to prevent vice is really pro-

tective of vice, because all such legislation saves the
vicious man from the penalty of his vice. Nature's
remedies against vice are terrible. She removes the vic-
tims without pity. A drunkard in the gutter is just where
he ought to be, according to the fitness and tendency of
things. Nature has set up on him the process of decline
and dissolution by which she removes things which have
survived their usefulness. Gambling and other less
mentionable vices carry their own penalties with them.

Now, we never can annihilate a penalty. We can only
divert it from the head of the man who has incurred it
to the heads of others who have not incurred it. A vast
amount of "social reform" consists in just this operation.
The consequence is that those who have gone astray,
being relieved from Nature's fierce discipline, go on
to worse, and that there is a constantly heavier burden
for the others to bear. Who are the others? When
we see a drunkard in the gutter we pity him.
If a policeman picks him up, we say that society
has interfered to save him from perishing. "Society"
is a fine word, and it saves us the trouble of thinking.
The industrious and sober workman, who is mulcted of a
percentage of his day's wages to pay the policeman, is
the one who bears the penalty. But he is the Forgotten
Man. He passes by and is never noticed, because he has
behaved himself, fulfilled his contracts, and asked for
nothing.

The fallacy of all prohibitory, sumptuary, and moral
legislation is the same. A and B determine to be tee-
totalers, which is often a wise determination, and sometimes a necessary one. If A and B are moved by considerations which seem to them good, that is enough.
But A and B put their heads together to get a law passed

which shall force C to be a teetotaler for the sake of D, who is in danger of drinking too much. There is no pressure on A and B. They are having their own way, and they like it. There is rarely any pressure on D. He does not like it, and evades it. The pressure all comes on C. The question then arises, Who is C? He is the man who wants alcoholic liquors for any honest purpose whatsoever, who would use his liberty without abusing it, who would occasion no public question, and trouble nobody at all. He is the Forgotten Man again, and as soon as he is drawn from his obscurity we see that he is just what each one of us ought to be.

THE TRAINING OF INTELLECT [1]

WOODROW WILSON

(From a Stenographic Report)

In any work it is the thought that is important. The attention of the student should be directed to the ordering of that thought. That this is true, not only of the written essay, but also of the spoken word, is illustrated by the following speech made by President Wilson, then President of Princeton University, before the Phi Beta Kappa Society at Yale. As the speech is taken avowedly from stenographic reports, the paragraphing, as pertaining to the stenographer rather than to President Wilson, may be disregarded. He opens, then, with a section purely introductory, conforming to the accepted type of after-dinner speech. Then follows the statement of the general principle that the function of a university is to train the intellect. This is expanded and fully illustrated until the audience accepts it. Then, as in case of Professor Sumner, the principle is applied in a number of cases, almost illustrations, in which there is the greatest room for dissension. He closes with an assertion of the principle. In form, therefore, it is very similar to the preceding essay by Professor Sumner. As such it shows the range and vividness of appeal of such a type.

MR. TOASTMASTER, MR. PRESIDENT, AND GENTLEMEN:
— I certainly considered it a compliment to myself when Mr. Phelps made the comparison he made a few moments ago, but it was hardly a compliment to Princeton.

I do not feel that in coming to Yale I am coming among strangers. I believe that a man who is accustomed to

[1] From *The Yale Alumni Weekly* for March 25, 1908, by permission of the editor.

living among college men finds everywhere the same spirit, the same atmosphere. I feel toward you as a friend of mine felt toward an acquaintance who slapped him on the back familiarly. He looked at the fellow coldly and said, "I do not know your name, but your manners are very familiar." And so I feel with regard to every college gathering that their manners are familiar, but I also feel that there is a quickness of mutual comprehension that is very reassuring to a speaker. And then I feel particularly at ease in appearing before a strange audience because they have not heard my stories, and, moreover, because it is not so difficult to maintain a boast of dignity where you are not known as it is where you are known. When I appear before a Princeton crowd and try to live up to an introduction, I feel like the old woman who went into the side show at the circus and saw a man reading a newspaper through a two-inch board. "Let me out of this place," she exclaimed, "this is no place for me to be with these thin things on." I have an uncomfortable feeling in such circumstances that the disguise is transparent, but perhaps I can maintain a disguise for a little while among you.

I must confess to you that I came here with very serious thoughts this evening, because I have been laboring under the conviction for a long time that the object of a university is to educate, and I have not seen the universities of this country achieving any remarkable or disturbing success in that direction. I have found everywhere the note which I must say I have heard sounded once or twice to-night — that apology for the intellectual side of the university. You hear it at all universities. Learning is on the defensive, is actually on the defensive, among college men, and they are being asked by way of indulgence to bring that also into the circle of their interests. Is it not time we stopped asking indulgence for learning and proclaimed its sovereignty? Is it not time we reminded the college men of this country that they have no right to any distinctive place in any community, unless they can show it by intellectual achievement? that if a university is a place for distinction at all it must be distinguished by the conquests of the mind? I for my part tell you plainly that that is my motto, that I have entered the field to fight for that thesis, and that for that thesis only do I care to fight.

The toastmaster of the evening said, and said truly, that this is the season when, for me, it was most difficult to break away from regular engagements in which I am involved at this time of the year. But when I was invited to the Phi Beta Kappa banquet it had an unusual sound, and I felt that that was the particular kind of invitation which it was my duty and privilege to accept. One of the problems of the American university now is how, among a great many other competing interests, to give places of distinction to men who want places of distinction in the classroom. Why don't we give you men the Y here and the P at Princeton, because after all you have done the particular thing which distinguishes Yale? Not that these other things are not worth doing, but they may be done anywhere. They may be done in athletic clubs where there is no study, but this thing can be done only here. This is the distinctive mark of the place.

A good many years ago, just two weeks before the midyear examinations, the Faculty of Princeton was foolish enough to permit a very unwise evangelist to come to the place and to upset the town. And while an assisting undergraduate was going from room to room one undergraduate secured his door and put this notice out, "I am a Christian and am studying for examinations." Now I want to say that that is exactly what a Christian under-graduate would be doing at that time of the year. He would not be attending religious meetings no matter how beneficial it would be to him. He would be studying for examinations not merely for the purpose of passing them, but from his sense of duty.

We get a good many men at Princeton from certain secondary schools who say a great deal about their earnest desire to cultivate character among our students, and I hear a great deal about character being the object of edu-cation. I take leave to believe that a man who cultivates his character consciously will cultivate nothing except what will make him intolerable to his fellow men. If your object in life is to make a fine fellow of yourself, you will not succeed, and you will not be acceptable to really fine fellows. Character, gentlemen, is a by-product. It comes, whether you will or not, as a consequence of a life devoted to the nearest duty, and the place in which character would be cultivated, if it be a place of study, is a place where study is the object and character the results.

Not long ago a gentleman approached me in great excitement just after the entrance examinations. He said we had made a great mistake in not taking so and so from a certain school which he named. "But," I said, "he did not pass the entrance examinations." And he went over the boy's moral excellencies again. "Pardon me," I said, "you do not understand. He did not pass the en-trance examinations. Now," I said, "I want you to understand that if the Angel Gabriel applied for admission to Princeton University and could not pass the entrance examinations, he would not be admitted. He would be wasting his time." It seemed a new idea to him. This boy had come from a school which cultivated character, and he was a nice, lovable fellow with a presentable character. Therefore, he ought to be admitted to any university. I fail to see it from this point of view, for a university is an institution of purpose. We have in some previous years had pity for young gentlemen who were not sufficiently acquainted with the elements of a preparatory course. They have been dropped at the examinations, and I have always felt that we have been guilty of an offense, and have made their parents spend money to no avail and the youngsters spend their time to no avail. And so I think that all university men ought to rouse themselves now and understand what is the object of a university. The object of a university is intellect; as a university its only object is intellect. As a body of young men there ought to be other things, there ought to be diversions to release them from the constant strain of effort, there ought to be things that gladden the heart and moments of leisure, but as a university the only object is intellect.

The reason why I chose the subject that I am permitted to speak upon to-night — the function of scholarship — was that I wanted to point out the function of scholarship not merely in the university but in the nation. In a country constituted as ours is the relation in which education stands is a very important one. Our whole theory has been based upon an enlightened citizenship and therefore the function of scholarship must be for the nation as well as for the university itself. I mean the function of such scholarship as undergraduates get. That is not a violent amount in any case. You cannot make a scholar of a man except by some largeness of Providence in his makeup, by the time he is twenty-one or twenty-

2 A

two years of age. There have been gentlemen who have made a reputation by twenty-one or twenty-two, but it is generally in some little province of knowledge, so small that a small effort can conquer it. You do not make scholars by that time, you do not often make scholars by seventy that are worth boasting of. The process of scholarship, so far as the real scholar is concerned, is an unending process, and knowledge is pushed forward only a very little by his best efforts. And it is evident, of course, that the most you can contribute to a man in his undergraduate years is not equipment in the exact knowledge which is characteristic of the scholar, but an inspiration of the spirit of scholarship. The most that you can give a youngster is the spirit of the scholar.

Now the spirit of the scholar in a country like ours must be a spirit related to the national life. It cannot, therefore, be a spirit of pedantry. I suppose that this is a sufficient working conception of pedantry to say that it is knowledge divorced from life. It is knowledge so closeted, so desecrated, so stripped of the significances of life itself, that it is a thing apart and not connected with the vital processes in the world about us.

There is a great place in every nation for the spirit of scholarship, and it seems to me that there never was a time when the spirit of scholarship was more needed in affairs than it is in this country at this time.

We are thinking just now with our emotions and not with our minds, we are moved by impulse and not by judgment. We are drawing away from things with blind antipathy. The spirit of knowledge is that you must base your conclusions on adequate grounds. Make sure that you are going to the real sources of knowledge, discovering what the real facts are before you move forward to the next process,

which is the process of clear thinking.   By clear thinking I
do not mean logical thinking.   I do not mean that life
is based upon any logical system whatever.   Life is essentially illogical.   The world is governed now by a tumultuous
sea of commonalities made up of passions, and we should
pray God that the good passions should out-vote the bad
passions.   But the movement of impulse, of motive, is
the stuff of passion, and therefore clear thinking about life
is not logical, symmetrical thinking, but it is interpretative
thinking, thinking that sees the secret motive of things,
thinking that penetrates deepest places where are the
pulses of life.

Now scholarship ought to lay these impulses bare just
as the physician can lay bare the seat of life in our bodies.
That is not scholarship which goes to work upon the mere
formal pedantry of logical reasoning, but that *is* scholarship
which searches for the heart of man.   The spirit of scholarship gives us catholicity of thinking, the readiness to understand that there will constantly swing into our ken new
items not dreamed of in our systems of philosophy, not
simply to draw our conclusions from the data that we have
had, but that all this is under constant mutation, and that
therefore new phases of life will come upon us and a new
adjustment of our conclusions will be necessary.   Our
thinking must be detached and disinterested thinking.

The particular objection that I have to the undergraduate forming his course of study on his future profession is this — that from start to finish, from the time
he enters the university until he finishes his career, his
thought will be centered upon particular interests.   He will
be immersed in the things that touch his profit and loss,
and a man is not free to think inside that territory.   If
his bread and butter is going to be affected, if he is always

thinking in the terms of his own profession, he is not thinking for the nation. He is thinking for himself, and whether
he be conscious of it or not, he can never throw these
trammels off. He will only think as a doctor, or a lawyer,
or a banker. He will not be free in the world of knowledge
and in the circle of interests which make up the great
citizenship of the country. It is necessary that the spirit
of scholarship should be a detached, disinterested spirit,
not immersed in a particular interest. That is the function of scholarship in a country like ours, to supply, not
heat, but light, to suffuse things with the calm radiance
of reason, to see to it that men do not act hastily, but that
they act considerately, that they obey the truth whether
they know it or not. The fault of our age is the fault
of hasty action, of premature judgments, of a preference
for ill-considered action over no action at all. Men who
insist upon standing still and doing a little thinking before they do any acting are called reactionaries. They
want actually to react to a state in which they can be
allowed to think. They want for a little while to withdraw from the turmoil of party controversy and see where
they stand before they commit themselves and their country
to action from which it may not be possible to withdraw.

The whole fault of the modern age is that it applies to
everything a false standard of efficiency. Efficiency with
us is accomplishment, whether the accomplishment be by
just and well-considered means or not; and this standard
of achievement it is that is debasing the morals of our age,
the intellectual morals of our age. We do not stop to
do things thoroughly; we do not stop to know why we do
things. We see an error and we hastily correct it by a
greater error; and then go on to cry that the age is
corrupt.

And so it is, gentlemen, that I try to join the function of the university with the great function of the national life. The life of this country is going to be revolutionized and purified only when the universities of this country wake up to the fact that their only reason for existing is intellect, that the objects that I have set forth, so far as undergraduate life is concerned, are the only legitimate objects. And every man should crave for his university primacy in these things, primacy in other things also if they may be brought in without enmity to it, but the sacrifice of everything that stands in the way of that.

For my part, I do not believe that it is athleticism which stands in the way. Athletics have been associated with the achievements of the mind in many a successful civilization. There is no difficulty in uniting vigor of body with achievement of mind, but there is a good deal of difficulty in uniting the achievement of the mind with a thousand distracting social influences, which take up all our ambitions, which absorb all our thoughts, which lead to all our arrangements of life, and then leave the university authorities the residuum of our attention, after we are through with the things that we are interested in. We absolutely changed the whole course of study at Princeton and revolutionized the methods of instruction without rousing a ripple on the surface of the alumni. They said those things are intellectual, they were our business. But just as soon as we thought to touch the social part of the university, there was not only a ripple, but the whole body was torn to its depths. We had touched the real things. These lay in triumphal competition with the province of the mind, and men's attention was so absolutely absorbed in these things that it was impossible for us to get their interest enlisted on the real undertakings of the university itself.

Now that is true of every university that I know anything about in this country, and if the Faculties in this country want to recapture the ground that they have lost, they must begin pretty soon, and they must go into the battle with their bridges burned behind them so that it will be of no avail to retreat. If I had a voice to which the university men of this country might listen, that is the endeavor to which my ambition would lead me to call.

THE RESPONSIBILITY OF AUTHORS [1]

BY

Sir Oliver Lodge

The utility of the deductive form may be illustrated also by this essay of Sir Oliver Lodge. As the footnote states, the question to be discussed was in regard to the value of a censorship over books. Against this, the author wishes to make a definite convincing protest. His last sentence gives the important conclusion that he wishes his readers to adopt. Every paragraph and every sentence in the essay is chosen with this last dominating sentence in mind. He begins, however, with a generalization that is so accepted that it is a platitude. "A work of literature is a real work of creation"; there is nothing here that can be objected to by any one. But if the reader grants this, by careful deduction he shows step by step that the final thought that censorship is undesirable, is the inevitable conclusion. The process by which he passes from the first to the second is therefore worthy of careful study.

A work of literature is a real work of creation. Authors must often have felt that their characters had a will of their own, that they would not always do what was expected of them, that they took the bit between their teeth sometimes, that they were not puppets. Persons in a book or drama ought not to be puppets, and should not be "put back in the box"; nor must they be forcibly

---

[1] An address to the Society of Authors in 1909 in special connection with a proposed Library censorship, whereby, if any three Librarians agreed that a book in course of publication was undesirable, it would be forbidden at all circulating libraries.

Reprinted from "Modern Problems," by permission of George H Doran Co.

coerced by their creator to a predestined end independent of their character and conduct. If they have been properly created they have a real existence of their own, an existence for which the author is responsible, and a certain amount of free will and independence of action.

Coercion to a predestined end is bad art. If that statement is true it is important. It affects the doctrine of predestination. A good work of art throws light on many problems of existence. For instance, the old and fundamental question, "Why is there any pain and sorrow in the world?" can be answered from this point of view. For it is a familiar fact that pain and sorrow are not kept out of a work of art designed and created by man. Why not? Why make trouble and pain artificially, over and above what inevitably exists? Because they are felt to be necessary, because they serve a useful end; they rescue existence from insipidity, they furnish scope for the exercise of human functions, — their endurance is justified, and felt to be "worth while."

King Lear, for instance, is a work of pain and sorrow and beauty. To achieve the beauty the pain was necessary, and its creator thought it worth while. He would not have it otherwise, nor would we. So it is in real life. Creation is "good," even "very good," but not perfect. We are still living amid imperfections; there is always room for improvement. Why is there any imperfection? Because without it evolution and progress, of the high kind which we are privileged to take part in, could not go on. Creation of free and responsible beings, who go right not by compulsion but because they choose, who move forward not because they *must* but because they *will*, cannot be an easy task — may we not venture to say that it must be a strenuous task? — even to Omnipotence.

Every worthy achievement demands certain conditions; and one of those conditions is toil and effort. The effort of Creation is surely a real effort. Difficulty is a necessary sequel to the gift of Freedom.

The construction of the physical universe, the interlocking of atoms and ether that we study in the material sciences, is beautiful and wonderful in the extreme; but it is all a kind of intricate, and high-grade machinery — perfectly obedient, strictly under control, never rebellious. So, though vastly beyond and above mechanism arranged by man, it is not hopelessly and unthinkably of a different kind, — saving always for the unthinkable problem of existence itself. But with the introduction of life and mind and will, difficulties of a superlatively higher order begin. The possibility of things going wrong, not through oversight but through active mutiny and rebellion, the possibility of real *vice*, can no longer be ignored. Compulsion might be easy, but the introduction of compulsion would be a breaking of the rules — an abandonment of the problem. The state of the world is surely as good as it has been possible to make it — given the conditions, — and exhibits infinitely more promise for the future than any mechanically perfect system could sustain; else it were blasphemy to say that there was ever imperfection, else the struggle for existence were a fiction and a sham.

There is undoubtedly a struggle, but there is also much joy, — the joy of achievement sometimes, the joy of preparation always. The joy of achieved existence manifests itself in beauty. Life is pressing forward amid troubles and trials, pressing forward to realize itself, to blossom and bud like a briar among ruins, even amid hardship and decay, — because — because existence is worth its price. Seen in this light the present pain and sorrow lend themselves to Optimism. How splendid must the future of the race be, if all this trouble and all the millions of years of preparation that science tells us of, were needed as its prelude! Each step is presumably essential, as it is in a good work of art. Nothing is there wasted — each word, each scene, each act, *tells*. So I assume it to be with real existence; each step, however painful it may be, is an essential part of the whole.

So an extraordinary responsibility belongs to the artists of the pen. They represent the truth of the present age to itself and to the future : and not only do they represent it, they also prepare the way and to some extent determine what the future shall be. The influence exerted on the living generation by those writers who have its ear, and to whom it listens, must be incalculable. No wonder that an effort is made from time to time to check and control the distribution of the works produced. People of very different ages exist in the world, and not everything is wholesome at every age. Vicious people also exist, and it behoves parents and guardians to exercise some super-vision — as much as they may think wise.

Nevertheless, freedom is essential to literature and the other arts; and their essential freedom must not be jeopardized because of some slatternly and opprobrious stuff which presumes to masquerade under a sacred title. Everything on earth can be misused, and the divinest gift can be prostituted; parents and guardians may properly feel responsibility, but they must not attempt to shift it to the shoulders of others. The danger may easily be exaggerated; and, whatever the danger, it gives no justification for a hasty trade-sifting process applied to works issued by reputable publishing houses and to the writings of sane and responsible authors. Coddling of that kind, even if practicable, would defeat its own end. Youth cannot be isolated and kept sound and sweet by means such as these. A robust is better than an anaemic virtue; and, from the Garden of Eden downwards, though a warning is issued against forbidden fruit, the tree on which it grows is not the tree which by decree of Providence is made impossible of access.

The gentlemen who own circulating libraries have realized what they think is *their* responsibility in this matter, and they very properly decline to circulate anything they think vicious — they desire to issue only good literature; but unfortunately the outcome of this wholesome desire has taken the impracticable form of a scheme for hasty amateur censorship of literary production generally. Such a scheme must be futile. A censorship of the Press by the State — if an attempt were made to reintroduce that — might indeed be a serious thing, against which it would be necessary to invoke the shade of Milton and to quote the *Areopagitica*. Indeed, the utterances of that mighty artist, who must be credited with a sympathetic attitude to all that is reasonable in the Puritan position — are so germane to the supposed need for censorship generally, that I shall not refrain from a few extracts : —

"For though licensers should happen to be judicious more than ordinary, which will be a great jeopardy of the next succession, yet their very office . . . enjoins them to let pass nothing but what is vulgarly received already. . . .

"If there be found in his book one sentence of a venturous edge, uttered in the height of zeal (and who knows whether it might not be the dictate of a divine spirit?), yet, not suiting with every low decrepit humour of their own, though it were Knox himself, the reformer of a kingdom, that spake it, they will not pardon him their dash; the sense of that great man shall to all posterity be lost, for the fearfulness, or the presumptuous rashness of a perfunctory licenser. . . .

". . . Wisdom we cannot call it, because it stops but one breach of license — nor that neither: whenas those corruptions which it seeks to prevent, break in faster at other doors, which cannot be shut. . . . It cannot praise a fugitive and cloistered virtue. . . .

"We should be wary, therefore, what persecution we raise against the living labours of public men, how we spill that seasoned life of man, preserved and stored up in books; since we see a kind of homicide may be thus committed, sometimes a martyrdom; and if it extend to the whole impression, a kind of massacre, whereof the execution ends not in the slaying of an elemental life, but strikes at the ethereal and fifth essence, the breath of reason itself; slays an immortality rather than a life."

Censorship of the Press was not slain by Milton's attack; it survived and presumably flourished during the productive era of the Restoration; but, its impotence having become manifest, it perished some fifty years after Milton's death.

Censorship of the drama, oddly enough, we are living under now; and though comic in its manner and execution, it is yet serious in its effect and outcome. It has prevailed to stop some good work; it does not avail to stop the foolish and the bad, but it stops some of the good — that is what censorship always does — and a censorship by a combination of circulating librarians cannot hope to achieve anything better. It can perturb the freedom of production in the literature of to-day; but over the literature of yesterday no one imagines that it has any control. The writers of the past have the freedom which it is proposed to deny to the writers of the present. Thus some good work has anyhow escaped destruction. There may be tares among the wheat — quite true — no doubt there are; but we have been warned against the danger of prematurely uprooting tares, lest we uproot the wheat also. It is safer to let both grow together. Fortunately the good has a longer life than the bad, and will survive and be full of influence long after the rubbish has retreated to its proper obscurity.

"But of the harm that may result hence . . . first is feared the infection that may spread; but then all human learning and controversy in religious points must remove out of the world, yea, the Bible itself."

If some now universally recognized works of literature — let us say if the classic novels of Henry Fielding — were to be brought out to-day, they would surely under the proposed arrangement be banned. As it is, they can be bought anywhere for a trifling sum. There was some outcry, I remember, about Kingsley's *Hypatia* — amazing as the fact sounds now. Yes, and *Adam Bede*, too, was objected to by some. In my youth *Jane Eyre* was a book half forbidden.

Here is part of a letter from Kingsley to Bishop Wilberforce on the subject of *Hypatia* so late as 1873 : —

"Your letter, I say, touched me deeply, and all the more, because it came from one who had been a sailor. But your kind words about *Hypatia* touched me more than those about *Westward Ho!*; for the former book was written with my heart's blood, and was received, as I expected, with curses from many of the very Churchmen whom I was trying to warn and save. Yet I think the book did good. I know that it has not hurt me, save, perhaps, in that ecclesiastical career to which I have never aspired."

At a time much earlier, in 1851, when *Yeast* appeared, it was received with a torrent of hostile criticism, which though partly clerical and political, was damaging not only to a clergyman but to any reputable citizen. Here, for instance, is an extract from *The Guardian* of that date : —

"A man in the position of the author of *Alton Locke* (if he be the writer) commits a grave offence when he publishes such a book as this. Professing to aim at religious earnestness and high morality, its tendencies are really to the destruction of both. . . . It is the countenance the writer gives to the worst tendencies of the day, and the manner in which he conceals loose morality in a dress of high-sounding and philosophical phraseology, which calls for plain and decided condemnation. . . . Doctrines, however consecrated by the faith of ages, practices, however recommended by the lives of saints, or the authority of wise and good men, are to be despised if they interfere with what he thinks the full development of our nature, tend to check the wildest speculations of the intellect, or even to restrain (if we understand the teaching of his character) the most entire indulgence of the passions."

And so on, with sentences in which the phrases "youthful profligacy," "selfish gratification," "impure philosophy," sufficiently exhibit the charges made.

Indeed, such was the agitation about Kingsley's conscientious utterances at that time that he was actually forbidden by the Bishop of London to preach in London, until the Bishop had had an opportunity of looking into the matter.

A poem of Clough's, too, seems to have been attacked; for we find Kingsley writing to a friend in the following strongly worded style in 1848: —

"As for Clough's poem. I am game to 'go in' fiercely against all Manicheans, Hermann-and-Dorothea-formalists, and other unclean beasts, to prove that Clough knows best what he wants to say, and how; and that taking the poem inductively, and not *a priori* (as the world, the flesh, and the devil take works of art), there is a true honest harmony, and a genial life in it, as of a man who, seeing things as they were, and believing that God and not 'taste' or the devil settles things, was not ashamed to describe what he saw."

It is plain, then, that contemporary criticism may be mistaken, and that a hasty censorship may commit much injustice.

" But that a book, in worse condition than a peccant soul, should be to stand before a jury ere it be born to the world, and undergo yet in darkness the judgment of Radamanth and his colleagues, ere it can pass the ferry backward into light, was never heard before."

As to the accusation of "blasphemy," we can comfort ourselves with the thought that the holiest saints in the past did not escape that. "The Christian faith — for that was once a schism!" The real adjective to apply in these cases is "unconventional" — contrary to accepted convention — if that is what is meant; then we should know where we were. But this adjective is not sufficiently strong and damaging to be injurious. It has even been regarded as semi-complimentary; consequently, when Mr. Bernard Shaw magnanimously wished to assist critics in applying opprobrious epithets to his own plays, he suggested the use of the word "immoral" instead.

But such an application of this word would be merely misleading and most unwise. The significance of the term "unconventional" should be strengthened, till it conveyed what was intended. The conventions of society are quite useful things, the result of ages of experience, and any conduct or writing that runs counter to them must be prepared to stand the test of criticism and to justify itself thoroughly; but it should not be condemned unheard.

The importance and responsibility of free criticism, too, should be fully recognized; and the social ostracism which it can be the means of inflicting is the appropriate and legitimate penalty for needlessly or prematurely infringing the conventions of society. All good customs have their day, and in due time will cease to be. Premature attacks, like premature attacks in chess, are bound to fail. But, every now and then, attacks upon conventions must be made, and when the time is ripe will succeed. An open and above-board attack is far better than one that skulks in holes and corners, and it is best to permit things to be said when they are seriously thought. That is why freedom of the Press is so necessary and valuable, not only as a reforming agency, but also as an outlet for malicious humours, which else might accumulate in the body politic and are better purged.

A writer or publisher who infringes the criminal law is rightly liable to severe penalties, and thereafter to restriction; but occasional abuses of this kind give no adequate ground for curtailment of legitimate freedom. Freedom is the noble and dangerous gift that has been bestowed upon the human race — the power of choice and full responsibility therefor. This responsibility already rests heavily on the shoulders of every artist, every writer. Upon him has been bestowed the gift of insight into life above his fellows. He can see what they see, but he can see it more clearly; he can see more and further than they can. He cannot only see, he can say; he has the gift of utterance, and he is bound to utter what he seriously feels to be his message. There were times when he was threatened with the rack or the stake if he did not hold his tongue. The early scientific discoverers were suppressed in every possible manner. But the more they were suppressed, the more a great deal they published it; and through their labors we have attained to our present large and beneficent freedom. With a great price our ancestors attained this freedom, but we were free-born. We are not going at the beginning of the twentieth century to lose this birthright, at the dictate of any three persons, however estimable, however well-meaning, however able they may be.

FILIAL RELATIONS [1]

BY

JANE ADDAMS

One of the great modern problems is that of the position of woman, and concerning it there is no more careful thinker than Miss Addams, who herself embodies her conception. The following essay was one of a series of lectures delivered before academic audiences. Since an audience imposes its characteristics upon the lecture, the following essay is abstract and very carefully reasoned. It begins with the point of view of the audience, namely an exposition of the position of the conservative element. Then by slow degrees the dominating principle of the demands of Society upon the daughter is elaborated. From this follows the deduction that much of the misery of the modern household lies in the imperfect recognition of the conflicting claims of the Family and the State. It is interesting to notice how very slowly Miss Addams develops her thought. Each position is stated very fully before the new step is taken. Also notice how academic are her illustrations. They are drawn from the life of Saint Francis of Assisi, from Switzerland, and finally and elaborately from the drama of *King Lear*. In each case it is clear that she is addressing not only an audience that thinks, but one that reads. Consider what would result to her argument if the reader were not familiar with *Lear* ! To what extent does an essay like this gain and lose in the limitation of its appeal ?

THERE are many people in every community who have not felt the "social compunction," who do not share the effort toward a higher social morality, who are even unable to sympathetically interpret it. Some of these have been shielded from the inevitable and salutary failures which the

[1] From "Democracy and Social Ethics," by permission of The Macmillan Co.

trial of new powers involve, because they are content to attain standards of virtue demanded by an easy public opinion, and others of them have exhausted their moral energy in attaining to the current standard of individual and family righteousness.

Such people, who form the bulk of contented society, demand that the radical, the reformer, shall be without stain or question in his personal and family relations, and judge most harshly any deviation from the established standards. There is a certain justice in this: it expresses the inherent conservatism of the mass of men, that none of the established virtues which have been so slowly and hardly acquired shall be sacrificed for the sake of making problematic advance; that the individual, in his attempt to develop and use the new and exalted virtue, shall not fall into the easy temptation of letting the ordinary ones slip through his fingers.

This instinct to conserve the old standards, combined with a distrust of the new standard, is a constant difficulty in the way of those experiments and advances depending upon the initiative of women, both because women are the more sensitive to the individual and family claims, and because their training has tended to make them content with the response to these claims alone.

There is no doubt that, in the effort to sustain the moral energy necessary to work out a more satisfactory social relation, the individual often sacrifices the energy which should legitimately go into the fulfilment of personal and family claims, to what he considers the higher claim.

In considering the changes which our increasing democracy is constantly making upon various relationships, it is impossible to ignore the filial relation. This chapter deals with the relation between parents and their grown-up daughters, as affording an explicit illustration of the perplexity and mal-adjustment brought about by the various attempts of young women to secure a more active share in the community life. We constantly see parents very much disconcerted and perplexed in regard to their daughters when these daughters undertake work lying quite outside of traditional and family interests. These parents insist that the girl is carried away by a foolish enthusiasm, that she is in search of a career, that she is restless and does not know what she wants. They will give any reason, almost, rather than the recognition of a genuine and dignified claim. Possibly all this is due to the fact that for so many hundreds of years women have had no larger interests, no participation in the affairs lying quite outside personal and family claims. Any attempt that the individual woman formerly made to subordinate or renounce the family claim was inevitably construed to mean that she was setting up her own will against that of her family's for selfish ends. It was concluded that she could have no motive larger than a desire to serve her family, and her attempt to break away must therefore be wilful and self-indulgent.

The family logically consented to give her up at her marriage, when she was enlarging the family tie by founding another family. It was easy to understand that they permitted and even promoted her going to college, travelling in Europe, or any other means of self-improvement, because these merely meant the development and cultivation of one of its own members. When, however, she responded to her impulse to fulfil the social or democratic claim, she violated every tradition.

The mind of each one of us reaches back to our first struggles as we emerged from self-willed childhood into

a recognition of family obligations. We have all gradually learned to respond to them, and yet most of us have
had at least fleeting glimpses of what it might be to
disregard them and the elemental claim they make upon
us. We have yielded at times to the temptation of ignoring them for selfish aims, of considering the individual
and not the family convenience, and we remember with
shame the self-pity which inevitably followed. But just
as we have learned to adjust the personal and family
claims, and to find an orderly development impossible
without recognition of both, so perhaps we are called upon
now to make a second adjustment between the family
and the social claim, in which neither shall lose and both be
ennobled.

The attempt to bring about a healing compromise in
which the two shall be adjusted in proper relation is not
an easy one. It is difficult to distinguish between the
outward act of him who in following one legitimate claim
has been led into the temporary violation of another,
and the outward act of him who deliberately renounces a
just claim and throws aside all obligation for the sake of
his own selfish and individual development. The man,
for instance, who deserts his family that he may cultivate
an artistic sensibility, or acquire what he considers more
fulness of life for himself, must always arouse our contempt.
Breaking the marriage tie as Ibsen's "Nora" did, to obtain
a larger self-development, or holding to it as George Eliot's
"Romola" did, because of the larger claim of the state
and society, must always remain two distinct paths. The
collision of interests, each of which has a real moral basis
and a right to its own place in life, is bound to be more or
less tragic. It is the struggle between two claims, the
destruction of either of which would bring ruin to the

ethical life. Curiously enough, it is almost exactly this contradiction which is the tragedy set forth by the Greek dramatist, who asserted that the gods who watch over the sanctity of the family bond must yield to the higher claims of the gods of the state. The failure to recognize the social claim as legitimate causes the trouble; the suspicion constantly remains that woman's public efforts are merely selfish and captious, and are not directed to the general good. This suspicion will never be dissipated until parents, as well as daughters, feel the democratic impulse and recognize the social claim.

Our democracy is making inroads upon the family, the oldest of human institutions, and a claim is being advanced which in a certain sense is larger than the family claim. The claim of the state in time of war has long been recognized, so that in its name the family has given up sons and husbands and even the fathers of little children. If we can once see the claims of society in any such light, if its misery and need can be made clear and urged as an explicit claim, as the state urges its claims in the time of danger, then for the first time the daughter who desires to minister to that need will be recognized as acting conscientiously. This recognition may easily come first through the emotions, and may be admitted as a response to pity and mercy long before it is formulated and perceived by the intellect.

The family as well as the state we are all called upon to maintain as the highest institutions which the race has evolved for its safeguard and protection. But merely to preserve these institutions is not enough. There come periods of reconstruction, during which the task is laid upon a passing generation, to enlarge the function and carry forward the ideal of a long-established institution.

There is no doubt that many women, consciously and unconsciously, are struggling with this task. The family, like every other element of human life, is susceptible of progress, and from epoch to epoch its tendencies and aspirations are enlarged, although its duties can never be abrogated and its obligations can never be cancelled. It is impossible to bring about the higher development by any self-assertion or breaking away of the individual will. The new growth in the plant swelling against the sheath, which at the same time imprisons and protects it, must still be the truest type of progress. The family in its entirety must be carried out into the larger life. Its various members together must recognize and acknowledge the validity of the social obligation. When this does not occur we have a most flagrant example of the ill-adjustment and misery arising when an ethical code is applied too rigorously and too conscientiously to conditions which are no longer the same as when the code was instituted, and for which it was never designed. We have all seen parental control and the family claim assert their authority in fields of effort which belong to the adult judgment of the child and pertain to activity quite outside the family life. Probably the distinctively family tragedy of which we all catch glimpses now and then, is the assertion of this authority through all the entanglements of wounded affection and misunderstanding. We see parents and children acting from conscientious motives and with the tenderest affection, yet bringing about a misery which can scarcely be hidden.

Such glimpses remind us of that tragedy enacted centuries ago in Assisi, when the eager young noble cast his very clothing at his father's feet, dramatically renouncing his filial allegiance, and formally subjecting the narrow family claim to the wider and more universal duty. All the conflict of tragedy ensued which might have been averted, had the father recognized the higher claim, and had he been willing to subordinate and adjust his own claim to it. The father considered his son disrespectful and hard-hearted, yet we know St. Francis to have been the most tender and loving of men, responsive to all possible ties, even to those of inanimate nature. We know that by his affections he freed the frozen life of his time. The elements of tragedy lay in the narrowness of the father's mind; in his lack of comprehension and his lack of sympathy with the power which was moving his son, and which was but part of the religious revival which swept Europe from end to end in the early part of the thirteenth century; the same power which built the cathedrals of the North, and produced the saints and sages of the South. But the father's situation was nevertheless genuine; he felt his heart sore and angry, and his dignity covered with disrespect. He could not, indeed, have felt otherwise, unless he had been touched by the fire of the same revival, and lifted out of and away from the contemplation of himself and his narrower claim. It is another proof that the notion of a larger obligation can only come through the response to an enlarged interest in life and in the social movements around us.

The grown-up son has so long been considered a citizen with well-defined duties and a need of "making his way in the world," that the family claim is urged much less strenuously in his case, and as a matter of authority, it ceases gradually to be made at all. In the case of the grown-up daughter, however, who is under no necessity of earning a living, and who has no strong artistic bent, taking her to Paris to study painting or to Germany to

study music, the years immediately following her gradua-
tion from college are too often filled with a restlessness
and unhappiness which might be avoided by a little clear
thinking, and by an adaptation of our code of family
ethics to modern conditions.

It is always difficult for the family to regard the daughter
otherwise than as a family possession. From her baby-
hood she has been the charm and grace of the household,
and it is hard to think of her as an integral part of the
social order, hard to believe that she has duties outside
of the family, to the state and to society in the larger sense.
This assumption that the daughter is solely an inspiration
and refinement to the family itself and its own immediate
circle, that her delicacy and polish are but outward symbols
of her father's protection and prosperity, worked very
smoothly for the most part so long as her education was in
line with it. When there was absolutely no recognition
of the entity of woman's life beyond the family, when the
outside claims upon her were still wholly unrecognized,
the situation was simple, and the finishing school harmoni-
ously and elegantly answered all requirements. She was
fitted to grace the fireside and to add lustre to that social
circle which her parents selected for her. But this family
assumption has been notably broken into, and educational
ideas no longer fit it. Modern education recognizes
woman quite apart from family or society claims, and gives
her the training which for many years has been deemed
successful for highly developing a man's individuality
and freeing his powers for independent action. Perplexi-
ties often occur when the daughter returns from college
and finds that this recognition has been but partially
accomplished. When she attempts to act upon the assumption of its accomplishment, she finds herself jarring

upon ideals which are so entwined with filial piety, so rooted in the tenderest affections of which the human heart is capable, that both daughter and parents are shocked and startled when they discover what is happening, and they scarcely venture to analyze the situation. The ideal for the education of woman has changed under the pressure of a new claim. The family has responded to the extent of granting the education, but they are jealous of the new claim and assert the family claim as over against it.

The modern woman finds herself educated to recognize a stress of social obligation which her family did not in the least anticipate when they sent her to college. She finds herself, in addition, under an impulse to act her part as a citizen of the world. She accepts her family inheritance with loyalty and affection, but she has entered into a wider inheritance as well, which, for lack of a better phrase, we call the social claim. This claim has been recognized for four years in her training, but after her return from college the family claim is again exclusively and strenuously asserted. The situation has all the discomfort of transition and compromise. The daughter finds a constant and totally unnecessary conflict between the social and the family claims. In most cases the former is repressed and gives way to the family claim, because the latter is concrete and definitely asserted, while the social demand is vague and unformulated. In such instances the girl quietly submits, but she feels wronged whenever she allows her mind to dwell upon the situation. She either hides her hurt, and splendid reserves of enthusiasm and capacity go to waste, or her zeal and emotions are turned inward, and the result is an unhappy woman, whose heart is consumed by vain regrets and desires.

If the college woman is not thus quietly reabsorbed, she is even reproached for her discontent. She is told to be devoted to her family, inspiring and responsive to her social circle, and to give the rest of her time to further self-improvement and enjoyment. She expects to do this, and responds to these claims to the best of her ability, even heroically sometimes. But where is the larger life of which she has dreamed so long? That life which surrounds and completes the individual and family life? She has been taught that it is her duty to share this life, and her highest privilege to extend it. This divergence between her self-centred existence and her best convictions becomes constantly more apparent. But the situation is not even so simple as a conflict between her affections and her intellectual convictions, although even that is tumultuous enough, also the emotional nature is divided against itself. The social claim is a demand upon the emotions as well as upon the intellect, and in ignoring it she represses not only her convictions but lowers her springs of vitality. Her life is full of contradictions. She looks out into the world, longing that some demand be made upon her powers, for they are too untrained to furnish an initiative. When her health gives way under this strain, as it often does, her physician invariably advises a rest. But to be put to bed and fed on milk is not what she requires. What she needs is simple, health-giving activity, which, involving the use of all her faculties, shall be a response to all the claims which she so keenly feels.

It is quite true that the family often resents her first attempts to be part of a life quite outside their own, because the college woman frequently makes these first attempts most awkwardly; her faculties have not been trained in the line of action. She lacks the ability to apply her knowledge and theories to life itself and to its complicated situations. This is largely the fault of her training and of the one-sidedness of educational methods. The colleges have long been full of the best ethical teaching, insisting that the good of the whole must ultimately be the measure of effort, and that the individual can only secure his own rights as he labors to secure those of others. But while the teaching has included an ever-broadening range of obligation and has insisted upon the recognition of the claims of human brotherhood, the training has been singularly individualistic; it has fostered ambitions for personal distinction, and has trained the faculties almost exclusively in the direction of intellectual accumulation. Doubtless, woman's education is at fault, in that it has failed to recognize certain needs, and has failed to cultivate and guide the larger desires of which all generous young hearts are full.

During the most formative years of life, it gives the young girl no contact with the feebleness of childhood, the pathos of suffering, or the needs of old age. It gathers together crude youth in contact only with each other and with mature men and women who are there for the purpose of their mental direction. The tenderest promptings are bidden to bide their time. This could only be justifiable if a definite outlet were provided when they leave college. Doubtless the need does not differ widely in men and women, but women not absorbed in professional or business life, in the years immediately following college, are baldly brought face to face with the deficiencies of their training. Apparently every obstacle is removed, and the college woman is at last free to begin the active life, for which, during so many years, she has been preparing.

But during this so-called preparation, her faculties have been trained solely for accumulation, and she has learned to utterly distrust the finer impulses of her nature, which would naturally have connected her with human interests outside of her family and her own immediate social circle. All through school and college the young soul dreamed of self-sacrifice, of succor to the helpless and of tenderness to the unfortunate. We persistently distrust these desires, and, unless they follow well-defined lines, we repress them with every device of convention and caution.

One summer the writer went from a two weeks' residence in East London, where she had become sick and bewildered by the sights and sounds encountered there, directly to Switzerland. She found the beaten routes of travel filled with young English men and women who could walk many miles a day, and who could climb peaks so inaccessible that the feats received honorable mention in Alpine journals, — a result which filled their families with joy and pride. These young people knew to a nicety the proper diet and clothing which would best contribute toward endurance. Everything was very fine about them save their motive power. The writer does not refer to the hard-worked men and women who were taking a vacation, but to the leisured young people, to whom this period was the most serious of the year, and filled with the most strenuous exertion. They did not, of course, thoroughly enjoy it, for we are too complicated to be content with mere exercise. Civilization has bound us too closely with our brethren for any one of us to be long happy in the cultivation of mere individual force or in the accumulation of mere muscular energy.

With Whitechapel constantly in mind, it was difficult not to advise these young people to use some of this muscular energy of which they were so proud, in cleaning neglected alleys and paving soggy streets. Their stores of enthusiasm might stir to energy the listless men and women of East London and utilize latent social forces. The exercise would be quite as good, the need of endurance as great, the care for proper dress and food as important; but the motives for action would be turned from selfish ones into social ones. Such an appeal would doubtless be met with a certain response from the young people, but would never be countenanced by their families for an instant.

Fortunately a beginning has been made in another direction, and a few parents have already begun to consider even their little children in relation to society as well as to the family. The young mothers who attend "Child Study" classes have a larger notion of parenthood and expect given characteristics from their children, at certain ages and under certain conditions. They quite calmly watch the various attempts of a child to assert his individuality, which so often takes the form of opposition to the wishes of the family and to the rule of the household. They recognize as acting under the same law of development the little child of three who persistently runs away and pretends not to hear his mother's voice, the boy of ten who violently, although temporarily, resents control of any sort, and the grown-up son who, by an individualized and trained personality, is drawn into pursuits and interests quite alien to those of his family.

This attempt to take the parental relation somewhat away from mere personal experience, as well as the increasing tendency of parents to share their children's pursuits and interests, will doubtless finally result in a better understanding of the social obligation. The understanding, which results from identity of interests, would seem to confirm the conviction that in the complicated life of to-day there is no education so admirable as that education which comes from participation in the constant trend of events. There is no doubt that most of the misunderstandings of life are due to partial intelligence, because our experiences have been so unlike that we cannot comprehend each other. The old difficulties incident to the clash of two codes of morals must drop away, as the experiences of various members of the family become larger and more identical.

At the present moment, however, many of those difficulties still exist and may be seen all about us. In order to illustrate the situation baldly, and at the same time to put it dramatically, it may be well to take an instance concerning which we have no personal feeling. The tragedy of King Lear has been selected, although we have been accustomed so long to give him our sympathy as the victim of the ingratitude of his two older daughters, and of the apparent coldness of Cordelia, that we have not sufficiently considered the weakness of his fatherhood, revealed by the fact that he should get himself into so entangled and unhappy a relation to all of his children. In our pity for Lear, we fail to analyze his character. The King on his throne exhibits utter lack of self-control. The King in the storm gives way to the same emotion, in repining over the wickedness of his children, which he formerly exhibited in his indulgent treatment of them.

It might be illuminating to discover wherein he had failed, and why his old age found him roofless in spite of the fact that he strenuously urged the family claim with his whole conscience. At the opening of the drama he sat upon his throne, ready for the enjoyment which an indulgent parent expects when he has given gifts to his children. From the two elder, the responses for the division of his lands were graceful and fitting, but he longed to hear what Cordelia, his youngest and best beloved child, would say. He looked toward her expectantly, but instead of delight and gratitude there was the first dawn of character. Cordelia made the awkward attempt of an untrained soul to be honest and scrupulously to express her inmost feeling. The king was baffled and distressed by this attempt at self-expression. It was new to him that his daughter should be moved by a principle obtained outside himself, which even his imagination could not follow; that she had caught the notion of an existence in which her relation as a daughter played but a part. She was transformed by a dignity which recast her speech and made it self-contained. She found herself in the sweep of a feeling so large that the immediate loss of a kingdom seemed of little consequence to her. Even an act which might be construed as disrespect to her father was justified in her eyes, because she was vainly striving to fill out this larger conception of duty. The test which comes sooner or later to many parents had come to Lear, to maintain the tenderness of the relation between father and child, after that relation had become one between adults, to be content with the responses made by the adult child to the family claim, while at the same time she responded to the claims of the rest of life. The mind of Lear was not big enough for this test; he failed to see anything but the personal slight involved, and the ingratitude alone reached him. It was impossible for him to calmly watch his child developing beyond the stretch of his own mind and sympathy.

That a man should be so absorbed in his own indignation

as to fail to apprehend his child's thought, that he should lose his affection in his anger, simply reveals the fact that his own emotions are dearer to him than his sense of paternal obligation. Lear apparently also ignored the common ancestry of Cordelia and himself, and forgot her royal inheritance of magnanimity. He had thought of himself so long as a noble and indulgent father that he had lost the faculty by which he might perceive himself in the wrong. Even in the midst of the storm he declared himself more sinned against than sinning. He could believe any amount of kindness and goodness of himself, but could imagine no fidelity on the part of Cordelia unless she gave him the sign he demanded.

At length he suffered many hardships; his spirit was buffeted and broken; he lost his reason as well as his kingdom; but for the first time his experience was identical with the experience of the men around him, and he came to a larger conception of life. He put himself in the place of "the poor naked wretches," and unexpectedly found healing and comfort. He took poor Tim in his arms from a sheer desire for human contact and animal warmth, a primitive and genuine need, through which he suddenly had a view of the world which he had never had from his throne, and from this moment his heart began to turn toward Cordelia.

In reading the tragedy of King Lear, Cordelia receives a full share of our censure. Her first words are cold, and we are shocked by her lack of tenderness. Why should she ignore her father's need for indulgence, and be unwilling to give him what he so obviously craved? We see in the old king "the over-mastering desire of being beloved, selfish, and yet characteristic of the selfishness of a loving and kindly nature alone." His eagerness produces in us a strange pity for him, and we are impatient that his youngest and best-beloved child cannot feel this, even in the midst of her search for truth and her newly acquired sense of a higher duty. It seems to us a narrow conception that would break thus abruptly with the past and would assume that her father had no part in the new life. We want to remind her "that pity, memory, and faithfulness are natural ties," and surely as much to be prized as is the development of her own soul. We do not admire the Cordelia who through her self-absorption deserts her father, as we later admire the same woman who comes back from France that she may include her father in her happiness and freer life. The first had selfishly taken her salvation for herself alone, and it was not until her conscience had developed in her new life that she was driven back to her father, where she perished, drawn into the cruelty and wrath which had now become objective and tragic.

Historically considered, the relation of Lear to his children was archaic and barbaric, indicating merely the beginning of a family life since developed. His paternal expression was one of domination and indulgence, without the perception of the needs of his children, without any anticipation of their entrance into a wider life, or any belief that they could have a worthy life apart from him. If that rudimentary conception of family life ended in such violent disaster, the fact that we have learned to be more decorous in our conduct does not demonstrate that by following the same line of theory we may not reach a like misery.

Wounded affection there is sure to be, but this could be reduced to a modicum if we could preserve a sense of the relation of the individual to the family, and of the latter

2 c

to society, and if we had been given a code of ethics dealing with these larger relationships, instead of a code designed to apply so exclusively to relationships obtaining only between individuals.

Doubtless the clashes and jars which we all feel most keenly are those which occur when two standards of morals, both honestly held and believed in, are brought sharply together. The awkwardness and constraint we experience when two standards of conventions and manners clash but feebly prefigure this deeper difference.

THE IRONY OF NATURE [1]

BY

RICHARD BURTON

In the delightful Foreword to his "Little Essays in Literature and Life," the volume from which the following essay is taken, Professor Burton tells us that the ambition of the familiar essayist is "to speak wisdom albeit debonairly, to be thought-provoking without heaviness, and helpful without didacticism." Here he wishes to have the reader feel that there is a communion with nature so sweet and strong and sustaining that it is counted among our most precious experiences. That is his objective point. In the deductive type of essay that sentence would be placed very early, illustrated and explained, and the attention would be focussed finally upon one typical phase. Notice that here exactly the contrary method is followed. The essay begins with an anecdote, illustrating the irony of character. Then follows a statement of the irony of nature. She crushes not individuals only, but whole cities. The pessimism induced by such a calamity is staggering. But it may be due to a false valuation. And there is a communion with nature. In proportion, the last paragraph occupies over one quarter of the space. The value of this method lies in the fact that the reader, beginning easily, is carried to a broad conception. The author, as it were, forces the reader to make his own generalization. Consequently, though more difficult, it is more effective than the other forms.

IN his delightful reminiscences, "Thirty Years of Paris," Alphonse Daudet tells of his companionship with Turgenev in those memorable evenings when he, Goncourt, Zola, and the mighty Russian ate supper together and talked of literature and life. He recalls how Turgenev gave him every evidence of friendship and affection;

[1] From "Little Essays in Literature and Life," by permission of The Century Co.

but long after his death, Daudet read certain words of his friend, wherein the author of "Fathers and Sons" sneers at his French *confrère* as "the lowest of my kind." And Daudet, with that wonderful Gallic lightness of touch which hides yet reveals the deep things of the heart, sighs over the disillusionment, and exclaims: "I can see him in my house, at my table, gentle, affectionate, kissing my children. I have in my possession many exquisite, warm-hearted letters from him. And this was what lay concealed beneath that kindly smile. Good heavens! How strange life is, and how true that charming word of the Greek language, *eironêia !*"

Yet this is the irony of character and circumstance. There is in life one deeper yet and more terrible: the irony of Nature. You feel that the Daudet episode might possibly be straightened out, that "the faith between friends" may haply be restored. But the other is different, hopeless. Hawthorne's "The Ambitious Guest" narrates how a family of cheerful folk sit talking with a guest for the night, in their house far up in the White Mountains, and discourse of human fate and their particular desires. Of a sudden they are interrupted by a sound of awful omen; there is a landslide, and when they realize that destruction is upon them they rush forth from the house to seek a place of safety, only to be buried under the avalanche, one and all. But the house in which they sat escapes scot free. Had they remained about the fire and continued their friendly converse, they would not have perished. Acting for what seemed to be the best, they were ruthlessly exterminated, since the processes of Nature, represented in this case by the landslide, pay no heed to that petty creature, man, and move on their mysterious ways, as if in mockery of his ineptness and ignorance of the fall of events. At such a juncture, a Plato, a Cæsar or a Shakspere is as helpless as the commonest of the earth.

Here is that irony which, sooner or later, confronts every thoughtful mind and no doubt often shakes the very foundations of faith. And surely it is far sadder than the irony which inheres in character, because it is, or seems, irremediable. Millions of human beings in the world's history have taken steps to the best of their judgment and actuated by the highest motives, only to be precipitated into calamity and to lose their lives in a manner so disastrous as to make the looker-on shudder with horror. Nature, magnificently indifferent to the animalcule who for a brief term of time struts and prates upon the earth, conducts her business according to great general laws, utterly refusing to consider the convenience, comfort, or welfare of such an unimportant item in the teeming universe. Often the ironic scene is on a scale of epic grandeur. Not men as individuals, but whole cities go down to death : Pompeii lies buried beneath the lava, San Francisco goes up in smoke, Messina is shaken into ruins.

At first, the spectacle of this cruel unconcern of Nature is of staggering effect ; that sometimes it breeds pessimism can well be understood. How, in truth, can this seemingly heartless procedure on the part of Nature — meaning by the word a personification of the laws and processes operative in the physical universe as observed by man — be explained, so that we may return to the soothing thought that not a sparrow falls unnoted, and that, in the forever lovely words of Coleridge,

> He prayeth best who loveth best
> All things both great and small ;
> For the dear God who loveth us,
> He made and loveth all.

Of course, all such inquiry can be dismissed on the ground that man is not intended to understand, that his limitations make mystery inevitable, and that faith is thus exercised as it faces the vast and curious antinomies of human life and the course of Nature. If we could comprehend all, there were no proper place for that spirit of trust — yea, even though it slay us! — which is the very basis of religion.

Perhaps another thought helps a little when one's mood is darkened by the apparent irony, whether of man or Nature. Why may it not be that all such catastrophic occurrences are but a reminder to us worldlings of the false valuations which are set upon life? Since it is natural for all to die, the manner of going is secondary; and so-called catastrophes are, as a rule, horrible to the observer rather than to the victim, who most often is painlessly and instantly removed from consciousness. But even if we conceded the suffering, it still remains true in a high and holy sense that nothing evil can happen to a good man, — worldly evil, yes, in plenty, but not that evil which is the only true tragedy to the philosopher: spiritual failure. What we call our tragedies are, speaking by and large, merely violent and unexpected interruptions of pleasure. And it is certainly salutary to be reminded, although in a way that is repellent, that one whom physical disaster overcomes can yet sleep with that smile upon his face which is a sign of triumph, and the certificate of a rest well won. The solemn saying of the Greek, "call no man happy until he is dead," was not uttered in cheap cynicism, but had in mind the fact that each day until the end is a chance for the spiritual success or defeat; and that, therefore, we may not claim the victory until all the days be numbered. It may well be, therefore, that what is known

as the "pathetic fallacy" in literature, the mood of loving
trust which makes Wordsworth see beneficent intention
in "earth's diurnal course," and sing in his own winsome
way,

> One impulse from a vernal wood
> May teach you more of man,
> Of moral evil and of good
> Than all the sages can,

— expresses a truth, a spiritual fact, deeper than any
process of logic, and more trustworthy than all self-
conscious reasoning.   Explain it as we will, and whatever
be the testimony of the brain, there is, as countless stricken
souls are aware, a communion with Nature so sweet and
strong and sustaining that it is counted among our most
precious experiences, and, once over, laid away in the
lavender of memory forever.   And when we no longer see
through a glass darkly, but face to face, it may then
become plain that behind the grim look and the chastise-
ment was the benign countenance of the friend, and the
unspeakable yearning of the mother heart.   Irony, in
the last analysis, may resolve itself into a masked goodwill.

ON SEEING TEN BAD PLAYS[1]

BY

Frank Moore Colby

Mr. Colby wishes the reader to make the generalization that the crude state of the drama is due to the crudity of the American public. Like Professor Burton, he starts with the particular fact that he has just seen ten bad plays. A long paragraph is devoted to an analysis of the audiences. A long paragraph, including the succeeding one of illustration, is devoted to the drama. The obvious induction is that these are correlative. Consequently there must be poor plays, since the American public is crude. In contrast with Professor Burton's subtle and allusive style, Mr. Colby hits with sledge-hammer blows. His witty phrases are not subtle, but they are most effective. He holds the attention, not as does Professor Burton with an aroma of lavender, but with humorous over-statement. You laugh — but you also remember the conclusion.

Had I an artist's soul I should be somewhat soured by what I have gone through. As it is, I have fought down all bitterness of heart by the aid of a little philosophy. A man needs philosophy more for the commonplaces of this world than he does for its miseries, ennui being a steadier foe than pain. I therefore offer my philosophy of the commonplace in the American drama and literature. It is not deep, but it is at least bland, and it may help to allay irritation in certain moods. There is enough of polished sarcasm, and of cynicism there is already too

[1] From "Imaginary Obligations." Copyright, 1904, by Dodd, Mead & Co. By permission of the author and publishers.

much.   What we need is something that will aid us in matters of routine.

In the first place I swear by all that is holiest in democracy — by the boiled onions of the plain people, by their even plainer wives, by the firesides of Tom, Dick and Harry, by the sanctity of the bigger figure, by the sacred whoops of the majority — that the usual man is not to blame for wanting the usual thing.   Hallcainery has its place in the world.   Indeed, I believe it altogether healthy, hopeful, and respectable, and if I thought otherwise I should lose all faith in representative institutions.   There are a few who never weary of saying spiteful things about literary mediocrity.   They have no patience with development or kindliness for beginnings; they would condemn every tadpole as a sort of apostate frog.   Why are they so petulant with majorities?   Humanity would pine away on masterpieces; yet many would have you think that the journey from savagery to high art must be made in total silence, with nothing to read on the way.   Our plays are relatively good, being no further below the drama than they are above tomtoms and human sacrifice.   Blessed is vulgar "reading-matter," for without it people might eat one another.   No race ever sinks from Hallcainery into barbarism; it rises from barbarism to Hallcainery, whence in time it may emerge.

And who shall say that our plays are not as good as our politics, or our writers as our Senators?   Do we expect brilliancy in our statesmen?   We are thankful enough in this country for a good candidate, let who will be clever. If a large city can, after intense intellectual efforts, choose for its mayor a man who merely will not steal from it, we consider it a triumph of the suffrage.   So moderate are our expectations in this field that if ordinary intelligence be superadded, it seems a piece of luck. We are overjoyed at any sign that the nation's choice is up to the nation's average ; and time and again you hear a thing called statesmanlike, which in private life would be just on the safe side of sanity. Mr. McKinley's refusal of a third term was regarded as a masterstroke of wisdom, and we have all read praises of Mr. Roosevelt's achievements which are deserved as well by anybody we ever knew. Nobody praises us when we come home sober of an evening, or speak a good average sentence, or draw a good average breath ; and sturdy virtues that keep us out of the police court for weeks at a time are not even mentioned by the family. But by these negative signs you can often tell a statesman, for politics is a place of humble hopes and strangely modest requirements, where all are good who are not criminal and all are wise who are not ridiculously otherwise. Any one who is used to the accidents of majorities should acquire this habit of mind. But the literary and artistic people persist in the most exorbitant demands at a point where the least should be logically expected, that is, the tastes of a crowd. And if the majority is against them, they scold it and the thing it chooses, and having lost their tempers and tired their friends, and troubled a number of honest creatures who have not the least idea what it is all about, they feel that they have been doing wonders for what they call artistic standards. Right enough views, but the wrong occasion. We expect only peace in a cable car ; for ecstasies we must look somewhere else.

If high art deserves its ecstasies, low art deserves its consolations ; and if there is any way of making better terms with humdrum and escaping the spasms of reform, it is our plain business to find it. St. Paul said, keep the body under. I say unto you, keep the mind under on seeing American plays. Be "contentit wi' little and canty wi' mair"; smile though the smile looks sometimes like a rictus; get the point of view of the original erect ape-man (*pithecanthropus erectus*); and if at any time you are afflicted by a play that is particularly bad and popular, consider the growth of our manufactures and sing "My Country, 'Tis of Thee." To express one's own tastes is reasonable, but to worry too much over other people's leads to a useless violence. Some wish to murder Hall Caine. I believe it would be inexpedient to do so, and possibly wrong. I believe Mr. Clyde Fitch as truly represents New York as Senator Peffer did Kansas or Mr. Bryan the West; and the more I see of audiences the surer I am that to massacre is the only way to reform.

Unwilling to be dependent longer on the bounty of her rich guardian the high-spirited *ingénue* in light blue leaves her luxurious home to teach school in a distant village. Being very much of a lady she is obliged to walk as if the stage floor were red hot, and to speak in a high trilling voice with a foreign accent — a course that instantly wins for her the love of every one she meets. But the guardian comes to urge her to return to what, as a gentleman of wealth and refinement, he is obliged to call "me home." They are talking alone, but as soon as she begins to explain that self-respect will not permit her to remain with him, now that she knows the fortune is not really hers, the violins play softly and from every door and alley the villagers come pouring in. A sentimental conversation between people they barely know will draw villagers to the spot for miles around. So when the heroine and her guardian are at their saddest everybody is punctually in place. It is all very exasperating, and the superior person, who has no business to be there, will ask you if it is Art. It is not Art, but the stout lady in the seat behind you is nearly bursting with sobs, and a large number of pocket handkerchiefs are fluttering in the aisles. With this particular audience Art could do nothing at all. Then comes humor in its more awful forms. Thrice-explained humor, with long waits for the effects; humor accompanied by the hilarious roars of the man who made it. And for half an hour there is as genuine enjoyment as you ever saw, and at the very heaviest of horse-plays the stout lady behind you says, "Isn't that rich?" Elevate the stage? Perhaps you can, but it will be a good many generations before those people will be ready for it. A quarter of an inch elevation would spoil the whole thing for them.

There is plenty of room for a good theatre, but there is no use in hoping that it will draw away the crowds from the class of plays that are now successful. These plays will continue, or others just as bad. They are wonderfully adapted to the people who go to see them, and as time goes on this element of the population is bound to increase. There are more below than above them. It is absurd for the superior person to ask them if it is Art. He would not take on like that about a ball game or a merry-go-round. And at a country fair or sociable or "sugar eat" he would not be so savage about bad taste. But a simple, hearty New York audience abandoning itself to the innocent, if rude, pleasures of the average play has no mercy from him for the amazing reason that it is not Art. As if simplicity required a background of hen roosts and apple orchards and all primitive men tucked their trousers in their boots. He is a child of nature, the New York playgoer, even if he is not picturesque, and he has an honest and wholesome regard for whatever is atrocious in art. Put him on the diet of the superior person and he would soon starve.

There must be bad plays. You cannot civilize the whole crowd of us at once, and those hideous early stages of artistic appreciation cannot be skipped. There is much cheerless writing on a subject that from certain points of view is almost cheerful. Compare the worst successful New York play with a war dance or with certain Zulu sports. Things have greatly improved. How did the same class use to amuse themselves? As to moral lessons, the poorest of successful plays is remarkably vigorous and insistent. No sign of decay there. In fact, the worse the art the more blatant the moral. No New York playgoer is likely to forget for one moment that virtue is an admirable thing. Is it not cheerful to think of the big audiences going night after night to have the same elementary moral lessons pounded in? You want your moral lesson served artistically or you will not take it at all. Perhaps you would as lief see the wicked triumph for a change. But these people are content with virtue in the raw. They are not after new ideas, but want some one to say a good word for those they have already. On no account must you meddle with their minds.

The moral of all this is that one ought to try and see the bright side of the situation, if such a thing is to be found, and suppress those murderous feelings toward what after all is a worthy class of citizens and good building material for the state. In spite of artistic merit and intelligence good plays may succeed, and some day the experiment will be tried on a large scale; but in the meanwhile all the philosophy that you can summon and patience with those who like the plays they have. The undiscriminating benignity of audiences almost drives you mad. Why do they not rise from their places and burn and slay? How easy to lynch the manager, if they only knew. But they are having a good time for all your splutter about Art, and if you can see any signs of demoralization in their pleasant moon faces you are a cynic at heart. For whatever our stage is, it supplies the unseasoned food that is relished in the lusty infancy of Art.

A STEPDAUGHTER OF THE PRAIRIE [1]

BY

Margaret Lynn

Quite another type of essay from those preceding is that in which the thought is subordinated to the emotion. In such an essay the writer tries to reproduce the impression or series of impressions caused upon him by scenes or incidents. Naturally, therefore, there can be no logical relation between paragraphs; what relation there is must be emotional. Thus Miss Lynn's "Stepdaughter of the Prairie" is a record of certain soul experiences, vague imaginings of childish dreams. The effort to transform the prairie into the landscape of Tennyson is quaintly pathetic, — to find there alien beauty and, in the attempt, to overlook the wonder that was no wonder because it was always there! And the trees on her horizon spelled l-i-f-e.

FAR away on the almost bare line of the prairie horizon a group of trees used to show. There was a tall one, and a short one, and then a tallish crooked one and another short one. And to my childish eyes they spelled l-i-f-e, as plainly as any word in my reader was spelled. They were the point that most fascinated me as I knelt at the upstairs window, with my elbows on the sill and my chin on my folded arms. I don't know when I first noticed them, for they had been there always, so far as I could remember, a scanty little bit of fringe on a horizon that was generally clear and bare. There were tips of other woods farther to the south, woods that were slightly known to me; but

[1] From "A Stepdaughter of the Prairie," by permission of the author and of The Macmillan Co.

this group of trees at the very limit of seeing appeared to lie beyond the knowledge of anyone. Even on the afternoons when I was allowed to go with my father on some long ride, and we drove and drove and drove, we never came in sight of it. Yet, when I next went upstairs and looked from the window, there it stood against the sky.

I had no sense of making an allegory out of it. At that age to the fairy-tale-fed child, the line between allegory and reality is scarcely perceptible, anyway. The Word on the horizon was only a matter of course to me. An older person, had it occurred to me to mention the matter, would perhaps have seen something significant, even worthy of sentimental remark, in the child's spelling out life on her far horizon. But to me, mystery as it was, it was also a matter of fact; there it stood, and that was all. Yet it was also a romance, a sort of unformulated promise. It was related to the far distant, to the remote in time, to the thing that was some day to be known. So I rested my chin on my little arms and watched.

I suppose the fact that the trees were evidently big and old — ours were still young and small — and perhaps a part of some woods, was their greatest interest to me. For no one can picture what the woods mean to the prairie child. They are a glimpse of dream-things, an illustration of poems read, a mystery of undefined possibilities. To pass through our scant bits of woods, even, was an excursion into a strange world. From places on the road to town we could see pieces of timber. And on some blessed occasions when a muddy hollow was impassable or when the Howell Bridge, the impermanent structure of a prairie country, was out, we went around through the Crossley woods. That was an experience! The depth of greenness — the prairie had nothing like it. I think that my eyes were born tired of the prairie, ungrateful little soul that I was.

And the summer shadows in the woods were marvelous. The shadow of the prairie was that of a passing cloud, or the square shade of some building, deepest at noonday. But the green depth of the woods' shadows, the softly moving light and shade, were a wonderful thing. To me these trips put all probability on a new basis. Out on the bare prairie, under the shining sun, stories were stories, even the dearest of them inventions. But in these shady depths, where my eyes were led on from green space through green space to a final remote dimness, anything might be true. Fiction and tradition took on a reality that the glaring openness would not allow. Things that were different might happen in a wood. I could not help expecting a new experience. But it never came; we passed out of the timber to the prairie again.

But at least expectation had been stirred. The possibility that something might happen seemed nearer. For Romance was always just around the corner, or just a little way ahead. But out on the prairie how could one overtake it? Where could the unknown lurk in that great open? The woods seemed to put me nearer to the world on whose borders I always hovered, the world of stories and poems, the world of books in general. The whole business of life in those first reading years was to discover in the world of actual events enough that was bookish to reconcile me to being a real child and not one in a story. For the most part, aside from play, which was a thing in itself and had a sane importance of its own, the realities of life were those that had their counterpart in books. Whatever I found in reading, especially in poetry, I craved for my own experience.

2 D

There is no bookishness like that of a childish reader, and there is no romanticism like that of a child. For good or ill, I was steeped in both. But the two things, books and the visible world that the sun shone in and the prairie spread out in, were far apart and, according to my lights, incompatible. I always had a suspicion of a distinct line between literature and life, at least life as I knew it, far out in the Missouri valley. Who had ever heard of the Missouri in a novel or a poem? No essays on Literature and Life had then enlightened me as to their relation; I didn't know that they had any. I wished that life could be translated into terms of literature, but so far as I could see I had to do it myself if it was to be done.

One must admit that it was little less than tragic to read of things that one could not know, and to live among things that had never been thought worth putting into a book. What did it avail to read of forests and crags and waterfalls and castles and blue seas, when I could know only barbed-wire fences and frame buildings and prairie grass?

Of course there were some elements of our living in which I discovered resemblances to what I had found in my reading, and I was always alert to these things, however small. I admired my pretty young-lady sister, for instance, but I admired her most when she put on the garments of romance; when she wore a filmy white muslin with blue ribbons, a costume stamped with the novelist's approval from the earliest times; or, better still, a velvet hat with a long plume sweeping down over her hair. For some reason I cannot explain — possibly because I knew him then better than I do now — I associated her appearance then with that of some of Scott's heroines. She rose in my estimation — as did anyone else — whenever she managed, however unconsciously, to link herself with romance. When I found after a time, as I grew sophisticated, that she was capable of exciting those feelings in the masculine breast that are depicted with some care in novels, especially in those which were forbidden and which I was obliged to read by snatches and in inconvenient places, I gave her my unqualified approval for all time.

As I have said, there is no bookishness like that of a small bookworm. In my own little self I did try to make a point of contact between what I read and what I saw. I wished that I dared to use the language of books. I did occasionally indulge in the joy of borrowing a literary phrase. To the grown-ups who heard it, it was doubtless a bit of precocious pedantry or an effort to show off. I sometimes saw visitors smile at one another, and with sudden amused interest try to draw me out; and in stammering prosaic embarrassment I shrank away, no literary fluency left. In reality I was not showing off. I could not resist the shy delicious pleasure of making my own a phrase from one of our yellow-leaved books of poetry. It linked reality with romance. In some way it seemed to make me free of the world of folk in books, whose company I craved. The elders never guessed the tremor with which I ventured on my phrase from Tennyson or Lowell, though I might have been rolling it under my tongue for half an hour. But it would not do, I saw, to use the sacred language lightly before unproved hearers, so I generally reserved it for my little talkings to myself. I had my small code of phrases for my private purposes, and a list of expletives rich but amazing. They were gleaned all the way from Shakespeare to Scott; modern writers are pitifully meager in expletives.

But that was after all a thin delight. And to live in one kind of country and feed on the literature of another kind of country is to put one all awry. Why was there no literature of the prairie? Whatever there was did not come to my hands, and I went on trying to translate the phenomena of the Missouri valley into terms of other-land poetry. But even such things as we had, appeared in unrecognizable guise. We had wild flowers in abundance, but unnamed. And what are botanical names to a child who wants to find foxglove and heather and bluebells and Wordsworth's daffodils and Burns's daisy? We — I was not alone in this quest — wanted names that might have come out of a book. So we traced imagined resemblances, and with slight encouragement from our elders — *they* came from back east where well-established flowers grow — named plants where we could.

There was a ruffly yellow flower with a vague pretty odor, which we forced the name primrose upon. For the primrose was yellow, in Wordsworth at least, and some agreeable visitor had said that this might be a primrose. We invented spurious pseudo-poetic names, trying to pretend that they were as good as the names we read. There was a pink flower of good intentions but no faithfulness, which retired at the approach of the sun, and which we christened "morning beauty." We had other attempts at ready-made folk names, crude and imitative, but I have forgotten them. What a pity the prairie did not last long enough to fix itself and the things that belonged to it in a sort of folk phrases! At least we ought to have had enough flower lore at our command to give us the sweet real names that may have belonged to its blossoms or their relatives in other lands. When we did learn such a name for some half-despised flower, how the plant leaped

to honor and took on a halo of merit! Some elder occasionally went with us to the woods, some teacher, perhaps,
hungry for her own far-away trees, and we found that
we really had a genuine sweet-william and dog-tooth
violet and Jack-in-the-pulpit and May apple, and even
a rare diffident yellow violet. They were no more beautiful than our gay, nameless flowers of the open, but they
grew in the woods and they had names with an atmosphere
to them. In our eternal quest for names, some learned
visitor — for we had many a visitor of every kind — would
give us crisp, scientific terms loaded with consonants. But
how could one love a flower by a botanical name?

As days went by, however, even before it was time for
me to be taken from the little country school and sent
east to learn other things, some conditions had changed.
Chance seeds of different flowers and grasses came floating
west. In a neighbor's field were real daisies — we did not
know then that they were not Burns's — brought in the
seed with which the field was sown, most unwelcome to
the farmer, but worshipped by us. Our own groves,
planted before we children were born, were growing up
and already served for the hundred purposes to which
children can put trees. But the ones most generous in
their growth and kindest in their service to us we regarded
with ungrateful contempt. Who had ever heard of a
a cotton-wood in a book? The box-elder was distinctly
unliterary. The fact that these trees had been quickest
and most gracious in redeeming new homes from bareness
was nothing to us. Even the maple was less valuable when
we learned that it was not the sugar-maple, and that no
matter how long we waited we could never have a sugar-
ing-off. The trees we were most eager for came on
slowly. It seemed as if the oaks would never have acorns.

They did come at last, and we were able to satisfy ourselves that they were not edible, either green or ripe,
and to fit our pinky fingers into the velvety little thimbles
of them, the softest, warmest little cups in the world.

Our grove was an experimental one, as a grove in a new
country must be, and held all sorts of things, which we
made our own one by one. There were slender white
birches, to become beautiful trees in time, from which we
stripped bits of young bark. It was quite useless, of
course, a flimsy, papery stuff, but we pretended to find
use for it, as we had read of others doing. There were
handsome young chestnut trees, bravely trying to adapt
themselves to their land of exile. The leaves were fine for
making dresses and hats, and we spent long July afternoons
bedizened like young dryads. There were so many
things to do and to investigate in the earlier months that
it was midsummer before we reached this amusement.
But we watched year by year for the fruit of the tree.
And at last, when the first ones came, we carried them
proudly to school to exhibit them for the wonderment of
the other pupils, and to apply them surreptitiously to
the natural uses of a chestnut burr.

One spring day, in the dimmest part of the maple grove,
we found a tiny fern-head coming up from a scanty bed of
moss. We watched it for days, consulting at intervals
the pictures of ferns in the encyclopedia, and at last, when
hope trembled on the brink of certainty, we solemnly
led our mother out to identify it. Was it really a fern or
only a weed that looked like a fern? No sacred oak was
ever approached with more careful reverence. Our
mother, an exile from her own forest country, talked of
bracken shoulder-high and rich moss on old gray stones
or broad tree stumps. We used to draw in our breath at

the wanton riches of fallen trees and stumps. *Big* trees, to cut down! We viewed our mother enviously. But our little frond was something. It drew as great ecstasy from our little hearts as a bracken-covered hillside has ever done. We saw the bracken in epitome, and dreamed of conventicles and royal fugitives.

How I hoarded my little borrowings from the actual to enrich the ideal! A neighbor had a stake-and-rider fence. No doubt he was a poor footless sort of farmer or he would never, in that country, have had one — where all good farmers had barbed-wire, or, at best, rail fences. My father had some hedges, and I was proud of them. They were not hawthorn, but one must be thankful for what gifts fate brings, and I felt some distinction in their smooth, genteel lines. But that Virginia rail fence — I coveted its irregular convolutions and deep angles, where the plough never went and where almost anything might grow. Whether it was an older place than ours or a worse-cared-for one, I don't know. But, if the cause were bad farming, it had a reward out of proportion, in my estimation; for the deep fence corners held a tangle wonderful to investigate, of wild grape and pokeberry and elderberry and an ivy the leaves of which must be counted to see if it were poison. They either should or should not be the same as the number of my fingers; but I never could remember which it was and had to leave its pink tips of tender new leaves unplucked. There were new little maples and box-elders, where the rails had stopped the flight of the winged seeds from the small grove about the house. There were tiny elms with their exquisite little leaves. No beauty of form I have ever found has given me more complete satisfaction than did the perfect lines and notches of those baby leaves. There were other plants that I never learned to know. How much better it would have been had all fields had a border like this, ornamental and satisfying, instead of the baldness of a wire fence. The possession of it gave the O'Brion children an eminence that, while I knew it was factitious, I could not help recognizing.

On our part we had a stream, such as it was. The muddy little creek — we called it *crick* — was to me a brook, secretly. Poor little creek! It did to wade in and to get muddy in, but that was all. It had no trout, no ripples over stones, no grassy banks. It ran through a cornfield and a bit of scanty pasture where its banks were trodden by the feet of cattle; and it did not babble as it flowed. Try as I might, I could not connect it with Tennyson or Jean Ingelow. But I could at least call it a brook to myself. I had other names of secret application. In the spring the dull little stream used to overflow its banks. Then the word brought to the house by one of the men would be, "The crick's out." But to myself I said freshet, and I suppose I was the only one in the whole section to use the old word.

There was an odd little hollow on the hillside above the brook. It was an unromantic spot enough, treeless, distinguished only by its dimple-like contour. But I called it a dell, or in intenser moments a dingle or, when I was thinking largely, a glen, and used to make a point to cross it. This was partly because I sometimes found bits of pebbles in the cup of the hollow, and any stone indigenous to the country was a treasure trove. I called the little level place below the hollow a glade, and the hillside a brae, and the open hill-top a moor or heath. Had I used the dictionary more freely I might have applied more terms, but I did not know what a wold or a tarn or a down was, and, lazily, kept them in reserve, fine as they sounded. My private vocabulary, as can be seen, was largely Tennysonian, and I loved an archaism, as something remote from the practical. Whatever excursions I made into other poets, Tennyson was, first and last, my dear delight. My feet were turned over and oft, by the guardians of my reading, into the easy paths of American poetry. I found due pleasure in them, but it was always tempered by a sort of resentment that, though American, their country was not my country. For New England was farther away than Old England, and I always went back to Tennyson. I used to sit in the dingle in bald sunlight and listen to such unpretentious noise as the creek made, and chant to myself, "How sweet it were, hearing the downward stream!"

The beauty of the prairie is not of the sort that a child perceives. The bigness of it, for instance, I had been used to all my life, and I can't remember that in those earlier days it conveyed any sense of expansiveness to me. In our long drives over it — interminably long they seemed once! — my chief recollection is of greenness and tiredness, a long succession of rolling hills and hollows, and a little girl so weary of sitting up on a seat and watching the horses go on and on. I thought the prairie was just green grass in summer and dry grass in winter. Children are not usually awake to shadings and modifications of color. The coral pink at the roots of the dried prairie grass, the opal tints of the summer mists in the early morning, I did not discover until I had reached a stage of greater alertness.

And the prairie was not suggestive to me at this early time. Looking back now, I guess that it was because it did not hint at the unknown. It should have, of course, but it did not. It did not carry me away and away to new possibilities.　I knew that beyond these grass-covered hills there lay others and then others — and that was all there was to it.　When I saw it face to face I seemed to know it all — and who wants to know all about anything? This was not only because I was a book-stuffed little prig, as I suppose I was.　I had imagination of a sort, as it seems to me now, when I recall my pleasure in certain things: in the dim, hovering suggestiveness of twilight and the unanalyzable reverie it put me into; in the half-heard sounds of mid-afternoon in the orchard; in the bend of the young trees in a storm at night, when I slipped from bed to watch them in the flashes of lightning.　There was a white pine near my window, "an exile in a stoneless land," that responded to the rush of the western wind with a beautiful bend and swing.　But when in the broad daylight I looked out on the green hills I, in those earlier days, saw no changing colors, none of the exquisite variety of view that must have been there.　I saw only green hills.

But had the prairie had a literature — if I could only have been sure that it was worthy to put in a book! If Lowell and Whittier and Tennyson — most of all, Tennyson — had written of slough-grass and ground squirrels and barbed-wire fences, those despised elements would have taken on new aspects.　I was a wistful peri longing for a literary paradise.

But the Word on the horizon was something.　It was far away, but it was real.　I did not try to analyze its promise, but it was there.

YOSEMITE [1]

BY

ARTHUR COLTON

As Miss Lynn's object was to give the impression of the prairie on the mind of a child, so Mr. Colton's desire is to interpret the effect of the Yosemite upon himself. There is very little of formal description, and none of the guide-book variety. He assumes on the part of the reader a knowledge, if not first-hand, at least second-hand, of this famous valley, and even of the details. He feels it unnecessary to describe or locate the "Bridal Veil Falls," the "Half Dome," or "El Capitan." There is no attempt to send the reader away with a picture of the Yosemite in his mind. His endeavor is to interpret the effect upon himself so that the reader will be in a mood analogous to that which he would experience were he in the Yosemite. To do this, Mr. Colton gives us the fanciful, suggestive, picturesque, and imaginative reflections that the Valley caused in him. In other words, to interpret the Valley to another, he records the ideas that flowed through his mind under this stimulus, exactly as a musician, to interpret a symphony, may record his reactions under that stimulus. Since from the nature of the case there can be no dominating thought, an essay of this type is good in proportion as the sensitive mind responds to the appeal.

THE traveler into Yosemite still goes by stage, or by his own conveyance of horse or foot. He is expected, presently, to enter by trolley up the Merced River, and this is thought by many to be a lamentable thing.

But Yosemite is already shorn of freedom and solitude. Shops and cottages are there, a hotel, permanent camps, regulations, and even the parasite called "graft," that

[1] From the author's manuscript, by permission.

411

final seal of a fledged society. The trolley will make it a convenient outfitting station to the High Sierras and their better solitudes.

A didactic poetess once wrote:

> "Laugh and the world laughs with you,
>   Weep and you weep alone";

and bestowed a familiar quotation on many who have perhaps no further acquaintance with the didactic poetess. She appeared to intend not only the statement of two facts in nature, but also to advise that you avoid sorrow because it is lonely, and cultivate cheerfulness because it attracts company. The two facts seem to be, in tendency, as stated, but the advice is open to qualification; first, because sorrow has some other results than solitude, and laughter than companionship; second, because solitude has its own values, and company its own drawbacks. Why should company, if gathered by your cheerfulness, be advisable, and company, if gathered by your trolley car, be lamentable?

But the knowledge of the survival of the fittest as a working law, makes for that calming philosophy which leans to a faith in the rightness of things that survive, and the power of time to prove it. Certain it is that no one but time can prove it; no one else has a rhetoric that applies to the case; no one else can so cause the works of man and nature to lie down together like a lion and a lamb at the millennium, and reconcile them as English villages and the hill towns of Tuscany are reconciled to their places. One foresees a generation to which the hotel shall seem at rest in Yosemite, the trolley car and the Merced River harmonious in their commotions; when the tourist shall quote poetry at Half Dome, Half Dome urbanely criticize the quotation, and shops and cottages be on easy terms with the dignitaries of the Sierran hierarchy.

Nature, brought into literature, was once hailed as the bringing in of a new sincerity. We have heard it ring false enough. Literature has been introduced to nature still oftener insincerely. Yet, if one honestly sets the poets and the plunging waters of Yosemite face to face, there is candor between them. Cataracts are no bad critics. They have their opinion of Coleridge's

> "Your strength, your speed, your fury and your joy,
> Unceasing thunder and eternal foam";

of Wordsworth's

> "Stationary blasts of waterfalls,"

and his

> "The cataracts blow their trumpets from the steep";

of Longfellow's

> "Rivulets rejoicing run and leap
> And wave their fluttering signals from the steep";

of Tennyson's

> "Pause and fall, and pause and fall,"

his

> "Thousand streams of dangling water smoke
> That like a broken purpose waste in air,"

and his

> "Some like a downward smoke,
>   Slow dropping veils of thinnest lawns, did go
> And some through wavering lights and shadows broke,
>   Rolling a slumbrous sheet of foam below."

In the "Valley" it is noticeable that Yosemite Falls prefers the Coleridge passage, that the Bridal Veil and

Vernal Falls approve of the third Tennyson, and several high wind-blown streams of the second Tennyson. Tennyson they all commend as the most observant and accurate, though lacking Coleridge's enthusiasm and Wordsworth's imaginative leaps and metaphors that go up with a rush. "Your Longfellow," they say, "can hardly be a Sierran poet; rather, on the whole, of some country where nature does not perform on a large scale, but closer to human proportions, a land where you Lilliputians can feel at home without over-expanding your minds. His 'fluttering signal' is a diminutive. Now, your Tennyson belongs, does he not, to a fixed society, somewhat heavy with customs, refinements, luxuries, morals and leisures?" "Dangling water smoke," wasted like "a broken purpose," Yosemite Falls once remarked in my hearing, "is more accurate than imaginative, and more promptly moralized than I care for." And it added, "Have any of your poets noticed my white rockets?"

I think not. Yet every long tumultuous waterfall shoots downward through its mists those round-headed missiles, half water and half foam, ghostly comets with a trailing splurge. Or noticed either, for that matter, the metallic clang of waterfalls if heard at some distance, the crash like the first attack of thunder shorn of its following roll; or noticed either, at the base of a waterfall, the heavy monotony of its voice, not a sound of "fury" or of "joy," but of fatality and despair; or taken to heart the gray breath of waterfalls, the pallor and chill of the blown spray, where it is ill for humanity to linger long in the sense of cold encircling mystery and its own delusion, of driving power and its own helplessness.

It is better to go down to the green Merced River and the meadows. The god of things as they should be meant that his worshippers — whose lives are spent in the pursuit of a lost chord, a missing harmony between ourselves and things not themselves — should contemplate Yosemite from the standpoint of its meadows. The spirit of Yosemite is defined, human, sufficient, sheltered from high, desolate and Sierran ambitions. The spirit of the Cañon of the Colorado is compact of color and immensity; the essence of Yosemite is not immensity but proportion and charm — white water falling in the distance, green water gliding in the shadow, still water reflecting blue groves and many colored flowers in level fields, and the right relation of all these to the smooth gray domes and those framing walls, whose height is not for terror but to make the pines that feather their keen edges look delicate as ferns.

Admitting that there is an element of freakishness about Yosemite, yet the sense of it soon dies away and leaves the charm. The cliffs shoot up from a flat valley, through whose green fields and woods goes a swift green river. The contrast is startling, and so far merely sensational, but time brings out their rightness in relation. The climbers to the hanging rock and sheer abyss of Glacier Point are seekers after sensation rather than beauty. The sensationalist is the same in the wilderness as in literature and at the theater. He feels no values but emphasis. Grass and sliding water are not emphatic. Grass is the standing example of things gracious by their indistinction, by their numbers and community, the swarming proletariat of the meadows. The orders and ranks of flowery aristocracy over it, gold, blue, red and white, are ornate persons given over to pomp and heraldry.

Some one has remarked on the prevalence of blue flowers

over red, and set it down to the facts that flowers are propagated through the agency of their banqueting visitors : that bees are more attracted by blue, and humming-birds by red; and that bees are many, while humming-birds are few.

Are flowers more frequently blue than red? Do bees prefer the blue, and if so, how did they come by the preference? The matter seems disputable throughout. The colors of flowers are doubtless derivative. They represent solutions of the advertising problem. The bill-board that disfigures the countryside and the flower that decorates it owe their characteristics to the same law and condition — the condition that in order to live they must be noticed. They are competitors for business, and every flower color represents success. It has some established relation to the taste of some visiting insect. But what the first elements of this taste may be is probably an unanswerable question.

Putting aside the composition and physics of color, if one looks about for the large insistent aspects of the world — those phenomena in respect to color whose constant presence to generations innumerable and forgotten has made us what we are, to see and feel as we do about color — the following seem to be the principal phenomena — so all generations have looked about them, and this is what they have seen.

The great blue was the sky, and its darkened reflection in water. Green appeared as the chief color of living growth, for, as a rule, whatever the earth brought forth in the vegetable kingdom, in field or forest or sea, was mainly green. Yellow was the color of the sand of shore and desert, and of most of those forms which, after a green life, had perished by drouth or cold; so it might have seemed the color of death and barrenness, but it was also the sun's color — an eminent contradiction — as well as that of the moon and stars. Brown was the color of the soil. White appeared mainly in water out of its normal condition, as in cloud, snow and foam. Black, they probably connected with night, or the closing of the eyes. Gray was the commonest rock color and tree-trunk color, but a larger fact than those was the gray of the shadowed cloud, and of the rain and mist. Red was not seen in the same masses and proportions as the others; no single immense aspect of nature was red; it was the color of blood from a wound, of the weather-beaten or flushed face; it was momentary in sunrises and sunsets, subsidiary in dead forest leaves; in part it was the color of fire, that mystery, which, leaping out of wood and stubble, destroyed them and vanished, leaving a red ember.

The preferences, if any, of bees and humming-birds and the tangled web of feeling, by which and to which the painter makes his human appeal, must somehow in the main hark back to these, the largest, oldest and most constant phenomena of color. One cannot see all the connections, but it is a pretty speculation in Yosemite, a useful speculation; lest we forget that out of wild nature we are come, that our instincts are great and our wisdoms little, that the main current of the will runs deep like the green Merced River and our reasoned choices are like the flutter of foam on its surface, that we became citizens but yesterday and were bred in the wilderness.

There have been four significant books put out within the last generation on the subject of the desert; of which Mr. Van Dyke's "Desert" is the Salton Basin in Southern California, Mrs. Austen's "Land of Little Rain" is the

2 E

Mojave, Mr. Hudson's "Idle Days in Patagonia" has the desert not so much for its subject as for its principal interest, and Mr. Hichens' "Garden of Allah" is a novel in which the Sahara is more vivid than the plot. They are significant for this reason :

The desert was a more dominant aspect of nature to the earlier than to the later civilization from which we derive, because of the place where the earlier happened to occur, southwestern Asia and northwestern Africa. It was an aspect almost wholly hostile. The center of events moving away into rainier Europe, the desert dropped out of prominence in recording literatures. But the new and forested wilderness was also a foe, the mountain a difficulty, the desert half forgotten or bitterly remembered. Our histories of culture have pointed out, with some exceptions and qualifications, that the great movement toward a conscious friendship and intimate communication with nature, as far as the possibility of a Wordsworth, is only some four or five generations old.

None of the four books above mentioned is simple description of the desert. Like Wordsworth's mountains and Thoreau's woods, something passed from the desert into the spirit of each writer and became expressive there. They are significant, because they announce that the desert too has been assimilated, brought within the sweep of the movement and put on confidential terms with humanity. After long absence it has returned to recognition and record. We have taken one more step in an acquaintance with the earth, toward making ourselves at home in our domicile, toward the exploration of its attics and cellars. Once we lived mainly in the kitchen. After all, the earth is a palatial dwelling, with art galleries, music rooms and interesting rat holes.

"I'm but a stranger here,
    Heaven is my home," —

is the astonishing statement we sometimes sing to a tune
none too thrilling, but we know better.   Even in a heaven
of our own ideals we would be but embarrassed aliens.
It were odd to have so long occupied the earth, and be
strangers there, with an offish and distant demeanor toward most of the household.   The intimacy with nature
attained by Mr. Gilbert Chesterton, to whom

"The million forests of the earth
    Come trooping in to tea,
The great Niagara waterfall
    Is never shy with me:

" I am the tiger's confidant
    And never mention names,
The lion drops the formal 'Sir'
    And lets me call him 'James,'"

looks like an intimacy on the point of becoming oppres-
sive, and yet the satirist uses for the purposes of satire a
manner of speech much the same as Emerson used in order
to present the profoundest facts that he knew ·

"River and rose and crag and bird,
    Forest and sun and oldest night,
To me their aid preferred,
    To me their comfort plight.
Courage !   We are thine allies,
And with this hint be wise."

The thing is somehow true in spite of the satirist.   More
and more in these latter times we turn to the wilderness for
consolation, for happiness.   Strangely enough we find it.
It appears that there are few methods of pursuing happiness so successful.   The moral of the old apologue was
that happiness was not to be found by pursuit at all, and

of most methods of pursuit it seems to be an observable fact. But the seekers of the wilderness have come upon certain odd habits of this furtive divinity, this happiness, whose shy, here-and-gone ways are like those of a wilderness animal, and have learned among her whims and usages how apt she is, at the end of the hard day, to glide like a shadow out of the forest, to sit silently beside the camp fire; or at noon on the mountain top, while one fancies he has no company but solitude, suddenly there are three on the mountain top, a weary body, a wide outlook and a world well reconciled.

It appears then that the solitude of the wilderness somehow makes for happiness, that happiness gathers company, whose happiness demands a trolley line into Yosemite and the banishment of solitude to the higher Sierras. And it appears that the god of things as they should be meant Yosemite to uplift the many rather than to transport the few, to popularize beauty rather than to discover it. For as regards this intimacy and mutual understanding between man and nature, there appear to be two kinds; one of which arises when their labors stand reconciled by time, as the hill towns with the hills in Tuscany, and this relation is like that of man and wife who have grown by long communion to resemble each other in spirit and even in feature; and the other arises when we come, weary of artifice, into the wilderness, and is like the meeting of man and maid, who look into each other's eyes and see eternity. And if, as appears, Yosemite is destined for the friendship of comforting usage rather than of superb recognitions, in the first place it is always well to be reasonable with destiny, and in the second, one's impression is that destiny had this idea in mind when Yosemite was first conceived and given its proportion and its restful charm. If, then, destiny comes in a trolley car to take possession, it is likely that time will follow with the title deeds, that the flowers will not be made self-conscious by spectators, and that Half Dome will attend to its own dignity.

THE BOWERY AND BOHEMIA [1]

BY

H. C. BUNNER

Clearly with this type of essay, without the unifying presence of a dominating thought, there is a tendency to disintegration. Both Miss Lynn and Mr. Colton held the essay together by confining the impressions to those of a single mind. Their work is subjective. Bunner, on the contrary, is objective. The rambling tour of lower New York, called *Bowery and Bohemia,* is made for the purpose of giving different vivid impressions. The essay opens with an anecdotal account of the old Bohemian circle, passes to a discussion of Bohemianism in general, and by the route of Mulberry Bend arrives at the Bowery, with which, from all that may be deduced from the essay, the Bohemians had little to do. Nor is there any very clear connection between Fitz-James O'Brien and the Polish Jew who hides chickens in his back yard. Thus the very title, Bowery and Bohemia, suggests a peddler's pack in which there is a little of everything. Theoretically the attempt is impossible; practically the essay is charming, with the flavor of a fine personality, in full control of his artistic medium. And the reader lays the book down with the feeling that New York is greater than he thought and with the wish to study it more deeply.

ONE day a good many years ago an old gentleman from Rondout-on-the-Hudson — then plain Rondout — was walking up Broadway seeing the sights. He had not been in New York in ten or twelve years, and although he was an old gentleman who always had a cask of good ale in his cellar in the winter-time, yet he never tasted the strange German beverage called lager-beer, which he had

[1] From "Jersey Street and Jersey Lane," by permission of Charles Scribner's Sons.

heard and read about. So when he saw its name on a sign he went in and drank a mug, sipping it slowly and thoughtfully, as he would have sipped his old ale. He found it refreshing — peculiar — and, well, on the whole, very refreshing indeed, as he considerately told the proprietor.

But what interested him more than the beer was the sight of a group of young men seated around a table drinking beer, reading — and — yes, actually writing verses, and bandying very lively jests among themselves. The old gentleman could not help hearing their conversation, and when he went out into the street he shook his head thoughtfully.

"I wonder what my father would have said to that?" he reflected. "Young gentlemen sitting in a pot-house at high noon and turning verses like so many ballad-mongers! Well, well, well, if those are the ways of lager-beer drinkers, I'll stick to my good old ale!"

And greatly surprised would that honest old gentleman have been to know that the presence of that little group of poets and humorists attracted as much custom to good Mr. Pfaff's beer-saloon as did his fresh, cool lager; and that young men, and, for the matter of that, men not so young, stole in there to listen to their contests of wit, and to wish and yearn and aspire to be of their goodly company. For the old gentleman little dreamed, as he went on his course up Broadway, that he had seen the first Bohemians of New York, and that these young men would be written about and talked about and versified about for generations to come. Unconscious of this honor he went on to Fourteenth Street to see the new square they were laying out there.

Perhaps nothing better marks the place where the

city of New York got clean and clear out of provincial
pettiness into metropolitan tolerance than the advent
of the Bohemians. Twenty-five years earlier they would
have been a scandal and a reproach to the town. Not
for their literature, or for their wit, or for their hard
drinking, or even for their poverty; but for their brotherhood, and for their calm indifference to all the rest of
the world whom they did not care to receive into their
kingdom of Bohemia. There is human nature in this;
more human nature than there is in most provincialism.
Take a community of one hundred people and let any ten
of its members join themselves together and dictate the
terms on which an eleventh may be admitted to their band.
The whole remaining eighty-nine will quarrel for the
twelfth place. But take a community of a thousand, and
let ten such internal groups be formed, and every group
will have to canvass more or less hard to increase its number. For the other nine hundred people, being able to
pick and choose, are likely to feel a deep indifference to
the question of joining any segregation at all. If group
No. 2 says, "Come into my crowd, I understand they
don't want you in No. 1," the individual replies: "What
the deuce do I care about No. 1 or you either? Here are
Nos. 4, 5, 6, and 7 all begging for me. If you and No. 1
keep on in your conceit you'll find yourselves left out in
the cold."

And as it frequently happens to turn out that way, the
dweller in a great city soon learns, in the first place, that
he is less important than he thought he was; in the second
place, that he is less unimportant than some people would
like to have him think himself. All of which goes to show
that when New Yorkers looked with easy tolerance, and
some of them with open admiration, upon the Bohemians

at Pfaff's saloon, they had come to be citizens of no mean city, and were making metropolitan growth.

A Bohemian may be defined as the only kind of gentleman permanently in temporary difficulties who is neither a sponge nor a cheat. He is a type that has existed in all ages and always will exist. He is a man who lacks certain elements necessary to success in this world, and who manages to keep fairly even with the world, by dint of ingenious shift and expedient; never fully succeeding, never wholly failing. He is a man, in fact, who can't swim, but can tread water. But he never, never, never calls himself a Bohemian — at least, in a somewhat wide experience, I have known only two that ever did, and one of these was a baronet. As a rule, if you overhear a man approach his acquaintance with the formula, "As one Bohemian to another," you may make up your mind that that man means an assault upon the other man's pocket-book, and that if the assault is successful the damages will never be repaired. That man is not a Bohemian; he is a beat. Your true Bohemian always calls himself by some euphemistic name. He is always a gentleman at odds with fortune, who rolled in wealth yesterday and will to-morrow, but who at present is willing to do any work that he is sure will make him immortal, and that he thinks may get him the price of a supper. And very often he lends more largely than he borrows.

Now the crowd which the old gentleman saw in the saloon — and he saw George Arnold, Fitz-James O'Brien, and perhaps N. P. Shepard — was a crowd of Bohemians rather by its own christening than by any ordinary application of the word. They were all young men of ability, recognized in their profession. Of those who have died, two at least have honor and literary consideration to-day;

of those who lived, some have obtained celebrity, and all a reasonable measure of success. Mürger's Bohemians would have called them Philistines. But they have started a tradition that will survive from generation unto generation; a tradition of delusion so long as the glamour of poetry, romance, and adventure hang around the mysteriously attractive personality of a Bohemian. Ever since then New York has had, and always will have, the posing Bohemian and his worshippers.

Ten or fifteen years ago the "French Quarter" got its literary introduction to New York, and the fact was revealed that it was the resort of real Bohemians — young men who actually lived by their wit and their wits, and who talked brilliantly over fifty-cent table-d'hôte dinners. This was the signal for the would-be Bohemian to emerge from his dainty flat or his oak-panelled studio in Washington Square, hasten down to Bleecker or Houston Street, there to eat chicken badly *braisé*, fried chuck-steak, and soggy spaghetti, and to drink thin blue wine and chicory-coffee that he might listen to the feast of witticism and flow of soul that he expected to find at the next table. If he found it at all, he lost it at once. If he made the acquaintance of the young men at the next table, he found them to be young men of his own sort — agreeable young boys just from Columbia and Harvard, who were painting impressionless pictures for the love of Art for Art's sake, and living very comfortably on their paternal allowances. Any one of the crowd would think the world was coming to pieces if he woke up in the morning to wonder where he could get his breakfast on credit, and wonder where he could earn enough money to buy his dinner. Yet these innocent youngsters continue to pervade "The Quarter," as they call it; and as time goes on, by much drinking of ponies of brandy and smoking of cigarettes, they get to fancy that they themselves are Bohemians. And when they get tired of it all and want something good to eat, they go up to Delmonico's and get it.

And their Bohemian predecessors, who sought the French fifty-cent restaurants as *their* highest attainable luxury — what has become of them? They have fled before that incursion as a flock of birds before a whirlwind. They leave behind them, perhaps, a few of the more mean-spirited among them, who are willing to degenerate into fawners on the rich, and habitual borrowers of trifling sums. But the true Bohemians, the men who have the real blood in their veins, they must seek some other meeting-place where they can pitch their never-abiding tents, and sit at their humble feasts to recount to each other, amid appreciative laughter, the tricks and devices and pitiful petty schemes for the gaining of daily bread that make up for them the game and comedy of life. Tell me not that Ishmael does not enjoy the wilderness. The Lord made him for it, and he would not be happy anywhere else.

There was one such child of fortune once, who brought his blue eyes over from Ireland. His harmless and gentle life closed after too many years in direst misfortune. But as long as he wandered in the depths of poverty there was one strange and mysterious thing about him. His clothes, always well brushed and well carried on a gallant form, often showed cruel signs of wear, especially when he went for a winter without an overcoat. But shabby as his garments might grow, empty as his pockets might be, his linen was always spotless, stiff, and fresh. Now everybody who has ever had occasion to consider the matter knows that by the aid of a pair of scissors the

life of a collar or of a pair of cuffs can be prolonged almost
indefinitely — apparent miracles had been performed in
this way. But no pair of scissors will pay a laundry bill;
and finally a committee of the curious waited upon this
student of economics and asked him to say how he did it.
He was proud and delighted to tell them.

"I — I — I'll tell ye, boys," he said, in his pleasant Dub-
lin brogue, "but 'twas I that thought it out. I wash them,
of course, in the basin — that's easy enough; but you'd
think I'd be put to it to iron them, wouldn't ye, now?
Well, I've invinted a substischoot for ironing — it's me
big books. Through all me vicissichoods, boys, I kept me
Bible and me dictionary, and I lay the collars and cuffs in
the undher one and get the leg of the bureau on top of
them both — and you'd be surprised at the artistic effect."

There is no class in society where the sponge, the toady,
the man who is willing to receive socially without giving
in return, is more quickly found out or more heartily dis-
owned than among the genuine Bohemians. He is to
them a traitor, he is one who plays the game unfairly,
one who is willing to fill his belly by means to which they
will not resort, lax and fantastic as is their social code.
Do you know, for instance, what "Jackaling" is in New
York? A Jackal is a man generally of good address,
and capable of a display of good fellowship combined
with much knowledge of literature and art, and a vast
and intimate acquaintance with writers, musicians, and
managers. He makes it his business to haunt hotels,
theatrical agencies, and managers' offices, and to know
whenever, in his language, "a new jay comes to town."
The jay he is after is some man generally from the smaller
provincial cities, who has artistic or theatrical aspirations
and a pocketful of money. It is the Jackal's mission to

turn this jay into an "angel." Has the gentleman from Lockport come with the score of a comic opera under his arm, and two thousand dollars in his pocket? Two thousand dollars will not go far toward the production of a comic opera in these days, and the jay finds that out later; but not until after the Jackal has made him intimately acquainted with a very gentlemanly and experienced manager who thinks that it can be done for that price with strict economy. Has the young man of pronounced theatrical talent arrived from Keokuk with gold and a thirst for fame? The Jackal knows just the dramatist who will write him the play that he ought to star in. Does the wealthy and important person from Podunk desire to back something absolutely safe and sure in the line of theatrical speculation? The Jackal has the very thing for which he is looking. And in all these, and in all similar contingencies, it is a poor Jackal who does not get his commission at both ends.

The Jackal may do all these things, but he may not, if he is treated, fail to treat in return. I do not mean to say at all that Jackaling is a business highly esteemed, even in darkest Bohemia, but it is considered legitimate, and I hope that no gentleman doing business in Wall Street, or on the Consolidated Exchange, will feel too deeply grieved when he learns the fact.

But where have the real Bohemians fled to from the presence of the too-well-disposed and too-wealthy children of the Benedick and the Holbein? Not where they are likely to find him, you may be sure. The true Bohemian does not carry his true address on his card. In fact, he is delicate to the point of sensitiveness about allowing any publicity to attach to his address. He communicates it confidentially to those with whom he has business dealings, but he carefully conceals it from the prying world. As soon as the world knows it he moves. I once asked a chief of the Bohemian tribe whose residence was the world, but whose temporary address was sometimes Paris, why he had moved from the Quartier Latin to a place in Montmartre.

"Had to, my dear fellow," he answered, with dignity; "why if you live over on that side of the river they'll call you a *Bohemian!*"

In Paris the home of wit in poverty has been moved across the Seine to the south side of the hill up which people climb to make pilgrimages to the Moulin Rouge and the church of St. Pierre de Montmartre. In New York it has been moved not only across that river of human intercourse that we call Broadway — a river with a tidal ebb and flow of travel and traffic — but across a wilder, stranger, and more turbulent flood called the Bowery, to a region of which the well-fed and prosperous New Yorker knows very, very little.

As more foreigners walk on the Bowery than walk on any other street in New York; and as more different nationalities are represented there than are represented in any other street in New York; and as the foreigners all say that the Bowery is the most marvellous thoroughfare in the world, I think we are justified in assuming that there is little reason to doubt that the foreigners are entirely right in the matter, especially as their opinion coincides with that of every American who has ever made even a casual attempt to size up the Bowery.

No one man can thoroughly know a great city. People say that Dickens knew London, but I am sure that Dickens would never have said it. He knew enough of London to know that no one human mind, no one mortal life can take

in the complex intensity of a metropolis. Try to count a
million, and then try to form a conception of the impossibility of learning all the ins and outs of the domicile
of a million men, women, and children. I have met men
who thought they knew New York, but I have never met a
man — except a man from a remote rural district — who
thought he knew the Bowery. There are agriculturists,
however, all over this broad land who have entertained
that supposition and acted on it — but never twice.
The sense of humor is the saving grace of the American
people.

I first made acquaintance with the Bowery as a boy
through some lithographic prints. I was interested in
them, for I was looking forward to learning to shoot, and
my father had told me that there used to be pretty good
shooting at the upper end of the Bowery, though, of course,
not so good as there was farther up near the Block House,
or in the wood beyond. Besides, the pictures showed a
very pretty country road with big trees on both sides of it,
and comfortable farmhouses, and, I suppose, an inn with
a swinging sign. I was disappointed at first, when I heard
it had been all built up, but I was consoled when the glories
of the real Bowery were unfolded to my youthful mind,
and I heard of the butcher-boy and his red sleigh; of the
Bowery Theatre and peanut gallery, and the gods, and Mr.
Eddy, and the war-cry they made of his name — and a
glorious old war-cry it is, better than any college cries ever
invented : "*Hi*, Eddy-eddy-eddy-eddy-eddy-eddy-eddy-
eddy-eddy !" of Mose and his silk locks, of the fire-en-
gine fights, and Big Six, and "Wash-her-down !" of the
pump at Houston Street; of what happened to Mr.
Thackeray when he talked to the tough; of many other
delightful things that made the Bowery, to my young

imagination, one long avenue of romance, mystery, and thrilling adventure. And the first time I went in the flesh to the Bowery was to go with an elderly lady to an optician's shop.

> "And is this — Yarrow? — *This* the stream
> Of which my fancy cherished,
> So faithfully, a waking dream?
> An image that hath perished!
> O that some minstrel's harp were near,
> To utter notes of gladness,
> And chase this silence from the air,
> That fills my heart with sadness!"

But the study of the Bowery that I began that day has gone on with interruption for a good many years, and I think now that I am arriving at the point where I have some faint glimmerings of the littleness of my knowledge of it as compared with what there is to be known. I do not mean to say that I can begin to size the disproportion up with any accuracy, but I think I have accomplished a good deal in getting as far as I have.

The Bowery is not a large place, for I think that, properly speaking, it is a place rather than a street or avenue. It is an irregularly shaped ellipse, of notable width in its widest part. It begins at Chatham Square, which lies on the parallel of the sixth Broadway block above City Hall, and loses its identity at the Cooper Union where Third and Fourth Avenues begin, so that it is a scant mile in all. But it is the alivest mile on the face of the earth. And it either bounds or bisects that square mile that the statisticians say is the most densely populated square mile on the face of the globe. This is the heart of the New York tenement district. As the Bowery is the Broadway of the East Side, the street of its pleasures, it would be interesting enough if it opened up only this one densely populated district. But there is much more to contribute to its infinite variety. It serves the same purpose for the Chinese colony in Mott, Pell, and Doyers Streets, and for the Italian swarms in Mulberry Bend, the most picturesque and interesting slum I have ever seen, and I am an ardent collector of slums. I have missed art galleries and palaces and theatres and cathedrals (cathedrals particularly) in various and sundry cities, but I don't think I ever missed a slum. Mulberry Bend is a narrow bend in Mulberry Street, a tortuous ravine of tall tenement houses, and it is so full of people that the throngs going and coming spread off the sidewalk nearly to the middle of the street. There they leave a little lane for the babies to play in. No, they never get run over. There is a perfect understanding between the babies and the peddlers who drive their wagons in Mulberry Bend. The crowds are in the street partly because much of the sidewalk and all of the gutter is taken up with venders' stands, which give its characteristic feature to Mulberry Bend. There are displayed more and stranger wares than uptown people ever heard of. Probably the edibles are in the majority, certainly they are the queerest part of the show. There are trays and bins there in the Bend, containing dozens and dozens of things that you would never guess were meant to eat if you didn't happen to see a ham or a string of sausages or some other familiar object among them. But the color of the Bend — and its color is its strong point — comes from its display of wearing apparel and candy. A lady can go out in Mulberry Bend and purchase every article of apparel, external or private and personal, that she ever heard of, and some that she never heard of, and she

2 F

can get them of any shade or hue. If she likes what they call "Liberty" colors — soft, neutral tones — she can get them from the second-hand dealers whose goods have all the softest of shades that age and exposure can give them. But if she likes, as I do, bright, cheerful colors, she can get tints in Mulberry Bend that you could warm your hands on. Red, greens, and yellows preponderate, and Nature herself would own that the Italians could give her points on inventing green and not exert themselves to do it. The pure arsenical tones are preferred in the Bend, and, by the bye, anybody who remembers the days when ladies wore magenta and solferino, and wants to have those dear old colors set his teeth on edge again, can go to the Bend and find them there. The same dye-stuffs that are popular in the dress-goods are equally popular in the candy, and candy is a chief product of Mulberry Bend. It is piled up in reckless profusion on scores of stands, here, there, and everywhere, and to call the general effect festal, would be to speak slightingly of it. The stranger who enters Mulberry Bend and sees the dress-goods and the candies is sure to think that the place has been decorated to receive him. No, nobody will hurt you if you go down there and are polite, and mind your own business, and do not step on the babies. But if you stare about and make comments, I think those people will be justified in suspecting that the people up-town don't always know how to behave themselves like ladies and gentlemen, so do not bring disgrace on your neighborhood, and do not go in a cab. You will not bother the babies, but you will find it trying to your own nerves.

There is a good deal of money in Mulberry Street, and some of it overflows into the Bowery. From this street also the Baxter Street variety of Jews find their way into the Bowery. These are the Jew toughs, and there is no other type of Jew at all like them in all New York's assortment of Hebrew types, which cannot be called meagre. Of the Jewish types New York has, as the printers say, "a full case."

But it is on the other side of the Bowery that there lies a world to which the world north of Fourteenth Street is a select family party. I could not give even a partial list of its elements. Here dwell the Polish Jews with their back-yards full of chickens. The police raid those back-yards with ready assiduity, but the yards are always promptly replenished. It is the police against a religion, and the odds are against the police. The Jew will die for it, if needs be, but his chickens must be killed *kosher* way and not Christian way, but that is only the way of the Jews: the Hungarians, the Bohemians, the Anarchist Russians, the Scandinavians of all sorts who come up from the wharfs, the Irish, who are there, as everywhere, the Portuguese Jews, and all the rest of them who help to form that city within a city — have they not, all of them, ways of their own? I speak of this Babylon only to say that here and there on its borders, and, once in a way, in its very heart, are rows or blocks of plain brick houses, homely, decent, respectable relics of the days when the sturdy, steady tradesfolk of New York built here the homes that they hoped to leave to their children. They are boarding- and lodging-houses now, poor enough, but proud in their respectability of the past, although the tide of ignorance, poverty, vice, filth, and misery is surging to their doors and their back-yard fences. And here, in hall bedrooms, in third-story backs and fronts, and in half-story attics, live the Bohemians of to-day, and with

them those other strugglers of poverty who are destined
to become "successful men" in various branches of art,
literature, science, trade, or finance. Of these latter our
children will speak with hushed respect, as men who rose
from small beginnings; and they will go into the school-
readers of our grandchildren along with Benjamin Franklin
and that contemptible wretch who got to be a great
banker because he picked up a pin, as examples of what
perseverance and industry can accomplish. From what
I remember I foresee that those children will hate them.

I am not going to give you the addresses of the cheap
restaurants where these poor, cheerful children of adversity
are now eating *goulasch* and *Kartoffelsalad* instead of the
spaghetti and tripe *à la mode de Caen* of their old haunts.
I do not know them, and if I did, I should not hand them
over to the mercies of the intrusive young men from the
studios and the bachelors' chambers. I wish them good
digestion of their goulasch: for those that are to climb,
I wish that they may keep the generous and faithful
spirit of friendly poverty; for those that are to go on to
the end in fruitless struggle and in futile hope, I wish
for them that that end may come in some gentle and
happier region lying to the westward of that black tide
that ebbs and flows by night and day along the Bowery
Way.

EVOLUTION [1]

John Galsworthy

In these last essays, the line of demarcation between exposition, description, and narration has become very thin — as it often does outside of rhetorics. Bunner's essay suggests description, and suggests narrative. It is a story without a plot. As the characters and the scenes are there, the reader at any moment half expects it to blossom into a short story. Still more is this true of Mr. Galsworthy's *Evolution*. Is it a story or is it an essay? For the first, it consists of a single dramatic episode with definite characters. For the second, however, the pathos of the situation is not individual but belongs to a class. The thought is that while evolution is necessary and desirable for those that survive, the struggle is hard for those that do not survive. This might be illustrated by the strikes in England with the introduction of machinery into the cotton mills, when thousands were thrown out of employment. It might be illustrated by the Venetian gondolier who finds his work taken from him by the motor-boat. Actually the particular illustration chosen is that of a cab-driver. This is presented with consummate art, detailed and definite. And the essay is omitted. But it is implicit. The tragedy presented is not that of an individual, but that of a class. And in this way Mr Galsworthy forces the reader to be himself the author. This type, then, represents the extreme limit of the expository form.

Coming out of the theatre, we found it utterly impossible to get a taxicab; and, though it was raining slightly, walked through Leicester Square in the hope of picking one up as it returned down Piccadilly. Numbers of han-

[1] From "The Inn of Tranquillity." Copyright, 1912, by Charles Scribner's Sons. By permission of the author and of the publishers.

soms and four-wheelers passed, or stood by the curb, hailing
us feebly, or not even attempting to attract our attention, but every taxi seemed to have its load. At Piccadilly
Circus, losing patience, we beckoned to a four-wheeler
and resigned ourselves to a long, slow journey. A sou'-
westerly air blew through the open windows, and there was
in it the scent of change, that wet scent which visits even
the hearts of towns and inspires the watcher of their myriad
activities with thought of the restless Force that forever
cries: "On, on!" But gradually the steady patter of
the horse's hoofs, the rattling of the windows, the slow
thudding of the wheels, pressed on us so drowsily that
when, at last, we reached home we were more than half
asleep. The fare was two shillings, and, standing in the
lamplight to make sure the coin was a half-crown before
handing it to the driver, we happened to look up. This
cabman appeared to be a man of about sixty, with a long,
thin face, whose chin and drooping grey moustaches
seemed in permanent repose on the up-turned collar of
his old blue overcoat. But the remarkable features of
his face were the two furrows down his cheeks, so deep and
hollow that it seemed as though that face were a collection
of bones without coherent flesh, among which the eyes
were sunk back so far that they had lost their lustre. He
sat quite motionless, gazing at the tail of his horse. And,
almost unconsciously, one added the rest of one's silver to
that half-crown. He took the coins without speaking;
but, as we were turning into the garden gate, we heard
him say:

"Thank you; you've saved my life."

Not knowing, either of us, what to reply to such a
curious speech, we closed the gate again and came back
to the cab.

"Are things so very bad?"

"They are," replied the cabman. "It's done with — is this job. We're not wanted now." And, taking up his whip, he prepared to drive away.

"How long have they been as bad as this?"

The cabman dropped his hand again, as though glad to rest it, and answered incoherently:

"Thirty-five year I've been drivin' a cab."

And, sunk again in contemplation of his horse's tail, he could only be roused by many questions to express himself, having, as it seemed, no knowledge of the habit.

"I don't blame the taxis, I don't blame nobody. It's come on us, that's what it has. I left the wife this morning with nothing in the house. She was saying to me only yesterday: 'What have you brought home the last four months?' 'Put it at six shillings a week,' I said. 'No,' she said, 'seven.' Well, that's right — she enters it all down in her book."

"You are really going short of food?"

The cabman smiled; and that smile between those two deep hollows was surely as strange as ever shone on a human face.

"You may say that," he said. "Well, what does it amount to? Before I picked you up, I had one eighteen-penny fare to-day; and yesterday I took five shillings. And I've got seven bob a day to pay for the cab, and that's low, too. There's many and many a proprietor that's broke and gone — every bit as bad as us. They let us down as easy as ever they can; you can't get blood from a stone, can you?" Once again he smiled. "I'm sorry for them, too, and I'm sorry for the horses, though they come out best of the three of us, I do believe."

One of us muttered something about the Public.

The cabman turned his face and stared down through the darkness.

"The Public?" he said, and his voice had in it a faint surprise. "Well, they all want the taxis. It's natural. They get about faster in them, and time's money. I was seven hours before I picked you up. And then you was lookin' for a taxi. Them as take us because they can't get better, they're not in a good temper, as a rule. And there's a few old ladies that's frightened of the motors, but old ladies aren't never very free with their money — can't afford to be, the most of them, I expect."

"Everybody's sorry for you; one would have thought that —"

He interrupted quietly: "Sorrow don't buy bread. . . . I never had nobody ask me about things before." And, slowly moving his long face from side to side, he added: "Besides, what could people do? They can't be expected to support you; and if they started askin' you questions they'd feel it very awkward. They know that, I suspect. Of course, there's such a lot of us: the hansoms are pretty nigh as bad off as we are. Well, we're gettin' fewer every day, that's one thing."

Not knowing whether or no to manifest sympathy with this extinction, we approached the horse. It was a horse that "stood over" a good deal at the knee, and in the darkness seemed to have innumerable ribs. And suddenly one of us said: "Many people want to see nothing but taxis on the streets, if only for the sake of the horses."

The cabman nodded.

"This old fellow," he said, "never carried a deal of flesh. His grub don't put spirit into him nowadays; it's not up to much in quality, but he gets enough of it."

"And you don't?"

The cabman again took up his whip.

"I don't suppose," he said without emotion, "any one could ever find another job for me now. I've been at this too long. It'll be the workhouse, if it's not the other thing."

And hearing us mutter that it seemed cruel, he smiled for the third time.

"Yes," he said slowly, "it's a bit 'ard on us, because we've done nothing to deserve it. But things are like that, so far as I can see. One thing comes pushin' out another, and so you go on. I've thought about it — you get to thinkin' and worryin' about the rights o' things, sittin' up here all day. No, I don't see anything for it. It'll soon be the end of us now — can't last much longer. And I don't know that I'll be sorry to have done with it. It's pretty well broke my spirit."

"There was a fund got up."

"Yes, it helped a few of us to learn the motor-drivin'; but what's the good of that to me, at my time of life? Sixty, that's my age; I'm not the only one — there's hundreds like me. We're not fit for it, that's the fact; we haven't got the nerve now. It'd want a mint of money to help *us*. And what you say's the truth — people want to see the end of us. They want the taxis — our day's over. I'm not complaining; you asked me about it yourself."

And for the third time he raised his whip.

"Tell me what you would have done if you had been given your fare and just sixpence over?"

The cabman stared downward, as though puzzled by that question.

"Done? Why, nothing. What could I have done?"

"But you said that it had saved your life."

"Yes, I said that," he answered slowly; "I was feelin'
a bit low. You can't help it sometimes; it's the thing
comin' on you, and no way out of it — that's what gets
over you. We try not to think about it, as a rule."

And this time, with a "Thank you, kindly!" he touched
his horse's flank with the whip. Like a thing aroused
from sleep the forgotten creature started and began to
draw the cabman away from us. Very slowly they
travelled down the road among the shadows of the trees
broken by lamplight. Above us, white ships of cloud
were sailing rapidly across the dark river of sky on the
wind which smelled of change. And, after the cab was
lost to sight, that wind still brought to us the dying sound
of the slow wheels.

BIOGRAPHICAL INDEX

ABBOTT, WILBUR CORTEZ. Born 1869, Kokomo, Ind. B. A., Wabash College, 1892; B. Litt., Oxford, 1897. Formerly instructor in history in University of Michigan, Dartmouth, and the University of Kansas. Professor of History in the Sheffield Scientific School since 1908. Contributor to English and American historical reviews, The Nation, Yale Review, etc.

ADDAMS, JANE. Born 1860, Cedarville, Ill. B.A., Rockford College, 1881. Two years in Europe. LL.D., University of Wisconsin, 1904, Smith, 1910. One of the founders of Hull House, Chicago, 1889. Head Resident, Hull House since founding. Writer and lecturer on political and social reforms. Author of: Democracy and Social Ethics, Newer Ideals of Peace, The Spirit of Youth and the City Streets, Twenty Years at Hull House, A New Conscience and an Ancient Evil, etc.

AVEBURY, JOHN LUBBOCK (first Baron). Born 1834, London. Died 1913. Banker, politician, naturalist, and author. Much of his work was popularizing natural history. Author of: The Origin and Metamorphoses of Insects, British Wild Flowers, The Pleasures of Life, The Beauties of Nature, The Use of Life, etc.

BALDWIN, CHARLES SEARS. Born 1867, New York City. B.A., Columbia, 1888, Ph. D., 1894. Formerly Professor of English at Yale. Professor of Rhetoric at Columbia. Author of books on composition and English literature; also of essays and reviews.

BEERS, HENRY AUGUSTINE. Born 1847, Buffalo, N. Y. B.A., Yale, 1869, M.A., 1887. Professor of English in Yale College. Author of: The Thankless Muse, A Suburban Pastoral, The Ways of Yale, Points at Issue, A History of English Romanticism (eighteenth and nineteenth centuries), and other poems, stories, essays, and works on English and American Literature.

BENNETT, ENOCH ARNOLD. Born 1867, North Staffordshire, England. Began his career as a journalist. Author of many novels, among which are The Old Wives' Tale, Anna of the Five Towns, Clayhanger, etc., and plays, such as What the Public Wants, Milestones (with Edward Knoblauch), and The Great Adventure.

BIRRELL, AUGUSTINE. Born 1850, near Liverpool. B.A., Cambridge,

1872; LL.D., St. Andrews. Lawyer and professor of law. Author of numerous volumes of critical and general essays, among them: Obiter Dicta; Res Judicatae; Men, Women, and Books; In the Name of the Bodleian, etc.

BRYCE, JAMES (VISCOUNT). Born 1838, Belfast. B.A., Trinity College, Oxford, 1862, D.C.L., 1870; LL.D. from various British and American universities. Formerly Regius Professor of Civil Law at Oxford. Active in English politics; member of Parliament. Ambassador to the United States, 1907–1912. Fellow of the Royal Society. Author of historical and governmental works, among them: The Holy Roman Empire, The American Commonwealth, The Hindrances to Good Citizenship, University and Historical Addresses, etc.

BUNNER, HENRY CUYLER. Born 1855, Oswego, N.Y. Died 1896. Journalist and editor. Best work done as editor of Puck. Author of: Airs from Arcady, and other volumes of poetry; Short Sixes, Made in France, Jersey Street and Jersey Lane, and other short stories and sketches.

BURTON, RICHARD EUGENE. Born 1859, Hartford, Conn. B.A., Trinity, 1883; Ph.D., Johns Hopkins, 1888. Literary editor of the Hartford Courant, 1890–1897. Associate editor of Warner's Library of the World's Best Literature. Now head of the English Department of the University of Minnesota. Author of: Lyrics of Brotherhood, Rahab, From the Book of Life, Forces in Fiction, Literary Likings, Little Essays in Literature and Life, and other volumes of poetry, essays, and critical works.

CANBY, HENRY SEIDEL. Born 1878, Wilmington, Del. Ph.B.,Yale, 1899, Ph.D., 1905. Assistant Professor of English in the Sheffield Scientific School. Assistant editor of The Yale Review. Author of: The Short Story in English, English Composition in Theory and Practice, etc. Contributor of short stories and essays to the magazines.

CHESTERTON, GILBERT KEITH. Born 1874, Campden Hill, Kensington, England. Began literary work by reviewing art books for the Bookman. Has written for various magazines as contributor and editor. Author of poems, novels, and essays, among which are The Man Who Was Thursday, The Flying Inn, Heretics, Orthodoxy, etc.

COLBY, FRANK MOORE. Born 1865, Washington, D.C. B.A., Columbia, 1888, M.A., 1889. Instructor in History and Economics at Amherst, Columbia, and New York University. Author of: Outlines of General History, Imaginary Obligations, Constrained Attitudes, and other historical works and general essays.

COLTON, ARTHUR WILLIS. Born 1868, Washington, Conn. B.A., Yale, 1890, Ph.D., 1893. Author of: The Delectable Mountains, The Debatable Land, The Cruise of the Violetta, Harps Hung Up in Babylon, and other novels and volumes of poetry; contributor to Atlantic Monthly, Harpers, Scribners, and other magazines.

CURRAN, HENRY HASTINGS. Born 1877, New York City. B.A., Yale, 1898; LL.B., New York Law School, 1900. For a number of years newspaper reporter and editor in New York. Member of the New York Board of Aldermen since 1911. Was Chairman of the Board of Aldermen's Committee which investigated the Police Department in 1912-1913. At present Chairman of the Board's Committee on Finance, and Majority Leader in the Board of Aldermen.

DANA, CHARLES ANDERSON. Born 1819, Hinsdale, N. H. Died 1897. Educated at Harvard. Member of Brook Farm. Was on the staff of the New York Tribune as correspondent, and later as managing editor. Special agent of the War Department under Secretary Stanton. Editor and part owner of the New York Sun from 1868 till his death. Author of: The Art of Newspaper Making, Reminiscences of the Civil War, and other works; but best known for his articles and editorials in The Sun.

FLANDRAU, CHARLES MACOMB. Born 1871, St. Paul, Minn. B.A., Harvard, 1895. Author of: Harvard Episodes, a volume of college short stories; The Diary of a Freshman, Viva Mexico, Prejudices, and of other stories and essays.

GALSWORTHY, JOHN. Born 1867, Coombe, Surrey, England. Educated at Harrow, and at New College, Oxford. Was called to the bar in 1890, but soon turned to literature as a profession. Author of: Jocelyn, Fraternity, The Patrician, The Dark Flower, and other novels; also poems and essays, among them Songs and Doggerels, and The Inn of Tranquillity. Much of his later work has been in the form of plays — The Silver Box, Strife, The Fugitive, and others.

HARRISON, FREDERIC. Born 1831, London. Honorary D.C.L., Oxford; Litt. D., Cambridge; LL.D., Aberdeen. Author and editor. Among his publications are: The Meaning of History, Order and Progress, Victorian Literature, American Addresses, Memories and Thoughts, The Philosophy of Common Sense, and other historical and general works.

LANG, ANDREW. Born 1844, Selkirk, Scotland. Died 1912. Educated at St. Andrews University, and at Balliol College, Oxford. Poet, journalist, critic, historian, and Homeric scholar. Among his publications are: Ballades in Blue China, Grass of Parnassus, Collected Rhymes,

Homer and the Epic, The Homeric Hymns, Homer and His Age. He was also the author of works on folk-lore, primitive religions, and English and Scotch history.

LEACOCK, STEPHEN. Born 1869, in England. Educated in Canada and the United States. Head of the Department of Political Science at McGill University. Author of: Sunshine Sketches, Nonsense Novels, Behind the Beyond, etc., also of works on political economy.

LODGE, HENRY CABOT. Born 1850, Boston, Mass. B.A., Harvard, 1871, LL.B., 1874. Has held various public positions in his state and in the nation. Senator from Massachusetts since 1893. Author and editor of works on American history and politics, such as The Life of Washington, History of Boston, Story of the Revolution, A Frontier Town and Other Essays, etc.

LODGE, SIR OLIVER JOSEPH. Born 1851, Penkhull, Staffordshire, England. D.Sc., London; D.Sc. (Hon.) Oxford, Cambridge, Victoria, and Liverpool; LL.D., St. Andrews, Glasgow, and Aberdeen. Fellow of the Royal Society. Principal of the University of Birmingham since 1900. Scientist, and author of works on Physics and related subjects. Author of: Modern Views of Electricity, Mathematics for Parents and Teachers, The Substance of Faith, Man and the Universe, Parent and Child, Modern Problems, etc.

LUBBOCK, SIR JOHN (see Avebury).

LYNN, MARGARET. Born and reared in northern Missouri. B.S., Tarkio College, 1889; M.A., University of Nebraska, 1900. Taught at the University of Nebraska, and at the University of Kansas, since 1901. Associate Professor of English Literature at the University of Kansas. Author of A Stepdaughter of the Prairie, and other western sketches, and contributor to the magazines.

MORE, PAUL ELMER. Born 1864, St. Louis, Mo. B.A., Washington University, 1887, M.A., 1892; M.A., Harvard, 1893; LL.D., Washington University, 1913. Formerly instructor at Harvard and Bryn Mawr, and literary editor of the Independent. Editor of the New York Evening Post since 1903, and of the Nation from 1909 to 1914. Member of the National Institute of Arts and Letters. Author of poems and translations. Has published eight volumes of critical and general essays under the title The Shelburne Essays.

PHELPS, WILLIAM LYON. Born 1865, New Haven, Conn. B.A., Yale, 1887; M.A., Harvard, 1891; Ph.D., Yale, 1891. Professor of English Literature in Yale College. Member of the National Institute of Arts and Letters, contributor to the magazines on literary topics, and public lecturer on literature. Editor of numerous English classics; author of: The Beginnings of the English Romantic Movement, Essays on Modern Novelists, Teaching in School and College, Essays on Russian Novelists, Essays on Books, etc.

RHODES, JAMES FORD. Born 1848, Cleveland, Ohio. Educated at New York University, and University of Chicago. LL.D., Harvard, Yale, and Princeton; Litt.D., Oxford. Lecturer at Oxford on the American Civil War, 1913. Author of History of the United States from the Compromise of 1850, also of Historical Essays. President of the American Historical Association, 1899. Corresponding Fellow of the British Academy. Member of the American Academy of Arts and Letters, and of other societies.

SUMNER, WILLIAM GRAHAM. Born 1840, Paterson, N.J. Died 1910. B.A., Yale, 1863, LL.D., 1909. Professor of Political Economy and of Sociology at Yale. Author of: History of American Currency, Lectures on the History of Protection in the United States, What Social Classes Owe to Each Other, Protectionism, Folkways, etc.; also of: War and Other Essays, Earth Hunger and Other Essays, The Challenge of Facts and Other Essays, volumes published since his death.

TAFT, WILLIAM HOWARD. Born 1857, Cincinnati, Ohio. B.A., Yale, 1878; LL.B., University of Cincinnati, 1880. Jurist and statesman; twenty-seventh President of the United States. Professor of Constitutional Law in Yale University since 1913. Author of: Political Issues and Outlooks, Present Day Problems, The United States and Peace, and other essays and addresses on politics and government.

TINGFANG, WU. Eminent Chinese statesman and diplomat. Formerly Minister to Peru, Spain, and later to the United States. More recently Minister of Foreign Affairs, and Minister of Justice for the Provincial Government of the Republic of China. Lecturer and essayist.

WHISTLER, JAMES ABBOTT MCNEILL. Born 1834, Lowell, Mass. Died 1903. Artist and lecturer on art. His etchings first brought him to notice while he was an art student in Paris. Did similar work in England. His work very distinctive and original. The portraits of his mother and of Carlyle, and his Nocturnes are among his best-known paintings. The Gentle Art of Making Enemies is the book in which he explains his theory of art, and replies to some of his critics, notably John Ruskin.

WILSON, WOODROW. Born 1856, Staunton, Va. B.A., Princeton, 1879; LL.B., University of Virginia, 1881; Ph.D., Johns Hopkins, 1886. Formerly Professor of Political Economy and Jurisprudence and later president of Princeton University. Governor of New Jersey; twenty-eighth President of the United States. Author of : Constitutional Government in the United States, A History of the American People, Division and Reunion, Mere Literature, and other volumes of history and essays.

WOODBERRY, GEORGE EDWARD. Born 1855, Beverly, Mass. B.A., Harvard, 1877. Various honorary degrees. Professor of English at the University of Nebraska, and of Comparative Literature at Columbia. Fellow of the American Academy of Arts and Sciences, Member of the American Academy of Arts and Letters. Editor of English classics; biographer of Poe, Hawthorne, Emerson, and others; author of poems, essays, and critical works.

Printed in the United States of America.

Write to please yourself

If you have dressed yourself sufficiently
you will necessarily please others

M. Cummings   4
T. Doyle   4
M. Tolitidy   1
L. Petrutti   1
myself   4
R. Larmer   2